Mentsh

Mentsh

On Being Jewish and Queer

Edited by

Angela Brown

alyson books
los angeles

MANUFACTURED IN THE UNITED STATES OF AMERICA.

THIS TRADE PAPERBACK ORIGINAL IS PUBLISHED BY ALYSON PUBLICATIONS,
P.O. BOX 4371, LOS ANGELES, CALIFORNIA 90078-4371.
DISTRIBUTION IN THE UNITED KINGDOM BY TURNAROUND PUBLISHER SERVICES LTD.,
UNIT 3, OLYMPIA TRADING ESTATE, COBURG ROAD, WOOD GREEN,
LONDON N22 6TZ ENGLAND.

FIRST EDITION: AUGUST 2004

04 05 06 07 08 a 10 9 8 7 6 5 4 3 2 1

ISBN 1-55583-850-2

LIBRARY OF CONGRESS CATALOGING-IN-PUBLICATION DATA
   MENTSH : ON BEING JEWISH AND QUEER / EDITED BY ANGELA BROWN.—1ST ED.
      INCLUDES BIBLIOGRAPHICAL REFERENCES.
      ISBN 1-55583-850-2 (PBK.)
      1. HOMOSEXUALITY—RELIGIOUS ASPECTS—JUDAISM. 2. JEWISH GAY MEN. 3. JEWISH
   LESBIANS. 4. BROWN, ANGELA, 1970–
   BM729.H65M46 2004
   296'.086'64—DC22   2004048571

CREDITS
• COVER ILLUSTRATION BY SUSAN SYNARSKI.
• COVER DESIGN BY MATT SAMS.
• PORTIONS OF AARON HAMBURGER'S "EXILE" PREVIOUSLY APPEARED IN *THE VIEW FROM STALIN'S HEAD*, RANDOM HOUSE, 2004.
• LESLÉA NEWMAN'S "ONE HUNDRED YEARS OF GRATITUDE" PREVIOUSLY APPEARED IN *LILITH MAGAZINE*, VOLUME 23, NUMBER 4. REPRINTED BY PERMISSION OF THE AUTHOR.

"Seek the good in everyone,
and reveal it,
bring it forth."

—Rebbe Nachman of Bratslav

"Everyone entrusted with a mission is an angel...
All forces that reside in the body are angels."

—Maimonides, "Guide for the Perplexed"

for my rabbi, who keeps pulling
my head out of the sand

and for Becky,
who sneaks in during Aleinu

Contents

Foreword
Rabbi Lisa A. Edwards

In our youth in an acculturated Jewish suburb of Chicago, my brother and I gained some notoriety among our Christian public school teachers for being the only Jewish students to attend class on Rosh Hashanah and Yom Kippur (albeit only in the afternoons after attending services in the morning and the night before). I loved being one of two students in my classroom on those days (the other was the only non-Jewish kid in my class). Our indulgent parents didn't mind letting us go to school, since few of their Jewish friends knew or cared where the children were on Holy Day afternoons. Most of our friends, we knew, were just taking a "vacation day" those days anyway. Any opportunity to miss school was a welcome one to them, but not to me or my brother.

There was no mistaking the value placed on secular education in our household. And I sometimes wonder if our teachers would have been as surprised as our parents were years later when both my brother and I became rabbis.

It doesn't seem surprising to either of us, however. In our house the Jewish and the secular often served one another. Hanukah when we were children became known as "Booknikah," for on each of the eight nights we received a new book, on many different topics, Jewish and not. Our father often read aloud to us from those Booknikah books before we went to sleep each night.

No wonder I became addicted to stories, and learned to listen for the voices telling those stories...and came to associate the telling of stories with being Jewish. Tell stories, listen to stories—that's what Jews do. I knew it unconsciously from my earliest years, and more so later on, as I studied the sacred texts of Judaism. The Torah itself teaches mainly through storytelling, and later generations continued to teach through their own literary forms—*aggadah* (from the Hebrew root meaning "to tell") and *midrash* (from the root meaning "to seek")—writing their own legends intended to answer the questions left unanswered by the stories of Torah.

In part due to my Booknikah years, my reading tastes went toward biographies and stories early on, many about and by Jews. And it doesn't take long to realize that those of us who write, and those of us who read, do so not only to hold up mirrors in front of our own faces, but also to reach out our hands to others: We search not only for self, but also for community. Reading can be a private experience, but seldom a lonely one (even if a loved one isn't reading aloud to you), for from the very first page you have company.

When I was in graduate school the "Jew as outsider" was already a well-established literary convention, but the recognition of the queer person (let alone the queer Jew) as outsider had barely begun. My own recognition of myself as outsider (Jew, lesbian, and then later: woman rabbi, lesbian rabbi) was just surfacing. As I struggled to integrate all the seemingly disparate parts of myself, I realized other queer Jews were doing the same, and creating community in the process. Once I got a glimpse of what could be, my goal was unwavering, though the journey itself took years—on a road not yet completely paved—for me to emerge from my carrel hidden deep in the library stacks at a Midwestern university to my place as the rabbi of an already well-established, active, diverse, bustling West Coast Jewish community called Beth Chayim Chadashim—"House of New Life" (BCC)—known as the world's first gay and lesbian synagogue and seen today as "a welcoming, thriving community of all sexualities and a range of ethnic and racial groups."

Foreword

In the world in which I now live and work, being Jewish and gay/lesbian/bi/trans/queer is the norm. And yet when I venture outside it, I see how invisible or scary we still are to much of the rest of the world, and sometimes even to ourselves. But we are Jews after all, and so we know what to do when people do not see us, or do not understand what they see—we tell them (and ourselves) stories about us, so they (and we) will come to know who we are. We tell stories, and in so doing, are reminded of what Torah taught us way back—that the stories themselves are transformative; they change lives.

Whether you come to this book looking to understand a culture and experience not your own, or hoping to own one you've come to only late in life or with ambivalence, or eagerly anticipating within these pages common ground and common lives, you have come to the right place, to the right voices. This collection called *Mentsh* is *mentshlich* indeed—very human, very Jewish, very queer; tough and tender, sweet and sour, closeted and proud; each voice speaking with astonishing honesty. Herein are stories told by hearts and minds—by *mentshen*—you will come to care for in a matter of moments, though it has taken all of us all of our lives to get us here to these pages (and these pages here to us), where we can all meet and fall in love. Enjoy *Mentsh*, this new book of Torah, these sacred teachings of our sacred lives.

Introduction

We've all heard someone say, "He (or she) is a true *mentsh*," but what exactly is a *mentsh*? *Mentsh* is a Yiddish word most commonly defined as "a good person." But the word literally translates as "human being." Others have offered similar definitions, including "a person who possesses a degree of moral integrity that most of us aren't blessed with," "a special person," "a decent human being," "a real human being," and "the Jewish ideal of ethical behavior and its impact on the self and others."

The most intriguing definition I've come across, however, is found in a Yiddish proverb: "*A mentsh heyst a mentsh veyl er mentsht zikr:* A person is called a *mentsh* because he or she struggles." Jewish scholar David S. Ariel examines this idea in his book *Spiritual Judaism: Restoring Heart and Soul to Jewish Life.* He writes:

> The Jewish definition of a *mentsh* is one who struggles with being human and all the difficulties that entails, who works to bring out the best within oneself, who nurtures the divine spark within another person, and who allows each person to find a treasure within his or her own house.

It's no wonder, then, that I decided to call this volume of writings on being Jewish and queer *Mentsh.* To be both Jewish and queer is a double-whammy—and what a wonderful, magical double-whammy it is. It is to be twice-blessed, but this blessing is often accompanied by struggles: the struggle to come out to one's family and community, the struggle to fit into sometimes constraining traditions, the struggle to live in—or remain outside of—Jewish culture as well as straight culture.

To be a *mentsh* means choosing to be the best person you can be, no matter the pressure to conform. It means putting your nose to the grindstone to make tough decisions. It means bringing out the best in others. I opened this book with a quote from Rebbe Nachman of Bratslav, "Seek the good in everyone, and reveal it, bring it forth," because I firmly believe the best kind of *mentsh* seeks good wherever she or he ventures—in the workplace, in our communities, in our families, and in our social circles, and coaxes and nurtures that good in others.

How often have we as Jews, as lesbians, bisexuals, transsexuals, gay men, and genderqueer individuals been ignored or shunned by others because we are different? How often have we perceived others as having no merit because they were different? Although a *mentsh* may not always make the "right" decision, he or she struggles to do so, and in this struggle he or she embodies the highest ideal of Judaism.

To be a *mentsh*, as Ariel writes, is to "allow each person to find a treasure within his or her house." As *mentshen*, as queer Jews, we are treasures within the house of Judaism and in a vaster house called the world. Each contributor in this volume displays their *mentshlichkeit*, their humanity: the good, the bad, even the ugly. In Judaism, every person is said to have a *yetzer hatov* (a good inclination) and a *yetzer hara* (an evil inclination). According to our sages, we need our *yetzer hara*—in fact, our *neshamas*, our souls depend upon it—because our struggle with it characterizes the very Jewish belief that we are endowed with free will. The trick, according to Judaism, is how we put to use our good inclination and our evil inclination.

Without our *yetzer hara*, the midrash goes, no one would build a house, marry, or have children. The *yetzer hara* can be seen, in this way, as the selfish impulse, while the *yetzer hara* is the selfless inclination. The goal is to balance our desire to do for ourselves with our obligation to do for others; the goal is achieving *mentshlichkeit*, humanity.

Thus, a *mentsh* is a balanced person but not a perfect person—how boring would our world be then? Far from perfect, a *mentsh* is a flawed fighter. And that's exactly what we as queer Jews are: flawed fighters in a world that can be rather discouraging but which also grants us gifts of beauty, light, and discovery each and every moment.

The contributors—the *mentshen*—in this book reveal their complex, heart-breaking, stunning, enigmatic, radiant, and authentic worlds within our world. They invite us to kibbutzes. They bring us along as they come out to their families, their rabbis, their cantors. They buy Jewish sperm to make the perfect Jewish baby. They rescue Palestinian refugees. They take us to Boro Park, Brooklyn, where Jews spy on other Jews to make sure they aren't breaking the Sabbath. They recite kaddish for their lovers who have died of AIDS. They marry each other at San Francisco City Hall. They live, pray, fight, write, and love in Israel, Australia, Yugoslavia, Jordan, the Czech Republic, Canada, and across the U.S. They suffer electroshock treatment and conversion therapy. They *kvetch* as their gentile girlfriend lights a cigar off their Shabbos candle. And they honor their families—the accepting, the disgruntled, the loving, the anxious, the neurotic, the scared.

I first decided to compile this anthology because I wanted to read about people like me, queer Jews. What surprised me most (besides the number of vibrant, highly literate essays I received—well, why should that surprise me? We're Jews!) was the variety of stories that came in. In this volume you'll find essays by queer Jews in their twenties through seventies. You'll read essays by those recently out of the closet and those who have been firmly grounded in both their Jewish and queer identities for decades. You'll learn about those who come from Reform, Orthodox, Conservative, and secular backgrounds. Rural Jews and city Jews. A redheaded Irish

Jew and a Chinese-American Jew. Jews by Choice and Jews by Birth. Zionist Jews and pro-Palestinian Jews.

But although the stories in this volume at first glance may seem disparate, what binds them is that each writer *clings* to her or his identity as both queer and Jewish. As Moses instructs in the Book of Deuteronomy, "Listen to G-d and cleave to G-d, for G-d is your life and the length of your days." The contributors to *Mentsh*, although they may sometimes, like Jacob, struggle with G-d or even the idea of G-d, do in fact cleave to G-d and live G-d's will, by firmly owning who they are, by kindling the lights in themselves and others, by bringing forth and nurturing the good in those around them, by working toward *tikkun olam* (the repair of the world), by taking the risk to be a *mentsh*.

In the Yiddish language there's a special verb, which has no translation in most languages: *farginen*. It means to share pleasure, to create space to allow others to *kvell*, to express their joy, their happiness, and their triumphs. With *Mentsh*, I hope I—and the twice-blessed women and men in these pages—have done just that.

—*Angela Brown,*
Los Angeles, California

"Lead me to a rock that is
too high for me."

—Psalm 61:3

Growing Up
and Coming Out

Israel 90210
Raphael Simon

The night before I left for Israel, my father gave me a pack of condoms. We were sitting in his car in front of my mother's house—at least this is how I like to remember the scene—after a just-us-guys goodbye dinner of, let's say, pizza and root beer. I gave him a quick hug and was about to climb out the door when he slipped the little box into my hands.

"You never know what can happen in the Holy Land," he said with a kind of wry solemnity, as if he were winkingly participating in a ritual of as grave import as a bar mitzvah, or more apropos, a bris.

"Da-a-ad! Je-e-ezus!" I rolled my eyes, but I couldn't help being thrilled by the vote of confidence. I ran inside clutching the condoms in my pocket like I was hiding a hard-on, embarrassed and full of myself at the same time.

It was 1983. I was fifteen, and my sexual experience was limited to having once felt up a girl at summer camp. That and the odd Truth or Dare tongue kiss. How could I be friendly with so many girls and not have done it with a single one? In those days, before AIDS and Christian rock, abstinence was still a dirty word, and already I'd been subjected to some uncomfortable questions, as well as the usual teasing. Luckily, for my condition a condom wasn't just a prophylaxis—it was tantamount to a cure. Armed by my father, I resolved I would to lose my virginity in Israel. Twenty

Los Angeles teenagers would be going with me. Of these, thirteen were female. Surely with those odds I could convince someone to do the deed.

That night I shut myself in the bathroom and studied the picture of the romantic couple on the box of Trojans. Even back then it looked dated. It reminded me of those old Almond Joy commercials showing a man and woman running toward each other in a meadow. *Sometimes you feel like a nut. Sometimes you don't.* I tried to imagine my big moment. How would I feel? Wacky or romantic? Nutty or not? Perhaps I wouldn't do it with someone on my trip after all but with an Israeli girl. A *sabra,* as they were so sexily called. Now *that* would be something to write home about.

I freed a condom out of its packet and awkwardly unrolled it onto my penis. Checking the mirror to make sure I didn't look too silly, I started masturbating. The rubber reduced sensation but added a sense of purpose to the enterprise. I was no longer wasting seed—I was preparing for the consummation of my manhood. The Holy Land awaited.

✡

"How can you be a Jew and live in America? This is not Jewish. A Jew is a Zionist is an Israeli!" The tough young *sabra* looked at our gaping mouths with satisfaction. She knew she was being provocative; that was the point. She was a soldier. We were just another group of Americans who needed to be shocked out of our spoiled adolescent stupors. It was our first day in Israel and already one thing was certain: I wasn't going to make it with this *sabra.*

"Let me ask you a question," she continued. "If America went to war against Israel, which side would you choose?"

Nobody answered. We might have been politically unaware, narcissistic teenagers, but we knew enough to know Israel was America's closest ally. War against Israel? The idea was absurd, even more so then than it would be today. But from the look she gave us, it appeared she was dead earnest, as were all the other Israelis who asked us the same question during our stay. Our answer was supposed to be Israel—we would fight for Israel. When we searched our souls, we were supposed to discover that Israel was our true home and start planning to make *aliyah,* as the Israelis call a Jew's move "up" to Israel. I didn't respond well to the *sabra*'s speech. I was never one for group allegiances—my stint in Cub Scouts had been short—and the Zionist pep talk struck me as propagandistic, even cultish. At the Tel Aviv airport we'd been advised that it was customary for Jews arriving in Israel to kiss the ground. I was too rebellious—and too self-conscious—to make the gesture. As the *sabra* continued welcoming us to Israel, I grumbled that our trip was a plot to brainwash American teenagers.

One of dozens of nearly identical teen tours that until recently over-ran Israel every summer, the trip was sponsored by a Los Angeles Reform Jewish organization. At the orientation session back home, all the other kids had recognized each other: from Sunday School, from High Holiday services, from their temple's latest bagel brunch. I didn't belong to a temple. My parents had more or less left my religious upbringing to my grandparents, who, as socialists, didn't approve of organized religion. I'm not sure they approved of G-d either. But having lived through World War II, they had a deep appreciation for the perils of assimilation and wanted my brother and me raised with what they called "Jewish content" in our lives. Thus they had created an entire calendar's worth of alternative holiday rituals to be celebrated at home. By the time they sent me to Israel, my sense of Judaism was an eclectic and eccentric mix of anthropology, socialist ideals, and gender-neutral Bible stories. To my fellow teen travelers, as far as I could make out, Judaism meant membership—in this or that temple, or more often than not, in this or that country club. Yet as different as our conceptions of Judaism were, we all resented having our Jewishness challenged; the strident nationalism of the Israelis had the perverse effect of bonding us as Jewish Americans. Tel Aviv, we'd heard, resembled our own Los Angeles. But that first night, as we walked down Dizengoff Road,

5

center of Tel Aviv nightlife, it seemed to us inferior to the California original. Our burgers were better. Our clubs were better. The chief advantage of Israel, as far as we could tell, was that we didn't need fake ID's to order beer.

As the group sized up Israel, I sized up the group. At that age, I was a snob precisely to the extent to which I was uncertain of my own worth, and I'm sure I made all kinds of distinctions that would be lost on me now; but I remember dividing my peers into three geographical categories: First, there were the San Fernando Valley kids, who included Cory, my assigned roommate, as well as a few class-clown types. *Fast Times at Ridgemont High* had come out not long before and all the Valley guys tried to outdo each other with variations on Spicoli-style surf speak. Though shyer and more soft-spoken than the others, even Cory threw around a few "radicals" and "tubulars"—something I teased him about but which also emboldened me to try a few surfer words myself when he wasn't within earshot. After the Valley kids, there were the Westsiders, the largest, most anonymous group, and the group to which I belonged by virtue of my high school if not exactly my home address. If we Westsiders were the chorus, the stars of our show were three girls from Beverly Hills.

This last group immediately and effortlessly took command over the rest of us and held on tight for the duration. My favorite of the three was Liz. She was dark, sexy, and wise—in my mind, a younger Mrs. Robinson. Debra, in contrast, was a frosty blond, notable for her extreme laziness. Her biggest ambition for her trip—announced to anyone who would listen—was to buy a Fendi purse duty-free at the airport in Rome on the way back. The undisputed leader, Alexandra, wasn't as obviously pretty as her two friends, but what she lacked in looks she made up for in ferocity. She was rich and she was mean and she had mouth like a chain saw. She once told me her parents didn't allow her in the kitchen because she made the cooks cry. I got the sense she'd been sent to Israel as a punishment, a last-ditch effort to turn her around. Everyone else on the trip was terrified of this formidable trio—including the only slightly older and much less socially adept trip leaders, whom the Beverly Hills Girls teased and ridiculed relentlessly.

To me the Beverly Hills Girls were much kinder. They treated me with a sort of amused condescension and affected surprise that they hadn't seen me at any of their parties back home. But there was no doubt they were out of my league as far as sex—my biggest ambition for the trip—was concerned. From the moment I met them, I was more a little brother or pet than a potential lover. I remember talking to Liz on the bus one morning early in our stay. I had heard a rumor that certain guys at Beverly Hills High considered it cool to be bisexual and wear eyeliner. As casually as I could, I asked whether this was true. She nodded as if bisexuality were the most normal thing in the world. Her friends pitched in from the seat behind us: Some guys looked great in eyeliner. Just think of Duran Duran. They pulled my face around and examined me critically. Why didn't I try it? I had the right kind of face. Before I knew it, I was being attacked with an eye pencil. I ducked, blushing.

Our defensive American smugness crumbled when we made the short trip from Tel Aviv to Jerusalem. Nothing in our burg of Los Angeles prepared us for the city's ancient golden rock, the timeless golden light, the centuries of history so palpable at every turn. Our arrival coincided with Tish B'av, the holiday that commemorates the destruction of Jerusalem's First and Second Temples. When we visited the last remains of the Second Temple—the famous Western Wall—we found ourselves swept up in a much larger crowd. Tish B'Av is traditionally a day of mourning, but the scene was far from dour; it was almost joyous. "I must confess to have been moved…." I later wrote to my grandparents. "Everyone in Jerusalem was at the Wall—the Chassids, the Israelis, the Europeans, all of us West L.A./Bev. Hills Jews. (I bumped into more friends at the Wall than I bump into at home.) All coming together as one culture—exciting." It was the closest thing to a religious sentiment I'd ever had, but I wasn't about to let myself undergo a conversion. At the bottom of the letter I added, "Don't worry, I'm still my same old cynical self underneath."

The carnival atmosphere of Tish B'Av stayed with us for the next six weeks, as we followed a well-worn itinerary across this astonishingly tiny country. Whether we were inspecting the Lebanese border in the Galilee, or climbing Masada by moonlight, Israel's battlegrounds were our playgrounds. Notwithstanding our tight schedule, few of us had ever experienced so much freedom. Other Jews had escaped persecution by coming to Israel; we had escaped our parents. As horribly ironic as it sounds today, Israel felt to us like the safest place on Earth. Even our exhausting two weeks on a kibbutz in the Negev, where we were awakened every morning at four to work in the fields, had an unreal quality that made the hard work seem if not like play, then like a dream. Missing from this pastoral idyll however was the girl running toward me through the fields. My personal Almond Joy commercial was only half-complete.

The most obvious candidate to fill the role was Jill, my best friend for much of the trip. Jill was also from Beverly Hills, but she was too weird to be on the inside with the others. She was very skinny and her back was covered with soft downy hair—a symptom, I later learned, of anorexia. She may not have eaten much, but she sure liked to talk about food, and we spent long hours on the kibbutz, where meals tended to be extremely plain, planning elaborate and fattening imaginary feasts. Once, after a particularly flirtatious conversation about what was coincidentally her favorite dish as well as mine, tortellini with pesto, we started making out. I think we both felt obligated; after all, we were a boy and a girl alone in a cabin on a hot afternoon. She was so bony I felt I would break her and I quickly made an excuse to stop. She seemed relieved. We never touched each other again.

As the weeks wore on, it began to look like I would never break out the condoms. For every girl in our group, I found a brand-new basis for rejection. This one had big ears, that one had mousy hair. Those who weren't objectionable were unavailable. The prospect of a long, sexless life stretched out in front of me. I confided my dilemma to Cory, my roommate, and he admitted that for him too, sex was a so-far uncrossable divide. Unlike me, however, he didn't seem to be in a rush. We had our whole lives to have sex. But we had only a short time to experience Israel. Why not enjoy it? His equanimity on the subject of his virginity shocked me. But I decided to try to adopt his attitude as my own. Perhaps the trip to Israel would benefit me in some unexpected, nonsexual way, if only I would allow it.

Mild-mannered Cory was our group's most ardent Zionist. When others scoffed at the *sabras'* dire predictions of anti-Semitism in America, it was Cory who reminded us that before Hitler the German Jews had scoffed too. At Cory's urging, I began reading *Exodus,* Leon Uris's turgid but engrossing history of Israel, which I'd been given as a parting gift by my grandparents but which I'd resisted opening. For a couple days I was lost in the novel. When I finished, I looked around me with new eyes: The kibbutz was no longer a drab group of buildings capriciously placed in the middle of a sweltering desert but a brave outpost of hope in a Promised Land reclaimed against all odds by Jewish grit and determination. I picked pears with a new energy. I even imagined returning some day for a longer stay. Maybe they were right, I thought. A Jew outside of Israel was like a bee away from the hive; eventually it was time to fly home and make some honey. I owed it to my ancestors' memory and my children's future to be a part of building this great Jewish nation. Fiction had accomplished what all the *sabras* had not: I was convinced I wanted to be a Zionist pioneer.

My cynicism came rushing back at the springs of Ein Gedi, Israel's legendary lovers' grotto, where our guides read from the "Song of Songs." "My beloved is unto me as a cluster of camphor in the vineyards of Ein Gedi." How corny, I inwardly groaned, it's like the Jewish *Blue Lagoon.* Still, I couldn't help feeling rueful about my lack of luck in the love department. Hadn't I come to Israel to make love in just such a desert spring? As I mulled over my uncoupled fate, a hand shoved me from behind. "C'mon, jump already, dude!" It was Steve, dripping wet at the head of a line forming along a ledge above the springs. Lost in thought, I'd been keeping everybody waiting. I stared at him. And something inside me turned upside down, even before I leaped off the edge.

For most of the trip I hadn't paid much attention to Steve. One of the wanna-be surfers from the Valley, Steve failed on almost every count the silent test to which I subjected all my peers. He wasn't particularly smart or sarcastic. His hair was too long. His rugby shirts were at least three years out of fashion. Mysteriously, none of that mattered now that Steve had taken his clothes off. At sixteen, he was tall and lean and growing into his body. Dark-skinned, long-nosed, he had the beginnings of what nowadays we would call a six-pack and a high, tight ass. Back then, I didn't have such an advanced physiological vocabulary, but I couldn't stop looking at his body. As we jumped in and out of the no longer so corny-seeming springs of Ein Gedi, his bathing suit clung to his crotch, and clusters of camphor danced in my head.

One of the girls whom I'd dismissed as a potential girlfriend, even while she made it clear she had a crush on me, was Erica. As fair as Steve was dark, Erica was blond, blue-eyed—and adorned with glittering braces on her teeth. Although I wasn't attracted to her, she fascinated me with her knowledgeable discussion of sexual intercourse, which she claimed to have experienced several times. One afternoon soon after our stop at Ein Gedi, Erica and I were engaged in that ever-popular pastime: rating other people's looks. I brought up Steve's name. She said she thought he was pretty cute. "You think he has a good body?" I asked, maintaining the straight-boy fiction that I wasn't capable of making that judgment on my own. She nodded, smiling.

"Would you do it with him?" I asked her.

That night, as we arrived back in Jerusalem, I told Steve she had said yes. "She wants you."

"Really?" He seemed confused. "I thought she liked you. You guys are always all talking and shit." Later that evening, I saw their eyes lock, but they didn't speak to each other. My attempt at matchmaking had led a creeping shyness to settle in between them. But by then I was concocting a plan that would bring us all together.

On our last day in Israel, we made a final visit to the Western Wall. Between the rocks of the wall so many visiting Jews had stuffed notes—the wishes, prayers, remembrances of year upon year—that the paper was indistinguishable from mortar. When I slipped my note in with the others, I felt a tingling in my fingertips. For a second I even fancied I could hear the heart of the Jewish people beating within the rock walls. But I wasn't certain whether it was a religious or sexual charge. On my note I had written, as if they were a Hebrew incantation, the evocative words "ménage à trois."

I don't know where I got the idea to have a ménage à trois, other than that I always had a pretentious predilection for French phrases. But I thought it was my best shot at having sex with Steve, or at least having sex in his vicinity. Erica was game. Perhaps she thought the idea had a continental flair. Perhaps she thought this was the surest way to get to have sex in *my* vicinity. Her only condition was that I be the one to ask Steve. As we got off the plane in Rome, and the Beverly Hills girls led the group on a frantic duty-free treasure hunt, I screwed up my courage and took Steve aside.

"Dude, you were right," I whispered. "She likes both of us. And…" I paused dramatically. "She wants to do it with both of us. At the same time."

"What!? No way!"

I nodded. "What do you say, man? Are you up for a threesome?"

He laughed nervously. "Sure…Totally!"

I grinned, relieved. "Cool."

"You, um, done this before?"

"Yeah, sure…" I told him. "But, uh, with two girls."

When I first learned we weren't getting any free time in Rome, and that we were to stay in our hotel the entire night, I'd been disappointed. Now I was thrilled with the sudden show of discipline; nothing would distract from my plan. I arranged to meet Steve and Erica by the rooftop swimming pool after eleven, which was the official lights-out. The group had managed to acquire several bottles of booze at the airport, and when I left

Cory sleeping in our room, I had a two-thirds full bottle of vodka in my hand. Nobody saw me as I took the elevator up to the top floor and walked out onto the roof. The view from the hotel, which was only minutes from the airport, was somewhat grim and institutional, more Soviet bloc than Spanish Steps. But the air was warm and the pool empty of guests. A perfect setting for what I had in mind. Whether it was the G-d of the Hebrews or a god of Ancient Rome, I felt sure that a divine force was operating in my favor.

Within seconds, a wary Erica emerged and sat next to me on a bench. We waited for Steve for about half an hour, sipping vodka.

"Maybe he saw somebody and had to go back to his room," I said, breaking a long silence. "Let's give him a couple more minutes."

Five more minutes passed. Then Erica looked at me. "Face it, he chickened out."

I slumped, miserable. "Guess we should go to bed."

Erica took a breath. "Well, just 'cause he won't doesn't mean we can't…"

"You mean, the two of us…? You can't have a ménage à trois with two people!," I sputtered.

"Suit yourself." She started to stand. I reconsidered her proposition.

"I don't know. I'm so drunk I'm not even sure I could get it up."

"Is that a dare?" she giggled. "To see if I can make you…?"

Was it a dare? My crude attempt at a pass? Or was the drunkenness an excuse to avoid doing something I never wanted in the first place? I don't know. But I remember the slight feeling of dishonesty that went along with the statement. And I remember the sense of determination with which I then fell into the role of horny guy. It was a case, I decided, of now or never.

"Yeah. Go ahead and try," I told her.

"Right here? Right now?"

"Why not? Nobody can see us."

And so she leaned over and unbuckled my pants. A few minutes later, she asked if I had a condom; she didn't know I'd been carrying at least one in each pocket since the first day of the trip. We had sex on the cement next to the pool. Later, I was able truthfully to tell people I'd lost my virginity on a rooftop in Rome. What could be more romantic? But the reality was a hard, cold, awkward affair—slow to get going and quick to finish. I don't think either of us enjoyed it much.

Afterward, I tiptoed into my hotel room, trying not to wake Cory. But he was waiting up for me.

"You're drunk," he said.

I nodded.

"That was my vodka."

I nodded.

"I should kick you out of the room."

I nodded.

Then I sat down on the bed.

"You stink! And get that smirk off your face." He swatted me with a pillow.

"Hey! You better treat me with respect. I'm a man now."

His eyes widened. " You mean…?"

"Uh-huh."

"With who?"

I hesitated. "Erica."

"But you don't even like her!"

The force of the accusation surprised me. It was if I had betrayed him in some way. As if he were jealous.

"Like you said, I was drunk."

He gave me a disgusted look.

"I know, it was pretty stupid," I said sheepishly.

After that admission, Cory grew friendlier and we talked for a few hours, eventually giving up on getting any sleep before the morning flight. I asked him if he was still planning on going back to live in Israel. He said he thought so, but he also admitted that sometimes the hard line taken by the Israelis had put off even him. "You know," he said, "I didn't like it when they told me I wasn't Jewish just because I was American."

I told him the trip had completely confused me about what it meant to be Jewish.

"At least you completed your mission," he offered.

"You think it counts if it wasn't in the Holy Land?" I joked.

"Depends. As an American, you're now a man, but not a Jew. As a Jew, you're still a boy. Actually, you don't exist…"

"Yeah, well what about you? You're not a man anywhere. Not even in Rome."

"I'll show you what a man is!" He hit me with a pillow, and we tussled, laughing.

It was the teen movie equivalent of a Talmudic argument. And, as in most teen movies, the homoerotic subtext in the hotel room remained unacknowledged. In retrospect, I think I would have gotten much further with Cory than I had with Steve, if only I'd tried. At the time, however, my closet door was shut too tight. A fantasy threesome was one thing, a real encounter with a friend another. I never saw Cory again. But whenever I hear news about Israel, which, alas, is all too often, I wonder if he made *aliyah* as he had planned, and if he is living there now. A gay soldier, perhaps, in a too-busy army.

One Hundred
Years of Gratitude
Lesléa Newman

When I told my siblings I was a lesbian, they had identical responses, though they live a thousand miles apart: "You're not going to tell Mom and Dad, are you?" Of course I was going to, and when I did, my parents had a similar, albeit more vehement response: "Don't you dare tell your grandmother."

But I did dare, despite my family's puzzlement over why she "had to know." After all, my grandmother was ninety-nine years old, and had "more important things to worry about," according to my mother. And even I had to admit my grandmother's plate was full. The year she turned ninety-nine, my grandmother's eyesight failed, her hearing declined, and worst of all, she was forced to give up the tiny Brooklyn apartment she had lived in for more than forty years to move into a nursing home.

I was well aware my grandmother had plenty of *tsouris;* I spoke to her on the telephone every day. When she had something to *kvetch* about, it was my ear she sought and vice versa. We were extremely close. I am her only daughter's only daughter and I am named for her husband, the grandfather I never knew who died a few months before I was born. Yet how close were we really, when I kept such a profound truth about my life a secret from her?

The truth is, I came out to my grandmother because I loved her more than anyone else in the world and I couldn't stand to see her suffer. And every time we talked on the phone, she spoke of the same pain: the pain of knowing she was not long for this world and once she was gone, I'd be left all alone. My grandmother was an expert on loneliness; she had been a widow for thirty-three years. "I talk to the walls, just to have someone to talk to," she'd tell me, "and I don't want that should happen to you." Other times she'd look at me baffled for I was her favorite granddaughter, in her eyes the smartest, prettiest, most talented girl in the world. So why didn't I have a "fella"? This made absolutely no sense to my grandmother, and as her hundredth birthday drew near, she grew more and more agitated about it.

"I only want to dance at your wedding, *mameleh*," she'd say. "Then I can die happy."

"Then I'm never getting married," I'd answer. "That way you'll live forever."

"Stop talking nonsense." My grandmother wagged a red painted nail. "It's no good to be alone. A stone is alone. Not a person."

Though I was far from alone, I couldn't face telling my grandmother that I lived with Mary, the woman I was in love with, the "friend" whom she had met many times. Instead I pointed out that even though she had gotten married, she still wound up living a third of her life all by herself, so what did it matter? My grandmother's response to this statement was to roll her eyes and shake her head. I was talking nonsense again.

On a crisp autumn day, a week before *Rosh Hashanah*, I drove to Brooklyn to visit my grandmother with exciting news. Mary had given me a diamond ring and we were planning to have a ceremony to celebrate our lifetime commitment to one another. Could I tell my grandmother? How could I? But how could I not? I was still trying to decide what to do when I walked into the nursing home, and my grandmother decided for me. Though legally blind by this time, she spotted my ring before I could even take off my coat or open my mouth. "What's that on your finger, an engagement ring, I should live so long?" she asked. I took a deep breath as she lifted my right hand to her eyes for a closer inspection.

"Yes, Grandma, it's an engagement ring," I said. "Mary gave it to me. We're having a ceremony."

"What?" My grandmother dropped my hand like it was a hot potato and then did something I had never seen her do: She turned her head to the side and spit three times. "*Feh*," she said, crossing her arms. "Lezel, darling, you're ruining your life."

"I am not ruining my life." I folded my arms too, but there was no arguing with her. She had seen people "like me" on television, and they had changed, so why couldn't I? When I told her I had no intention of changing, that I was happy the way I was, she looked at me with disdain.

"Happy, what do you know from happy?" she asked. "You think you know what's best for you, you never listen to anyone, you think you're so smart, you think you know everything. Well, you know something? You're too smart for your own good. *Feh*." She spit again, then clapped her hands together like she was dusting flour off them, a gesture I was very familiar with. It meant, *That's all I have to say: case closed.*

I left my grandmother without kissing her goodbye and cried all the way home. Maybe my family was right, I thought. Maybe it would have been better if she had never known. Now I had upset her, and she needed more aggravation like she needed a hole in the head. I expected angry messages from my parents and my siblings on my answering machine waiting to greet me when I got home, which I also needed like a hole in the head. But when I opened the door, no blinking red light met my swollen eyes. In fact, the phone didn't ring at all until six o'clock the next morning.

"*Mameleh*, I didn't sleep the whole night, so upset I was that you was mad on me." My grandmother's voice was shaky with emotion. "Listen, darling, I thought it over and all right, if you're happy, I'm happy too. Okay, darling? You're my Lezel and you'll always be my Lezel. You could sleep with a dog and I wouldn't care, I would still love you."

Though Mary and I got a lot of mileage out of that comment

for years to come, all I could do was choke back the tears in my throat and say, "Really, Grandma? You mean it?"

"Of course I mean it. I'm an old woman, darling, I don't got a lot of time left, so let's not fight no more."

Unfortunately, my grandmother's words proved to be true; she died a few months after our phone conversation, and she never did dance at my wedding. But she did give Mary and me her blessing. In fact, she treated Mary very differently the next time she saw her. She treated her like—for lack of a better word—a son-in-law, taking great interest in her job, her income, her plans for the future. When the visit was over, she placed Mary's hand on top of mine and told us to take care of each other. She said to me, "I love you, darling," and then she said to Mary, "And I love you too, for taking such good care on her." When I started to cry, she said, "*Shah*," and turned away, but the quaver in her voice betrayed her: She was crying too.

Times Are Changing, Reb Tevye
Dan Fishback

I hear my mother conducting dinner downstairs. From the supermarket, she has brought home familiar smells, familiar ingredients. It's a familiar Passover, made cozy in its ease. That's dill in the air. That's chicken broth. That's Mom flinging directions across the kitchen, that's Dad scurrying out of the way. Of course. I've been away at school all year, collecting surprises, and now I can snuggle into unself-conscious expectation. And that's why I'm sprawled out on the carpet upstairs, above their heads, like the bubble in a comic strip, like they're thinking, *Dan.*

I curl up with a small, oblong tin box. It's painted to look like a diner, labeled "Open 24 Hours," with M&M cartoons prancing around in sunglasses, sipping milkshakes, dancing in freeze-frame beneath suspended quarter notes. I have no idea where I got it, but I retrieve it from my closet when I come home. I'll arrive, hang out with my family, but pretty soon my parents will get involved in something and my brother will disappear. I'll run in terror from the archaic modem connection and end up here in my room, holding this box. When I open it, tightly folded pieces of paper will pop out like prank snakes in a can. I'll be covered in scraps from high school. Notes we passed in class. Printouts of instant-message conversations. The few handwritten letters I saved, including the ones

I photocopied before sending, as if I knew someday I'd be sitting here, compelled to read what this fifteen-year-old voice had to say to...who? Does it matter now?

Downstairs, my dad unearths the haggadahs and brings them to the dining room. At our Passover dinner tonight, we will read from this book—the story of our people's exodus from Egypt. Families around the world will read the story aloud, but not everyone will read *our* haggadah—the "freedom seder." When I was little, Passover meant looking up at the adults talking about César Chávez, about striking workers, about our responsibility as Jews to support the struggles of oppressed people all over the world. It meant thinking about my great-grandfather. When I was very young, the story went something like: "Great-Grandpa Sam traveled *under* a train to get to America." It always sounded odd, but I took it for granted. In time, it started to make more sense. The eldest son of a rabbi (in a long line of rabbis), Sam rejected tradition and ran away to the city. He became the printer of an underground socialist newspaper and was soon arrested by the czar and deported to Siberia. But in a comically undramatic turn of events (this is my favorite part of the story), he walked out. They figured no one could just walk away from Siberia without freezing to death, so it was apparently no big deal to mosey off. He found a train, lodged himself in the machinery (traveled *under* a train!), and rode out of Russia, settling eventually in New York, where he again printed a socialist newspaper, fighting for the disenfranchised. Just like Cesar Chavez. And Moses. It's all the same seder to me: Russia, Egypt, the czar, the pharaoh... The pieces of Passover sing to each other in my head, none of them quite possible in isolation. They murmur between my ears all year long, amplified whenever thoughts of oppression surface, which is often.

Upstairs, I sort through the scraps of paper. I'm so used to them that I recognize their content by the handwriting, the color of ink, the shape of the paragraphs. *That's a Katie note, from early sophomore year, not important.* I move some pages to the side. The hierarchy is obvious. Of all the things that happened in high school, two months were more rigorously documented than the rest. The vast majority of these notes—the ones I, for some reason, decided to keep—were written during March and April 1997.

When I think about these events, I don't just conjure the image of the scene—I see the note itself: the handwriting, the ink, the shape of the paragraph.

✡

March 10, 1997: blue computer ink, white printer paper. Bottom margin lined with smiley-face emoticons. Tyler slips me the typewritten note after rehearsal. We're in our drama club production of *Fiddler on the Roof.* My brother, Mike, undisputed star of the high school stage, is ending his illustrious career with a bang: Tevye, the role of a lifetime. I, an up-and-coming sophomore, am ascending to my first lead—Motel the tailor. Tyler is a cossack—a fitting role indeed because I simply don't like him. He comes across as arrogant, elitist, preppy. But one night in mid March, talking on the phone, Caitlin tells me of Tyler's summer romance with…a boy.

I'm stunned. I didn't even know he was gay. Well, perhaps I knew, but I never thought he would *tell* anyone. And he wasn't just gay. He had sex. With his body. I tingle all over and pull the blankets around me in bed, disturbingly aware of my thighs. It is now, for some reason, that I decide to tell Caitlin I'm gay. And when I hang up the phone, I realize I'm suddenly attracted to Tyler. I get comfortable under the sheets and go to sleep relaxed.

So it only takes this note, in blue ink, offering a shoulder to cry on and an understanding ear, to send me flinging my imagination unclothed into a future of Tylered possibilities.

The blue-inked letter begets a series of torn, wide-ruled notebook pages. We pass them to each other between classes as we rearrange our routes to see each other. I'm too dazed by this sudden flirtation to let my paranoia prompt anything but giddy cheer. Tyler's words grow more suggestive. I can't believe they're true with anything but my imagination, which perpetually saturates itself in cosmic erotic dramas of true love and covert consummation.

So I'm somewhat unprepared, in my week of hazy bliss, for a phone call on the Ides of March, with Christine's frantic voice: "Tyler can't use his phone right now, but he told me to tell you Caitlin told him that Amber told your brother you're gay!"

What? "Everyone's worried about you!" I become very aware of Mike in the next room—the fact of him, sitting there, doing homework, having mentioned nothing, notoriously reserved, except for an infamous temper. He's different around his friends. Personable. They like him. But at home he seems possessed by this alien tension. Usually methodical, almost eerily uniform, he'll suddenly snap at seemingly nothing, storm away, leaving my parents and me bewildered. "What the hell was that?" Inexplicable. Like a sort of malfunctioning robot—normally cold, conservative, collected, but at moments volcanic, desperate, seething.

I hang up the phone and sit in silence for a long while, staring at the wall separating our rooms. The air in Mike's room is always thick, the lighting dim. He sits on his floor often, surrounded by folders and stacks of paper, organizing his life. Grade-A worksheets back through elementary school. When you open his door, which is often closed, you stand face-to-face with a wall. You have to turn left to enter the actual chamber. And that's how I imagine my brother's room: a wall, and then this person sitting on his floor, surrounded by his achievements. The combined effect is dungeon-like. I don't like going in there.

Particularly not under these circumstances. I've been planning on being methodical—like him—about coming out, telling him before my parents, enlisting his help, planning strategically to break the news. But I've been putting it off—it's not going to be pretty. My brother constantly mocks my voice, presenting me as some sort of autistic Valley girl. As disgusted as he is by my personality, my sexuality might freak him out beyond gratuitous insult.

So I've been expecting an explosion of disdain, and yet he

hasn't said a thing. His room is quiet, which makes it all the more foreboding.

I knock on the door and walk in. "So I hear you talked to Amber today…"

He looks down. "Close the door."

Shit shit shit. I close the door. "Listen, Mike…"

"I am too."

His voice is small, shaky, projected down into his crossed legs. I think to myself what a poor sense of humor he has—what sad delivery. He's too wimpy to even look me in the eye as he unveils the punch line to his silence. He probably would have cracked up laughing. Who does he think he is, making fun of me like this? How could he take this so lightly?

"That's not funny. That's the most horrible joke you could possibly…"

"I'm not joking."

"Shut up! Stop it!" I start to cry. It's a joke. It's a joke. He's try-ing to milk it, trying to salvage a weak finale.

"I'm not joking." His face collapses. He's not joking.

He tries to explain his story—the confusion he's faced where I face certainty, the ambiguity that tortures him where desire tor-tures me; his revelation is paralyzing, while mine is nothing short of salvation. And all this time he's been reassuring himself that our parents would have at least one straight son—me!

No, no, no, this is not how it was supposed to happen. *I* was supposed to tell *him*, reassure him that everything would be fine, that Mom and Dad would be okay because *he'd* be there to do all those straight-son things—my brother, so straight he's practically asexual, never expressing desire beyond chaste respect. It's always been endearing, and I could envision his family: in sweaters, in bifocals, placid reserve punctuated by feral hostility—the perfect American family.

"Dan, it would kill them! Mom keeps talking about grandchil-dren!" His crying deepens, forces its way through his torso, shak-ing him. I try to tell him—that I've got a plan, that I'll come out over the summer, that they love me, and it'll be okay. But *both* of us now…

"Mike, what about you?"

"I'm not telling them." He pauses. "Not in the foreseeable future." He has settled. He is still. A recognizable brother has returned. I can't breathe a word of this to anyone, he says. We plan for the summer. We get organized. He seems more comfortable as we develop a strategy. *I'll come out; he'll stay in.* He'll deal some-how.

I make myself believe he's secure in his decision. If I can't talk about it, it's like it didn't even happen. We'll just act like he has no orientation at all, which is kind of true anyway, so it's a minor set-back really. If he doesn't want to deal with it, I'm certainly not going to. I have other things on my mind: I'm in love…

March 22: I seclude myself in a far corner of my aunt's New Jersey home, scribbling to Caitlin in my notepad. I write page after page, soon running out of ink, resorting to the crayons inexplica-bly in my possession. I didn't want to travel this weekend, the weekend of Elena Winningham's big birthday party, a party for which Tyler has stolen a pair of very tight plaid pants from the cos-tume room, a pair of pants that have been on my mind and in my notes all week long. I cross my legs at the thought. But my grand-mother is sick, and our presence is important.

And yet, perversely, I can think of nothing to do but write let-ters and fantasize about Tyler. No one in my family, not even my increasingly tense brother, is on my mind. As I switch from peri-winkle to red-orange, my written whine grows shrill with newly learned gay jokes, puns, media references I know Caitlin won't get. Feeling lonely and tragic in this vast quiet house, I describe my ideal boyfriend. The list of traits goes on and on, a mix of genuine desires and odd tips of the hat to gay culture: "someone who will cry in front of me…someone who'll know what to do with my hair…someone who wants children…someone who knows about burlesque theater…" On pages of fuchsia, sea green, and cobalt blue runs a list of non sequiturs, gaining urgency as they become more forced—the intensity of their source burning hotter the more effort it takes to sound creative, interesting, complicated. I write into existence…something. A rainbow of fantasy and pretension with too many heads, all breathing fire. It keeps me company, feeling vital as long as it expands, as long as I keep writing, until Caitlin calls to tell me she has spoken to Tyler and that "someone has a crush" on me.

As soon as she hangs up, I whip out my pad and unleash the magenta: "I JUST TALKED TO YOU!! I'M ON TOP OF THE WORLD!!!!"

March 25, a note from Tyler: "I had a lot of, um…fun yesterday—very thrilling!—same bat time, same bat place?" The previous morning, a Monday, I bring a change of clothes in my backpack. When I get to school, I run to the bathroom and squeeze into a spandex T-shirt and tight bell-bottoms. In my gayest outfit, I emerge into the hallway to meet the boy who likes me. We pass notes between classes, each getting more and more suggestive, until, by seventh period, we have become boyfriends. Tyler: "I realize we wouldn't be holding hands in the hallway, and especially not in front of Mike, but I'd be willing to make it work—hey, keeping it secret would be an adventure!" No one can guess why I'm so bouncy, staring down the clock, waiting for class to end, for rehearsal to begin.

In the auditorium, as the girls practice "Matchmaker, Matchmaker," Tyler asks if I want to go somewhere to talk, so we skip backstage to the boys' dressing room. It's a long room, one wall covered with mirrors. We sit along the opposite side on a ratty prop couch. When we drop ourselves down, facing each other, our thighs intertwine, and I'm blown away by his physicality, his mass. He has a body and it's right there. I'm only slightly distracted by our reflection on the other side of the room.

Soon, his head advances, and I move to kiss him, hoping he'll know what do, reminding myself how unbelievable this is—I'm about to kiss a boy!—and *BAM!* Our mouths collide—flat, failed. I blink and giggle: My fantasies have never accounted for stubble! I ponder that for a moment, but then he lunges forward again, this time openmouthed, breaching my lips with his tongue. It squirms inside me. He holds me tightly, frantically. The force of his face knocks my head back, and I go stiff all over, my mouth busted ajar, my limbs confused, twisted, bent every which way, like a squashed bug. I struggle to regain control: My hands find his shoulders and slide across his back (fingers twitching), my thigh slips over his legs, pulling my hips toward his lap (his lap! oh, G-d!), then (push! push!) my head finally dislodges itself from its neck (pop!), but—my tongue—what should it do?! It has nowhere to go, like my penis, itself crunched up against brutal denim, his pelvis pressing it into me (I think of trash compactors). Each twist for penis liberation sends my boxers scooching up my thighs, gathering in worn, nubbly bunches in my butt crack. I can't move a muscle without sentencing some poor body part to a humid torture chamber—and yet: Here is a boy! A *boyfriend*! Rubbing up against me!

His tongue still inside me, I turn my eyes to the dressing-room mirror, at two fifteen-year-old boys braiding themselves through each other. The rodeo in my mouth is shielded from view. *He wants me this much*, I reason. So, squelching tears and muffling laughter, I shove him back—our faces still fused together—and roll my whole body onto his lap, squeezing his waist between my thighs: He's surprised and reels in his tongue, followed desperately by mine, plunging across the border and entering his body.

We stop after a few minutes, not wanting to seem suspicious, and I run onto the stage, panting, late, to sing a love song to a girl:

> *Wonder of wonders, miracle of miracles,*
> *G-d took a Daniel once again,*
> *Stood by his side and, miracle of miracles,*
> *Led him through the lions' den!*

My song is infused with new energy. I don't need to act any-more—it's real. Motel spends his whole life thinking he's nothing, a poor tailor. He never expects to win the girl of his dreams, and

26

he's always too nervous to try. But finally he snaps, stands up for himself, defies tradition, and gets his girl. I see Tyler in the audience and belt each note in a cackling frenzy, still semierect.

It seems natural, to slip into this Russian peasant's outfit every afternoon—it feels fittingly revolutionary. Breaking with tradition on this stage, in this makeshift *shtetl,* makes me feel like my great-grandfather. And so, oddly enough, does making out with my boyfriend backstage. Breaking tradition is my tradition. And now I get to embody it, literally.

But my brother is busy embodying a different Jewish tradition. (March 28, Tyler: "Did Mike say anything?") I watch him now, singing these grand songs—portraying a man who is rapidly becoming an anachronism. He isn't acting either. His twinges of confusion and rage are real, as each of his daughters betray tradition in the name of love. He resists: *"Where do they think they are? America?" "If I try to bend that far, I will break!" "This isn't the way it's done—not here, not now—some things I will not, I cannot allow!"*

He says to me, "You must be crazy, arranging a match for yourself!"

"Times are changing, Reb Tevye," I reply.

We don't speak much offstage. He doesn't want to hear about my daily dressing-room debauchery with Tyler, and I don't want to be distracted from it. Every day is a prologue to the feverish, frantic kisses I will suck from my boyfriend's mouth; my muffled groans as he gropes my body, reassuringly, as if to say, "Yes, this ass is acceptable. Yes, this thigh too. You pass inspection—you're a person."

His notes grow infrequent. Mine do not, but I don't remember what I wrote (March 29, Tyler: "You know, I have all the notes you've written me."). My words have vanished now. All I have are his, as they taper off, each signifying more and more time: the classes spent scribbling "Dear Tyler" letters, the rehearsals spent itching to get backstage, waiting to feel my life happen to me, waiting to feel my body happen to me.

With April comes a burst of notes from my friends: "Are you okay?!" "What did he do?!" "I'll kill him!"

There's something wrong with him on April 7—he's not so

eager to make eye contact. He asks me to come to the dressing room, and this time he actually *does* want to talk.

When he's finished breaking up with me, I stand up, nauseous, barely breathing, and rack my brain for something cinematic to say. "Well it's been fun," I finally blurt out. He winks at me and smiles. "Don't look at me like that!" I scream and run out the door. I end up in the girls' dressing room, where I collapse, sobbing, "I can't do this alone! I can't do this alo-ho-hone," feeling at first like a sham, like the serious thirty seconds of a badly written sitcom. But the sting of mimesis doesn't last—I soon feel at home in my tears, in my wailing. I set up house there. The girl playing Golde hands me paper towels as I look into the dressing room mirror, my red eyeballs making their green irises look fierce, poisonous. I feel wronged, and powerful in my wrongedness—but "alo-ho-hone."

So I tell all my friends. I write them notes, remembering the really sizzling phrases from the most apocalyptic Tyler fights, and repeating them for each new audience. They pass the notes back: "What an asshole!" "Tyler sucks now." "If you need anything, call me." So I call, and I talk about my feelings in excruciating detail, whisking the phone into the basement, hiding from my parents—who've caught on to *something,* but they clearly don't know what—and from my brother, who receives news of my breakup with expressionless disinterest. I recite for my friends the unfolding Tyler drama, full of fiery confrontations and a cast full of Jewish peasants taking sides.

Tyler has leaked top-secret, shocking information to the general populace: Dan Fishback is gay. Yes, it was obvious; yes I was planning on telling them eventually anyway, but the premature outing leaves me numb. He's a thief. He stole my revolution. He's deprived me not only of my coming-out party but of my body—my chance to feel it all happen—and it's because he's deprived me of *his* body, of something to rub up against. In its stead he's left me with something to kick against. Not his body but his character. I grow nasty when we all gather in the dressing rooms during rehearsal. Some of the villagers rally around me, others around him—most have no idea what they're fighting about. But rehearsals are growing tense, and there's much to gossip about afterward.

But my friends have better things to do than listen to me bitch and whine—things like homework. So I often end up online, browsing aimlessly through Tori Amos Web sites, feeling tragic and broken. One day I get an instant message from a stranger. The message goes something like, "Hey, my name's Kris—I used to know Tyler and he was really mean to me. I heard what he did to you, and I think it sucks." Kris offers his ear—the very thing Tyler had promised me but had taken away. I unleash the floodgates. I begin to blabber.

Every night I come home from rehearsal and talk to Kris on my parents' computer. He's jarringly interested in everything I say. He responds supportively and fuels my rage. So I type and type. After a week or so, I find myself attracted to him. I don't understand it, since I know virtually nothing about him. But it feels so good to talk to this boy—this gay boy—who understands and believes in me. And it feels so good that my parents don't know. I'm recapturing my revolution: whispers, secrets, power. But through all our deviant chitchat, I'm aware of Mike sitting in his room. He will never have this. He will never know a misery this sweet—this alive. He will never have stupid teenage epic anything. His pain is different. It knows no stage. It has no lights, no orchestra. This musical we're in at school—this is his only chance to do something with his despair—to turn it into something (*anything*) other than a five-second temper tantrum. When we're done, all he'll have is a costume. And what a costume. A fake beard. A cap. Khakis and a buttoned shirt, tucked in.

Nonetheless, I'm more concerned with my tortured chastity than his drab reticence—for he claims his is voluntary, and I'm eager to believe him. Right now I'm preoccupied with next week's show. *Kris says he's going to come.*

I pass a note to Anna in fourth period pre-calc: "Kris is coming to the show! I'm so excited. I hope he's cute!" Anna reads the note gravely, frowning. She passes the note back: "Dan…Kris isn't real. It's Tyler."

I lose it in the parking lot, hours later, as my brother is about to drive me home. He says something vaguely aggressive or insulting, and I snap, shrieking out my tears, fumbling into the car. I tell him what happened—that I had a crush on someone who didn't exist, that Tyler's been playing cruel games. It starts to rain, and we pull out onto the street. My brother is silent as my heaving dies down to a slow, steady moan. Despite my display, which Mike usually brushes aside as nonsense, I can feel heat from the driver's seat. He's pissed off. And not at me. At Tyler. He feels...protective. "That asshole," he says. So I don't mind much that, driving in our station wagon, he's the safe and noble son, and I'm the foolish and broken one. I don't mind that he's traditional and upright, and I'm radical and beaten. There is no "I told you so" in his manner—just compassion, solidarity. His pain tips its hat to mine. "Sorry," it says. "Same to you," mine replies. For the first time in ages, it feels like we're on the same side of something.

The next week, we perform.

When I'm not onstage, I hang out in the wings, watching the show…

Tevye/Mike hauls his milk cart onstage. He is tired. He talks to G-d: *Sometimes I think when things get too quiet up there, you say to yourself, "Let's see what kind of mischief I can play on my friend Tevye."* He feels played upon, the object of a sick joke. Burdened. With what? With the reality of his life? The desires he must confront? Perhaps it's the cart itself—the job of Papa, the list of chores: *Who day and night must scramble for a living, feed his wife and children, say his daily prayers?* And the perk: *Who has the right as master of the house to have the final word at home? Who? The Papa-a-a. The Papa.*

He gets up from the cart. He dances: *I would yadadada-yadadada-dadadadadie… All day long, I'd biddy-biddy-bum…* If he were Papa. If he could feed his wife and children, say his daily prayers. *Without our traditions, our lives would be as shaky as…* Yes, and *with* our traditions? What do you have? This still, still man—this emotionally motionless boy struggling to contain himself, to resist himself, to halt. He is tectonic, scarred with fault—something must give! What do you want him to do? *Lord who made the lion and the lamb, You decreed I should be what I am! Would it spoil some vast eternal plan?* His arms flail, his eyes unfocused, seething, desperate, sweat spilling from his fake beard, like the beard itself is weeping, itself scorched under the spotlights. I see a breakdown.

But not the audience—they are silent, wide-eyed, slack-jawed. No one has seen high school theater this brilliant. Awe abounds. Tevye/Mike fills his body with pain. It sends him flying around the stage. He looks grand, important—he is, for once, the Papa (*the Papa-a-a!*). He heaves his last note into the air, flooding the room in a shockwave of sound and desire, what he fears, what he craves, what he glories in performing: *Ma-a-an!*

He embraces me after curtain call, both our faces dribbling helplessly. "Keep it going," he says. "Tradition."

✡

Now, lying on my carpet, covered in paper, I hear my family clunking around downstairs, laughing. I smile—my brother has discovered alternative traditions. We have both come out to our parents, who are now equally traditional: My mother organizes LGBT outreach programs for local synagogues; my dad has joined a committee to make public schools safer for gay kids; my brother teaches identity politics to seventh-graders. He's out to them. He's even had a boyfriend. He's even…happy. They're all tapping into the revolutionary tradition, a tradition of horror and redemption—at first: "They enslaved us in Egypt," "They desecrated our temple," "They destroyed our village," but then: "We escaped from Egypt," "Mattathais would not bow," "Great-Grandpa Sam traveled to America *under* a train!" They slaughtered us in gas chambers, but we are still here. So of course my parents are supportive—we're Jews—we know what it feels like to be persecuted even if we don't know what it feels like to be persecuted. We hear the stories. Again and again: *Never again.* So middle-school bullies were nothing new. Tyler was nothing new. No pain is new to me. We know what it feels like to be persecuted. Even if we don't. We know.

I know. I seem to have made it my business. I gather the notes, stuff them back in their box. A rabbi somewhere places a Torah in its Ark. We're Jews because we remember. We remember being victims. We recite in constant rotation our cultural memoirs, our story of anguish and survival. When it ends, we unroll the scroll back to its beginning and start over, knowing full well the story didn't end there. That wasn't the half of it.

Why do we do these things? I'll tell you…I don't know. But it's a tradition! A peanut M&M jitterbugs beneath the painted sign: "Open 24 Hours." I close the box but keep the stories. *Never again!* Every boy is a cossack now. Every touch an invasion. Every kiss a sign of impending disaster, a mnemonic device: *Playing with matches, a girl can get burned.*

My brother is forging ahead, open to love and life. So why do I feel so cold, after all this time? Why do I feel so melodramatic?— so tragically, tragically underkissed and so unwilling to do anything about it? I hold the box in my hands and I don't let go. I wait for a long time. I don't want to go downstairs. I don't want to see my family; I want to sit here with my stories.

I hear voices in the kitchen. They're talking about politics, about Israel. Someone says something about Palestinian rights. Someone says something about the Holocaust. I hear the word "paranoia." I hear the word "traumatized." I hear all sorts of words: "crazy," "understandable," "overreaction," "irrational." Someone says, "ghetto mentality."

I don't want to listen to politics. I don't want to listen to anything. I open the box again. I look for the beginning—for blue ink on white paper. I start to read:

"March 10, 1997…"

Oh, My Godzilla
Bonnie Kaplan

To my mother, camp was a four-letter word for baby-sitter. It didn't matter what type of camp I went to as long as I was off-site and out of her hair. She had even negotiated to get me into camp at an early age (for free) by letting the director borrow our 1961 Chevy station wagon. By my early teens I had been to dozens of camps. I was happy to go; I loved shopping at the military surplus store for duffel bags and footlockers. And it was great to get out of the suburbs. I would finally learn to barrel stitch a lanyard.

Around my thirteenth birthday, my mother was running out of camps to send me to. They were all specialized and I didn't need to lose weight and I was allergic to horses. My friend Melissa was involved in the Baptist Church youth fellowship. The church had a retreat each summer in the Sierra Mountains. Suddenly, my mom had an idea: Baptist camp for three weeks, even though I'd be the only Jew there. I was a Jewish tomboy from the San Fernando who skateboarded and lived in cutoffs. I was eager to try pot, and being saved was the furthest thing from my mind that summer.

Upon arrival we gathered in the large cafeteria. I didn't know the Christian songs. They didn't sing the usual rounds and folk songs I'd grown up with. I soon realized I was surrounded by hundreds of teenagers—an army of youths being trained to go forth and save souls. It was if someone had sent them a divine gift, a Jew to practice on. I was sure if I didn't exist, the campers would have elected someone to be the nonbeliever. Still, I wanted to make friends. I wanted to fit in and play their games.

On my first full day at camp, a boy with long brown hair approached me and asked me where I stood with Jesus. I told him I wasn't sure. He asked me to come sit on the hill so he could tell me more about The Word. I listened intently until he leaned forward to kiss me, at which point I ran down the hill to my cabin. That's when I saw Lori lying in her bunk riffling through her latest care package. "Pringles? Beef jerky? Red licorice?" she offered.

"Red licorice," I smiled.

Lori was beautiful: tall and slim with silky black hair past her waist. She loved camp and was going to stay the whole summer session. She was very tan, made even more striking by the white tank top and puka shells she wore. I was dreaming of Lori the night I sleepwalked. While asleep, I climbed down from my bunk and sat on one of my fellow campers, "Get off me, you crazy person!" the girl wailed. I was sound asleep and continued to sit on her chest. In my somnambulist displacement, I began to shout for *her* to get off *me*. I remember waking up mortified. All I could think was, "Thank G-d it wasn't Lori."

I was a budding lesbian. I was the only Jew in the place. I couldn't be trusted in my sleep. Needless to say, I wasn't making many friends. But the next day, I managed to make things even worse. That morning in the latrine I noticed there was no toilet paper. "Oh, my G-d...there's no paper in here," I winced.

A voice came out of the next stall: "It's *my* G-d too."

"What do you mean? What are you talking about?"

"You used G-d's name in vain," she said.

"Ah, okay, oh, my God...zilla." I quickly made up a solution to the problem.

"I'm sorry," she said, "but that's not going to work."

"Yes, it is," I said louder. "Oh, my Godzilla, would you give me some toilet paper, please?" A hand appeared under the stall with a moderate amount of camp-quality tissue. I got out in time to see her scuttling off, proud of her admonishment. For the rest of the summer, to the shock and dismay of my Baptist campers, I continued to replace the word "G-d" with "Godzilla" whenever I caught myself speaking in my natural Valley Girl vernacular.

By the second week of camp, the pressure for me to convert was starting to wear on me. "Can I get one of those books?" I asked the girl who bunked below me. *The Way,* a youth Bible, answered difficult questions for teens, like "Why do my parents fight?" by referring them to specific scripture. In addition, fellow campers before me had carved all kinds of religious graffiti into the Lincoln Logs that made up our cabin. Sitting on the top bunk, I'd proudly proclaim, "Matthew is my favorite!" and quote the passage I had discovered on the cabin wall. I'd sit up at night read the Bible by flashlight. I promised myself I was going to finish it because I couldn't take it home.

Twice a day everyone walked quietly to attend a sermon in the little church at the edge of camp. I enjoyed the short hike to the church. A few of the hymns began to roll out of me. I ate bread out of the basket that was passed around during the meetings. My friend told me I wasn't supposed to do that. "Now you're Baptist," she said with a look of mild shock. "You can't go back now. You've consumed his body, his flesh."

"No, I didn't," I told her. "I just ate some bread from a basket that was being passed around." From then on, I was careful not to eat the bread when it was handed down the row. "Jewish," I would whisper, and they'd pass the basket high over me.

During the last week, a special trip was planned off-site, but the camp hadn't planned for enough bus transportation. A couple of flatbed trucks pulled up with wooden slats for containment.

"Are those cattle trucks?" I asked.

"Not if there ain't cattle in 'em," the driver said.

I didn't have a choice; if I wanted to canoe, raft the rapids, or do whatever they'd planned for us, I had to get on that truck. I had a vision of Jews being loaded onto a similar truck. I protested, but they convinced me it would be fun and helped me into the truck. The campers were squeezed in tightly. The driver started the climb along the sharp curving mountain road. My fellow campers sang songs of joy and rebirth. They bounced and slid along the flatbed without a care. The blood began to drain from my face; I felt hot and cold at the same time, and then I threw up all over the wooden floor of the truck.

The trucks dropped us off at a natural waterslide, a gently sloping river where campers slid down foaming rapids over smooth rocks. I let the water pull me over the rocks and down the river first on my back and eventually on my belly. Hallelujah! It was invigorating, it was cleansing, and it was fun. *Perhaps this is what it means to be reborn,* I realized. For weeks fellow campers had been trying to get me to experience a second birth, but I'd resisted their every explanation. All along, it was my mom who had shown me The Way. She had sent me to camp so I could hike and hug pine trees. She had given me this spirituality, one seeped in ghost stories and marked by lanyard key chains. The entire camp experience had been spiritual—but not because I had read The Way. My mother knew a childhood of watching shooting stars and singing "Kumbaya" was meant for me.

At the end of camp I gave back the New Testament I had borrowed. Soon I would be home. I was pretty sure I was Baptist. I'd eaten the bread, sung the hymns, and slept among the psalms. I was too embarrassed to discuss my possible conversion with anyone. My Jewish neighbor intervened after I'd come home and while swimming in his backyard, he found me singing, *"When I get to heaven, gonna walk with Jesus..."*

"Where did you learn that song?" he asked.

"I just came back from Baptist camp," I told him. "I was there three weeks."

"You know, Bonnie," he said, "our temple has a youth group, and we'd be glad to take you next Saturday afternoon." Before I knew it I was going to a camp where they served bagels, lox, and cream cheese on Sunday mornings.

Oh, my Godzilla, I was home.

On Becoming a Man
Jeffrey Bernhardt

These were the days after my bar mitzvah, the day I supposedly became a man, the day friends and relatives watched as I entered manhood. I remember standing on the bimah on that cold January day, snow falling outside the large gray-stoned building that housed the octagonal sanctuary. The sanctuary was capped with a striking dome, which inside created an ornate ceiling with large hanging light fixtures. Including the balcony, the space could probably have seated a thousand. I stood before the sacred scroll, the silver filigreed pointer in my shaking hand, frustrated at my inability to control the trembling. I heard the words of the rabbi and cantor, though my anxiety hardly allowed me to make sense of them. On this day in the dimly lit sanctuary the Shabbat crowd was larger than usual, though spread amongst the many seats, the number still seemed thin. I imagined a day years earlier when hundreds of the seats might have been filled by the many Jews who had previously lived in the neighborhood.

The walls of the sanctuary were made up of large gray stones, reminiscent of the Western Wall in Jerusalem. The stained-glass windows high up on the walls allowed in little light on this cloud-filled day. There was a cold, cavern-like hollowness in the room. I stood by the rabbi and cantor waiting for what seemed to be hours. As the speech continued, my eyes moved through the crowd, most everyone there for *me*. I felt the air in my stomach bubbling and the gases gurgling. My heart was racing. My parents stood to the side, and I saw myself as I thought they saw me. I stood five foot something, taller than average for my age. Medium-length brown hair framed my smooth, light face, not yet marked by acne. It was the start of the bicentennial craze, and my suit jacket was a red-white-and-blue tweed, my tie the same colors. Draped over my shoulders was the traditional white tallis with blue stripes. I wondered what else my mother and father saw as they looked upon their oldest child at this rite of passage.

Suddenly the rabbi's words were over, and the time had come for me to recite the blessings. My voice still high, I chanted on key but with a nervous rhythm. I felt the eyes of parents, grandparents, cousins, friends upon me, the heat of their stares causing hundreds of drops of perspiration to form on my forehead.

I stood facing the rabbi after finishing my chanting as well as my speech. The rabbi was like a kindly grandfather, soft-spoken, offering a generous smile whenever he saw me. I felt comfort in sensing he liked me. He stood before me in his black gown and headpiece (almost a black crown of sorts) and smiled down on me, his translucent blue eyes meeting mine. He began to speak in his deep voice, and I tried to maintain eye contact though it was awkward and the scene surreal. I began to feel soothed by the smooth, steady waves of his words. I looked at my parents, who stood behind the rabbi and to his right. Their eyes were mist-covered as they looked upon the scene. They smiled lovingly at me, my mother all the while dabbing her eyes with a white hankie.

"Jeffrey," I heard the rabbi say at one point, "today you are a man." His voice continued on though the words remained muffled and indistinguishable. I continued to look at the rabbi as he spoke, but I imagine my eyes were vacant as I found myself obsessing over what it meant to be a man. Could I be a man if I had spent years unself-consciously playing with my sister's Barbie dolls? Could I be a man if I had no interest in the Mets or Yankees and couldn't care less about the Super Bowl? Could I be a man if I found myself fantasizing about Keith Partridge, Peter Brady, and Dick Grayson?

Suddenly I felt naked on the bimah, vulnerable before my parents and friends. What did they see when they looked at me? Hardly a man, I imagined.

During those years I typically went to synagogue on Shabbat once or twice a month. There were few others my age, so I received a lot of attention and doting from the elderly congregants who formed the majority of the thirty or forty service attendees. During the Torah service I'd struggle to follow along in the old blue Torah volumes, the binding peeling off. But it was during the end of the Torah service that I was most captivated, for there was a young man, most likely college age at the time, who would lift the Torah. On cue from our venerable white-haired rabbi we'd rise out of respect for the Torah. This tall, beautiful, olive-skinned young man stood before us, his button-down white sport shirt covered with an oversize tallis he folded neatly over his broad shoulders. His white sleeves were rolled to below the elbow, revealing his strong, tanned forearms covered with light brown hairs. He'd stand before the podium, bend his knees, and with ease and grace lift the Torah in one smooth movement. He'd turn for a few moments, with his back to the sparse congregation, so we could see the words of the holy scroll. Right then it felt as though he were revealing a secret to me, whispering the truth in my ear. He'd then move to an ornate padded red chair with arms and legs painted gold, and sit with the scroll as someone else wrapped and covered it and then placed the silver ornaments upon it. He'd remain seated with the Torah against his shoulder, arms embracing it, keeping it safe. I imagined being that Torah. Being held in his arms, my face rubbing against the young stubble of his cheeks and chin. I wanted to run my hand through his black curly hair and feel the soft hairs on his manly forearms as I mindlessly rubbed my hand up and down his arm like a young boy on his father's lap.

On one of those Shabbat mornings, as happened occasionally, I was invited up for the honor of wrapping the Torah while he held it. The tall young cantor stood in the ceremonial black robe and black head covering, instructing me on how to place each object (the silver crown with small jingling bells, the silver pointer used to follow the place in the scroll, the breastplate) and in which order. I accomplished each task with as much self-confidence as I could muster, at times placing the objects just before the cantor could give his instruction. I vowed not to appear ignorant in the presence of the object of my admiration. As I performed my appointed tasks I remained focused and feared eye contact as though my stare would betray my longing for this beautiful man. At the end of the job I extended my hand to him, offered the traditional words "*yeshar koach*," and only then and only briefly looked him in the eye. I did this as if it were part of the ritual, as if it meant nothing more to me than any other required act. But maintaining my composure took a great bit of effort as I felt the softness and strength of his bigger hand when his palm touched mine. And when I looked into his face, ever so briefly, and he smiled and returned the traditional words, I quickly smiled back. Then I nervously moved on, turning quickly to shake hands with the cantor and the rabbi as was the custom. When I returned to my seat I stole glances at this beautiful, rugged, and seemingly devout man. I rubbed my fingers against the palm of my hand as though I felt his presence in the palm he had just touched. I secretly moved my young fingers to my nose and breathed in his scent. At the end of the Shabbat services I typically did not have the courage to even approach him to wish him "Shabbat Shalom," for fear that even in that small and traditional gesture, my words, my tone, my awkwardness would reveal my desire.

✡

It was on one of those Shabbat days that Mr. Feldberg, the regular Shabbat usher, approached me during the Torah service. "Jeffrey, we need you to lift the Torah this week," he said. All the other congregants were too old and weak, he told me, and the usual lifter had broken his arm. I had earlier stealthily looked over at the young man whom I continued to admire when in his presence and had begun to fantasize about when I was not. I typically tried to find a seat that would keep him in my view, but only at this time, having had it pointed out, did I see the cast covering his right arm. There was something strangely arousing about this as it seemed to point out his strength, his athleticism, as I fantasized about how he might have broken his arm. Perhaps it had happened while he was playing baseball or, even more exciting, during a wrestling match with another good-looking college student.

Feeling cornered, I accepted the honor from the usher, which instantaneously raised my anxiety as I had never before lifted the Torah. It could be quite heavy, and depending on how far into the annual reading we were, one side could be significantly weightier than the other. The job required strength and confidence, neither of which were my strong suit. In any case, I had accepted the task, and now I dreaded what felt like the moment of truth—when my strength, my manhood would be put to the test. Through the rest of the Torah service as the moment grew closer, I became more and more anxious. In addition to worrying I might look weak, I was concerned about dropping the Torah, for while I'd never witnessed it, all kinds of Jewish suburban myths circulated among children about what would happen if you did drop it (required fasting for forty days being the most popular of these).

When Mr. Feldberg motioned for me to ascend the bimah, the young man in the cast came up as well. I supposed he'd be wrapping the Torah as we'd be switching roles for the day. Now I had to show him how strong I was. I had to pull together every last bit of strength to impress this man whom I so badly wanted to desire me, to acknowledge me in something other than casual or ritual way. With as much confidence as I could muster, I moved toward the podium where the Torah scroll rested. The rabbi motioned to the congregants to stand. The cantor and the young man stood to the side. I felt my palms get clammy and my heart begin to beat faster. The air and gases in my stomach were churning wildly. This was the moment when all eyes were on me. At this moment I *would* be a man. I would emulate the movements I had seen during previous synagogue visits as I had raptly watched the young man lift the Torah, biceps and triceps stretching his upper shirtsleeve. I subtly wiped my perspiring hands on the edges of my tallis, as though the gesture was part of the ritual. I put one hand on each of the two carved wooden handles and began to bend my knees. I maneuvered the scroll toward me so I could lift it up. I must not have elicited the confidence I'd hoped, as I felt the three men move in a little closer (just like the other boys on the softball field when it was my turn to bat). I felt a pang of embarrassment and was determined to prove them wrong, prove their exercise in caution was unwarranted. I began to lift the Torah scroll. The three moved in closer still. I felt the congregation watch my every move. As I lifted the Torah I felt it wobble a little, and once again the rabbi and cantor's protective arms moved in, not yet touching the Torah but ready to catch it if necessary. I moved directly over to the chair with the cantor and the young man following closely beside me. I had skipped the whole turning around and displaying the words for the congregation. My only thought had been to sit down before the scroll wobbled and fell, and my forty days of fasting would begin.

The young man maneuvered the dressing of the Torah and placed the ornaments with his one good hand and with several fingers on the hand with the cast. I was mesmerized by those light brown fingers poking out from the hard white cast. As he moved in closer to adjust the silver ornaments I could smell his manliness. It was an aroma I would long for, seek out. I wanted to look him in the eyes and have him look into mine, to smile, to acknowledge I'd done a good job, that *he* admired *me*, that *he* secretly longed for *me*. But his focus seemed to be on doing his job as respectfully and efficiently as he could, given that his dexterity was limited by his injury.

I was beginning to feel relieved that my job was over, that I hadn't dropped the Torah, that I'd been successful and shown them I could do it, albeit not with the natural flair that the young man could. I rationalized that he'd had a lot of practice and that perhaps I'd done as well as he had on his first try. I was catching my breath and exhaling the anxiety that had climaxed as I'd lifted the heavy sacred scroll. The act now accomplished, my manhood was intact.

He was completing his task, and I was recovering from mine. The sensory stimuli, which had become background noise, were once again becoming defined as I grew aware of the congregation chanting the end of the traditional melody that accompanies the lifting and dressing of the Torah. As the sound of their voices, cracking and off-key from age, faded away, the rabbi motioned for the congregants to sit. This portion of the service was over, and my dignity was intact.

Just then the cantor, with his toothy smile, said nonchalantly, "You must not have eaten your Wheaties this morning."

I froze. I had thought it was over, that I had accomplished my job fairly competently. I'd been able to breathe easily again, my stomach was calm, my heart rate had returned to normal. And then, a punch in the stomach. I'm sure my eyes betrayed my shock, opened at full attention as if I'd been hit in the stomach by a school bully or had been called "fag" by a taunting classmate in front of my peers. But the shock was multiplied, as I never would have expected to receive the blow here, in the synagogue and in front of the man I so wanted to impress.

I tried to regain my composure as if this wasn't a stinging comment but a joke shared by guys palling around in the locker room. I was just one of the guys, and it was my turn to be the butt of the joke. Next time it would be one of them. I smiled back awkwardly. The young man smiled as well. A good joke at my expense. But inside my stomach had dropped, sent reeling by a right hook. I felt my face become hot and imagined it turning red.

I continued to smile awkwardly, but I felt a tear form in my eye. The young man absently shook my hand firmly, said "*yeshar koach*," and returned to his seat in the congregation, seeming not to give it another thought. The cantor returned to his designated seat on the bimah as the rabbi continued the service. I couldn't look at the cantor. I moved my hand, the one the young man had held a moment earlier, and attempted to nonchalantly wipe the tear from my eye. I adjusted my body in the padded chair, hoping to sink into it and disappear from sight. I held the Torah close, shifting it to my right shoulder to serve as a shield, blocking the congregation and especially the young man from seeing my shamed face. I looked up at the rabbi as he began his sermon. I let his words gently roll toward me through his calm voice. As he finished I heard him recite the priestly blessing, his voice gently resonating through the sanctuary:

May the Lord bless you and keep you.
May the Lord shine His Presence upon you and be gracious unto you.
May the Lord turn with favor unto you and give you peace.

Despite the humiliation I had suffered at the cantor's thoughtless words, the rabbi's soothing voice pulled me into his words. Perhaps these words were for me. Perhaps one day I would find peace.

What About the Children?
Ronni L. Sanlo

It was 1958. I fell in love with Annette Funicello. I don't know which was more upsetting: that she was a girl like me or that she wasn't Jewish. Of course I didn't tell anybody. I figured they'd lock me up and throw away the key if either of those things were true. It'd be worse than getting caught smoking my first cigarette behind the old shul. But I suspected the fact that Annette was a girl was far more a breach of family etiquette, not to mention a severe violation of the image of perfection we were so carefully taught. So I learned to live a parallel life: nice Jewish Ronni and queerer-than-queer Ronni. I somehow—quickly and early—learned the word *queer,* or, more accurately, *faygeleh,* from my North Miami Beach beginnings. But I referred to myself as queerer-than-queer because I thought only men were *faygelehs.* I didn't know women could be too. Such a dummy. Actually, whenever I looked into a mirror, I referred to myself in the third person as "that damn queer." Yeah, such a dummy, and so much shame…

In fifth grade at Sabal Palm Elementary, Wendy. Not Jewish. In sixth grade, Nadine. Not Jewish. In seventh grade at North Miami Beach Junior High School, Paulette. Not Jewish. In tenth grade at Miami Norland Senior High, Sandra the jock. Not Jewish. (Back then Jews weren't jocks anyway. Oh, maybe we're still not.) To my growing horror, I was developing a desire—though unrequited—for *shiksas*! To redeem myself in my own eyes, I dated Jewish boys, not so much because they were Jewish but because they were the only boys I knew, and it was expected of me by everyone in my entire world and I needed to hide my attraction to all these girls. *Oy!* Which was worse, *shiksas* or girls? I struggled. It finally occurred to me it didn't matter. If anyone found out, neither was good.

In my everyday life I was a great student, decent surfer—if one can decently surf on Miami Beach's mini-waves—a community organizer, and extremely active in my synagogue, Beth Torah in North Miami Beach. (You know, the one designed by Frank Lloyd Wright that looked like a Mogen David from the friendly skies and whose front window looked like the Torah scrolls my mother replicated in Glass Wax on our sliding glass doors every year for the neighborhood Chanukah-decorating contest.)

But in my Walter Mitty-Schmitty teenage life, I was a suave, debonair woman who swept other women off their feet, who was Bogey to Bacall, who was Tracy to Hepburn, who was Hudson to Day. What always confused me was that I had no desire to be a man, so I took those dashing male personae and re-created them to be dashing women. (Heck, it was *my* daydream, so I could do anything to them!)

And then 1967 happened. I was a junior at the University of Florida and fell in love with Marilyn. She was Jewish. Oh, shit! Too close to my real life. I had absolutely no desire to have my real life and my fantasy life intersect. As long as the objects of my affection weren't Jewish, they could remain in the deep realm of my closeted hidden dreams. But now my real life and my fantasy life were banging up against each other—well, not actually, but I wish that had been so! Marilyn. I heard her tell her mother that if I were a guy, she'd marry me. I *heard* it. I was sitting right there. I didn't want to be a guy, but I thought if I went to Sweden and had things done to my body, the woman of my dreams would be mine. A fleeting, frightful thought.

After we graduated from college in 1969, Marilyn moved to Los Angeles with me. My family had moved there from Miami two years earlier. Marilyn and I shared a one-bedroom apartment in Encino. While I never told her—or anyone, for that matter—how I felt, I was profoundly happy to have established a home with Marilyn. We didn't date anyone else. We just had each other, and we had become our own nonverbalized family of choice. No sex, no outward physical affection, but lots of love nonetheless. I was happy even if I did have to keep my feelings a giant secret.

In the summer of 1971 my grandfather said to me, "You're almost twenty-five and not married. What are you, funny or something?" He moved his right hand back and forth in AC/DC fashion, depicting, well, what? Did he know about me? I freaked. *He knows! How does he know? I've never, ever uttered a word to anyone about my sexual orientation. Jews aren't queer. No one in my family or even in my realm of acquaintances were queer. We aren't queer. We're a perfect, loving, happy—did I mention perfect?—Jewish family and no one is queer!* I never told anyone. I never acted on it. How did he know?

So I called this guy I used to date in college—no, he wasn't Jewish—and asked if he still wanted to get married. I had declined his invitation two and a half years earlier and hadn't spoken with him since. He said yes.

My parents were horrified. I'm the oldest of four children. It never occurred to my parents that any of us would consider marrying a *goyim*, least of all me! I was the one who'd wanted to be a rabbi, even when it was impossible for women to go to rabbinical school. I constantly heard, "You don't want to be a rabbi. You want to be a rebbetzin." A rebbetzin? But I don't cook! And I *did* want to be a rabbi. I became neither. Instead I became the wife of a middle school band director. My mother didn't talk to me for weeks when I announced I would be marrying John. He wasn't Jewish. *What about the children?*

My parallel life: In my dreams I was marrying Marilyn. In real life, John. On the morning of my wedding day, I felt I had two options: get married or commit suicide. Coming out in 1971, admitting I was a lesbian, wasn't an option for me. Even though it was two years post-Stonewall, I still thought I was the only woman in the world who felt the way I did. Queerer than queer. Since I didn't know how to commit suicide, and I didn't want to make a mess in my family's perfect house, I got married and moved to my husband's home in Orlando, 3,000 miles away.

I made babies. I made dinner. I made curtains. I made myself nuts. I was a stay-at-home mom with two beautiful children. I knew every song on *Sesame Street*. I needed grown-ups in my life, so I got a part-time job at Burdines department store, where I met two delightful gay men named Tony and Richard. They're dead now, but back then they saved my life. They did two things for me. First, when they thought I was simply a wonderful ally, they gave me a copy of Rita Mae Brown's *Rubyfruit Jungle*. Then they took me to a gay bar, not *any* gay bar, but the Parliament House in Orlando.

I remember that night in the spring of 1978. My husband and I and another couple were going to be Tony and Richard's guests at the Parliament. My husband decided not to go, but I knew I had to. I remember walking into the huge room where hundreds of people were mingling. I saw men dancing with men, but far more important for me, I saw women dancing with women. While I'm not much of a drinker or a party person, and while I didn't know a soul, I knew I was home among my people. These unknowns, these dancers and drinkers and shmoozers and cruisers—these were my people and I was finally home. G-d help me...

I still had never said the words aloud, but now, in the fall of 1978, the feelings were surfacing. The self I had kept in check, kept in hiding and isolation for so long was begging to finally become real. During the 1978 University of Florida homecoming weekend, I called an old college roommate who I suspected—no, hoped—was a lesbian. She was. I told her I thought I was too. She chuckled as she said, "What took you so long?" It was time to be free.

It took several more months before I had the courage to tell anyone else, including John, that I was a lesbian and wanted a divorce. I spent that time thinking about the past couple of years. When Anita Bryant was waging her anti-gay campaign in 1977 in Miami, three hours down the road from me, I was totally oblivious, completely unaware that as a result of her Save Our Children campaign, the Florida legislature had created anti-gay laws that would soon devastate my world. Two years later, in 1979, at the ripe old age of thirty-two, I finally came out. I finally acknowledged my lesbian identity twenty-one years after I'd fallen in love with Annette Funicello, ten years after Stonewall and after I had graduated from the University Florida, and two years after Anita Bryant.

When I came out in 1979, I lost custody of my two children, then ages three and six, because I didn't know about laws and rules and terms like "in the best interest of the children." I didn't know our history as LGBT people. I knew only what I'd learned from school and community. It wasn't much, and it wasn't pretty.

John was threatening to call my parents to tell them about me. I knew I was in for a battle and needed their support, so I called them myself. I would have preferred to tell them in person, but they were 3,000 miles away and I was deeply frightened at the thought of losing my children. When I told my parents I was a lesbian, the only words I heard were from my mother: *"But what about the children?"*

My children were taken away from me, so when I came out, I was one angry dyke. Though I didn't know the laws and I sure didn't know our history, I *did* know that losing my children wasn't fair and wasn't right, and I committed myself to doing everything I could to try to make this world a better place for us. Within eighteen months of my coming-out I became the executive director and lobbyist of the Florida Task Force, then Florida's lesbian and gay civil rights organization. From there it was a bumpy journey first into HIV work and then higher education. Eventually, as a doctoral student, I was hired by the University of Michigan to do work for them for which I had been repeatedly fired for doing in Florida. I accepted the job as the LGBT Center director. Four years later I was recruited by the University of California, Los Angeles, to do similar work.

What about my children? Today, my children are adults. Though we were estranged for many years, we are now intimate and loving parts of one another's lives. We've come together as adults to honor the love and process the history we share. I was present at the birth of both of my two precious granddaughters. While I missed many years of my children's youth, I'm blessed that these two wonderful young people are now friends and guides in my life. Not to long ago my son and I had an e-mail conversation about reflection. He wrote:

I was doing nothing but introspection and reflection. I had to in order to make the transition from focusing on what was behind me to focusing on what is ahead of me. I was so desperately looking for who I was. Eventually I found out that changing myself changed my world at the same time. Even though you can only change yourself, don't think that won't change your world and those in it. You played the largest role in teaching me that, so now I impart the message to you. I always have a degree of introspection going on, which allows me to change, and I imagine the same holds true with you. It's all about survival, remember, Mom? And about love.

Indeed, my son. It's all about survival and truly about love. Isn't that, after all, the core of my life as a Jewish woman and a lesbian? So, *nu*, let's cook dinner.

Portrait of the Artist as a Young Faygeleh
Adam Seth Rosen

I sit in my family's polite suburban St. Louis living room, holding a portrait in my hands. I look at this face, this observant *shaynah* face. He exudes a delicate yet naïve confidence, of the kind only shown once or twice at eighteen. Yet his confident smile betrays a residue of the loneliness of that sensitive, introverted thirteen-year-old with no friends at all to invite to his bar mitzvah party. Now the face I see in front of me is a bold, expressive, fearless, Jewish, queer, poet, composer, and visionary: in other words, Hitler's worst nightmare! Yet today, I still have some of those pregraduate, late-night, first-breakthrough, showcase-writing jitters most senior English majors get when they first receive the opportunity to make their literary mark on the world. So, here's the story of how a Jewish-American, gay youth found the right-size frame for the *faygeleh* inside his high-school graduation portrait.

Portrait of a Suburban, All-American, Nice Jewish Boy

Even before I came out of the womb, my mother had an inkling I was going to grow up to be an artist. She humorously relayed to me a prebirth tale about feeling me kick to the beat of "One Singular Sensation" when she attended the first touring production of *A Chorus Line* at the Kiel Opera House, back in the summer of 1978. Both of my parents always hoped I was going to make a difference in the world. Little did they know how different I would be. Yet, like those of all Jewish boys, my penis had to suffer the consequences of that ancient, patriarchal ritual that ties every Jewish male together. But for some reason my dick failed to understand this ironic covenant between G-d and his people, marked by a permanent surgical incision involving the destruction of its foreskin, juxtaposed with the stampede of relatives grazing on the catered smoked fish at my bris.

From eight days to five years old, I followed a schedule governed by the rhythms and flows of mainstream Jewish life. My earliest memory is being dunked in the JCC pool by the first in a long line of bullies. I can still recall the almost out-of-body sensations of being submerged under water as my nameless tormentor turned me upside down in the celestial, womb-like environment of the swimming pool. As I came up 180 degrees from where I first stood in the shallow end, gasping for air, the moderately handsome eighteen-year-old lifeguard arrogantly smirked at my inability to cope. You'd think a five-year-old could handle a little water! As painful (and fluid) as this first memory sounds, something good did come out it: I learned at a young age how the strong prey on the weak—and Jewish boys in an all-Jewish setting tend to act like normal boys in any setting.

From the ages of eight to twelve, I attended Ross Elementary. Every Tuesday and Thursday afternoon after school I went to Hebrew school at the Central Agency for Jewish Educational (CAJE). In retrospect, elementary school felt more like a real "cage." The harassment started the first day of second grade. Some cocky kid sitting next to me asked what was my favorite music group. Having not the slightest idea of what he was talking about, I naïvely replied, "Well, I like Beethoven's Ninth symphony and stuff by Mozart." I guess he thought I was some nerdy snob or something, because the next words out of his mouth were, "Hey, are you a fag?" I don't remember what I said in return, not knowing what "fag" even meant. But my intuition told me being myself was a doorway not open to me. This was contrary to the patriotic sludge we were later force-fed in third grade social studies about how America is the land of the free and the home of the brave. I'll be the first to admit that at least the latter part of this phrase is accurate. After all, being a soft-spoken, Jewish, nonmasculine, classical music–listening, hypersensitive eight-year-old, you have no choice *not* to be brave if you are going to survive young, straight, white, male, Christian, all-American bullies. There was one in every classroom. Yet life wasn't really that different in Hebrew school, where the kids asked me why I talked and walked so funny.

I soon discovered that as long as my body was physically breathing, there was nowhere in life I could hide. If I wasn't getting wood chips shoved down the back of my pants at recess, then I be getting gum smeared on the back of my scalp on the school bus. If I wasn't getting spit on in the hallway, then I was getting pinched, poked, prodded, and (yes) even fondled in the classroom, regardless of whether a teacher was in the room. In the five hellish years I spent at Ross Elementary, I was called "fag," "queer," "cocksucker," "Jew-boy," "retard," "wuss," "spaz," "nerd," "freak," "pussy," and words I can't see fit to repeat again. It's no wonder, then, that some lesbian and gay youths would rather kill themselves than face these kinds of school conditions on a daily basis. What rational human beings would subject their children to such a revolting educational environment? Unfortunately, one of those human beings was my father. As a professional therapist with a doctoral degree in clinical psychology, he gave me the following advice: "Adam, don't let them get to you. Try to make friends." I lashed out at those words that did not comfort. Still, I did learn something from his parental inadequacy: A parent can understand you only to the degree you understand yourself.

Portrait of a Queer-Youth Activist

So how did a frightened Jewish twelve-year-old with zero social skills become an eighteen-year-old openly gay talk-radio host who took a same-sex date to both his junior and senior proms? Easy! He stopped worrying what everyone else thought about him when he realized he wasn't popular enough to be a prom king and had nothing more to lose by simply being himself. Actually, it wasn't that easy to get to that level of self-acceptance. I had to pass through two years of junior high, where I was sexually harassed in gym class by homophobic jocks (who, more than likely, would have fooled around with me outside of a locker-room setting, at least in my fantasies). The only way I fully came to accept myself was by being aware of every part of myself. This self-awakening coincided with my bar mitzvah, the ritualized celebration of a Jewish boy's passage into adulthood. While preparing for this unprecedented milestone through weekly *Maftir* lessons, slowly I became aware of how men's bodies made me feel. One random Wednesday night, while watching a rerun of *Charles in Charge*, I got my first homo-conscious boner. And it was directed toward the '80s teeny-bopper actor Scott Baio! Finally I understood why all of those nameless bullies were calling me a fag. But this new knowledge wasn't the end of my self-hatred. It wasn't enough to know my feelings had a label. I had to discover I wasn't the only one who felt this way. At this time, which was before Internet chat rooms and online instant messaging, the only tools an isolated gay youth had at his disposal were books and rare images of gay life in the media. Because openly gay and lesbian television characters were still years away, it's no wonder I bolted to the library. I'd frantically devour every book I could find that related to being gay. And my mother, G-d bless her, put her embarrassment aside to satisfy the curiosity of her adolescent son and checked out the taboo books that were reserved for adults.

But now that I had internally come out of the homosexual closet, I found myself coming out in a totally Jewish context to the entire congregation of Shaare Zedek Synagogue on August 31, 1991. As I stood on the bimah, pretending to smile like a winner for my family, inside I felt about as welcome as *treyf* at Shabbos dinner. I knew I would never be able to fulfill the biblical expectations of the Jewish community to be fruitful and multiply. And as the rabbi called me forward to receive the blessings of *Ha-Shem,* I trembled not with humility but with trepidation. Here I stood in front of the congregation, but I didn't feel like a man. The rabbi reminded me of my place in Jewish tradition, but framed by my tallis, I realized I couldn't fulfill this important mitzvah. I would never marry under the chuppah. But I was beginning to know where I stood. That was the last day I regularly came to Saturday morning services. The rules and rituals of Conservative Judaism no longer applied to me. I would have to look elsewhere for my spiritual home.

Actually, finding home was easier than clicking my heels together. It came in the form of a book. What initially attracted me to *Reflections of a Rock Lobster* was not the pop music title but the handsome face of its author, Aaron Fricke. Tears of joy dripped from my eyes as I read the story of how an eighteen-year-old won the legal right to take another guy to his senior prom. The injustice of it all hit me like a thousand swinging baseball bats as I learned what it was like to be young, gay, and brave in the early '80s. Aaron's courage in taking on the homophobic authority of his principal provided an emotional blueprint for my budding social consciousness. As for me, thirteen was a lie, fourteen was a lie, and fifteen was a lie. Each birthday was a promise left unkept as I wrestled with coming out. Yet at sixteen, within three short weeks I came out to my parents, both sets of grandparents, my brother and sister, and eventually the entire student body of Parkway North High. After reaching a point of no return, I broke down the closet door and found that as a society, the American closet holds more people than we can imagine. Classmates I'd never spoken to thanked me for being the first openly gay student at PNH. Both girls and guys confided in me about divorce, substance abuse, weight problems, and other social challenges. I had been a shy, scared kid who spoke to no one, and now suddenly almost everyone was speaking to me.

In March 1995, I finally met other gay and lesbian youths like myself when I first opened the door to Growing American Youth, St. Louis's LGBT youth group. And only months later I was given a rare opportunity that turned me into the artist and activist I am today. Through the offer of a scholarship, I soon found myself attending the first-ever Youth Leadership Training Institute sponsored by the National Gay and Lesbian Task Force. Nestled in the rolling hills of Northern California's Marin County, the homey Walker Creek Ranch housed twenty-four queer youth activists from across the country. At sixteen, I was the youngest and least experienced. Yet I learned my youth was a tremendous asset, as many of my newly acquainted twenty-something friends gave me priceless advice on how to organize effectively for social change. In short, we discovered each of us could be an activist in small and large ways, often by just being visible. Our activist training concluded with each of us creating a project to take back to our home communities.

Armed with the media skills I would later use on the air, I was a bit unnerved coming home to St. Louis. Would I be able to make my dream project a reality? At the Training Institute I told myself I wanted to make the world a better place for LGBT youth. When I volunteered to be interviewed on a gay and lesbian talk-radio show after the training, my dreams found an unexpected way of coming true. The cohosts of *Out & Open* liked our interview so much they asked me and my friends Mike and Shauna if we would like to produce a monthly segment of the show devoted exclusively to the needs of LGBT youths. I couldn't believe my good luck, and on October 20, 1995, the nation's first-ever queer youth talk-radio show was on the air. My once cold and lonely world had now become a blazing, passionate universe. The phone began to ring off the hook as I became the poster child for gay youths in St. Louis. I was barely able to focus on homework as I began to research upcoming topics for the show. We called it the *Gay '90s*, and in 1996 our segment grew into a weekly half-hour show.

Now my life had a clear sense of direction. Every week we rotated responsibilities and planned at least one topic. One of my favorites was the show we did on the pros and cons of taking a same-gender date to the prom. I was elated to report to the entire St. Louis metropolitan area that I'd successfully taken my cohost Mike to my junior prom. A few listeners called in to ask why I would subject myself to possible ridicule and harassment. I answered that after surviving seventh and eighth grades intact, taking a guy to prom was, like, no big deal. I also told the listening audience about how one brave gay youth wrote a book about fighting for the right to do what my generation now considers a rite of passage. The radio-show years were some of the happiest of my life. I was definitely gay but didn't think it was important to be Jewish.

In September 1997 I left the show, graduated from high school, and went to college. I thought by moving somewhere else—otherwise known as Wisconsin—I'd find a new kind of affirmative world. The student body of Lawrence University, however, was overwhelmingly heterosexual, Christian, and remarkably unfamiliar with gay or Jewish students.

Many of them had never met a Jew, and their questioning made me wonder if they just wanted to see my horns. These farm-fresh kids couldn't understand how I could be both gay and Jewish, yet they were much more intrigued with meeting a real-live Jew. Although I joined a gay student group, I was surprised to find myself gravitating to the few Jewish kids on campus when none of my other gay friends in St. Louis were members of the tribe. Anne Frank's diary and stories of the Holocaust entered my consciousness for the first time. The history of the yellow star became my history, and I learned who had first worn the pink triangle.

Reluctantly, I led the Jewish student *chavurah* my sophomore year in order to connect with the Jewish identity thrust upon me by the rest of the student body. Lawrence has an active lesbian and gay student group, which gave me access to the school's queer student body, but no one seemed as out as I was. And though the cheese and beer in Wisconsin were filling enough, I was starving for the world I had left behind. There was literally a church on every corner, but I did band together with other non-Christian students. Some were pagan, some were Buddhist, and many were agnostic. Because of the Christian-dominated environment of the Fox Valley area, we were forced to find each other. Though I did enjoy majoring in musical theater, I was, in truth, a fish swimming up the wrong stream.

What finally sent me packing was the day a fundamentalist cult illegally came into one of the student dorms distributing salvation propaganda. The Bible verses quoted in their brochure said "effeminates" could never get into heaven and so must repent to Jesus lest we suffer the consequences of violating G-d's law. I'm already sensitive to the age-old stereotype of the nonmasculine Jew, from the Crusades to the Holocaust, so the double sting of being "effeminate" was too much to bear again. I thought surviving my high school years as an activist meant the end of fighting for my place. I had foolishly assumed college would be free of the childish prejudices of my earlier world. And I was surprised that my old insecurities resurfaced. The day after our queer student group organized a meeting in response to the incident, we heard on the news that a twenty-one-year-old Laramie, Wyoming, college student had been beaten to death for being gay. None of us ever forgot the name Matthew Shepard.

PORTRAIT OF THE AUTHOR AS A TWENTY-THREE-YEAR-OLD FAYGELEH

Coming home was one of the hardest things I'd ever done. I wasn't sure if I was retreating in defeat or gravitating toward the safety of my friends back home. At Lawrence, I was looking forward to completing independent study in musical theater. My original plans included composing and orchestrating a rock musical based on my youth group experiences. With all the middle-class privileges I'd been fortunate enough to have in life, I wanted to use those privileges to make a difference in the world. But there was still a missing piece of the puzzle I had to solve. While doing summer work at the same library where I first found the story of my hero, Aaron Fricke, I stumbled upon another book that opened the final door to the closet of my self. As I was shelving some books downstairs, the title *Twice Blessed* caught my eye. I read the book from cover to cover the next day, and I finally found myself on the page. Everyone had their own story to tell, but the common experience of being gay, Jewish, and human had never been made more clear to me. No longer did I have to live in separate worlds, never feeling fully a part of either. I discovered there were generations of *faygelehs* before me—Leonard Bernstein, Stephen Sondheim, and Jerry Herman to name a few—all outsiders who had defined the American experience on Broadway for the entire world. However, they didn't put my world on the stage, let alone dare to tell their own stories.

My musical is still unfinished. I like to think it's a work in progress. But I am making my professional debut this summer, composing an original theatrical score for the St. Louis premiere of *The Laramie Project*. Matthew Shepard's tragic story never left me. Though I was once a vulnerable college student in a small town, I will now stand with pride when my *mishpucha* gathers for the premiere. I don't know if our rabbi will attend, but I do know this *faygeleh* has done his family proud. And in years to come, I hope they will gather again at the opening of my own musical, *Identity*. Now it's up to my generation to tell the stories of our lives as we really lived them.

Coming Out at Sixty-Five
Roy Liebman

When someone was quoted recently about coming out at the "pathetic" age of thirty-six, I briefly wondered how he might describe me. I was almost thirty years older when I had, as I like to call it, my "epiphany." So am I *beyond pathetic?* Frankly, my dear, I don't give a damn. I may be the personification of "better late than never," but I'm proud I finally did it. Of course, people ask me why I waited so long to come out, but not any more than I've asked myself. What was I waiting for—a dramatic deathbed declaration?

When I was younger, I used to tell myself I had good reasons for remaining in the closet: It was my parents; it was the times in which I grew up; it was my desire to have children; when I did have children it was so they would respect me. I had an unending list of excuses. All of them were true, but I conveniently used those excuses to avoid the decision I finally had the courage to make.

To put it mildly, it's certainly true my parents weren't receptive to the idea of homosexuality. They were both born while Queen Victoria was on the throne (although she didn't register much in the tenements of New York's lower east side). My parents were probably adults before knowing such a thing even existed.

My mother, born impossibly long ago in 1896, waited forty years for her little red-haired Roy to be born. She understandably doted on me. Not for nothing was I a fat little *boychik* stuffed with foods that probably hardened my arteries before I had a chance to defend myself. My father was a few years younger, emerging with the new century in 1900, almost exactly one hundred years before my granddaughter was born in the present century. I soon learned there were three things Jewish families discussed in whispers because of their "disgraceful" nature: divorce, homosexuality, and any need to consult a mental health professional. My family's occasional use of Yiddish in front of me was partly to cover up discussion of such unspeakable topics.

My parents remained true to their social code. They might have been miserable together for fifty-three years, but they never thought of divorce. They and various relatives may have been highly neurotic—or worse—but they never consulted anyone who could have helped them, at least not that they would admit publicly.

And homosexuality? My parents would have had me committed for "treatment" if they had suspected there was anything roiling beneath my quiet, unathletic surface. My mother always said, accusingly, "You think too much." It's a good thing she never knew what I was thinking about. Homosexuality was considered a mental aberration then, and forced commitment wasn't such a remote possibility.

Ironically, in my parents' generation there was one presumably sexless bachelor or "old maid" in nearly every large family. It was never considered anything but a natural fact of life. He or she simply had never met the right person and were quietly and fondly pitied for not having a family of their own. I wonder now whether many of those seemingly placid people secretly hungered for something else they could never have.

Yes, homosexuality was one of the unthinkables—except of course for the *one* neighborhood *faygeleh*. Apparently my Brooklyn neighborhood consisted of all perfectly normal people, except for the *one* person each who exemplified a different "sin."

First, there was the *one* young girl who got pregnant out of wedlock. Neighbors constantly hooted at her as she wheeled her baby carriage around the streets. More than once she had hot water thrown down on her from an upstairs apartment. A close second in condemnation was the *one* high school girl who wasn't a virgin. Her freely proffered wares apparently had been sampled by everyone but me.

Then there was the *one* man who made his money dishonestly. Everyone else made very little money, but at least they did it honestly. He was the neighborhood bookie, whom you could always spot because he dressed much better than anyone else while at his street-corner "office." (And truth to tell, he was more widely respected than the local police force that he supported with payoffs.)

Now, to the one *faygeleh*. The fact that he was a married man with children didn't stop the imprecations that both preceded and followed him as he went out walking with his family. Cries of "Here comes the *faygeleh*!" or "There goes the *faygeleh*!" were hurled loudly. I don't know if he actually was queer, but he was forever branded, and you could see the hurt on the faces of his family members.

There obviously was more than one gay person in the neighborhood. On one memorable occasion a crowd gathered outside a movie theater in which two men had been seen holding hands. All this didn't affect the usual teenage horseplay between totally "heterosexual" buddies. Only some of us were less hetero than others and enjoyed it for reasons other than pure male bonding. I'd sure like to meet those guys now, especially the one who blurted he "worshiped" me, then covered up his confusion with pretend laughter. I'd also like to reacquaint myself with a few I came across in the all-straight (just kidding, folks!) world of the U.S. Army. Ah, that shower room!

As my straight friends did, I joined a college social organization and insincerely smiled at remarks about certain professors who were known to favor good-looking male students. (Fraternities actually kept files on them.) In truth, I was reluctant to sign up for those professors' classes for fear they would easily see through me. When one of them did ask me, with probing suspicion, why I wanted to be a librarian, I had no doubt it confirmed his certainty that I was gay.

In college I double-dated "good" girls with my friends. In the 1950s Jewish girls generally waited until their wedding night to tumble into bed, for which I was profoundly grateful. It was an event I hoped to postpone as long as possible. I may have been aware from the age of three or so that I liked boys—and that I lusted in my heart for them—but I also never doubted I'd have my own wedding day. And in due course I did.

One of my first close encounters with what was then called the "third kind"—i.e., openly gay men—came after my move to California. By then I was engaged (for the second time) and of course firmly closeted. At a New Year's party given by some married friends of my fiancée was a male, hand-holding couple. (Interestingly, one of them had recently been propositioned by Rock Hudson, so I knew twenty years before most of the world of the actor's proclivities.)

These two men were brave to have been so open in those repressive times. But this fact wasn't on my mind then, only the fear of being exposed to my future wife—because of course they knew about me; I could tell by the looks they exchanged with each other. I barely opened my mouth the rest of the night, even though another guest had been a Marine buddy of Lee Harvey Oswald who had just killed President Kennedy. Looking back on it, that was certainly one of the more interesting parties I've attended— too bad I couldn't let myself enjoy it.

Not too long afterward I took on the protective cover of marriage. I wished even then that I could have been brave enough to come out. At least I took some (very scant) satisfaction in admitting to myself I was and always would be gay. I might have deceived others, but never myself. Having straight sex countless times during a thirty-year marriage did not, in my eyes, ever make me straight or even bisexual.

I well understood it isn't so much what you do with your body, it's what's in your head. And my thoughts were pretty much all gay, all the time. To turn an old adage on its head: I may have been quacking like a duck, but it didn't make me a duck.

Actually, my impending wedded bliss had almost ended before it began. Shortly before the marriage, the most gorgeous guy in my military reserve unit came on to me like gangbusters. Resistance seemed futile, especially after he showed up at my office to show me the tight pants he was wearing. Oy! But I did ultimately decide to opt for a "normal" life, one that increasingly came to be marked by marital strife. Although it was mitigated by the birth of two wonderful daughters, who sometimes made it all seem worthwhile, it was never really enough.

I had wanted even more children, but I knew deep down that no magic number of offspring would fill the void in my life. The yearning would never go away. At long last, I ended the marriage when I was almost sixty. In a way I was proud of myself because I did it in the face of uncertainty about the rest of my life. After all, I had traded security—albeit unhappy security—for an unknown future.

But I still wasn't thinking about coming out, for now I had a whole new set of "reasons": I might contract AIDS. I was too old to be attractive to anyone. One big decision—my divorce—was enough. And so on and so on. I also had to cope with the common after-divorce problem of who gets the friends. After all, if I didn't have my straight friends (and I surely wasn't ready to make gay ones), I'd be very lonely.

Fortunately, my friends, mostly all married couples, stuck by me, and for a couple of years my life seemed full. The first of my film history books was published and was the culmination of a longtime dream. I joined a local temple, the only time in my life I had ever been affiliated. Both my parents had been nonobservant; my mother even sought her succor in Christian Science. (This was something she always concealed from my Orthodox grandmother. Even so, my grandmother rarely came to our apartment rarely—probably because of the ever-present aroma of ham, bacon, and pork chops.)

There were also post-divorce dates with several nice ladies, one of whom remains a close friend. I was still convinced I was "fitting in," but fate—or my repressed subconscious—was sending me a different message. My temple had become intent on appealing to young families, and I didn't really fit in. I also realized that as caring as my friends were, I was always a third wheel to heterosexual couples. So I didn't fit in there either. And obviously the ladies weren't what I wanted. So what *did* I have to look forward to at the age of sixty-five?

Finally, my epiphany came: I wasn't ever going to fit in. My life wasn't working; it never had, and it never would if I persisted in denying the central core of my being. Was that how I wanted to spend whatever was the rest of my life?

When I finally faced that question, there could only be one possible answer. But why hadn't I faced it forty years ago? I'd always secretly hoped reincarnation was a fact and I'd be able make up for lost time in another life. But I wasn't through with *this* life!

After a lifetime of caution, I didn't immediately run out into the streets and proclaim myself—not in my white-bread neighborhood anyway. We're not talking West Hollywood here. Over time, a sympathetic gay therapist helped me along my now-determined but still shaky path.

At a seminar, I first heard the powerful phrase "toxic shame" to describe what many gay men feel about their sexuality. Perhaps that's what I had felt all those years. So here I was at sixty-five, the symbol of everything my Victorian family had talked about in whispers: a divorced *faygeleh* in therapy.

It wasn't too long before I was eagerly exploring gay Web sites and organizations. Through the Gay and Lesbian Center I heard about a senior support group that I finally plucked up the courage to attend. It was the first time I had come out to a group of people, but they couldn't have been more understanding and full of good tips for me. (Although some might possibly be a bit outdated? For instance, the availability of a "good time" at certain places forty years ago.)

I have also rekindled my interest in the spiritual side. I went to a service at the Los Angeles Reform temple Beth Chayim Chadashim. There I found an outstanding gay community of which I am now a member. I have made many new friends—and incidentally, openly kissing my male friends is something it took me all of two seconds to be comfortable with.

In common with everyone else who's ever come out, the biggest dilemma in my mind was *whom* to tell and *how* to tell them—-foremost being my children. Although I had suspected for some time that they were aware of my homosexuality, the subject had never been broached. When I began throwing out delicate "hints" (like "My life may be taking a new direction"), one of my daughters seized the moment to out me before I could fully out myself.

She said she and her sister knew I was gay, they were not judgmental, and it was just fine with them. As happy as I am to have that over with, I do balk at my daughters asking me whether I think this or that guy is cute. Perhaps I'm old-fashioned, but I draw the line at having "girl" talk with my daughters. Of course, with my gay friends it's different. It's very liberating to be able to express openly what I used to only whisper inside my mind.

In other ways, though, I'm not old-fashioned. Since my life has essentially started over, I'm like a kid craving things I could only dream of before. A potentially great adventure is still ahead of me; by the time I'm seventy, perhaps I'll be in my teen years again. Hopefully, they'll be sweeter than the original ones were.

Of course I know I have a long way to go. My gaydar certainly needs some fine-tuning. For instance, a straight colleague informed me, to my astonishment, that another colleague of more than twenty years was gay. And a friend said he thought my very own plumber was gay. *Really?* Well, I always did admire his tool belt.

I'm realistic enough to know I can never recoup the lost years— there were an awful lot of them. Too many prospective lovers have come and gone, and age does have a way of creeping—or leaping ferociously—upon one. But that's for the future; meanwhile, I'm savoring the present. When I look at my children and granddaughter, I know I paid some prices on the long, lonely road to coming out, but this is a new time.

I'm still here, and at long last I'm queer!

"How true Daddy's words were when he said: All children must look after their own upbringing. Parents can only give good advice or put them on the right paths, but the final forming of a person's character lies in their own hands."

—Anne Frank

Family

A Letter to My Great-Grandfather on Being Jewish and Gay

Warren J. Blumenfeld

Dear Great-grandfather Wolf,

Though I have never written to you, I have carried your image and felt your comforting presence ever since that day when your son (my maternal grandfather, Simon) told me about you and his mother—my great-grandmother Basha. One day when I was very young, I sat upon Simon's knee. Looking down urgently but with deep affection, he said to me, "Varn," (he always pronounced my name "Varn"), "you are named after my father, Wolf Mahler, who was killed by the Nazis along with my mother and most of my thirteen brothers and sisters." When I asked why they were killed, he simply said, "Because they were Jews." Those words have reverberated in my mind, haunting me ever since.

As you know, according to Ashkenazi Jewish tradition, a newborn infant is given a name in honor of a deceased relative. The name is formed by taking the initial letter of the name of the ancestor being honored. I had the good fortune to be named after you. As it has turned out over the years, you not only gave me my name, but you also gave me a sense of history and a sense of my identity.

Simon left Krosno in 1912 bound for New York, leaving you and nine of his siblings. (Already in this country were one brother and three sisters.) As he left, a series of pogroms targeting Jews had spread throughout the area. He often explained to me that he could travel only by night, with darkness as his shield to avoid being attacked and beaten by anti-Semites. He arrived in the United States on New Year's Eve in a city filled with gleaming lights and frenetic activity and with his heart filled with hope for a new life.

Simon returned to Krosno with my grandmother Eva in 1929 to a joyous homecoming—for this was the first time he had seen you since he left Poland. He took with him an early home-movie camera to record you on film. While in Poland he promised that once back in the United States he would try to earn enough money to send for his remaining family members who wished to leave, but history was to thwart his plans. During that happy reunion, he had no way of knowing this would be the last time he would ever see you and those others he left behind alive. Just ten years later, the Nazis invaded Poland.

Simon heard the news sitting in the kitchen of his home in Brooklyn. He was so infuriated, so frightened, so incensed that he took the large radio from the table, lifted it above his head, and hurled it against a wall. He knew what this invasion meant. He knew it signaled the end of the Jewish population in Eastern Europe as he had known it. He knew it meant certain death for people he had grown up with, people he had loved, people who had loved him.

Simon's fears soon became reality. He eventually learned from a brother who had escaped into the woods with his wife and young son that you, Basha, and a number of his siblings were tossed alive along with hundreds of other Jews into a massive bonfire in the streets of Krosno by Nazi troops. Other friends and relatives were eventually loaded onto cattle cars and transported to Auschwitz concentration camp.

Simon never fully recovered from those days in 1939. Though he kept the faces and voices from that distant land within him throughout his life, the Nazis also invaded my grandfather's heart, killing a part of him forever. My mother told me Simon became increasingly introspective, less spontaneous, less optimistic about what the future would hold.

In this country, my own father suffered the effects of anti-Jewish prejudice. One of only a handful of Jews in his school in Los Angeles in the 1920s and '30s, he returned home many afternoons injured from a fight. To get a decent job, his father, Edmond, was forced to Anglicize the family name, changing it from Blumenfeld to Fields.

My parents did what they could to protect my sister and myself from the effects of anti-Jewish prejudice, but still I grew up with a constant and gnawing feeling that I didn't belong. The time was the early 1950s, the so-called McCarthy era—a conservative time, a time when difference of any sort was held suspect. On the floor of the U.S. Senate, a brash young senator from Wisconsin, Joseph McCarthy, sternly warned that "Communists [often thought of as Jews in public perceptions] corrupt the minds and homosexuals corrupt the bodies of good upstanding Americans," and he proceeded to have them officially banned from government service. During this era there were frequent police raids on gay and lesbian bars, which were usually Mafia-owned; the U.S. Postal Service raided gay organizations and even published the names of their mailing lists in local newspapers, and people lost their jobs. Gays and lesbians were often involuntarily committed to mental institutions and underwent electroshock therapy; some were lobotomized.

Not knowing what else to do, my parents sent me, beginning when I was five and lasting for the next eight years, to a child psychologist because they feared I might be gay (or, to use the terminology of the day, "homosexual"). And as it turned out, their perceptions were correct.

While Simon was alive, my mother asked me not to discuss my sexual orientation with him—for he often expressed to me that it was now my responsibility to eventually marry and raise children so I could help perpetuate the Jewish people, a people who had been decimated in Europe. My mother worried information concerning my sexual orientation would upset Simon and that he probably wouldn't understand. Something within me, though, felt he knew anyway and most certainly did understand. I know it grieved him that I never married and never gave him great-grandchildren; I saw how it pleased him to be around the children of my cousins. It hurt me not to be able to be fully open with him. I think now, if I had, it might have ultimately brought us closer.

Great-grandfather Wolf, you would have been proud of Simon. He was a loving and caring father, grandfather, and great-grandfather. He gave me so much: my enjoyment for taking long walks and sitting in quiet solitude, pride in my Jewish heritage, and most of all, my ability to love.

My journey of coming out as gay over successive years was often difficult and painful, but it was certainly rewarding, for it has been the prime motivator for my work as a writer and social justice educator. I'm committed to this work on one level to ensure a better future for the young people growing up today. To be completely honest, though, my major motivation stems from the fact that I haven't felt safe in the world and therefore have a deep personal stake in the work I'm doing. Often, when I leave my university enclave, I feel like an outsider in my own country. Maybe that feeling will never completely leave me. I can take solace, at least, that my fear has diminished somewhat over the years.

A few years ago, Great-grandfather, I felt your presence, your touch strongly as I cofacilitated a workshop in eastern Massachusetts for thirty-one German teachers of English who were taking a summer course on U.S. culture at a local college. During the workshop I heard you telling me I was doing something exceptionally important. In my own small way I was having an impact on these teachers who soon would be traveling back home to Germany, teachers who themselves have an impact on German youth. I was proud to be an integral link in that chain. I knew I could never undo the terrible things that happened to you, but in some way I was doing my part to ensure it never happened again.

As I'm sure you're aware, I too have my biases and prejudices, which I acknowledge and am taking responsibility to heal. I automatically to stiffen whenever I hear the German language being spoken. Growing up with Simon, I was wary of even buying German products. I recall a conversation, or should I say an argument, between him and my sister, Susan, many years ago in which he voiced his immediate and vehement protest when Susan brought up the notion of purchasing a Volkswagen. Until that day I hadn't realized how deep his wounds were.

In my own case, on a number of occasions my wounds surfaced. For example, while attending an opera in Boston with a friend, I lost my ability to concentrate on the production as the German couple seated behind me spoke in their native tongue. Also, years before, while traveling through Germany en route from Holland to Copenhagen on a train, my anxiety seemed almost paralyzing until we finally reached Denmark, clear of the German border.

During the workshop with the German teachers, my apprehension collided with the reality that these teachers were warm, good people whom I could begin to trust. I was overwhelmed with conflicting feelings and felt as though I were blanking out. As my cofacilitator led the group through an exercise, I walked out into the hallway of the building and up a short flight of stairs. As I looked out the window onto a courtyard, I saw a young mother and her toddler son walking slowly below me. Flashes of the film that Simon and Eva took when they visited you back in 1929 played in my mind. In black-and-white images were pictured the inquisitive young children in their long nightshirts; smiling, proud women, some with small infants in their arms; horse-drawn carts at an open-air market; relatives of all ages self-consciously walking quickly toward the camera, for some inexplicable reason moving their arms around in tightly closed circles.

Great-grandfather, you know I am gay. Even though you lived at a time and place in which homosexuality was rarely discussed, your presence offers me support and comfort, for you saw firsthand how parallel forms of oppression run side by side and at points intersect. Though you may not have actually witnessed those "accused" of same-sex attractions being tortured and put to death, you no doubt heard about how they were treated. Hitler, in his ultimate fashion, showed the world the direct links in the various forms of oppression.

I recently looked up the word *holocaust* in the dictionary. Among the listings was the definition "genocidal slaughter." As I read this, the same nagging questions came to me as they did that first day Simon told me about your death—questions concerning the nature of human aggression, our ability for compassion, and, to those generations following World War II, our capacity to prevent similar tragedies in the future.

I write to you today, Great-grandfather, with both bad and good news. The bad news is that I fear we are repeating many of the mistakes of the past. With the rise of nationalistic movements throughout Eastern Europe, anti-Semitism, and other forms of racism, long suppressed, are once again resurfacing, where "ethnic cleansing" has become a sanitized term for hatred, forced expulsions, and murder. Hate-motivated vandalism and violence are on the increase in the United States too—for example, the series of incidents in 1999: fire-bombings at three synagogues in and around Sacramento; the shooting spree in Indiana and Illinois singling out Jews and Koreans; the spraying of bullets into a Los Angeles Jewish Community Center wounding a number of Jewish adults and children; and eventually, the killing of an Asian postal worker. We have witnessed the brutal attacks on Rodney King in Los Angeles; the barbarous slaying of James Byrd Jr. in Jasper, Texas; and the rape and murder of a seven-year-old girl in a Las Vegas casino bathroom.

In addition, the number of lesbian, gay, bisexual, and transgendered people who are the targets of bashings is escalating. Almost every week we hear of brutal and senseless attacks, so-called "gay bashings." In our schools and on our streets, groups of males wielding baseball bats and guns target anyone who acts or looks "different." For example, two men in Alabama bludgeoned to death Billy Jack Gaither, a thirty-nine-year-old gay man, with an ax han-

dle and tossed his limp body onto a pyre of burning tires. Brandon
Teena, a female-to-male transgendered person, was gang-raped in
Nebraska. Teena reported the incident to local police officials who
basically discounted his story. Soon thereafter, the perpetrators
entered Teena's home and murdered him along with two of his
nontransgendered friends.

There is a tradition in the western United States of ranchers
killing a coyote and tying it to a fence to scare off other coyotes and
to keep them from coming out of their hiding places. On October
6, 1998, two young men lured twenty-one-year-old Matthew
Shepard—a gay college student at the University of Wyoming in
Laramie—into their truck and drove him to a remote spot on the
Wyoming prairie, pistol-whipped him, and shattered his skull.
They then tied him to a wooden fence as if he were a lifeless coyote, where he was bound for over eighteen hours in near-freezing
temperatures. The message from his attackers seemed quite clear:
To all lesbian, gay, bisexual, and transgendered people, stay locked
away in your suffocating closets of denial and fear and don't ever
come out into the light of day.

Great-grandfather, as you know because you were there with
me, in the winter of 1991 I had the opportunity to travel with my
friend Derek to Amsterdam on vacation. This city is truly magical,
especially in winter when its intricate series of canals freeze over,
offering a veritable ice highway to a country of skaters. Of all the
amazing sites I visited, none attracted my interest more than the
Homomonument and the Anne Frank House.

The monument consists of three separate triangles of pink gran-
ite, which together form one larger triangle. Over one of the triangles hangs the inscription: "Homomonument commemorates all
women and men oppressed and persecuted because of their homosexuality, supports the international lesbian and gay movement in
their struggle against contempt, discrimination, and oppression,
demonstrates that we are not alone, calls for permanent vigilance."
The theme of the monument is "Past, Present, and Future," and the
three pink triangles relate to the three aspects of this theme.

Following my visit to the monument, I walked the short distance to the Anne Frank House. On my first visit to the house in 1972, I was too overcome with grief to remain for more than a few minutes. This time, as I mounted the narrow steps leading to her hiding place, I envisioned her faint image and could almost see her writing her secret thoughts in the diary that would one day become a chronicle, a testimony to all the world.

It is no coincidence that these two historic sites (one commemorating the Jews of Holland, the other memorializing a sexual minority) rest a mere few hundred meters apart. Though they are clearly not identical, there are connections between the pain and suffering endured by Anne, her family, and countless other European Jews, and by the gay and lesbian people forced into the camps under the pink-and-black triangle cloth.

In 2000 I again visited Europe, and this is the good news I alluded to earlier. The November before, when I was visiting my mother and sister at their home in Nevada, I checked my e-mail, and I found a personal invitation to present at an international colloquium to be held in Berlin the following February on the topic of *Die Verfolgung Homosexueller im Dritten Reich* (The Persecution of Homosexuals Under the Nazis). The colloquium organizers were aware of my work on this topic and were interested in having me give one of my slide presentations, titled "The German Homosexual Emancipation Movement From 1860 to 1933," to lay an historical foundation for the colloquium. Without hesitation, I immediately replied, accepting their kind invitation and expressing how enormously honored I was and how much I looked forward to joining what I believed would be a truly remarkable program.

Over the next few weeks before traveling to Berlin, however, the reality set in, filling me with a constant and overwhelming anxiety from which I could not escape. I lay in my bed late into the night unable to sleep, thoughts of you and Basha, Simon, and Eva flashing into my consciousness. Difficult and seemingly unanswerable questions filled my mind: *Will my going to Germany be tantamount to betraying my kin?* or *Would they approve of this trip?* and *What about my personal safety?* How secure is Germany for Jews today? Also, self-doubt concerning my abilities engulfed me: *What right do* you *have?* I questioned myself. *You're an American, you don't speak German, and you're traveling to Germany to present German history to Germans? What sense does that make?* My heart raced many nights as I cried myself to sleep. On a few occasions I nearly got out of bed to e-mail colloquium organizers that I in fact would not be able to attend. Throughout the days leading up to the colloquium, my apprehension was intense; I withdrew from friends, becoming increasingly melancholy, isolated, depressed. My friend Leah reached out to me, saying, "You bring with you a clear and resounding voice, one your relatives were denied. You can speak in their memory and speak in a way they never could." Her words resonated in my mind at Boston's Logan Airport as I boarded the Lufthansa plane that would transport me to Berlin, though the tears flowed uninterrupted throughout that long flight.

I arrived on a cloudy and drizzly morning. On the cab ride to my hotel, except for a small segment of the Berlin Wall that stood as a reminder of the city's not-so-distant past, the landscape appeared strangely familiar, for this could have been any of a number of European or even U.S. cities, with factories, small shops, rush-hour traffic, pedestrians toting raised umbrellas walking to work, and children on their way to school. Once in my hotel room, I turned on the TV and viewed a children's program in which a young girl and boy demonstrated the proper way to assemble a tropical aquarium. This seeming ordinariness was somehow reassuring to me.

I ventured downtown, walking through a number of neighborhoods and riding the subway. People appeared relaxed and friendly.

By the day of the colloquium, I'd begun to feel I'd made the right decision in coming here. The first panel was composed of preeminent researchers in the persecution of homosexuals under the Third Reich, followed by curators of Holocaust museums and concentration camps. Next, two gay men, both survivors of the death camps, gave moving testimonials. I then shared the platform

77

with a college student whom I had met in Florida one year prior and whom I invited to join me in the presentation.

As the lights lowered, I pressed the "advance" button on the remote-control switch to display the first slide. Toward the end of my presentation, I interjected a personal note. Choking back tears, I acknowledged, "This has been a difficult presentation for me, for I come to you today speaking not only as a gay man but also as a Jew. I feel honored to have been invited to come to Berlin to be able to speak on behalf of my family members whose voice was extinguished." I dedicated my talk to your memory, and to Basha, Simon, and Eva. I continued, "And to their memory, I raise a central tenet of Jewish tradition, which is *tikkun olam*, meaning the transformation, healing, and repairing of the world so it becomes a more just, peaceful, nurturing, and perfect place. As we look back over the unconscionable horrors of the Nazi era, I have a hope—a hope that we can all join together as allies to counter the hatred so we can make real the true potential of *never again*. I end then by asking us all to join and go out into our lives and work for *tikkun olam*. Let us transform the world."

Throughout the colloquium and my time in Berlin, I felt your presence, Great-grandfather, and the power of *tikkun olam*, for I continued my own healing journey as someone from the third generation, someone who has been touched deeply by the German Holocaust.

As you know, I'm by no means a very religious person, though I strive to become more spiritual and connected to you. Before the end of my days, for me to be able to say I have truly accomplished all I needed to accomplish in this world, I must travel back to Krosno. Though Simon's son, my uncle Jack, has informed me that your small village no longer exists—that the Nazis destroyed Krosno—I want and walk upon the soil you once walked upon, to witness the hallowed ground on which you prayed, and to feel the Polish sun nurturing me as it had once nurtured and illuminated you—that same sun which they eclipsed for you all too soon.

I don't know if there is a purpose to life, or if we're placed here for a reason. If, however, we all truly have a unique mission or calling in this world, I believe mine is to continue doing the work I am doing, with you as my guide. You are that still and quiet voice within me, that voice that keeps me on course and prevents me from sinking under the waters of doubt and fear. The mistakes I have made along my path most assuredly occurred when I refused to heed your counsel.

Being both Jewish and gay, I truly believe I am twice blessed. I ask that you now, Great-grandfather, stay with me and continue to be my teacher, my light, my guide. With you by my side, I can never be alone.

With love forever and ever,
Warren

The Thing Is Very Close to You
Angela Brown

This is my favorite quote from Torah:

"Surely, this Instruction that I enjoin upon you this day is not too extraordinary for you, nor is it beyond reach," Moses tells us. "It is not in the heavens, that you should say 'Who among us can go up to the heavens and get it for us and impart it to us that we may observe it?'.... No, the thing is very close to you—in your mouth and in your heart, to observe it."

I first fell in love with this passage when I was giving a drash on Parashat Netzavim at my synagogue, Beth Chayim Chadashim in Los Angeles, a couple of years ago. This quote comes from Moses' famous "choose life" speech, and in my sermon I spoke about how we choose the kind of person we want to be, how we choose all of our actions. Since then I've tried to figure out why these words from Moses move me so much. Part of my attraction to them has to do with the idea that everything we need is very close to us; it's a part of us. When I was a kid, I'd watch *The Wizard of Oz* wide-eyed year after year when it appeared on television each spring; part of my fascination with the film (besides the flying monkeys) was that Dorothy searched so hard for what she needed, when all along it was right with her. So this passage from Torah resonates with me, certainly, on that level: We have all the tools we need—to make our own lives better and to make the world a more peaceful place for those around us. In this way we choose who we are by trying to do what is right.

But this passage also compels me because of the line "the thing is very close to you." The word "thing" especially draws me in. It's so vague yet so vast. What is this "thing" Moses describes?

I didn't fully realize the power of this passage—or what this "thing" might be—until I became friends with Dr. David Neiman, a man who completely changed my outlook on the world and my identity. I met Dr. Neiman through his daughter, my good friend Becky. I wasn't raised in a Jewish tradition, although I had known for years, deep inside, that I was Jewish through and through. All along there had been a light burning inside me, but when I made the choice to become Jewish, the light burned even brighter. This is why later I chose for myself the Hebrew name Orly, which means "my light." After I decided to become Jewish, I spoke to Becky about it, and she immediately said, "You have to meet my father!" In fact, she said it about a dozen times in the course of our conversation. I hesitated—actually, I put her off for close to six months. I'd always been intimidated by meeting my friends' parents. And I had an irrational fear of older people (Dr. Neiman was around eighty at the time), because I confused them somehow with death and illness. I thought Becky's father, a Conservative rabbi and Jewish scholar, would judge me—a feisty, tattooed (oy) gentile (oy again) lesbian (triple oy) from a broken family. Looking back now, it all seems so ridiculous.

After I'd been studying Judaism for several months and meeting with my rabbi, Lisa Edwards, on a regular basis, I finally mustered the courage to meet Dr. Neiman, or Dr. N, as I like to call him. I attended a lecture he delivered called "Jesus the Jew" in a bank building in Studio City. Dr. N was well known in the field of comparative religion—in fact, he made history in 1966 at Boston College when he became the first tenured Jewish theology professor at a Catholic university in the United States.

Dr. Neiman had a broad, handsome face, beautiful white hair, and a smile that lit up the room. When I first met him, he was dressed to the nines in a gorgeous gray suit and crisp white dress shirt. (I would learn later that he dressed this way all the time, even for a trip to the grocery store.) But what impressed me most was the peaceful energy that radiated from him. After his lecture, Becky and I, along with two other friends, had lunch with Dr. N at a nearby kosher hot dog stand. What I remember most was his exclaiming, "I love being around young people!" Dr. N was as comfortable—if not more so—with people in their twenties and thirties as he was with scholars his own age. He glowed in the presence of younger people; he drew energy from them and returned it tenfold.

After that day, I spent more and more time with Dr. N and Becky. Our favorite pastime—and his especially—was to eat. So we'd go to a local diner, Twain's, and have sandwiches or fish 'n' chips on Shabbat or Sunday afternoons. We'd dine at old-school Italian restaurants where he'd proclaim, "The only decent egg-plant parmigiana is in Rome!"

Becky would snicker and say, "Well, Dad, you have to remember we're in the Valley."

One evening at Twain's with Becky and Dr. N, I ordered a tuna melt. I'd had the tuna melt several times, and it was quite good—especially with their incredible crinkle-cut fries. This time, however, I was surprised when I spotted a piece of bacon sticking out from beneath a slice of rye bread.

"Becky, it's bacon!" I said.

"Get that waitress over here now!" Dr. N cried out, as if we were surrounded by flames.

"Oh, I'll just take it off."

"No, it's not kosher. It's ruined. Becky, get the waitress."

Becky summoned the waitress, and an exhausted-looking woman approached the table.

"This sandwich has bacon on it!" Dr. N told her.

"It says right on the menu that the tuna melt has bacon on it," the waitress said.

"Well, I've gotten it before and it never had bacon on it," I offered.

"Can't you just take it off?" She looked so tired.

"That's not kosher! And whoever heard of a tuna melt with bacon?" Dr. N gave her a quizzical look.

I wanted to take the plate and everything on it and hide under the table, especially because my own family specializes in bitterly complaining to wait staff and enjoys pushing people's buttons wherever they go.

"We'd have to make an entirely new sandwich," the waitress protested.

"Well, then, that's what you'll have to do," Dr. N told her, his stage-worthy baritone resounding off the rock-laden walls of Twain's. He wasn't harsh with the waitress; he was just being his dogged self, fighting for a damsel in distress.

"Really, I can just take it off..."

Becky whispered in my ear, "Let him go. He's enjoying this."

"You can't take it off. It's not kosher!" Dr. N persisted. He turned to the waitress. "Bring her another sandwich, please...this time without the bacon."

"Okay, I'll take it back," the waitress finally conceded, clearly worn out. "It'll be a few minutes."

Becky and I smirked at each other, and I smiled inside. I was a bit embarrassed that such a fuss had been made over me, but I was secretly thrilled that a renowned Jewish scholar had fought for my kosher tuna melt at a cheap diner in Studio City. This was someone I wanted to keep in my life for a long time. This guy was a real *mentsh*.

And Cloud Nine had one more resident: David Neiman.

✡

After Pesach that year, Becky phoned me with some sad news. Her father had bone cancer, and it had progressed to stage four. He hadn't told Becky—or her sisters, Rachel and Rina—that he had been battling cancer for years. He was that kind of man, that kind of father. He wanted to spare them his *tsouris*, didn't want them to worry. Soon after, Becky sublet her apartment and moved in with him. Her life—and that of her sister Rina—was taken up with medication schedules, doctor's appointments, meal preparation, and keeping up her father's spirits—by discussing religion, politics, world history, and even Dr. Phil and Ben and J-Lo with him. (He accurately predicted the couple would break up within a few months.)

I, in turn, began to spend even more time with Dr. Neiman, bringing by cheesecake or Chinese food or watching television with him while he hung out with my dog, Harry. Dr. N was always very concerned about whether Harry liked him. *How funny*, I thought. He was such a strong man, so cerebral; he'd been through so much—his family had fled Russia in 1921 when he was an infant; he'd conducted ten archaeological expeditions to Israel; he'd mourned the death of his wife, Israeli guitarist and singer Shulamit Dubno, more than twenty-five years before; and he had raised three daughters as a single father—and yet he worried that my scrappy one-eyed dog didn't like him.

"You love your mother Angela, don't you?" he said, holding Harry's head in his hands and looking into his sole eye one night.

Harry stared up at him, expecting a treat. Dr. N liked to spoil him, even letting him gobble leftover chicken off his fork or lap up the remains of his cream of mushroom soup.

"And you're clearly in love with Becky," he went on, rather sorrowfully. "But you just like David, huh? Just like him. That's all."

✡

By Yom Kippur, Dr. N's health had declined further and he was unable to attend services at a temple. Becky's sister Rina arranged a service at his apartment, and we were joined by their cousins. Dr. N traded in his suit for a white terrycloth bathrobe, which he was now wearing almost constantly, and quietly conducted the service in his living room. His voice was quavering, and he was extremely weak, but he was determined to make it through the service. Each of us took turns reading from the machzor he had written, which contained poems and special passages on Jewish history—Dr. N's favorite area of study. After the service, Dr. N went to rest, and Becky and Rina and I broke the fast (a little early—please don't tell my rabbi) with frozen yogurt at a strip mall down the street.

As I sat there devouring a dish of peanut-butter chocolate, I looked at Rina and Becky, and thought, *These are my sisters. This family has taken me in and sees me as a whole person: as a lesbian, as a Jew; not as a Jew by Choice but as a Jew, as a member of their—our—tribe.* I'd been so scared to meet Dr. Neiman, so nervous about reaching out to someone I'd thought was so different from me, someone I assumed would judge me. I'd been so afraid to take the risk.

✡

Dr. Neiman passed away peacefully on Feb. 22, 2004, a shadow of his former self. But this is what I will remember most about him and keep with me forever:

David Neiman was my friend. I will miss his warm smile, his brilliant wit, and his playful sense of humor. I will miss his humanity. I will miss the way he could take down the house with his one-liners. I will miss the way he loved his daughters, fiercely and joyfully. He didn't tell me this; I could just tell.

I will miss the support and friendship he gave me while I studied to become Jewish, the way he approached me in the parking lot of Vitello's restaurant one month after I had my mikveh and bet din and asked, "How are you doing?"

I thought the question was strange considering we had just celebrated his birthday together. "I'm doing fine," I shrugged.

"No, how are you *doing*?"

I knew what he meant now: He wanted to know how I was doing now that I was Jewish.

"Oh, that! I'm doing great, just GREAT!" I told him.

He smiled and hugged me, and gave me a sweet kiss on the ear. He was the one person who could make me feel the most Jewish without saying a word. He had a gift for just being around people.

White, black, gay, straight, Jewish, gentile—it didn't matter. To him, all people were G-d's gift to the world.

I will miss him because he proclaimed that the New Year's Eve Becky and I spent with him this year watching *I, Claudius* episodes back to back to back was his best New Year's ever—and he had partied all night in Times Square in the '40s, he told us! "I'm past that," he said. "This is where I want to be. With you and Becky and Harry."

I will miss him most because he was the father I never had.

So what is this "thing" Moses describes in Parashat Netzavim? How did Dr. N teach me the meaning of this? Well, I think the "thing" is many things, but I know for sure that one of them is this: The thing that is very close to us is other human beings. Dr. Neiman, at his congregation in Brookline, Massachusetts, often saved up his recyclables for a homeless man who regularly stopped by the synagogue for help. While board members would shoo the man away, Dr. Neiman made it a point to bring in bottles and cans from home and have a conversation with him, ask him how he was doing, chat about the weather, compliment him on his industriousness. He was living Judaism. A scholar with 4,000 books in his home and office—in English, Hebrew, Latin, Aramaic, Spanish, Italian, French, Ladino, and more. A man who founded in New York the Academy for Higher Jewish Learning, now known as the Academy for Jewish Religion. A man who had taught at Brandeis and the Gregorian Pontificate in Rome. He nurtured his mind, his being, his soul, but knew all this was pointless without connecting with others, without taking giant leaps of faith and spirit—even when the prospect might be scary. This is Torah, this is what is close to us, this is what is in our mouths and hearts to observe. If we don't take risks, if we make our decisions out of shame or apathy or fear—which I've done often, as a Jew, as a lesbian, and as a person—we aren't living Torah.

One of my favorite quotations comes from Rabbi Samson Raphael Hirsch's *Nineteen Letters About Judaism*: "A life of seclusion, devoted only to meditation and prayer, is not Judaism."

I like to think David Neiman thought about this quote often.

The Cantor and Carol Channing
Eric Pliner

In her own mind, my Grandma Ruth was a modern-day Renaissance woman, skilled in and renowned for her work in the visual and performing arts. She was a lifelong entertainer at heart whose professional career was cut short early when her mother caught her walking down the street while skipping a day of school with two girlfriends to sing in an amateur contest. (She won.) Her most magnificent needlepoint hung proudly in her home's prize location—just above the living room TV—and included a small brass plaque with the inscription NEEDLEWORK BY RUTHE. ("Ruthe" was not a typo but a more flamboyant, imaginary stage name.)

Like many frustrated artists without an official audience, my grandmother hovered near performers for much of her life. She and my grandfather, Pop, spent several years as the managers of an ultimately unsuccessful singer named Mer-lyn, and were back-door neighbors with a gal named Reenie, who went on to 1960s one-hit wonder status as Diane Renee with a tune called "Navy Blue." ("Blue / navy blue / I'm as blue as I can be / 'cause my steady boy / said, 'Ship ahoy,' / and joined the na-a-avy.") Grandma loved to tell the story of having the Four Tops over to her house for dinner, a tale that was never complete without her crooning a few verses of "Sugar Pie, Honey Bunch." In the '80s, when she and Pop owned an arcade in the Woodhaven Mall, my grandmother could often be found in front of the store, untying her denim apron to try out a few moves with the break-dancing teens who presided over the place.

As she got older, Grandma's big, deep brown eyes lent themselves to spot-on impersonations of a boozy Judy Garland wailing "Over the Rainbow," and even more so of an aging Carol Channing. She kept a cued cassette in a nearby boom box, ready to entertain anyone, even strangers, at the slightest indication of interest, or without it. Of course, as I entered my teens—and was trying desperately to sublimate my own growing interest in show tunes and brassy impersonations—I wanted nothing more than to fit in, and Grandma's in-public antics quickly turned mortifying.

A typical Sunday (every third or fourth Sunday, that is) involved my dad hustling me and my brother, Todd, into his car for the half-hour drive from South Jersey to his parents' home in northeast Philadelphia. (He had given up on begging my mother to join us long ago.) After a brief visit, complete with time to put our feet up on the plastic-covered couches, eat a few of Grandma's favorite chocolate-covered potato chips, and hear her sing a Frank Sinatra ditty, we'd head to the Country Club—the Country Club Diner, that is—for lunch at the only restaurant Grandma and Pop would eat in for the last ten years of their lives.

The Country Club was Grandma's greatest performance venue and my personal adolescent torture diner. At the moment of our grand arrival, Grandma would gleefully remind me, "They're known for their baked goods!" and call out to Mike, her long-suffering restaurant-manager friend and only fan (and only by default, at that). Mike would escort us to a table in the back (never quite enough in a corner for my liking), and Grandma would serenade him with "New York, New York" or "My Way." Then we'd order—bagels and lox for me and Dad, whitefish for Todd, chicken breasts for Grandma and Pop, who were watching their sodium (except, of course, for the chocolate-covered potato chips).

Table by table, the restaurant would fill up with neighborhood families on their way from church, each one obviously less brash, more fashionable, less edgy, more relaxed, less Jewish, more blond (except for Grandma, who had been a bottle-blond for decades) than we. I hated them, and I wanted to be them. I wanted to be at the mall, I wanted to be hanging out with my friends (I wanted to have friends), I wanted Grandma Ruth to put away the piece of twine she had unfurled from her rhinestone-encrusted purse and stop singing "I've Got the World on a String." But instead I sat silently and slid a little farther down the red vinyl chair during each song in the set, until dessert—they were, after all, known for their baked goods—which I ate under the table with my brother.

These Sunday afternoon concert-lunches capped off preteen weekends that started with the holy ritual of Junior Congregation on Saturday morning, even though my parents and their friends never seemed to attend any sort of Senior Congregation. Besides our usual Hebrew and Judaica classes, we (forty or so awkward, adolescent Jews and one folksy cantor with an acoustic guitar) participated in a weekly Shabbat service. The cantor wore plain gray skirt-suits that came to just below her knees, a kippah and tallis, and flat shoes. We were about the same height. Every week we trudged through the familiar routine: The Amidah meant we were half-done (who would stand the longest during the silent part?). Aleinu meant we were almost done. Kaddish meant we were done except for a final song. It was all I knew, so I took it all for granted: that our cantor was a woman (at home, Dad sometimes referred to her as the cantress), that she had a great voice (and a perm!), that she played the guitar with Indigo Girls–like flair (it would be a good six years before I'd even hear of the Indigo Girls), and that she led us with sternness and structure but also affection and kindness. And we all took for granted that each of us, in a community of what has today grown to be more than 900 families, would get to study for our bar or bat mitzvah with the cantor.

I remember few details about her office (more of a large, converted supply closet, I think), except that she had a few filing cabinets, a guitar stand, a big desk, and a light-blue index card tacked to a bulletin board on the side wall. In red marker and her bold, block capital letters, it read, "CAN'T = WON'T." She never pointed at the index card or even referred to it. It spoke for itself. I spent more than one afternoon sucking on my braces and glancing sheepishly at that card while she admonished me that my bar mitzvah was not for her but for me and my family and that I needed to study my *haftarah*.

In the midst of a rather shoddy explanation about why I was unprepared one particular week, the cantor's phone rang, and she answered it. I tried not to eavesdrop. I looked at the bookshelves, I stared up at the ceiling, I reread the "CAN'T = WON'T" card. Twice. I pretended to study my portion, but my choice to prioritize a few hours at the mall with Orange Julius and Spencer Gifts over a few hours with G-d and the cantor's cassette left me with little idea what the Hebrew actually said.

So—forgive me—instead I listened. And what I heard sent me into a tailspin: The cantor had a life! I had never thought about it before. She had friends, she didn't live in the synagogue, she made dinner plans. I mean, right there in front of me, she made dinner plans! My mind started flying: Where was she from? Where did she live? Did she go on dates? Did she have a boyfriend? Who was on the phone?

I was stunned. I sat in front of this woman every Saturday for Junior Congregation, and once every few weeks for bar mitzvah tutoring, preparing for the most significant moment in my life to date, and she hadn't told me a blessed thing about herself. What nerve. I resolved, in that moment, to embody Yente, the great matchmaking heroine of *Fiddler on the Roof,* which my mother had made me watch as part of her mandatory Good Moral Lessons film series, which began soon after we acquired our first VCR in the early '80s and extended over a period of many years. (The series also included *My Bodyguard,* in which a skinny, intelligent, slightly nerdy but not unattractive young man gets a bigger, stronger, tougher, older boy to follow him around, take care of him, and protect him from bullies. I liked this one.)

I prepared my series of questions and my best seventh-grade Bea Arthur* impersonation. The cantor hung up the phone, but before I could begin the questioning, she quickly returned to her patient, gentle, and unyielding reminder of my upcoming performance in front of everyone I knew in the entire world. Ah, yes, that. Bea was not to be.

When the big day came, I did a decent job. The cantor stood next to me and quietly corrected my three (three!) mistakes. She spoke soft words of encouragement to me before I started to chant, and whispered wonderful, kind, congratulatory praise everyone could see but only I could hear during a public-private moment on the bimah immediately afterward. I exhaled and then glowed. The cantor glowed a little too.

At the party, Aunt Ethel complained that my friends were eating soap. (It was pastel-colored chocolate candy in the shape of Torahs and Stars of David that Mom had been making and freezing for three months.) Unsurprisingly, a great uncle (or two) kvetched about the woman with the guitar who led much of the service. They weren't used to seeing a woman leading much of anything (particularly in synagogue), and especially not a woman with a guitar.

Grandma Ruth, on the other hand, paid no mind to the complaints, and instead had a blast, flitting about the room, "befriending" the bandleader, and doing her infamous rendition of the Mummers' strut at the front of a conga line. Even Pop danced with her. She would talk about that day for a long time to come.

I went on high school and spent weeknights balancing confirmation and post-confirmation classes (every Tuesday) with significant suburban youth activities, like cashiering and homework and choir (oh, my!). And that's not even counting my considerable hours rehearsing to play the noteworthy role of Pippin's gay brother Lewis (eight lines, one singing line, and one dance number with Fastrada) in the spring musical. My connection to the cantor waned as I took on the identity of oppositional teen and

*Bea, whom I silently worshiped because of her role as Dorothy on *The Golden Girls*, had played Yente on Broadway, which I remembered from the original cast album Mom kept in our family room cabinet. And shame on you for not knowing.

she ushered ever-growing hordes of twelve-year-olds into the chamber of CAN'T = WON'T.

The summer between junior and senior years, I found out who the Indigo Girls were (some friends at a summer program sang "Closer to Fine" at the talent show), and I found out who I was (a counselor at the same program showed *The Times of Harvey Milk* and then came out to us). A couple of weeks later, when Mom and Dad found out who I was (I left a love note from J.J., who played Pippin's father, Charlemagne, hanging out of my yearbook), things took a turn for the worse in our household. We started fighting with extreme frequency, like once a minute.

One day after school, Mom and I took a break from bickering long enough to open the mail, which included a thick light-blue envelope from the synagogue. It was a lengthy social action survey, and it asked congregants to check off issues with which they had expertise or, conversely, needed help. Smack in the middle of page two was a line for "homosexuality." I was ready to whip out a big pink pen and check it off right then. (At that point, I would've started a PFLAG chapter in our living room, with or without my parents, had I known what PFLAG was.) But Mom quietly discouraged me by emitting smoke and flame from the rims of her eye sockets, clenching her jaw, and going into her bedroom, survey in hand. (She was much too clever to leave it within reach of me and my feathered pen.)

This was around the beginning of what Mom sometimes calls our "difficult time," which also included my brother getting caught drinking in the backyard and the first of my grandfather's strokes. Within the next year, we ate our last brunch (as I, now a sophisticated college queer, had taken to calling it) at the Country Club Diner, just in time for me to humiliate my entire family by joining Grandma Ruth in a verse of "Hello, Dolly." "Wow, wow, wow, fellas," we belted, chewing on the insides of our cheeks, smiling broadly, eyelashes fluttering. "Look at the old girl now, fellas!" (I had learned all the words after seeing Carol Channing herself croak her way through a bizarre Day-Glo thirtieth-anniversary revival. I gave her a great review in the *Tufts Daily*.) We capped it off with a passionate rendition of Judy doing "Over the Rainbow" at Carnegie Hall.

Pop's second stroke would land him in a nursing home, with Grandma next door at York House, an independent living facility for seniors. This meant she had her own apartment (which retained much of her old furniture, sans the nicotine-stained plastic covers) but ate lunch in a group dining room. It also meant she had a lot of free time and a lot of neighbors and therefore an instant audience. She traveled up and down the halls, and up and down the too-steep pathway to Pop's building, with her giant purse, stuffed with a pair of Grouch Marx–style plastic glasses with nose and mustache, a *Judy Garland's Greatest Hits* cassette, and an ample supply of yarn for the still-kicking "I've Got the World on a String" number. She filled her days with impromptu performances, dancing and singing to her own delight, to some residents' mild pleasure, and to other folks' utter horror. She missed living with my grandfather, of course—we all stifled tears when we saw the sweat-suited shell of his former feisty self—but Grandma Ruth managed to find a way to make something exciting out of her new circumstances: she made herself a star.

In the long hours between her treks to visit Pop, Grandma played bingo, did arts and crafts, and watched *Wheel of Fortune* and *Jeopardy!* ("I like to know a little bit about a lot of things," she'd say.) She also began to take advantage of the Jewish facility's Shabbat and holiday services and to forge a relationship with the rabbi who visited each week. It seemed odd to me, as my memories of Grandma and Judaism were limited to a killer (both in taste and in sodium content) matzoh ball recipe and a videocassette of *Yentl* (labeled *Yentle,* like Ruthe) that gathered dust atop her VCR for a good decade. But she was passionate about it, mentioning holiday dinners, humming tunes when she didn't know the words, and proudly proclaiming whatever syllables, in English or Hebrew, that she did remember from her childhood.

When my grandfather died (physically, as it seemed he had died mentally long before), Grandma seemed to take it in stride. As

Pop's ability to recognize her diminished, alongside her own energy, Grandma had begun to make the uphill journey every other day instead of every day. She started saying goodbye to her beloved husband sooner, I think, than any of us knew, and when the day finally came, Grandma Ruth held her head high and her hands steady. She was Pop's companion for nearly sixty years, and naturally she was to be the center of attention, together with our memories of him. In the limousine on the way to the cemetery (and for the subsequent days of shiva), Grandma softly wailed, "Oh, Freddy," any time the conversation diverted from her. She didn't do it to be malicious or even consciously manipulative—she just was who she was, being who she had always been. Though the day was particularly painful for my brave, patient, and compassionate father (an only child), I imagine the focus on Grandma Ruth is exactly what my grandfather would have wanted.

Our few remaining relatives—including Pop's brother Irv, who bore an unsettling resemblance to a younger, healthier version of my dead grandfather—along with an assortment of Dad's coworkers and family friends, attended the graveside service, which was led by the cantor. Though I had seen her a handful of times in the intermittent years (often from a great distance or on closed-circuit TV at packed High Holiday services), she looked older than I remembered, my brain frozen on a moment in time nearly ten years prior. Her skirt-suit was the same gray, and her hair was the same too but grayer. The synagogue community had been through some unexpectedly painful experiences, and the cantor was the only member of our clergy who had remained through major transitions. Regardless, given a choice, my parents wouldn't have had the service led by anyone else, as our family retained powerful, affectionate feelings for this strong, brilliant woman who had guided us—and, indeed, our entire community—through so many important moments in our lives.

At the funeral, the cantor showed her characteristic compassion for my grandmother, who needed it. Grandma followed through the service, calling out for my grandfather any time focus strayed from her or when we spoke in Hebrew for more than a minute and using a loud, strong voice to read along when she knew the words. (I will never forget the sound of her throaty letter "L" and her raspy voice as she recited the 23rd Psalm. I think of her every time I hear it.)

When the service was over, Grandma took my father's arm. "She's the same one that did the bar mitzvahs, right, Pat?" she asked him, as she had several times already. He took a deep breath, ever patient, and said yes.

Grandma was overflowing with gratitude and respect for the cantor, and thanked her profusely. The cantor gave her a long, slow look, listening intently and thoughtfully to my grandmother's words, followed by a firm, kind hug. "You have a good family, Mrs. Pliner," she told her. My brother and I each got a hug too, full of familiar warmth and strength and care. "How are you doing?" she asked us, one by one.

"Crazy," I wanted to say. Instead I said, "Okay."

In the following days, Grandma brought up the cantor every chance she could, trying my Dad's patience by repeatedly asking if she would be returning to our house to lead the services. Often her questions were an unsubtle way of criticizing that particular day's volunteer lay minyan leader as she or he left our house. No one, it seemed, could compare with the cantor—a concept everyone, even my mother and grandmother, could agree on.

By then, six years after I'd come out to my family, I had graduated from college, was working full-time in a program for lesbian, gay, bisexual, and transgendered students, and volunteered my free time as a member of Boston's pride committee. Along with these roles came a reasonably effective gaydar, though it didn't take Harvey Fierstein to figure out that our beloved cantor probably had more in common with the Indigo Girls than just the guitar. In the time since Mom had shot me a combustible glance and destroyed the synagogue survey, things had changed quite a bit in our home community. The rabbi had used the space of a Yom Kippur sermon to indicate his support for same-gender commitment ceremonies, and the cantor had begun to appear at some holidays and events with another woman, who was clearly a part of her family. (Of course, much of what I knew was hearsay, as my parents' occasional attendance at synagogue was something that hadn't changed much.)

Grandma lived about two and a half more years. Though she retained her lively spirit (and most of her props), her impressions and performances grew fewer and farther between. She spent many days watching soaps with her caregivers and filled her evenings with *Who Wants to Be a Millionaire* (she still liked to know a little bit about a lot of things) and extended sleep.

Even as her mental capacities dwindled, Grandma Ruth managed to maintain some of her self-awareness and even a bit of her once-prominent edge. About six months before I last saw her, she cornered me with questions, wanting to know why I hadn't had a girlfriend since high school and glaring at me with keen brown eyes over her yellowed bifocals. I squirmed at her questions, once again avoiding the conversation I thought we'd never get to have. (We never did.)

Except for Grandma, I was out to pretty much everyone else in my life, including my other grandparents, who acted as though they were thrilled. (My then-boyfriend, Adam, had somehow managed to replace me, my brother, and our two cousins as the favorite grandchild on that side of the family.) When Dad and I went to visit Grandma Ruth, though, Adam stayed at my parents' house, gossiping about us with my mother, and my identity as a gay man stayed with him. I struggled with the pain of this decision, that someone who I loved so much (and my most drag queen–like relative to boot) didn't know me as my full self. Still, during particularly argumentative times, my mother had once prophesied that coming out to any of my grandparents would probably kill them. Though she had been wrong so far, the dregs of my deeply ingrained shame, combined with Grandma's failing mental and physical health, made me more reluctant than ever to test the theory out on her. Each of our visits grew cloudier, as Grandma Ruth showed less and less of the woman she had always been, and I showed less and less of the man I was becoming.

The cantor wasn't available to lead the graveside service at Grandma's funeral, right next to the spot where we had buried Pop not quite three years before. Instead we rode in the limousine with the new rabbi, who made small talk with me about the synagogue on the block in Brooklyn where Adam and I lived. (It was a good connection: He had played basketball there while he was in rabbinical school; I knew what a basketball was.) I stood silently through the service, and broke down in the back of the car before we left the cemetery.

I knew the cantor would come to our home the next night to lead the shiva minyan, and I was looking forward to seeing her, both with curiosity and for comfort at yet another important moment in the story of our family. I knew I wanted to come out to her, and to thank her, even silently if necessary, for the ways that her strength and leadership had affected me.

I filled the day with easy distractions. Aunt Gloria, Aunt Bea, and a third well-meaning individual had all sent fish platters (platters that not only contained fish but were also in the shape of fish). We were overwhelmed with lox and herring, and the trays wouldn't fit in the refrigerator. Despite my protests, Mom kept one in the garage for a few hours, since the weather was unseasonably cold. I spent the afternoon calling food banks and synagogues to see who would take perishables. (I didn't mention the part about the garage.) I ate as much as I could.

At dusk, when the doorbell rang, I stiffened. I moved to get the door, but my mother beat me to it. She opened it, and the cantor was there on our porch. Mom smiled and the cantor smiled. From the corner, I half-smiled. (I was nervous, in mourning, and full of salty fish.)

"Hello, cantor!" Mom started.

And then, my loving mother, whose grand theatrical experience is limited to having directed first-graders in holiday pageants twenty years ago, managed a brilliant, rehearsed-sounding stage whisper, directed at the cantor but obviously intended for my ears too. (As it happened, she needn't have put forth the effort, as I was not-so-subtly eavesdropping near from in front of the hall closet.) "Thank you so much for coming," she sighed/projected. "I just want you to know your partner is welcome any time you come here."

I grimaced, said hello to the cantor, took her coat, and retreated to the living room to wait in hiding for the service to begin. I was mortified. I knew my mother meant well, but I took major offense. "She's working, Mom," I whined later that day. "It's like one of your kids' parents telling you Daddy is welcome to attend a parent-teacher conference."

"And that's such an insult?" she would respond. "People at work happen to be very fond of your father."

Of course, my aggravation was probably as much from feeling my mother's remark was inappropriate as from feeling she'd stolen my thunder. After years of self-blame, bickering, and using her fingers as gay-prevention earplugs, Mom had developed a new level of comfort with talking about queerness that appeared somewhere around the same time as the arrival of Adam and the premiere of *Will & Grace*. ("I love that Jack," she'd say. "Oh, and that Megan Mullally! She is a stitch!")

When it was over, I waited my turn to talk to the cutes with her before she had to leave.

The cantor smiled at me with her eyes, and after some pleasantries asked me what I was up to. I recounted the details of my New York life in a whisper not unlike that of my mother's earlier performance. Not because I felt the need to hide anything from the gathering of neighbors, Dad's coworkers, and Aunt Gloria, but because I wanted another public-private moment with the cantor, one that was just mine and hers, to be alone together amidst the mourning.

I twisted a paper napkin, and I started talking. I struggled to find words about being a writer. I talked about my job with the lesbian, gay, bisexual, and transgender youth program. I talked about Adam, about how he hadn't come because he had never met my grandmother and thought it would be awkward. I tore off more bits of napkin. I talked about our apartment and about our cat, Turner. I wanted to talk trash about my mother's greeting, but I restrained myself. I talked about Brooklyn, about living on the block with the synagogue with the basketball court that the rabbi had played on.

I don't know what I was expecting. I wanted her to say something, to acknowledge the immensity of what I felt and what I felt I had done. I wanted "Closer to Fine." With guitar.

She said nothing. What I got instead was a big smile (eyes and mouth), full of familiar sweetness and sternness and strength, and a hug.

Just right.

Maybe I chose to come out to the cantor at that moment because Grandma, the last close person in my life with whom I wasn't open about my queerness, was gone. Maybe it was because I chose self-absorption as a safe refuge from mourning. Maybe it was because I had felt I couldn't do it before then (couldn't, of course, = wouldn't). It was probably some combination of all three.

I like to think coming out to the cantor on the occasion of my grandmother's death was a tribute to Grandma Ruth—a way of being my brassy self without fear, of wearing my Groucho glasses and wailing "Diamonds Are a Girl's Best Friend" in a place known for their baked goods, no matter what anyone around thinks. I saw the cantor through different eyes that night—through Grandma's eyes, maybe—knowing that someone about whom I cared deeply, and even loved, might not sing along with me right then but would give me a hug and be proud. And perhaps, someday, someplace—maybe over a rainbow, maybe just at the diner, or maybe even in synagogue—we'd all stand up and sing together.

Conversion
Chana Wilson

"It didn't happen at all like that," Dad said. We were having our weekly bicoastal phone conversation, now that I, in middle age, had come to a certain peace with my father. I was telling Dad my memory of his consultation with Mom's psychiatrist at the mental hospital when I was seven. How the psychiatrist had said, "She's incurable."

"It was just the opposite," Dad insisted. "He said there was a lot of hope for her cure."

I was stunned. I was so sure of my memory, could see it in my mind's eye. My father weeping, face in his hands, before he spoke the words, "The doctor says your mother is incurable." The cold chill in my heart.

"What happened was this," Dad continued. "One day your mom's psychiatrist called me. Said he wanted to meet with me. He was a specialist who was called in by the hospital, because they didn't know what to do with your mom. They brought him all the way from up Manhattan, a couple hours' drive, because nothing they did seemed to help with her depression."

Then Dad told me what this psychiatrist specialized in: conversion therapy. That is, the therapy whose goal is to convert immature, perverted homosexuals into happy, maturely adjusted heterosexuals.

"The doctor told me not to lose hope," Dad said. "He assured me he had helped other homosexual patients. He told me to have faith. Then he gave me a book to read about a gay man who had become a successful heterosexual."

My G-d, all these years I had never known my mother's treatment was so blatantly directed at her lesbianism. My father had omitted that incredible detail.

When I had come out to my father, twenty-five years previously at age nineteen, he repeated that familiar gesture: put his face in his hands and wept. He finally raised his head, blew his nose, and explained, apologetic, that in the '50s when he had learned my mother was a lesbian, he had thought of leaving her. He decided to stay because he would certainly stay with her if she had tuberculosis. "That's how we thought of it then," he said, "as an illness. So, it is going to take me some time, with you."

Once I saw a movie, *Madame Rosa,* with Simone Signoret, she of the mournful eyes, in which she plays an aging Holocaust survivor living after the war in a sixth-floor Parisian walk-up. There's a scene where a young Algerian boy she's foster-parenting follows her as she sneaks off to her locked basement storage room in the apartment house. It's dark, windowless, hidden. She lights a menorah. "What is this place?" the boy asks her. "It's my Jewish hideaway," she tells him. "You must never tell a soul about this place. Never." I wept, something in the pain of the outcast and the tenacity of survival against all odds tugging at my heart.

Simone in her role as Madame Rosa reminded me of the Marranos. During the Spanish Inquisition, the Jews of Spain were given a terrible choice: Leave the country, or convert to Christianity. Leave their cities, homes, belongings, their network of kin and community, and be cast out into an anti-Semitic world. Or stay but renounce what was central to their culture and identity. Of those who stayed and converted, over time and generations, many forgot they had ever been Jews. Others became Marranos, secret Jews who publicly practiced Christianity but privately—in cellars, windowless rooms, and caves—continued fragments of Jewish ritual and faith.

In America in the 1950s, conversion therapy offered only the country of the nuclear family. There was no other nation for my

Jewish mother to go to. Once, after she was out of the hospital, she ventured fifty miles from New Jersey to a lesbian bar in Greenwich Village. She entered timidly, a shy émigré, disoriented by the butch-femme world, and made no connection with the sisters of that country. In the terror that overcame her, she never went back. Until much, much later.

✡

A few weeks after our conversation, my father called me. "I've been thinking about your memory, of the doctor saying your mom was a hopeless case," he told me. "You know, maybe both things happened. Maybe first I had that meeting where the psychiatrist gave me the book and told me to have faith. Then maybe later someone told me it was hopeless. I so wanted her to get well, I think I erased that from memory, but the truth is, she just wasn't getting better. They only let her go because the insurance ran out."

I had thought about it too: imagining the modern tools of torture bearing down on my lesbian mother. The straps and electrodes of electroconvulsive therapy. The grand inquisitor in the smiling guise of helpful psychiatrist. How a culture bears down on its deviates, pressing its hymn, the lyrics simple: *convert, convert, convert.*

My Big Fat Jewish Sperm Donor

Harlyn Aizley

At age eleven I attended my first and last Hebrew class. I knew failing to return meant I was forfeiting the right to a bat mitzvah, a party in my honor at which I would cash in big-time in the way of presents and money. Still, it didn't matter. It was a warm sunny day in suburban New Jersey. My neighbor Frankie DeMeo was riding his new Stingray up and down our block. My best friend, Lisa Perry, was at home listening to every one of her older brother's Beatles albums. Even my fellow Jew, Seth Berkowitz, was in his backyard creating a fort from old sheets and pieces of cardboard. Faced for the second boring time in two weeks with being driven by my father to the YMHA, where Hebrew lessons for the children of nonpracticing Jews were held, or joining my peers, I did what any eleven-year-old would do (perhaps with the exception of one growing up on a kibbutz).

"I don't want to go back," I told my parents. "Ever."

"All right," was their response. Both my mother and father had been forced to attend Hebrew school as children and apparently so deeply resented it that their daughter's impulsive decision to ride her bike all around the neighborhood rather than learn the history of her people was enough excuse for them to exercise—at long last—their spiritual free will. "We'll withdraw you from the class."

When I was eighteen and attending Brandeis University my father insisted I take a class in Jewish studies—"Anything! Just one!"—seemingly to make up for never having encouraged me to finish Hebrew, make bat mitzvah, or fast on Yom Kippur. "The Destruction of European Jewry" served the purpose. It was a devastating class all about the Holocaust, taught by an emotional and devoted scholar who believed simply attending his heart-ripping lectures was obligation enough and so gave everyone with perfect attendance an A. That's why I took the course. Because it was a gut. A Jewish gut.

It wasn't until twenty years later, when my girlfriend and I were scanning the catalogs of dozens of sperm banks across the nation in order to find a donor with whom to merge first one of my eggs and later one of hers that I became host to an unexpected awareness of my Jewish identity. Suddenly it mattered, the fact that I was Jewish and my girlfriend was Jewish, and—most important—that the sperm we were about to purchase be Jewish. It didn't have to do with Hebrew classes, bat mitzvahs, or the state of Israel. This abrupt piety had more to do with my grandmother's chicken soup and my uncle Freddie's dirty jokes, with the familiar ring of a Yiddish phrase, and knowing the difference between whitefish and sable.

Not being able to see or speak to our future children's biological father, we told ourselves a Jewish donor would be a guy who was appealing to us in some way, maybe even minimally attractive. When it comes to inseminating with the sperm of a total stranger, much like blind dating, conjuring up one's religious heritage is a way to assume some sense of connection. It's a tribe thing. I know that if I were to awaken one morning straight, single, and lonely, I most definitely would register with J-Date.

To prove our procreating hunch, my partner, Faith, and I called to mind every Jewish man we ever had befriended and forced ourselves to imagine having a baby with him. While unsettling in some cases, terrifying in others, the scenario always was better than the fantasy of mating with a casual Catholic acquaintance or an Episcopalian, even an atheist. Since we were Jews ourselves, even the ickiest of our race was in some way warm, fuzzy, and familiar. We could picture a Jewish donor's family, guess at the conversations that took place between his parents on long car rides, ("Well, it looks like Shelly Nussbaum finally had some work done. You could've hung a brisket off that shnoz of hers."). We could imagine his grandmother's cooking, almost smell the gefilte fish served at all of his seders. If we met our unknown Jew at a bar, we might not want to share a drink with him, but at least we wouldn't feel as alien as we might with a guy who didn't like Woody Allen movies or had never been in therapy. Our relief seemed perfectly sensible; we'd rather go wrong with one of our own.

Because we are Jews, to satisfy ourselves, we conducted an experiment. We paid a hundred dollars to register with a sperm bank in Georgia that featured photos of each of their donors. First we read the essays the men had written about why they wanted to donate sperm and then we jotted down the donor-ID numbers of those with the most articulate, well-written essays. Next we looked at pictures of all the men and made a new list containing the ID numbers of those we thought were the most physically appealing. Mind you, it was not drop-dead handsome we were after, just a friendly, benign enough face we could bear melding with our own and then have reflected back to us over breakfast each morning for the next eighteen years or the rest of our lives, whichever came first—a face that suggested the personality behind it might be generous of spirit, nonviolent, a democrat.

After three hours of strenuous research we were ready for the climatic unveiling, the cross-referencing of literacy and language arts skills. For two artists like ourselves, it was a moment so empirical, so reasonable, so scientific, it made us shudder. It was like we had stumbled upon the theory of relativity (also discovered by a Jew) or the Ten Commandments (and Moses, of course, was one too). I wondered if we should submit our findings to *The New England Journal of Medicine*. Faith, who had committed her life to writing musical comedies, mumbled, "You know, I've always thought I could be a doctor." There was no doubt, we were mature and objective partners entirely capable of making the decisions and choices necessary to bring a child into this world.

Voilà! While not every articulate essay had been written by a Jewish man, every Jewish man, indeed, had written an articulate essay! We yelped with joy, if not for having validated our Jewish intuition and rationalized our sperm-shopping approach, then for being Jews ourselves—daughters of an enterprising and creative people who valued education and could write so well. How easy selecting a donor now was going to be. Able to trust fully that he was a decent enough chap who could pen an essay, all we had to do was find a Jewish donor with a clean medical history at one of the two California sperm banks we were interested in using. (Despite their pleasant-looking and literate Semites, the Georgia sperm bank did not provide identity-release donors—those willing to meet their offspring if said children so desired when they were eighteen years of age—and so would not be getting any more cash from these two Nobel Prize–deserving lesbians.)

Deciding to use only a Jewish, identity-release sperm donor to make our family narrowed the sperm-shopping field dramatically. Out of hundreds of possible sperm donors nationwide we were left with approximately twenty from which to choose. Not to mention that an official at one of the sperm banks told us, "Jewish donors sell out fast."

So, comforted by our newly cherished Jewishness, Faith and I plunged. We found three identity-release Jewish sperm donors who fit the medical bill and numbered them in order of preference—1) Tall, Dark, and Handsome; 2) Unibrow; and 3) Baldie. Numbers 1 and 2 were no longer available. And so, three thousand dollars later, Baldie was granted the gift of biologically fathering our Jewish children.

In Judaism knowledge is revered, questions encouraged, lifelong learning held sacred. By extension, one should never assume they know the answer as to how anything will turn out, how they might feel in the future, or with whom they might be making a baby. Faith and I began inseminating the romantic way—at home with a syringe and a smoking cauldron of liquid nitrogen. When that failed, we decided to enlist professional sperm handlers and had a nurse at a fertility clinic inject Baldie's donation intracervically. When that also didn't work, we moved on to intrauterine inseminations, the insertion of chemically washed vials of Baldie's semen directly into my uterus. When four months' worth of intrauterine inseminations proved unsuccessful, the status of my fertility was called into question, invasive medical procedures initiated, and a recommendation for treatment with synthetic hormones kindly but firmly suggested.

Baldie had let us down six months in a row, under the most deliberate family planning conditions, even though his Jewish sperm were all present and accounted for, all swimming quickly and in the right direction. On a whim, and out of a tremendous fear of fertility treatment caused by witnessing my mother's battle with ovarian cancer—a disease some experts feel can be related to the taking of fertility drugs and for which I was at higher risk due both to my mother's diagnosis and to another predisposing factor: being Jewish—I called the sperm bank and asked if Baldie had gotten anybody else pregnant. Their answer: no.

More and more anonymous poop slowly hit the fan. It seemed that at least three other women had failed to conceive via Baldie, that the reason Baldie had chosen to donate sperm in the first place was that his spouse couldn't get pregnant and he wanted to get his genes into the next generation, and that despite his good sperm counts, the sperm bank now was questioning the status of Baldie's fertility and thereby taking him off the market.

"But," said the sperm official, "why don't we credit you five vials' worth of sperm from another donor."

Because I am Jewish, instead of accepting the offer to continue working with a sperm bank capable of allowing four women to inseminate month after month with a repeatedly unsuccessful donor, I wrote an articulate letter to the director of the sperm bank demanding they refund every cent we had invested in Baldie and the shipment of his Jewish blanks. And because I am Jewish, I told them I was sending a copy of the letter to a lawyer, also Jewish. Perhaps because the director of the sperm bank was Jewish, she knew better than to do anything but comply with this sister's demands.

Back at the sperm-shopping drawing board, everything was different. Incredibly, the days of looking for a Jewish donor were totally and utterly over. It's not just that there was not a decent Jew to be found (the other identity-release provider seemed to be running a special on Jews with mental illness). It was something else that had reared its fertile head—something deep and primordial, blindly determined, and hell-bent on success. It was my biological clock.

Demanding nothing less than pregnancy by the time I was forty (two months from the news of Baldie's infertility) and seeing how far our last Jew got us, I suddenly found myself wanting the seed of someone entirely different—from him, from me, from our people. Rather than grasp Judaism as the reproductive muse with which I might journey to parenthood, I once again was compelled to leave my religion in the dust. I imagined Baldie to have been so genetically similar as to be almost invisible, as if part of the problem was that my eggs didn't even notice his passive little sperm were there. Like spoiled, lazy familiar brats they entered my womb, sat down, and waited for my eggs to make the first move. No, this time I wanted foreign sperm, sperm that shouted "I'm here!" and looked so utterly different from my Ashkenazi eggs that they perked up and took notice. To hell with matzoh balls, bubbes with big bosoms, and the purity of our tribe. I wanted action. Raising children with our Jewish hearts and Jewish souls would have to be Jewishness enough because we were inseminating with the first identity-release donor with a clean medical history we could find, religious background be damned.

Two months and one vial of mixed-race sperm later, I was pregnant. The insemination with our new donor was the first time I'd ever had non-Jewish sperm inside me. As I lay back on an exam table, feet in stirrups, it struck me that all of my significant others, past and present, male and female, had been Jewish. Not once in my life had I leapt into the arms of a *goy*. Any man or woman I ever had fallen for, dreamed of spending my life with, regularly shared my bed and bodily fluids with, had been Jewish. Without having joined a temple, learned to count to ten in Hebrew, ever comprehended the meaning of Purim, or been impregnated via another Jew, I already was finding comfort and companionship in those with whom I shared the culture of Judaism. In fact, being Jewish had informed everything about me—from my sense of humor and taste in food to the process by which I decided first to use a Jewish sperm donor and then not to. My doctors were Jewish; my therapist was Jewish. And hadn't I gone and attended Brandeis? Jewish law aside, there was no way a child of ours could be anything but Jewish—at least in the way that mattered to Faith and me.

Nine months before Faith and I became doting Jewish mothers to a beautiful baby girl, I closed my eyes and imagined a school of uncircumcised spermatozoa crossing themselves before swimming toward my little Jewish egg. I hoped they weren't anti-Semitic, those microscopic Catholic-Buddhist sperm, hoped they would treat my egg with respect and roll back their foreskin before doing the deed. But do it, I knew they would, those mixed-race, potent crossbreeds who ran downstairs on Christmas morning all piss and vinegar and knew the proper way to hold a pair of chopsticks.

"Do it," I told them. "I know you can."

Because overly obsessive, neurotic thoughts of *not* doing it never would cross their tiny non-Jewish XY minds.

The Liberty Theater
Daniel M. Jaffe

Here's a secret my parents don't know: The three of us watched movies at the same porno theater. Although we all watched allegedly hetero porn, my take on it was definitely homo in orientation.

The incidents occurred after our move into a typical South Jersey 1960s suburb—a housing development with white-painted colonials, white-painted split levels, white-painted raised ranches, all with weed-filled backyards and grassy front lawns. Like everyone else, we had purple rhododendron and red azaleas out front (it was the rogue independent neighbor whose shrubbery dared bloom orange). Nonetheless, we were rather odd, the lone Jewish family on the block, although nobody could tell until December, when ours was the only house not to light up at night and twinkle.

One Saturday night the following May, my younger brother and I were left with the teenage baby-sitter from down the block, an Italian Catholic young lady who tolerated my Jewish boy's inquiries into the mysteries of Christianity. Fortunately, Dorothy's church was a broad-minded congregation, so she said she didn't hold me, at all of age ten, personally responsible for the murder of Jesus. I repeated defenses I'd grown up hearing it was the Romans, not the Jews, who'd done the evil deed. "Even if it was those Jews way back when," she said with a shrug, "it's not like it's *your* fault." But, for me, guilt by association was a genuine concern. Wasn't

Mrs. Levitsky, my new Hebrew school teacher—a short, waddling woman with a boxer's beat-up face and a wart on her tongue—always saying each of us was a Jewish ambassador in a non-Jewish world, that any misbehavior on our part reflected badly on our entire community and could lead to pogroms, maybe not by cossacks on horseback or by Nazi sympathizers with pitchforks like she'd experienced in Ukraine, but still? Each Jew was responsible for the entire community's welfare.

Seated on a brown sofa, Dorothy and I ecumenically discussed. Little did we know that while she was explaining Jesus' resurrection on Easter, while I was saying the Last Supper sounded an awful lot to me like Passover, while my little brother was zooming his cars and trucks around the family room, Mom and Dad were out watching porn.

I would hear the story only years later: From the address in the newspaper, Mom and Dad realized the movie theater was somewhere near the synagogue we'd recently joined, a temple located in an older, neighboring town and across the street from a Catholic church. They drove to the synagogue that night, found a policeman in the neighborhood, and asked him directions to the Liberty Theater. Removing his cap, the balding officer looked through my father's driver's-side window, across at my mother, and snickered.

How rude, thought Mom.

They followed the policeman's directions.

"Pretty shabby," Mom said inside the theater, noticing the lobby's worn red carpet, the off-white paint peeling from the walls. "And it smells like stale smoke."

My parents never smoked except for the occasional secret cigarette in the car, never in front of the children, who might develop bad habits, G-d forbid. My parents never drank but for ceremonial Manishewitz Extra-Heavy Malaga or social drinks with friends, never hard liquor in front of the children, who might develop bad habits, G-d forbid. My parents never cursed in front of the children, who might develop bad habits, G-d forbid, but on the rare occasions when they said "shit," they immediately apologized (like

111

the Thanksgiving Mom realized, way too late, that she'd pressed not the "Warm" button on the new oven but the "Self-Clean" button: "Shit!" she exploded, "I'm sorry." "Shit!" Dad muttered beneath his breath when later gnawing the world's cleanest, driest turkey, "*I'm* sorry").

No off-color jokes were ever heard at home, except for the one I told at the dinner table about the woman giving birth to an albino baby because her husband, "oh so very tricky…put lots of Clorox in his dicky." Mom gagged on her lamb chop, my little brother laughed with an exaggerated "ha, ha, ha" because I did, Dad jumped up, led me by the arm out of the kitchen and into the living room, asked if I understood what was so funny. When I answered honestly that I didn't, that I'd heard the older boys, the sixth graders, tell it at school, Dad explained the word "dick," a word I had previously thought of only in conjunction with "and Jane"; Dad cautioned me never to tell jokes I didn't understand and had me apologize to Mom, who, no longer choking and coughing, feigned ignorance of any faux pas having occurred. Ours was a polite and proper home where the parents tried hard not to embarrass the children so as not to instill complexes, G-d forbid.

So, what the hell were my parents, these prim and proper people, doing in a porno theater?

Well, it turns out Mom and Dad hadn't actually intended to see porn. As naïve as I was about "dick," they were about a movie titled *The Private Lives of Romeo and Juliet*. They thought they'd gone out for a cultural evening, to see a retelling that might not quite live up to Shakespeare's standards, but that would be elevating nonetheless.

Seated in the dark theater, Mom commented to Dad—wasn't it strange, on a Saturday night, for the theater's only patrons to be single men without dates? Especially since Romeo and Juliet was such a romantic subject? And what was with all the raincoats on a clear spring evening?

The film started, and Mom whispered to Dad that the costumes were fairly poor imitations of Elizabethan dress. Not to worry, the costumes soon came off. When Romeo and Juliet

112

started, respectively, fucking and licking Juliet's nurse, Dad realized his mistake (Dad had been in the Army and was worldly), grabbed a frozen Mom by the arm, led her out of the theater, fast. They rushed home, paid Dorothy the baby-sitter her full evening's wages ("It's not your fault, dear, that the movie was a disappointment"), hugged my brother and me a dozen times and declared that TV was better than movies any day of the week.

Life continued as before, I reached puberty, entered junior high and then high school. I never dated back then. Oh, to be sure, I played spin the bottle like everyone else in our early teens. And ironically, my own bar mitzvah party in my very own basement was the first spin-the-bottle session for me and my Jewish friends. Whenever my spin sent the bottle pointing to wavy-haired Larry Cohen or peach-fuzzy Davey Katz, I snickered with everyone else at the absurdity of random fate, then sighed inwardly, and spun again until the bottle pointed at someone acceptable like red-headed Cheryl Goldsmith or early-to-bloom Eileen Marcus.

Feeling nothing during my first kisses with those girls, I quickly realized the need for a system to maintain my masquerade, so, while kissing tall Linda Greenspan, I silently counted Mississippis to mark an appropriate passage of seemingly passion-filled time. By five-Mississippi, having felt nothing but wetness on my lips, none of the tingles I'd heard tell of, certainly none of the stirrings *down there,* I pulled back with "I'd better stop before I get carried away!" She grinned and the others giggled, so I knew my performance had been convincing. Fine. But then, several spins later, came the kiss with button-nosed Miranda Green. She and I, kneeling in the middle of the circle, kissed for a solid five-count; I duly moaned, pulled away with a hearty "Wow!" but Miranda pouted and announced flatly for all to hear, "You were kissing my chin." I vociferously insisted my blunder had been an intentional effort to avoid her bad breath. Sex performance was trickier than I'd thought.

Which is one reason I would later admire the porn star of the first X-rated film I ever saw. I was sixteen. One Monday afternoon, I leafed innocently through the local newspaper to find a movie, not some Disney film Mom and Dad would take me to with my younger brother, but a grown-up movie I could go see on my own the following weekend now that I had a driver's license. I noticed the listing for the Liberty Theater.

I had to have seen that listing before—it was among all the others. But the openmouthed woman sketched into the theater's logo suddenly expressed something more to me than "Oh, what a great film, oh!" And those three X's in bold print beside the theater's movie titles—they meant something too, didn't they? (Had there been no X's when Dad found the listing for *The Private Lives of Romeo and Juliet*? Maybe not—what did I know? Had my parents' own experience been the very one to prompt the imposition of movie ratings nationwide?) I finally understood. The three X's on the Liberty Theater's listing meant HOT HOT HOT. Right here in suburban New Jersey. Not in Philadelphia or New York, those big cities I never ventured into except on school field trips to the Liberty Bell or the Statue of Liberty. But at the Liberty Theater, just five miles away.

I contemplated the upcoming weekend's adventure. In bed every night, hands beneath the covers, I wondered what that movie would be like. Would they actually show naked bodies? *Forget it— disgusting.* Completely naked bodies? Naked men's bodies? No briefs or anything? *No way. Too risky. You're not going.* How much would I be able to see while they were doing it? Or were pretending to be doing it—I mean, they were actors, right, so they wouldn't actually be having sex. Or would they? *What could you be thinking? You, a good Jewish boy nerd at a porno movie? You?* Would I really be able to catch a glimpse of the man's naked butt going hump, hump, hump?

Forget it, I told myself. *Just forget it.* But I couldn't forget it, not for a second. As I struggled with logarithms in Algebra II, crystallization properties in Chemistry I, *le subjonctif* in French, conscience battled desire. And while watching *I Love Lucy* reruns and *All in The Family* and *Gomer Pyle, U.S.M.C.* While singing the kiddush with my family at the Friday night dinner table, while reading silent prayers during services on Saturday morning in our synagogue a few blocks from the Liberty Theater, I thought of blankets pulled down to reveal torsos "making the beast with two backs" (we'd just read *Othello* in English class), then with blankets tossed boldly aside to reveal butts, naked butts, naked men's butts hairy and muscular, all sweaty and jiggling up and down and if I don't see them soon I'm gonna die plain and simple. It was as if my biological urges, frustrated for years by the world's homophobia and my own, had redirected themselves to an attainable outlet—the Liberty Theater. *Liberté! Fraternité! Egalité!* (yep—the French Revolution in history class). With a driver's license, my parents' wheels, a historically respected ideology as justification, and a hard-on, I was ready.

On Sunday I told my parents I was going to spend the afternoon at the mall. Sin number one—lying; sin number two—dishonoring my father and mother. (I could never bring myself to tally the rest of the day's sins.)

When nearing our synagogue, I drove considerably faster than the twenty-five miles-per-hour limit. I didn't want to focus on the building where I'd become bar mitzvah, son of the commandment, where I'd won academic awards for religious scholarship, where scowling Mrs. Levitsky had designated us all plenipotentiaries whose individual actions would determine the fate of world Jewry.

I drove on, found the Liberty Theater without asking any policeman's assistance. (Can you imagine?) The theater was on a main road, so I parked my mother's gray Oldsmobile sedan three blocks away, on a narrow side street, out of view of passersby who might know Mom and recognize her car. I walked quickly but casually to the theater's entrance.

I knew I was underage. I knew I might be humiliated at the ticket booth and turned away. But still. If I could get in, if I could really get in, if I could only get in, maybe, maybe if the camera angle was just right or a blanket slipped for a second, maybe I could actually get a fleeting glimpse of…of…an erection other than my own. The fact that the men would be having sex with women didn't matter— an erection was an erection.

"One, please," I said in my deepest teenage baritone, chin pressed hard against chest (I'd practiced at home in front of the bathroom mirror). The Howdy Doody look-alike in the ticket booth didn't raise either of her makeup-encrusted eyebrows, didn't stare at me, didn't even look into my face, just grabbed my money, ripped a ticket in half, and handed over the stub. Whew!

Unlike my mother, I didn't notice the shabbiness of the lobby carpet, the paint peeling from the walls, or the odor of stale smoke. However, very much like my mother, I did notice the dozen or so men scattered in isolated seats throughout the theater. They, I was certain, were all here to see the naked women.

Waiting for the film to start, I began to worry: What if my father were to walk in and see me, not that I had any reason to think he frequented such a venue, but still? Would he wink and slap my shoulder? Or would he be able to tell I was planning to look at naked men? What if Mrs. Levitsky waddled in with a flashlight? She too might know, might know why I was here, and might then petition Abba Eban, Israel's U.N. ambassador, to denounce me at a meeting of the Security Council. Or worse: What if some of the men in the theater were actually undercover cops and when the film started, they led a raid on the place and put me on the six o'clock news as The Perverted Jew? Our neighbors would stone our house. Dorothy, my old baby-sitter from down the block, would lead a torch-wielding mob to chase us out of town, and the Catholic congregation across the street from our synagogue would picket, build bonfires, rekindle the Spanish Inquisition because they didn't want such wicked influences around their children, G-d forbid! All because of me.

The house lights went down; the movie began.

From what I could tell (the script was one of those masterpieces of minimalist dialogue) the opening scenes involved a husband and wife. They, fully dressed, were smoking cigarettes. Then they argued over money, and he threw her down onto the bed in a rage. This violence, for some reason I missed, excited her. She ripped off her dress (no bra, no panties) and started displaying her body, fondling her own breasts and then—oh my G-d—playing with herself, between her legs, right on camera! So far, although not excited, I was totally intrigued. Is this what married women did? My mother?

Then the porn husband removed his clothes: his shirt—skinny chest, pot belly—and his pants. (Apparently, this family did not believe in underwear.)

His dick. I wanted to cry. His dick was huge. I'd never considered the possibility of one being so large. My own erection, although harder in the theater than his in the film, couldn't have been more than half the size. I wanted him.

At this point, I felt I had definitely gotten my money's worth. But the film, of course, had only begun. He initiated sex with her. His titty licks and pussy laps did nothing for me, but when she lay back and he straddled her, positioning his erection over her face, and when he did push-ups into and out of her mouth, well…I was alone in my aisle…so…without moving my shoulder in any way that might be visible to all the respectable patrons in the theater, I moved my hand discreetly over the surface of my zipped jeans…gently back and forth…The notion of actually unzipping and exposing myself in the theater, in a public place where others might see, never occurred to me… How mortifying if any of the other men, those normal adults with nice Lord & Taylor raincoats on their laps, caught me doing something so disgusting…so I kept my jeans zipped and rubbed only on the cloth's surface.

I watched the porn star's push-ups, thought what a shame there was no Academy Award category for his area of expertise, and I imagined him doing push-ups into my mouth. My mouth. Oh, how terrible. Oh, how awful. Oh, how shameful. Oh, how wonderful how incredibly wonderful. Gurgle gurgle gurgle. Sighing ever so softly, I came, then looked around to check that no one had noticed, went back to watching the film.

Husband and wife screwed in various positions, then the wife went shopping. At that point their daughter arrived home. She looked the same age as her father, but he called her "Daughter," so I figured my perceptions were the ones out of synch with reality. "You're late!" said naked father to dressed daughter, "And must be spanked." Off with the dress (no underwear here either). Naked daughter over naked daddy's knees. Gee, she seemed awfully willing. He spanked her and this, oddly enough, turned her on. He did various things to her and then she knelt and sucked him. My hand moved into position again, on the surface of my tightly zipped jeans. Suck suck fuck fuck. I sighed softly a second time. My jockeys and pants were soaked.

Then the wife returned home, and the three of them did things together. But I was too drained to get involved. I watched to see how the story would end and to let my pants dry a bit before I walked out in public. Although feeling deeply ashamed, I also felt wildly free: Here was a place I could go, and despite the dark, the isolation, the need to masturbate furtively behind a closed zipper, I could share someone else's sexual fantasy, could project myself into a film, share with the porn stars, be one step closer than ever to experiencing real live sex.

Mother took daughter to bed—now, that was something I'd never imagined, how interesting, what clever scriptwriters they had…while the father, down to his last pack, went out to buy more cigarettes. Realism.

On a dark street corner, a stranger approached him, asked to bum a smoke. The porn hero reached into his pocket. At that exact moment, the stranger pulled out a huge butcher knife from within his trousers and thrust it deep into the porn hero's gut. (How right my parents had been to hide their occasional smoking from me…just look what cigarettes could lead to.) The stabber, stealing nothing, saying nothing, ran quickly away. Apparently, his only goal had been to stab.

The porn hero doubled over and collapsed, and the film, this hour and a half of sex, ended with thirty seconds of the camera panning a man dying in the gutter, blood spurting into the street, a huge butcher knife sticking out of his belly. He hadn't been shot or strangled or hit by a car. He'd been stabbed. And, his attacker had not been a woman, someone of the same gender as those he'd arguably been violating, but had been a man. Stabbed by another man. Symbolically fucked by another man, I wonder now? The ultimate horrific punishment.

The image might as well have been a cold floodlight dissolving my shadowy afterglow. I was shocked, horrified.

The film ended, and I stole out of the theater, avoided the eyes of everyone else who was stealing out and avoiding eyes. I walked quickly to Mom's car, drove slowly home.

My utopia had been atom-bombed.

Admittedly, the porn family had gone around without underwear, and had behaved rather loosely by Ozzie and Harriet standards. But still. Was murder typical for the end of a rollicking sex flick? If this was the director's vision of irony, his intentions escaped me.

Arriving home, I darted upstairs, peeled off my jeans and briefs and dropped them into the laundry hamper, washclothed myself, slunk to my room.

The film had lured me in, had made me think for a few minutes that maybe, just maybe, maybe in that dark place, the vicarious living out of fantasy was possible, even okay. Lying all curled up in bed, I tried to convince myself that the film was uplifting after all, that it was actually a very religious ending, albeit in a Christian sort of way—porn hero dies for our sinfulness, so the rest of us may live and jerk off… Well, it was possible, wasn't it? Sure it was. I knew if Dorothy, my old baby-sitter, were to hear my interpretation, she'd obtain a papal ban or whatever it was the Vatican issued in condemnation of heretical bull. Here I was, setting Judeo-Christian relations back centuries. Was there no limit to the potential damage caused by my perversion?

Of course, I realize now the murder had been the requisite element of "redeeming social value" necessary to get the film past all those anti-obscenity censors jockeying for sainthood in the early 1970s. If you fuck on the screen, death will come. A biblical response in this land where church and state are as separate as sex and guilt.

I would recall the film night after night, would struggle to force the tainted, closing bloody image aside. And those moments when I succeeded in remembering just that enormous dick, the push-ups, those incredible push-ups, I would sigh in joy that I'd had the chutzpah to go. But afterward, as I'd try falling asleep, I would twist around in bed, would struggle to fend off the lurking notion that there was, somehow, a link between the porn hero's fate and my own. But what exactly was it? He hadn't been having sex with men, so the film wasn't advocating the death of creepy homos like me…and I would never (truly never) have sex with wife or daughter, so there was no chance I would be like him that way…and I sure as hell didn't smoke. So…I reasoned there was no link between us and our fates after all. Whew!

I'd fall asleep.

But the next night I'd run through the entire litany again, feeling a connection I couldn't define—his death frightened me, made me feel as cold as the trickle on my belly. What exactly was going on?

In my mid twenties, my parents finally shared with me the story of their Liberty Theater misadventure. The three of us were seated on the brown family-room sofa where Dorothy and I had sat discussing great theological issues in years past. A commercial appeared on TV, an advertisement for yet another remake of *Romeo and Juliet*. Mom, pressing lips together and dilating nostrils in what I could read as a strained attempt to stifle laughter, turned her head and looked across me at Dad. Dad's mouth didn't so much as twitch, but his eyes glistened wet. "Okay, guys," I said, "let me in on it." Mom exploded in a hiss, Dad guffawed. They reminisced and laughed at the policeman's amusement, laughed at the shabbiness of the theater and oddness of the crowd, laughed at their own shock once the movie began, the speed with which they drove home, laughed at their own naïveté. And I laughed as well, genuinely. This was so funny! What's more, they revealed I hadn't been the first one they'd told—apparently, the incident had found its way into my parents' storage closet of risqué anecdotes to be dusted off and shared at parties and family gatherings, although never in front of minor children, who might develop bad habits, G-d forbid.

Now that I'm more or less grown up, I can admit that, despite my parents' good intentions, I have, in fact, developed a G-d-forbidden bad habit or two. Yet I've never told my parents about my relatively tame experience at the Liberty Theater. I didn't tell them that night in my mid twenties in the family room, even though I so very much wanted to feel included in the riotous family story and to find a way of laughing at my own experience. The furtiveness of what I'd done in the theater kept me silent and apart, the furtiveness and sense of shame exaggerated by the porn hero's murder.

In the interest of perspective, I should make clear that I have not exactly been obsessing about this set of incidents for the past thirty years. In fact, I rarely think of the Liberty Theater at all. Sure, it would be a solid decade before I could drag myself to a porn cinema again, but in the meantime I discovered enough compensatory pornographic magazines to nearly induce tendinitis in my right forearm. And, card-carrying homo that I am now, I have the requisite Chi Chi LaRue, Kristen Bjorn, Falcon, and Colt collectibles secreted away in my bedroom (no, I won't disclose exactly where…they're *secreted*). The Liberty Theater didn't sour me forever on the sweet joys of porn, just left a bitter aftertaste.

And here's the precise source of that bitterness, of the shadowy discomfort I couldn't fully understand at age sixteen: if porn Romeo and porn Juliet had, true to their Shakespearean fates, actually died on-screen, and if Mom and Dad had stayed in the theater long enough to witness their deaths, would Mom and Dad have been as shaken by their viewing experience as I'd been by mine? Probably not—everyone knew Romeo and Juliet were destined to die, so their deaths would not have been shocking; they were fated to die at their own hands rather than at those of a murderer crazed by nicotine withdrawal; and, as sympathetic as the audience might have been toward the young lovers, the porn versions would have, after all, been engaging in marital relations without the marital sanctions of church and state, so punishment would have been inevitable. In this latter regard, they were very different from my married parents, whose wedding had been conducted by a state-licensed rabbi. Mom and Dad were safe.

On the other hand, I was very much akin to my murdered porn hero. True, he was straight and married, but those distinctions between us didn't seem to matter; what mattered was that just as he had engaged in sex far beyond the bounds of church-state approval, I knew the kind of sex I would one day (hopefully) engage in would lack approval as well. Always and forever. Every single sexual encounter of my entire life would lie beyond the synagogue-state pale. I was destined to be as wicked and profane as the porn hero. No wonder I identified with him. No wonder I felt so upset at his murder. For if the murder of that "immoral" man was considered artistically appropriate or justified or socially redeeming, then might not the murder of me, someone just as "immoral," one day be considered socially redeeming as well?

Ay, there's the rub.

Oy Vey, the Kids Are Gay
Beverly Kopf

It's the night of the Academy Awards. Bobbie and I look stunning—her silver-spiked hair and Paul Newman–blue eyes sparkle in head-to-toe Armani. I'm sheathed in lavender Pamela Dennis. To my right is Kevin Spacey, who has just come out to Barbara Walters and now proudly smooches with his former "assistant." Cameron Diaz has the stage all to herself. She opens the envelope. "And the Academy Award for Best Original Screenplay goes to...Beverly Kopf."

I'm overcome with emotion but remain remarkably cool. Kevin kisses me... I kiss Bobbie and walk gracefully up the stairs, allowing the slit of my gown to reveal my perfect thighs. Taking my cue from Adrien Brody, I give Cameron a passionate kiss. Unlike Halle Berry, she kisses me back. I command the microphone and look to the sky. "Barry, this is for you. I know your spirit is with me because...I was never this funny...you were the funny one. Remember?

Suddenly I wake up. I'm having a hot flash and so is Bobbie. Our sheets are drenched and we're engaged in our nightly menopausal tennis match—flinging our covers back and forth in a futile attempt to cool off. In an instant I'm sobbing uncontrollably. I miss my brother and I always will.

Memories come flooding back—the life of a good Jewish girl

who happened to be queer. And one night in particular—a balmy night in 1995 when gaggles of lesbians gathered all across America. I wrote this poem, which I called "For Bobbie."

I have loved you like no other
Through the sunshine and the rain
I have listened and remembered
Only you, my heart, remain.

There are turns in every lifetime
That travel far and wide
There are yearnings and caresses
And the grace on which we glide.

Come with me this very moment
Sprinkle moonbeams on my way
Let our passion pour us onward
We are proud and free and gay.

This is our drop of madness
We are the chosen few.
Love me, love me, love me, love me
Love me let me say I do.

After more than twenty-five years of agonizing uncertainty, of tiptoeing out and charging back in, if Ellen was coming out—by G-d, so was I.

I guess you could say I got my first taste of how treacherous coming out might be in my mother's womb. Either I was determined to be an Aquarius instead of a Capricorn or I was already feeling the pressure of my parents' expectations even then—but I was three weeks late to my own birth. Of course I didn't find out till much later about the doctor who, early in the pregnancy, told my mother to fling herself down a flight of stairs to induce a miscarriage. Imagine carrying that terror for nine long months? The truth is, she had been carrying around a much greater terror all of her life. And like a baby born addicted to heroin, I was born addicted to my mother's terror.

My mother swears this story is true, although to this day I have trouble believing it. Her parents were first cousins who got married in Russia and came here to start a new life. Their first son died of the measles at age three. Then came my aunt Sadie—the beauty. Their second son was born circumcised—the sign, the Torah says, of a true *tzadik*. All my grandfather had to do was remind the *mohl* right before the bris not to cut the foreskin. Only he forgot. "Come on, what are you talking about? How could he forget something so important?" I would cry. "What can I say? He had a lot on his mind. He forgot," my mother would patiently reply. "But what about the *mohl*? Was he blind?"

The *mohl* literally moved in to try and save him, but after a few days the *tzadik* bled to death. My grandfather disappeared inside his own grief and would remain there for the rest of his life. Yet somewhere between the death of his precious son and the desolation of the Wards Island mental institution to which he was committed, my mother was conceived. Her birth certificate lists her name as "female." When people commented how pretty she was—my grandmother would say, "You should see my other daughter, Sadie." My mother, renamed Bessie, never knew her father...but she would never stop trying to fill the hole he left in her mother's soul.

And so by the time I was born, as my mother tells it, her milk was so infused with hysteria and heartache that her doctor forbade her to breast-feed me. Overfeeding seemed to provide the perfect substitute. By the time I was a toddler, I had been labeled the good eater—the chubby apple of my parents' eye. My brother, Barry—four years older and the bad eater—was already misbehaving, rebelling against the strict Orthodox Jewish rules that governed our existence. But as I did with the big bowls of Cream of Wheat placed before me every morning, I swallowed every bite.

When I was four we moved from my grandmother's apartment

in the projects on the lower east side of Manhattan to our very own house in Bellrose, Queens. I hardly remember what it looked like except it had a big front lawn where Barry fell and broke his collarbone. I would be left home every morning with my grandmother—too young for kindergarten—while my mother shlepped Barry to the Yeshiva of Central Queens, fourteen miles away. I felt like a hostage, locked inside this enormous, empty house, because I wasn't allowed to play with the kids next door. The explanation was simple—my mother was convinced our very lives were in peril. "Hymie, look around," she beseeched my father, "We're surrounded by *goyim*." Finally, her terror had a face.

Bessie Keller and Hymie Kopf had met as teenagers at the neighborhood synagogue—both already deeply wounded by the harshness of life. It was love at first sight—each seeing in the other a chance for a better life. My mother—a spunky brunette barely five feet tall—desperately needed someone to take care of; my dad—a wisecracking, skinny scholar, with a frail father and a cold-hearted mother—desperately needed to be nurtured and held. Until that moment, he had put his faith in no one but G-d and the religion that raised him and would soon turn him into an honest, hardworking, rigid man. Black and white, good and bad, life would forever be made up of rules that could not be broken...not even when his children's lives were at stake.

They were married without my bubbe's blessings—she didn't want her son marrying into a family of lunatics. And then, to make matters worse, they moved in with my grandmother—a fierce woman with sagging flesh, devious ways, and a steady stream of illnesses. Growing up, I don't remember a single week that she didn't need to be taken to a clinic or rushed to an emergency room or when she didn't have an opinion on how the "kinda" should be raised. My mother wanted to escape her past. Instead, she brought it into her future. And as for my dad, he would never be skinny or naked again. This was a man who came out of the shower in a shirt and tie. And when it came to the children, the women were in charge. Other than a kind of sarcastic humor that felt like pinpricks in my eyeballs and a particular way that he had of raining on my parade—my father rarely got involved.

So, after only a few months in our dream house in Bellrose, we were back in a cramped three-bedroom apartment, only this time it was in the Sheepshead Bay section of Brooklyn. Why they chose this G-d-forsaken neighborhood, I will never know. But my father's favorite synagogue—a Young Israel—was within walking distance, so my father was happy, and there was a kosher butcher right down the block, which I guess convinced my mother that other Jews were close by. Barry and I were enrolled in Yeshiva Rambam and although we looked alike—both with big brown eyes and irresistible smiles—we headed out in entirely different directions. Barry became the screw-up and I began a life of trying to please—first my parents, then my teachers, then everyone who ever laid eyes on me. I wore big bows in my ponytail, went to shul every Shabboth, and absolutely radiated happiness. Were there signs even then that I was headed for a complete nervous breakdown? Obviously, not to my family. Things escalated in high school.

Because I had convinced my parents to let me enter a two-year accelerated program at Rambam, I was a scant twelve years old when I entered Yeshiva University High School for Girls. But in reality, thanks to my mother's desperate need to be needed, I was a pudgy three-year-old in the guise of a peppy preteen, spending grueling days at a gloomy, competitive, fire hazard of a school. To say I was in over my head would be like saying Bessie was just your typical Jewish mother. The pressure I felt to make up for something I didn't even understand was turning into an uncanny ability to beat myself into a pulp.

Every morning, my mother woke me with an eight-ounce glass of orange juice. "Ma, let me go to the bathroom first," I begged. "No, mamala, drink this…quickly… It's fresh-squeezed, full of precious vitamins." Then she would drive me to school because I was afraid to take the city bus. She brought me mint chocolate chip ice cream late at night while I studied round the clock because I just had to get straight A's. I would send her shopping for the perfect baby-blue handbag to match my new plaid suit and if the color wasn't exactly right, I made her go again, because deep down I knew my looks meant everything. Their perfect child was becoming a binge-eating, ass-kissing monster with the prettiest clothes and the most ingratiating personality in all of Brooklyn.

And then the unthinkable happened. My big brother, my soul mate, the one person who could make me laugh at just about anything, pulled the rug out from under me.

Barry was seventeen when he went away to an Orthodox Jewish camp in the Catskills and—freed at last from my mother's relentless scrutiny—allowed himself to act on the feelings he had been harboring all his life. How long did it take my mother to discover his "dirty little secret"? Eavesdropping on phone conversations, stealing crumpled pieces of paper hidden in his pants pockets, following him in her big blue Buick—maybe ten minutes?

Of course it was left to my father to make sure I found out. He was the designated killjoy in our house.

"Barry's gay?" I was stunned. "Does that mean he doesn't love me anymore?"

"Of course not," my mother replied, like she had a clue what it meant. "It's only a phase he's going through. It'll be over before you know it. We're sending him to a psychiatrist."

And there it was. Life went on. My mother would close her bedroom door to scream and rage at G-d—but only after she had served dinner, done the dishes, vacuumed, finished the laundry and driven my dad to his board meeting at the Young Israel. My dad stuffed his rage and turned to G-d for solace, even as he shut the rest of us out. He was being punished for something—if only he could figure out what. We became strangers gathered together on Sunday nights to watch *The Ed Sullivan Show*.

Barry moved out of the house and checked out of our lives. He dealt with us in a simple and effective way: He lied, telling my parents absolutely anything they wanted to hear, and then swearing it was true. He swore he was attending classes at Yeshiva University where they had forced him to go. He never even set foot on the campus. He swore he was going to the shrink they found for him but convinced my mother to make the checks out to him. If the hook that attached me to my mother was food, Barry's was money. Just like Jenny Craig pays people a million dollars to lose weight— so what if they gain it all back—my mother paid her son to go straight. How much? Let's just say that for most of his troubled life, my brother couldn't earn a living on his own.

And me? The chasm between the pretty pretend girl who made her parents proud and the angry lost soul inside became so wide you could drive a truck through it. More studying, more starving myself, more matching shoes to purses. I wanted my brother back. He had a missing piece of me, even if I didn't know what it was.

Still on the fast track, I went to Brooklyn College, graduated magna cum laude in three and a half years, and tried desperately to get engaged. That was all that really mattered to everyone. But even though I had lots of "good catches" pursuing me—Benji, the deep, compassionate medical student; Daniel, the snooty scion of a wealthy family; Henry, the repressed financial genius; Mel, the earnest ophthalmologist; Joshua, the gorgeous rabbi—I rejected every last one of them. The occasional guy I became obsessed with wouldn't give me the time of day. That was part of his appeal. My best friends had names like Renee, Michele, and Vivian. They had mothers who took them to the ballet, fathers who taught them tennis, and their bodies were smooth and strong. I wore padded bras and panty girdles—no one could get in, not even close. I seduced with my smile.

Then came the beginning of the end. I convinced my parents to let me go to the University of Michigan graduate school with my classmate Jane. I had gotten a full fellowship in my major, speech pathology, and they reluctantly agreed. I had never seen so many *goyim* in my entire life. My professors were hitting on me, and I was hitting the big boxes of raisins Jane kept stashed away in our kitchen cabinets. Within six months, I was stealing Sara Lee cheesecakes from the clinic where I worked. I knew I was in trouble. And then I binged on Yom Kippur. It wasn't the first time I had strayed from my Orthodox upbringing—but it was the most blatant and devastating. I called my mom—she was there the next day. I came home and gained thirty pounds. I lived in a lavender bathrobe. I tried to kill myself and ended up in the emergency room at Sheepshead Bay Hospital with my stomach pumped twice and my hair caked in vomit.

My first shrink should rot in hell or at least in a state penitentiary. I became his last patient of the day so he could fondle my breasts. He fucked me on my mother's dime. Then he got engaged to his research assistant and I became catatonic. He prescribed shock therapy and we were all too numb and too terrified to resist. My mother drove me in my lavender bathrobe from Brooklyn to the upper east side of Manhattan, to a lime-green waiting room packed with methadone patients. It reeked of human suffering. I was twenty-three years old. They put me on a stretcher with my shoes tucked under my feet, and a devilish doctor would smile and tell me how beautiful I was as he covered my face with a mask that would render me unconscious to the electric jolts he applied to my brain. I walked out sometime later and didn't have a clue what day it was…only that I was ravenously hungry.

When my mother left in the morning to drive my father to the subway station, I would sneak down to the corner deli to stock up on Pepperidge Farm cookies, M&M's, and trail mix—ready for another day of eating, television, and writing venomous words in black eyeliner on my lilac wall. If my poor mother dared to knock on my door, I would scream bloody murder. It was all her fault and she was going to pay.

I was going down for the count. I had almost convinced Bessie and Hymie to commit me to a mental ward, like my grandfather, when they persuaded me to see a prominent doctor who would give me a battery of psychological tests. I looked at this elderly gentleman, so dapper and kind, and I saw the face of G-d. He said, "Don't give up on yourself. You've got a long way to go, but you can make it." And I believed him.

I went through every kind of cockamamy therapy imaginable and some I'm sure were made up as we went along. My primal therapist, the exotic and egomaniacal Otto, took total control of my life. He had his assistant weigh me in every morning, and if my weight went above a hundred pounds, he threatened to terminate me. But it worked. I moved out of my parents' home and within two years I was a writer at *Good Morning America*.

Then I met Liz, a pot-smoking, sex kitten who lived in Philadelphia with her husband, a kinky dentist. I can still taste her. My sexual feelings terrified me so much that I plunged into a committed relationship with a woman I wasn't attracted to—Kate—an angry, angular actress who wanted to be Ethel Merman. My parents were in shock. How much more could they take? Grandchildren... what about grandchildren? My brother and his boyfriend, Michael, were living in Los Angeles, and that's where I wanted to be. We packed up the Pontiac that Kate had won as a contestant on the game show *Concentration,* and headed west. I knew I would feel right at home in La-La Land.

We were together about three years when I realized I didn't love her anymore. The next day we bought a house together. I was a segment producer at *Entertainment Tonight* when I met Pauline. Dark and juicy, she reminded me of myself—a Jewish princess hobnobbing with celebrities so she could feel special. Of course she wasn't gay either—except when she got me into her hot tub. Then I fell in love with a Hawaiian inner-game-of-tennis instructor named Jordana. She was a free spirit. We watched fireworks from her porch in Santa Monica and camped on the beach in Malibu—our tent overflowing with gardenias. I left her for a Second City wanna-be named Steve.

My insanity was affecting my career. Despite my best efforts at sabotage, I was becoming much more successful than I could handle. It was time to run away. For two years I lived up near La Tuna Canyon channeling Mary Magdalene and Jesus in a spiritual community we called "The Stream." We were the walking wounded, hoping G-d—in the guise of a tiny, birdlike New York

Jew named Sheba—would give us the courage to face our demons. Having grown up in an Orthodox Jewish family, I felt right at home in a cult. My brain enjoyed being washed, and I was accustomed to believing G-d wanted strange and mysterious things from his flock.

Only this was different. None of my winning ways worked on this group. I was finally busted. Okay, so I knew Cindy Crawford and had slept with Arthur Ashe. *But who was I?* For two years they helped me to find out, to actually have the sensation of saying how I really felt whatever the consequences. But then a funny thing happened—they wouldn't let me go. Like the pressure I felt from my mother to stay dependent on her, this group had a hold on me. Once again, I had to run for my life, back to the only world I knew: show biz.

Through these wacky years, Barry and I drifted in and out of each other's lives. Sure, we lived in the same city and loved each other unconditionally, but it seemed we were once again headed down different roads. I found him slippery and unscrupulous; he found me half a bubble off. Then Michael got sick. One day he was taking a shower and noticed a lump, within a month he was diagnosed with AIDS. Barry and I became inseparable. I was finally able to be there for him in a way I never could before. I went to bed every night with my suitcase packed—just in case he needed me. And as I watched my brother take care of his dying lover, he was transformed before my eyes into a caring and dependable human being—a real mentsh.

Barry swore he was negative—and I believed him. I was so proud of him; I was ready to forgive all the lies, all the disappearances—if only he would stay in my life for good. But he would disappear one more time.

In 1998, when Maria Shriver hired me for a new show she was creating for NBC News, I was feeling pretty good about myself. Of course my sexuality was still totally fucked. I was driving my friends crazy—the "In and Out Beverly Burger," they called me, after the popular L.A. fast-food chain. And then fate intervened.

Maria wanted to make history. She put me in charge of researching and booking a special we would call *The Gay '90s*. Every day I soaked up more and more of the energy of the community I had resisted for so long. And every day the thought of being gay became less and less abhorrent to me. I was beginning to reclaim the piece of me that my brother had held in safekeeping for so many years.

Determined to kick-start my newfound lesbian identity, I signed up for an Olivia cruise to Alaska. And there, amid a sea of closeted couples parading around in togas or jogging around the deck, I found my Bobbie. Who knew I would fall for a Wyoming cowgirl? She was unlike anyone I had ever met before—part clown, part Casanova, part Cecil B. DeMille. Everything I know about anything—I learned from her. When my brother met her for the first and only time, he couldn't believe his eyes. "Finally, a real lesbian" were his exact words, forever etched in my brain. And when I introduced Bobbie to Maria, she took her aside and warned, "If you don't make her happy, you'll have me to answer to." She had nothing to worry about.

After Michael's death, Barry moved to San Francisco. Before long he quit smoking, had a "great" new job, and was even dating again. Then, out of the blue, I got a call from his boss. In twenty-four hours, if he didn't get the money my brother owed him, he was going to issue a warrant for Barry's arrest. None of the numbers I had for my brother were in service. What had gone wrong? The next thing I knew, Barry was living in his car—so my parents moved him to their retirement community in West Palm Beach. "Ma, what are you talking about? What will Barry do in Century Village?" I was baffled. "Whatever he wants to do," she told me. "He's our son and he needs us."

Barry wanted to become a massage therapist. My parents paid his tuition. He graduated first in his class. They got him a red Camaro, a brand-new wardrobe, and a membership at Gold's Gym. He never missed a day. We spoke on the phone—he always made me laugh. He had finally found something he loved.

Bobbie and I were together about two years, living in the Studio City hills, and I was taking my first stab at writing an *Intimate Portrait* of Vanessa Williams when the call came from my mother. Fly down to West Palm Beach immediately. While my parents had been away in Brooklyn for the summer, Barry had gotten very sick. By the time they returned, he had full-blown AIDS. No one knew. He had never been to the doctor, never tried to get on the cocktail, never confided in the person he trusted the most—me.

By the time I got there, he was practically unconscious. The nurse told me he had been waiting for me. He wanted to die, and only I could help. I screamed and cried and begged, "Are you sure? Barry, please we can fight this. How could you let this happen? Please don't leave me. Yes, of course, I'll help you. I love you. Please don't leave me."

My parents were in shock. They didn't even know he was sick and now he wanted to die? I was in charge. "He wants to be with Michael," I tried to explain. "He's tired of the struggle." For two weeks we watched my brother get worse and worse. It was the only time I raged at my father. "How could you choose religion over your own children? Do you really believe this is G-d's will?"

I was in the shower when my favorite nurse—Barry's angel, I called her—phoned. Time to go to the hospital. We walked into his room. The curtains were drawn, but light was streaming through the blinds. Barry had an oxygen mask covering his nose. He was the color of chalk. With one eye closed and the other open, part of him had already left. My mother started screaming. "Shut up!" I commanded. "This is not about you." She and my father sat by the window and never uttered a word. I pulled up a chair and sat beside my brother. I was calm and clear, as if everything in my life had brought me to this moment. I put one hand on his heart, the other on his head, and reached out him. Like a mother to a child, I whispered, "It's okay. Everything is okay. I'm here and G-d is here and you are safe. I love you so much. Michael is waiting for you and you are in G-d's loving hands. You have been the best brother in the whole world and I am so proud to be your sister. I will keep you with me always."

I felt him take his last breath.

It was ten-thirty on a Friday morning and Shabboth was at five. The body would have to be taken to Miami to be cleaned, but my mother refused to wait till Sunday for the funeral. We rushed home and made all the arrangements. My parents' friends at Century Village were like an army battalion brought into battle. The rabbi was notified, the cemetery plot picked and paid for, the egg salad and pickled herring prepared for my parents' shiva—my brother would be buried before Shabboth.

The funeral felt like a Woody Allen movie. About thirty of my parents' friends were there. Apparently they loved Barry too. The skies clouded over, rain was threatening—no Barry. Torrents of rain came pouring down—some people stayed, some ran to their cars—no Barry. The traffic was terrible and the drive from Miami was taking longer than expected. Only my brother would be late to his own funeral.

And through it all—holding my mother up when they lowered her son into the ground; reminding my father to breathe when he seemed ready to keel over; thanking every single person who had come to honor my brother's memory—I became the good Jewish girl I had set out to be. Only this time it was authentic, and I was being my true self.

It has been almost eight years since my brother died, and my life has never been the same. I moved back to New York to be close to my parents and to accept a job as the writer of *The View*. As an out lesbian writing a national show for women, I was in a unique position to influence every conversation we had that involved gay issues. Once I even talked Barbara Walters into kissing k.d. lang—on camera!

Bobbie has become part of our family—my mother adores her unabashedly and even my dad loves her in his way. Sure, they still wish I was happily married with grandkids all around, but they no longer think Barry and I came out to punish them. They never disowned us, never stopped loving us, but to this day have never told a single relative, a single friend about their two gay children. We make the best of what we have. My dad says "I love you" out loud, and my mom encourages me to live my own life, even as she reminds me to drink my fresh orange juice every day. Bobbie and I recently celebrated ten years together, and even though I still own a lavender bathrobe—not the same one—I'm no longer hiding.

But not a day goes by that I don't miss my brother. Since his death, I've been on a mission to show the world what I can do—because he never got the chance. Okay, so I still dream of winning an Academy Award—but you'd be surprised how many of my dreams have already come true.

O.M.: Ode to the Maccabees
Carol Frischman

How did a nice Jewish family, in the heart of Miami Beach in the 1950s, come to celebrate Chanukah, Christmas, Passover, Easter, and everything in between? Well, my mother made us believe all holidays were an excuse for merriment. Mom would have gone wild over some of the newer holidays—on Martin Luther King Day we'd probably have a cake with "I have a dream" written in pink icing. César Chávez Day we'd be singing folk songs while roasting tofu dogs over a camp fire. Kwanzaa would add a new African-American doll to my sister's overflowing collection.

Actually, I think it's human nature; my mom wanted to be the best mother on the entire the planet—no, make that in the whole galaxy. What better way to get this stamp of approval than to make every occasion a fiesta. It's important to understand that the celebration of Jewish, Christian, or Native-American (my mom was part Native-American, something for another story) holidays was in no way associated with religious meaning. We were simply exercising our rights as Americans—freedom to separate religion from celebration. Consciously or not, yontiff (explained best in Leo Rosten's *The Joys of Yiddish* as "holiday: what better way to send the Pope an Xmas greeting…good yontiff, Pontiff!") was dipping apple in honey and egg in saltwater. In case you haven't discovered by now, this was simply a ruse for getting us all to gather, eat, and be happy.

Besides my birthday, with cupcakes in the morning and my favorite meal and desert for dinner (and being all about me), my favorite time of year was December. What young person (and maybe older too) wouldn't have fallen for a celebration that lasted eight days (translated in our household as eight presents)? In order to give these presents their rightful place, we all decorated boxes big enough to fit eight various-size presents. I remember each year wanting to have the best box in the house, and I think we all felt that way, because our boxes were pieces of art by themselves.

And the party didn't stop there. Decorating a tree—often live and easier to find than you might think in Miami Beach—became a mini-celebration of its own: pulling from the closet the dusty, sometimes moldy boxes of lights, ornaments, and tinsel as well as recently purchased candy canes. You might think this hard to believe, but I loved the kitschy personalized stockings (including one for each of the animals in our family) overflowing with surprises. Topped off with the chance to catch Santa live with cookies and milk—I rest my case. And this is how Chanumas evolved. It simply became one celebration.

December was just the beginning of our ongoing celebrations. January marked three birthdays—Dad's, my brother Larry's, and mine. February, besides Valentine's Day, was mom's birthday month. March and April marked Passover, Easter, and my sister Bobbi's birthday. Not to slight Passover—which later would become one of my favorite holidays, full of powerful rituals and the chance to author my own feminist haggadah—I have to confess what I remember best is not the storytelling or sacrificial shank bone. What captured my imagination and memory was the coloring of the eggs, the Easter hunt, and for me, the chocoholic, the Easter basket overflowing with candy, including my favorite—malted milk balls in the shape of little eggs. Summer was one big holiday, with road trips crisscrossing the country and weeks in summer camp. The two last holidays that hold special memories for me are Halloween and Thanksgiving. Mom was incredibly creative, and she and I would come up with some of the best costumes, often taking first prize at parties and in contests I entered. There's no doubt these costumes would be the envy of any serious West Hollywood drag queen during the annual massive parade of All Saints Day down Santa Monica Boulevard in the heart of Gay Town, U.S.A.

Most likely the appetizer for all the upcoming celebrations in December was Thanksgiving. I think this was part of Mom's *big* plan: use Thanksgiving to hypnotize us for the grand finale of the year. I guess the closest association to religion for all these celebrations was my unconscious thought that this is what heaven must be like.

A few years later and I came out—as a Jew, meaning calling out loud to whoever would listen. I stopped celebrating Christmas and Easter. In its place I created rituals and celebrations that reflected me: lesbian, feminist, Jew, vegetarian, jock. But I wasn't always heard. In fact, it took years for my father to finally stop sending me Christmas cards.

Fast-forward to the present: It's 5764. Mom must be kvelling because I'm returning to my love of celebration and ritual. During my rising feminist consciousness, holidays were filled with commercialism, void of the sacred, and filled with patriarchal meanings. Though much of that hasn't changed, I needed to reclaim celebrating life and love and everything in between. Coming out— wanting to celebrate holidays and life, but this time from my own feminist, Jewish perspective—brought me full circle.

To Mom: Thanks for being the best mother in the galaxy and giving me the desire to create happiness and joy. For me, carrying on your traditions begins with connecting to my family, friends, colleagues, and even strangers, since most connections revolve around six degrees of separation. Like my journey to complete the AIDS Life Cycle ride from San Francisco to Los Angeles, life is as much about the ride, if not more so, than the presents and the finish line.

"Gravitation is not responsible
for people falling in love."
—Albert Einstein

Relationships,
Marriage, and Sex

Creating a Little More Room Under the Chuppah
Ina Turpen Fried

Dear Friends and Family,

As you may or may not know, my partner, A.J., and I will be celebrating our commitment to each other in a wedding ceremony at the end of this year—December 28, to be exact. For the past three years, A.J. and I have built an incredibly strong and supportive relationship. More recently, we have begun to build a home together. Our relationship is different, in several ways, from what you might be used to. Both A.J. and I identify as transgendered, meaning that our biological sex does not line up with the way we see ourselves. A.J. identifies more as male and I identify more as female. Our complex genders are often difficult for others to understand, but for us they are just one of many common things we share.

We want our ceremony to honor our complicated genders and the way we see ourselves. We plan to use the pronouns that are most comfortable for us—"he" for A.J. and "she" for me. You may know me as Ian, Michael and Doris's child, but for the wedding I plan to use the name Ina, a name I use with my friends in San Francisco. We also want to recognize the dual nature of our genders in what we wear. We both plan to wear dresses at the ceremony and tuxedos at the reception.

We are planning to have a relatively traditional Jewish wedding, albeit with more egalitarian language and, clearly, a few twists. We're very excited about our union and for the opportunity to affirm our love in front of our friends and family. At the same time, we understand not everyone will be comfortable attending the ceremony. If you are, or if you are willing to try something new, we would love to have you share in our celebration. If not, we understand.

There is no need to decide now. We will be sending formal invitations closer to the actual event. In the mean time, if you have any questions, feel free to call or e-mail us.

Love,
Ina and A.J.

There it is, all neat and laid out. But it didn't start out that way.

For a long time I couldn't even picture our wedding, let alone plan it. I thought I might need two weddings, a conventional one for my family and coworkers and "the real one" for my friends. I thought there would be the one where I played the boy and A.J. played a girl, and we tried hard to pretend we were what our chromosomes said we should be. And then there would be another wedding, probably a smaller one, in which we privately affirmed "the real us" in front of our community.

Deep down, though, that wasn't good enough. I wanted to marry A.J., the boy I loved. And I wanted to do it as the girl I was in the process of becoming. So we waited, both of us ready to spend the rest of our lives together, but neither of us quite sure how to express that intention.

The commitment was already there. We'd been dating for more than two years. We'd adopted a cat and moved in together. And then there was the moment when I knew for sure. There, in the basement of Sears, it hit us. We were buying a washer-dryer. This was serious. This was it. We drove back in silence, both stunned by the enormity of what had transpired.

But I wanted more than just our internal recognition that we were together for life. The events of September 11 had served as a final hint that it was time to make manifest the feelings of my heart. So a few weeks later I took A.J. to the Palace of Fine Arts, his favorite place in San Francisco, and asked him to marry me. (He said yes.)

Once we decided to get married, there was a lot to do. First I had to tell my parents. All I wanted from them was a simple, unqualified "I'm so happy for you two." But I had the unfortunate circumstance of phoning them just as they were having a heated discussion on whether my dad should change jobs. Plus, A.J. was never exactly the person they had pictured me with. In their minds I was destined to end up with a straight woman, in all likelihood an upper-middle-class, college-educated one. A.J. was everything I wanted in a partner, but he was none of those things they had come to expect.

Their support was present but somewhat strained.

Next we met with our rabbi.

"I usually meet at least three times with any couple," she told us. "With gay or lesbian couples, it usually takes at least five." With us, the rabbi said she would need at least seven meetings. "What kind of ceremony do you envision?" she asked.

"Maybe we should start with what we want to wear," A.J. offered. "We plan to wear dresses during the ceremony and tuxedos at the reception."

"Uh-huh," the rabbi said, gears clearly grinding inside.

"It also honors us, since I identify as a dyke and A.J. as a fag," I offered, unhelpfully.

By this point I had to assume the rabbi was counting the number of hours between now and our ceremony to see if she could possibly sort this out.

I can understand how tough it is for people to wrap their head around our relationship, our genders, and our sexual identities. We had our doubts ourselves. When A.J. and I first met, we were trapped by all of the labels that make our relationship so confusing to everyone else. He was becoming a boy and wanted to date other boys. I was becoming a girl and wanted to date other girls. It seemed like we were headed in opposite directions. Logic said that even though we were attracted to each other, we were never going to be what the other was looking for. That's what logic said. But something inside me, and I think inside both of us, said to dig deeper. Call it fate, call it the hand of G-d, or just two people searching for the right someone and willing to look in unlikely places.

Despite having no words to describe our relationship, nor necessarily to describe our resulting sexual identities, we headed into the relationship. Even after we were dating, I had my uncertainties about us. Could we make it? Was I prepared to be with a man? Was A.J. prepared to be with a woman? What did this all mean? It took a while to really let go of the labels, to not worry what my dating him said about me, to figure out I was as little or as much of a dyke as I was going to be and whom I dated wasn't going to change that.

I had no question about A.J., though. He was undoubtedly the sweetest and kindest person I had ever known, constantly bringing flowers, writing me notes, and reminding me of our blossoming love. We had fabulous adventures together, discovering places around the city and discovering new things about ourselves.

One thing that impressed me early on was our mutual ability to seek out joy. We were both tired one night after work but decided to walk for a bit in our neighborhood. On the way back, with a view of downtown, we saw fireworks in the distance. We stood there arm in arm and enjoyed the unexpected show. I told A.J. I thought there was a reason we had such good dates, or perhaps several reasons. It was part luck, to be sure, part divine providence, perhaps. But a big part, I felt, was that we walked around with open hearts, ready to receive life's unexpected treasures.

One of the best things about our relationship, right from the start was our ability to be ourselves and be accepted as such. I was used to putting a lot of effort into trying to appear to people the way I wanted to be seen. Initially I thought I'd have to do the same with A.J. Very quickly I learned I didn't have to do that, nor did he with me. It's often hard for nontransgendered people to appreciate the power of being accepted as who you are, without having to take external steps, such as putting on makeup, taking hormones, having surgery, etc. I think the power of our mutual acceptance nurtured our relationship and allowed the other aspects of the relationship to develop.

A.J. also started coming with me to temple, which was a challenge in some ways. I wanted to share my faith, and I also knew religion was where a lot of A.J.'s wounds were. He'd been raised as a fundamentalist Christian and had been active in church youth groups, but he lost his friends and spiritual community when he came out as a lesbian after high school.

I was glad A.J. was finding a comfortable place at our temple, but I didn't want to push anything. I was so afraid of appearing to push Judaism that I think I was less supportive than I could have been. With no urging from me, however, A.J. took an Introduction to Judaism class and later decided to convert.

Our rabbi had presided over his conversion, and we were hopeful she could preside over our ceremony as well. Unfortunately, our schedule didn't mesh with hers. So we went on a rabbi hunt. There were a number on our list. We learned that, odd as it may seem, it can be hard to find a rabbi to marry you around Christmastime.

Finally we found a rabbi who was both available and uniquely prepared for a ceremony such as ours. A..J knew her as one of many rabbis who'd spoken in his Introduction to Judaism class. But he also knew her son, who's also transgendered.

While my parents were definitely still coming to terms with what our wedding meant, they were also trying to embrace the event. And, therefore, my mom wanted to invite *everyone*, which meant we had to find a way to explain our complicated genders to a whole lot of people, some of whom I didn't even know. That's where the letter came in.

Planning for our wedding was a really positive experience. It forced everyone to stop hiding. My parents finally opened up to more of their family and friends. And out of necessity I was forced to tell some old friends and coworkers. That was a humbling experience and a reminder of how hard it can be to come out.

Amazingly, the response was almost all positive. My cousin wanted the screenplay rights, and another friend wanted to film a documentary. Perhaps even more impressive were the responses from those we knew less well—the people for whom the letter was intended.

About a week after the letters went out, I received a call from the daughter of one of my mom's childhood friends.

"I just wanted you to know how wonderful your letter was," she told me.

A few weeks later, a postcard arrived from Norway from my cousin Herbert:

"Dear Ina, Thank you for your thoughtful letter bringing me up to date on what's important in your life. I look forward to the invitation so I can share my eighty-first birthday with you and your friends."

The reactions were sometimes amusing.

When we asked our friend Sarah—a very butch-looking dyke—to be in the wedding, she was immediately excited. But then it hit her. "What do I have to wear?" she asked.

That was the same question I heard from my straitlaced cousin Kurt when I asked him to be in the wedding. My mind flashed back to the previous summer when he had awkwardly held his wife's purse when she used the restroom at Golden Gate Park.

Sarah and Kurt were both relieved they could wear a tux.

My parents also rose to the occasion. My mom gave me her wedding dress to wear. When we unpacked the dress, sealed for thirty years since her wedding day, we were amazed to find it fit me nearly perfectly.

Still, there were struggles. The idea of their son getting married as a girl to a boy who used to be a girl was not an easy one. But all things considered, planning the wedding were going reasonably well. At least as well as could be expected. Until about the middle of June, anyway.

That's when A.J.'s dad decided that after years of struggle, he needed to deal with the fact that *he* was a transsexual. Up until this point A.J. and I had been managing our soap opera of a life pretty well. But the thing with A.J.'s dad—that nearly sent us over the edge. It nearly sent A.J.'s dad over the edge too. It only seemed fair that he should be able to wear what ever he wanted to the wedding. But what were we going to tell everyone? We had already mailed the letter. Would we have to send an addendum?

A.J. and I decided to wait a while on that one. In the meantime we still had plenty of work to do to.

We made our way through some of the rituals. After much searching, we finally found a *ketubah* (wedding contract) with egalitarian language that described the partnership we were looking to create. Thankfully it had space for two names, instead of using the terms bride or groom, roles neither of us felt particularly comfortable with.

As the wedding day approached, it felt like we'd already done what we set out to do—create a little more room under the chuppah. We were unprepared, however, for the gifts we would receive on our wedding day.

The day started with me, my mom, and my eighty-six-year-old great-aunt Hilda going to the beauty parlor to have our hair and makeup done. It was great to have Hilda there, especially since none of my grandparents had lived to see my wedding day. I'm not sure how they would have reacted to their genderqueer grandkid, but my aunt Hilda was great about everything. Having three generations of us together, each with our very different paths to womanhood, was an incredible experience. It's not the scene either my mom or I had envisioned, but I know it's one we'll both cherish forever.

As if the emotion was too much for the sky to bear, the heavens let loose torrential rain as our final layers of makeup were applied. Luckily, A.J. was a knight in shining armor, whisking each of us to the car without ruining the hours of work.

✡

The wedding itself was magical. Our close friend (and now the Reform movement's first transgendered rabbinical student) Reuben sang as we entered and chanted the Sheva Brachot (seven blessings). A.J.'s parents walked him down the aisle and mine did the same. Not one but two rabbis offered their blessings, as did friends and family. When it came time, we both stepped on the glass—which didn't break at first despite the heft of the white Doc Martens we managed to procure on eBay. I think it was a reminder that even with all that love and support, marriage is something that takes work. Eventually we managed to shatter the glass and Reuben's singing resumed, droned out shortly thereafter with a rousing chorus of "Siman Tov und Mazel Tov."

The reception was an amazing sight—and not just because we managed to change from dresses to tuxes so quickly. For many people, the big Kleenex moment was my dad's speech

"I've known Ina since before she was wearing dresses," he began with a joke, as is his way. "I don't know quite what to say. I guess the thing I really want to say is that Ina and A.J. are really very, very brave. As a young person I thought I was brave. I did a lot of things I thought were brave. But they're *really* brave. And I respect that. I wish you all the joy and happiness the world has to offer. I love you both."

For me, the most poignant moment came a few minutes later, with the first dance—a slow song during which we invited everyone to dance together. There, swaying to the beautiful words of Tracy Chapman, were families dancing with children, couples who had been married for years, and couples who were still not allowed to get legally married. There were straight couples and gay couple, tranny couples, boy couples, girl couples. and indeterminately gendered couples—all celebrating together. That was it; I was in tears and my mascara just could not bear the weight.

What a blessing. What a mitzvah.

A Lesbian Intermarriage
(Or, the Date from Gehanna)
Siobhán Houston

How did my brother Kieran and I wind up as redheaded Jewish kids with Irish names? My father, an Irish-American WWII vet, met my much younger Jewish mother at a Hillel event, the first either had attended at Wayne State University. Two years later they married at a Detroit courthouse with no one in attendance but another interfaith couple (my mom's family was sitting shiva for her at the time).

I also ended up in an intercultural marriage, with a woman of Bohemian ancestry from the Midwestern heartland. Raised nominally Methodist, my spouse had never had a Jewish partner, been in a synagogue, or spent much time around *Yidden,* so certain ethnic customs like pickled herring consumption shocked her at first. I tried to explain that herring to a Jew is like *kolaches* (filled pastries) to a Czech. Rae and I have agreed that I won't eat herring in her presence, but I may store it in the refrigerator if it's hidden really well. This rule also applies to gefilte fish.

If I had fallen in love with a Jewish woman, I wouldn't have come up against this and other cultural hurdles. On Sunday mornings my Jewish lover and I would happily scarf down fresh onion rolls with chopped liver and smoked whitefish salad, *The New York Times* spread out messily on the dining room table. My Jewish lover wouldn't expect me to sleep in a campground posted with signs warning: BEWARE! YOU ARE IN BEAR COUNTRY! My Jewish lover would understand why I bring along a surfeit of food for any activity or trip. And my Jewish lover wouldn't even notice my wild hand gestures when I talk. Being partnered with a Jew might have been an easier life in some ways. Before I met Rae, I *did* try to date another Jewish lesbian, really. But my first and only date with another Jew turned out to be an unredeemable disaster.

Single and newly relocated to Denver, I'd placed a personal ad on a local gay Web site. M., "an intellectual, fit, spiritually oriented advertising account manager," responded with a smart and humorous e-mail. Her missive intrigued me, even though I had some misgivings about dating a Jew. This was something I'd avoided my whole life for a host of unexamined reasons. Perhaps I feared feeling suffocated by *yiddishkeit,* or maybe I worried about pleasing my mother. Maybe I was afraid of being with someone too much like me. (I personally think one vocal, high-strung, over-bearing, and excessively cerebral woman in a relationship is enough.) After M. and I chatted on the phone, however, I thought I'd give it a go. Our repartee had been easy and amusing, and I looked forward to meeting her. I hoped this time the dating sweep-stakes would finally pan out for me.

I arrived at the restaurant for our Saturday brunch date. Racine's is a trendy eatery in downtown Denver, furnished with overstuffed booths, brass fittings, and light oak paneling. Since it's near the Colorado capitol, it attracts legislators, lobbyists, and downtown businesspeople as well as theatergoers and queer folk of all persuasions.

On the morning I was to meet M., the hostess seated me at a window table with a view of the trellised patio filled with patrons. I was dressed casually in silky olive green pants and a matching Ultrasuede jacket, the perfect color to set off my long auburn tresses. A few minutes later a woman matching M.'s self-description strode into Racine's lobby. She had short wavy brown hair and a scatter-ing of freckles across her nose, and she wore jeans and a green

sweater embroidered with alpine pictographs, reindeers, and pine
trees. Our eyes caught each other's, and she mouthed my name
with a questioning look. I nodded with a smile, and M. joined me
at the table. I knew immediately she wasn't my romantic type. She
looked too much like one of my cousins, and anyway she wasn't at
all butch enough. Maybe we could be friends.

I ordered a cheeseless Mexican omelet, and she ordered eggs
benedict, served up quickly by our efficient and sociable waiter. We
introduced ourselves, and almost instantly I knew something was
wrong. She hardly looked at me, and when she did, it was with irri-
tation and boredom. I tried to keep the conversation light and
fluid, but M.'s churlish attitude continually stymied me.

"So how was your business trip to St. Louis?" I asked her.

"Fine," M. replied as she pushed her oozing eggs around the
plate and shifted uneasily in her chair.

"Mmm, had you ever been there before?"

"Yes."

You're not giving me much to work with here, I thought irritably.
"Aren't you from the Midwest? I remember you told me you went
to school in Madison. What did you study there?"

"Marketing." She stared glumly into her coffee cup.

I made another attempt at civility. "My omelet is delicious. I
love the flavor these ancho chilies give it. How's your meal?"

"Those aren't ancho chilies in your omelet. They're chipotles."

"Actually, they're really mild-tasting, which is why I think I
they're anchos. And they have this certain taste."

"I've had that same dish before, and I know for a fact they only
use chipotles in it." M. seemed ready to fight *mano a mano* over the
genotyping of my peppers. Most of my Jewish family has this same
character trait; a mania to triumph in any argument however
mindless the dispute. My brother (also gay) and I have had violent
quarrels over the most absurd things. Once we fought bitterly to
determine if the Yiddish word *mentsh* was used colloquially to refer
to women. (I argued vociferously that while *das mentsh* is a neutral
noun in the grammatical sense, have you ever heard a woman

described as a "real mentsh"? I rest my case.) I believe this reflex harkens back to the time-honored rabbinic practice of *pilpul,* where Talmudic scholars hold lengthy disputations over legal minutiae.

I took a deep rich hit of oxygen and released it slowly and surreptitiously through my mouth, willing myself to relax. Obviously she hated me. G-d forbid she should ask any questions about me or smile. Initially I thought there might be a chance we could cobble together a friendship. That naïve notion vanished quickly, replaced with the pure and desperate motive of surviving this encounter and getting the hell out of there.

I decided to cut my losses. I did the unthinkable. I conceded the argument.

"You know, you're probably right. I think these *are* chipotles," I said brightly.

She glared at me as if cheated. She knew hers was a hollow victory.

Eating quickly in order to hasten our escape from each other, we paid the check and left the restaurant abruptly after exchanging quick goodbyes. As I stepped outside, the intense Rocky Mountain sunshine blinded me for a minute, even though it was winter and patches of snow and ice slicked up the sidewalks. I leaned against my Saturn for a few minutes, watching people stream in and out of Racine's and wondering why this rendezvous had gone so awry. The contrast between our effervescent phone conversation and our calamitous in-person meeting was puzzling. Possibly an untreated mood disorder, I thought charitably. (Hers, not mine—mine was responding well to Effexor.)

As I unlocked the car and got in, I decided to write off the episode as one more unfortunate blind date experience, of which I'd had remarkably few. Not a bad record, considering that at the time dating was practically my second job. After this debacle I courageously kept on meeting women but drew the line at any more Jewish dykes, even though logically I knew M. wasn't a representative sample.

When I met my spouse-to-be a couple of months later, it

turned out she and M. were acquainted with each other. Rae told me she always thought M. was strange and inappropriate and avoided her at lesbian social events, so perhaps it wasn't anything *I* did to cause her to act like an escapee from Gehanna.

And *danken Got,* being married to a *shiksa* is working out fine. Even though I was raised in a primarily Jewish milieu, I *am* half-Irish with a bit of Scots thrown in, so I know from gentiles. In fact, educating Rae about Jewish culture is proving to be fun. She's picked up some Yiddish words and I've begun introducing her to Jewish cuisine; she relishes *matzoh brie* and *rugalach.* (I think I'll hold off on the *kishka* for a while, though.) And she appreciates my ability to translate Yiddish words like *momzer* and *shtup* when we watch Mel Brooks movies.

For my part, I'm starting to like camping, although I'm never without my can of bear mace. And after several years together, I'm even getting used to her laconic and laid-back personality. Recently I explained to a Jewish lesbian friend of mine who's dating a Texan *shiksa:* "Don't assume because she's quiet that something is wrong or she doesn't like you. Gentiles don't talk as much as Jews, at least not the Protestants—they don't have that same compulsion for self-confession." (Actually, I think this disparity in communicatory styles explains why Catholics marry Jews at far higher rates than they do Protestants.)

My friend Sharon almost *plotzed.* "You mean some people don't need to talk incessantly about their feelings and thoughts but actually reflect on them for a while before sharing them? You mean they don't imagine every possible contingency and permutation of a situation, especially the most disastrous, and then worry aloud about all of them?"

Yes, *bubele,* a revolutionary concept that's hard to get used to, I know. But life with my *bashert* is teaching me to take things a little slower and not worry so much. *Shoyn tsayt* (it's about time)!

Top Man
Edward M. Cohen

I was always planning to break up with Ralphie, but somehow I never managed to. And was it any wonder? He threatened to murder me if I tried.

"Let them sentence me to the electric chair. Life is not worth living without you."

"First you say you'll murder me. Then I'm supposed to believe you love me?"

"What do you know about love?" he said. "Nineteen! When I was your age, I could have had any man in Georgia! Now all I do is wait while you're in class or studying for exams or having dinner with your fucking parents! Is it any wonder I drink too much and I'm getting so fat you'll dump me?"

"You were a lush before I met you," he said.

"You crawl out of my bed in the middle of the night, and I can't get back to sleep, counting the hours till I see you again. If you ever dump me, I'll die."

"I'll never dump you, Ralphie."

As soon as I'd said it, I knew it was a lie. The truth was that, fifteen minutes after I had left his bed, he called to make sure I hadn't stopped off at a bar halfway between his place and my parents'. It so infuriated me that I was often tempted to take the phone off the hook, but I was afraid he'd race from his door to pound on mine until he had crashed his way through.

In the morning, my mother would ask who had called in the middle of the night, and I'd answer that she must have been dreaming, and the poor woman was so intimidated because I was a psych major at Columbia that the conversation went no further.

I lived with my parents and also worked part-time to save money for my Ph.D. and then analytic training, not to mention the future costs of my own analysis and setting up a Park Avenue office. Besides, in order to build a practice, you had to be active socially. You had to attend conferences all over the world. You had to spend a lot on a wardrobe to get referrals. Ralphie begged me to move in with him, but I explained that he didn't understand the demands of my profession.

"I don't need to understand the demands of your profession. I understand the demands of your ass!"

"See what I mean? Imagine if you said a disgusting thing like that in front of my colleagues."

"I'm sure they would find it disgusting. It's disgusting when someone crawls along the floor and dribbles over your ass. It's the most disgusting thing in the world. Right, Sigmund?"

There was no winning an argument with Ralphie. He came from redneck Southern stock, and though there had been no money for college, his inheritance had been the stubborn belief that he was right and the world was wrong. He never questioned himself. He never apologized. He had never been in therapy. Matter of fact, he hated therapists, never failing to mention they were all Jews. Like me.

When he was being dunned by a department store or a collection agency or a former lover, he responded with contempt for the creditor. After a bad day at work, he carried on about his boss or coworkers or the customers, particularly the Jewish customers.

"It's always the Jews who make the most noise, cause the most trouble, end up with the money, and I'm always the one in the hole. Don't say it's not true!"

"Ralphie, you disgust me."

"Ah, I'm just talking the way they talk back home," he'd say. "You know I love you, baby."

My schoolteacher parents, who had never been well off in their lives, had brought me up to despise the likes of Ralphie and often, lying in bed with the taste of him in my mouth, I did.

I surely didn't love him. This could not be what all those songs and novels and movies were about. There were never any moments when we walked along beaches holding hands or danced beneath the stars. All we ever did was fight or fuck.

On weekends, Ralphie liked to rent a car. He owed money to every agency in the city, but he loved to drive because it reminded him of tearing up country roads in Georgia, wild dogs yelping at his wheels. He'd tell me stories about his youth, sliding a hand up my leg, unzipping me on the front seat. I was always afraid a passing trucker could look down through the window, so I'd squeal and pull away. But Ralphie liked that too, and what with the groping and giggles, we never got to where we were going but ended up turning onto side roads so I could blow him as he drove, which he loved the most because it reminded him of how things were done back home.

The weekend drives had become such a relief that when, one Saturday, Ralphie was told at the cashier's desk that his Visa card was overextended, I stupidly offered him mine. And he was so pleased when the shining car emerged that I could see the bulge forming in his trousers so I forgot to ask for the card back.

I was so careful with my money that I hardly ever used credit anyway, so the matter slipped my mind until at the end of the month, my statement revealed not only the car rental charge but a $600 cash withdrawal.

Ralphie didn't deny it. What the hell, he explained, the money was sitting in my bank account where I didn't need it, so all I had to do was foot the bill now and he'd pay me back when he could.

"That money is for my Ph.D. tuition. I certainly do need it!"

"You're not getting your Ph.D. this week, are you? This crazy guy's got a lien on my salary! I don't even remember what I bought from him, probably something for you."

"You've never bought me anything that cost $600!"

"Oh, yeah? What about the meals I make when you come over? I've never had a meal at your house that I can fucking recall. And the ice cream we eat in bed every night, who do you think pays for that?"

"Ralphie, $600!"

"Think of it as sixty bucks a week for ten weeks. That's how I'm going to pay you back. You're not getting your Ph.D. within the next ten weeks, are you?"

"That's not the point," I told him. You had no right to do this without asking."

"And have you say no on top of all the other evidence that you don't give a damn whether I live or die? I've got my pride, and here's your first installment!"

He dug for his wallet, red faced and furious.

"Here's twenty right off the bat. That's all I've got on me, see?"

I grabbed for the bills, speechless with rage. As soon as I'd slipped them into my pocket, he was behind me, nuzzling his chin into my cheek.

"You don't expect me to go to bed with you now?" I asked him. "Can't you see how upset I am?"

"Fucking Jew bastard," he hissed.

I stormed from the kitchen, planning to head straight out the door, but if I did, I figured, I'd never get my money back ,so I decided to grit my teeth and hang around for ten weeks until I had extracted every last penny and then I could dump him for good.

I sulked in the living room and heard him in the kitchen, pouring one drink on top of another. Finally he weaved in after me, trying to cuddle on the couch, whimpering about how his boss hated it when you had a lien on your salary because it made so much trouble for payroll.

He buried his head in my neck, playing contrite. I lunged from the couch, but he was quick on his feet, stronger and bigger, not nearly as drunk as I had expected, and he captured me in the vestibule, clear-eyed and laughing, so the more I struggled, the more he enjoyed it, until I allowed my body to go limp in his arms and he plunged his hot tongue into my mouth.

Wrestling me to the floor in a flurry of promises and kisses and flying socks and underwear, there, on the shag rug, he mounted me. But I had my own moment of triumph when he burst into tears as he came, weeping, "Please forgive me, baby. I'll die if you don't forgive me. Please. Please. I'm begging you not to dump me …" He fell asleep in my arms right there on the floor as I calculated that ten weeks brought us to Passover, when my parents took their annual vacation so I would be alone in the house and could let the phone ring all night. The minute Ralphie paid me back, I'd leave his bed without a sign that anything was wrong and head for the bar, where I'd get me a *shaygitz* to fuck and, when I had finished with him, I would find me another, the blonder the better, and all the time the phone would be ringing, and to make sure my message was clear, I'd stay out all night, the hottest top man in the place,

So if Ralphie came over to pound on the door and collapsed in a drunken heap in the hall, the super could sweep him out with the morning trash and, to make sure the job was done, douse his body with kerosene and set him on fire on the sidewalk.

Ralphie must have felt the heat rising from my limbs because he awoke and murmured how much he loved me and could he please, please fuck me again, he'd die if he couldn't, all his friends said he shouldn't get involved with Jews because of their strange powers and he had to admit it was true because he would crawl over hot coals if that's what it took to fuck me again and, since the fantasy was so enticing, I whispered that yes, he could.

From Mayo to Mishpucha
Liz Morrison

As a kid, I thought being Jewish meant you celebrated Christmas *and* Hanukkah. Each December, my mother (who was born into a Conservative Jewish home) broke out the complete set of Spode Christmas tree pattern plates only to serve latkes on them. We lit the menorah and decorated our Christmas tree all in the same evening. In the spring we ate matzos and Easter candy, in the fall we attended High Holy Day services, and I atoned for not knowing what the hell was going on. We were Jewish Lite—some of the rituals but all of the guilt.

Oddly enough, my parents insisted I attend Sunday school and be confirmed. At the time I thought it was torture, getting up early on Sundays and sitting through an hour of Jewish history followed by an hour of Hebrew lessons. I retained almost nothing from the Hebrew classes, but this slice of education saved me from total ignorance. Every once in a while when my partner and I attend services, I'll recognize a song and sing the words from memory. She'll look over at me, surprised, and say, "You *know* this one?"

My partner Ellen grew up in Riverdale, a Jewish enclave in the Bronx. There were synagogues on every corner, and the secular world, even during Christmas, was barely noticed. At thirteen she became bat mitzvah, and each summer she went to Hebrew camp.

161

At thirteen I was singing Handel's "Hallelujah Chorus" with my high school glee club. Being with Ellen showed me how much I still had to learn about Judaism.

The learning curve wasn't quite as steep when I came out. That process felt natural, and there was no foreign language to deal with. Right after finishing college, I flew out of the closet and immediately put a NOW bumper sticker on my Datsun station wagon, thinking an affiliation with feminism would slowly ease me into my new orientation. Instead I hooked up with a group of Jewish radical lesbian separatists. Their battle cry was, "Avoid the three M's—men, meat, and makeup."

My first all-woman seder felt like tea with the Mad Hatter. Nothing made sense. Because there were no animal products served, the lamb shank bone on the traditional seder plate was replaced by carrot carved into the shape of a goddess. The familiar rituals were sanitized of anything considered to be politically incorrect, so all the pronouns and names in the haggadah were changed to reflect female characters only. The celebration wasn't so much about deliverance from Egypt but deliverance from the patriarchy. It occurred to me that if we escaped a life of slavery in Egypt and wandered the desert for forty years with a group exclusively made up of women, there wouldn't be a whole lot of Jews in the world today. I didn't dare share this thought with my "sisters." Had *they* been around for the Exodus, the goddess surely would have provided plenty of frozen sperm and turkey basters.

After the seder experience, I didn't feel I had much in common with radical Jewish lesbians because they seemed to have a lot of rules. In addition to the Three M's, there were rules about boycotting certain businesses, shaving body hair, and the spelling of the word *woman*. I liked men and wasn't comfortable adding *womyn* and *wimmin* to my written vocabulary. Radical separatist politics felt too limiting, so I gravitated toward the more mainstream lesbians, most of whom were gentiles.

Even though I grew up with Christmas cookies and Easter candy, I wasn't prepared for the onslaught of unfamiliar foods that were presented to me by my non-Jewish girlfriends' families. There were hams for every occasion—Christmas, Easter, first communions, and birthdays. I had never seen so much ambrosia salad, or Jell-O molds with fruit and marshmallows, or fried bologna sandwiches on white bread, saturated with mayonnaise. And the pork—who knew there were so many ways to cook it? All parts of the forbidden pig became part of my regular diet.

After several years of high cholesterol and failed relationships, I decided it was time to meet a nice Jewish girl. Most of the gentile women I dated were bright and interesting, but they lacked that intangible quality I found only in other Jews. I wanted a *haimishe* life with matzo ball soup, correctly pronounced Yiddish expressions, and meals that didn't include any combination of white bread and mayonnaise. I wanted a girlfriend whose mother stage-whispered the words "divorced" and "cancer."

The local Jewish paper had a personals section, so I placed an ad hoping to find my *bashert. Attractive, thirty-something nice Jewish girl, East Coast sensibilities, looking to meet a haimishe woman with a little guilt and a lot of chutzpah. Please respond to nouhaulz@xyz.com.* The results were disastrous. My dates either spun long, convoluted yarns about their most recent ex-girlfriends or reminded me of one or both of my parents, and not in a good way. I was about ready to throw in the *tallit* when I connected with a group of nice gay Jewish boys through the local gay business owners association. We began spending time together, attending an occasional Shabbat service, and going out for deli. One evening, over corned beef on rye and Dr. Brown's sodas, they proposed an idea.

"So, *mameleh*," my friend Jeff said, "there's this new *chavurah* that's looking to recruit gay Jews. The rabbi is Reform and very open-minded. We're thinking about attending their Rosh Hashanah services." Jeff, a Scarsdale native with blue eyes and straight light brown hair, looked more like a farm boy from Iowa than someone who grew up in a Conservative Jewish home. But like me, he wanted to incorporate more Judaism into his life.

Mike added, "Most of the members are straight, but it's a really welcoming environment. Some of us went last year and found the rabbi to be very dynamic. You'll have a chance to meet her at the next business association meeting. She's coming to recruit."

Rabbi Ruth Rabinowitz (not her real name), a gregarious, Rubenesque woman in her late thirties, worked the room like a seasoned yenta. By the end of the evening she had the names of every gay Jew at the event. We spoke briefly and I learned she was divorced, had two kids, and loved what she did. She asked for my e-mail address so she could send me more information about the upcoming services. The next day my friend David called with some titillating news.

"Ruth Rabinowitz has a crush on you," he said. "She told me after the business association meeting." He could barely contain himself, but I had gayer fish to fry.

"David, she's straight. I'm looking for a nice *gay* Jewish girl, remember? The gay part is key. I don't want to be some soccer mom's sexual experiment."

Initially I ignored his news, but when e-mails started coming from Ruth, I became intrigued. The only rabbis I knew were old men who seemed solemn and unapproachable. Ruth was a woman, close to my age, and clearly interested in getting to know me. Why not become friends? I wanted to learn more about Judaism, and Ruth was an excellent source of knowledge.

We went from frequent e-mails to weekly lunches, and then to weekly Shabbat dinners at her home. Ruth was fresh out of a yearlong relationship with a man and needed validation. I was fresh out of spiritual purgatory and needed guidance. The sexual tension between us, however, was interfering with both my desire to keep our friendship purely about Judaism and my ability to access better judgment. I tried to keep in mind that sleeping with me wouldn't make her gay, it would just make her a little more interesting.

By Erev Rosh Hashanah, Ruth and I were involved in a secret tryst. As one of my friends aptly said, "Ruth put the 'bi' in rabbi." One thought ran continually through my head as I watched her lead the Rosh Hashanah service: *I just had sex with a rabbi. I know a rabbi in the biblical sense.* But our brief relationship wasn't only about sex. We had long discussions about Judaism, and I learned more about Jewish life in the few weeks we spent together than in eighteen years of living with my parents.

It wasn't long before things began to unravel between me and Ruth. She was paranoid and didn't want to be open about us, and I was far too out to put up with all the secrecy. In the end she went back to her boyfriend and eventually married him. When I told my mother about Ruth she said, "I knew you wanted to meet a Jewish girl, but you had to go right to the *top*?"

Ruth inspired me to be a better Jew and gave me a brief glimpse into what it would be like to date another Jewish woman. I wanted that experience again, but this time with a certified lesbian, complete with a toaster oven. To meet someone like that I had to stay on the path to becoming a more observant Jew. I went to stores that sold Judaica and asked a lot of questions. I bought books that explained prayers and rituals, and I went to Shabbat services on a more regular basis. Being a Jew genetically only was no longer enough. I wanted to live an active Jewish life with a partner, which included attending temple and keeping the rituals. If friends knew of a *shayna maidel* and wanted to fix me up, I had get over myself and meet her. It couldn't hurt.

"Relax. This is not a fix-up," Paula told me over the phone. "Ellen and I decided it was time to get to know more Jewish women, and we thought of you because I already know you and we saw you at High Holy Day services last year. Don't read into it." Paula, an attorney, was a closer friend with Ellen than she was with me, and Ellen and I only knew each other well enough to say hello. It sure felt like a fix-up, but I knew better than to argue with a lawyer.

I almost didn't go to our first get-together. Paula arranged for the three of us to meet for a beer on a Sunday afternoon, but I had bought a Miata the week before and wanted to spend that warm April day driving around with the top down and my face in the sun. This little avoidance tactic was challenged by the persistent *yenta* voice inside my head that said, *You can drive the car anytime. Here's your chance to meet a nice Jewish girl, someone who hasn't dated any of your friends.*

Even though this casual Sunday beer date wasn't technically supposed to be about matchmaking, I still felt the kind of self-conscious awkwardness that accompanies meeting another single lesbian. There was a level of expectation attached to this get-together that I wasn't able to suppress. I'd met Ellen a few years before through friends, and I already thought she was attractive. We'd see each other in passing on occasion, but we didn't hang out in the same circles so I didn't really know her. I only knew she was Jewish and had been out of a relationship for almost a year. Friends I had plenty of. My own secret *yenta* agenda for that afternoon contained a line item that read, *See if you and her have any chemistry.*

I tried on several different outfits before settling on a pair of jeans and an off-white shirt. My mother always told me to wear light colors to accent my dark complexion, but she would have chosen something in a tangerine or a bright yellow. Off-white felt a little less Hadassah. I wanted to wear something that said, *I'm relaxed. This is what I normally wear on a Sunday afternoon. I'm not trying to impress anyone.* But at the same time, I wanted Ellen to notice me. As I walked out the door, I imagined my mother saying, "You should bring a sweater."

Our meeting place was a cozy neighborhood bar with large French doors that opened out to the street, allowing sunlight and fresh air to fill the room. As I took the only available parking spot out front, Ellen pulled up next to me in a white Miata and said "Nice car" before speeding off in search of an elusive space for herself. I played that brief moment over and over in my head. Was she flirting with me?

As soon as I got inside, I ordered a beer so I'd have something to do with my hands and sat down at one of the small cocktail tables near the open doors. The room was cool and empty. At the front was a small stage with an electronic keyboard and a single microphone on a stand next to it. A bored-looking bartender stood behind a square wooden bar at the back of the room. I looked at my watch. Five P.M. Only three hours before the live entertainment began. I had three hours in this empty bar to make conversation with two people I didn't know very well, one of whom already made me nervous.

I knew Ellen would walk in at any moment, and I wanted to have a topic ready to avoid an immediate awkward silence. We could talk about our Miatas. Not being one of those I-can-change-my-own-oil type of lesbians, I didn't know how much I could say about the car. I knew the year, the make, and the mileage.

As I struggled to think of more interesting things to discuss, Ellen came in, walked directly to the bartender, and ordered a drink. Though I'd seen her before, I was struck by her olive skin and clear green eyes. Her light brown hair was cut short and accented her cheekbones. She wore jeans and a yellow cotton blouse that showed off her tan and looked good on her long frame. Height has always been an issue for me because I'm five-two; except for small children and certain family members, most people seem like Norse gods to me. I blushed as she came toward the table. *Way to go, poker face,* I thought.

"I told Paula not to be late," Ellen said as she sat down and surveyed the empty bar. I noticed she didn't look right at me, which was good. I didn't expect to feel such a strong attraction so quickly and I was afraid she'd be able to see it in my face.

"Afraid to be alone with me?" I joked. *Look who's talking.*

"That's not what I meant. It's just that Paula's always late…" Her voice trailed off, and she began playing with one of the cardboard coasters on the table. I took another sip of my beer and mentally calculated the distance between our table and the nearest door. Silence sat between us like a chaperone.

"So how long have you had your car?" I wasn't about to let the conversation die that quickly. After all, Ellen was a psychologist and talked to people for a living. How hard could this be?

"A couple of years. You?"

"A week." We both smiled with the relief of having made an

effort at something that resembled a conversation. What I really wanted to know was how she felt about being a Jew. Did she attend services regularly? How religious was her family? Was it important to her to have a Jewish partner? Could she make a decent noodle kugel? I intended to get these answers before the afternoon was over.

About twenty minutes later, Paula walked in. By then Ellen and I had finished our first beers and were beginning to relax and actually look at each other while we spoke. I noticed her eyes changed between green and blue and had small gold flecks surrounding the pupils.

Paula's presence took the pressure off Ellen and me to carry the discussion, and eventually the talk turned to Judaism. As it turned out, we were all temple shopping and began to debate the merits of one temple over another.

"Emanu El and Beth Israel both send contingents to march in the pride parade, so it's pretty clear they're encouraging gay people to join," Paula said.

"And they're both Reform, so those of us who aren't Hebrew scholars will know what's going on throughout most of the service," I added. They looked at me and laughed. Since they'd both been bat mitzvahed, reading Hebrew wasn't an issue for them.

By the end of the evening, I knew Ellen had grown up in a Reform home, attended Hebrew camp every summer as a kid, was interested in finding a Jewish partner, and loved to cook. She was funny, articulate, and *haimishe,* and I knew I wanted to see her again. I gave her my business card, and she promised to send me a *Miata Magazine,* the official publication of the U.S. Miata Club. I e-mailed her the next day, and we began an online correspondence. That weekend I took several deep breaths and dialed her number. We made plans to see each other the following Saturday.

Our first official date was an awkward breakfast where we both pushed the food around on our plates and had trouble making eye contact. Subsequent dates were more relaxed; after all, how long can two Jews go without eating? We became inseparable that summer, and months before, purely by chance, we had both booked the same August week in Provincetown.

That fall we attended our first High Holy Day services as a couple. At the end of Rosh Hashanah we fed each other slices of apple dipped in honey to guarantee a sweet beginning to the New Year. At *tashlich* we tossed our bread crumbs into the ocean, casting away our sins of the past year. My slate was clean. Along with my sins, I also tossed in all my unhealthy former relationships. I imagined repeating these same traditions with Ellen year after year. Even the Yom Kippur fasting wasn't so bad.

At this writing, we've been together six years. We've bought a house, posted mezuzahs on our doors, and hosted four seders. After test-driving several temples, we became part of a warm and welcoming Reform synagogue where we observe our families' *yarzheits*, attend Shabbat and High Holy Day services, and are out to our fellow temple members. At some point we plan to have a commitment ceremony using traditional Jewish vows and rituals. This is still in the discussion phase, however. Two Jews, three opinions.

My gentile friends have often asked me to explain why it was so important to me to be with another Jew. This has never been an easy thing for me to articulate. As much as I try to explain the shared history, familiar traditions, and common neuroses, there are some things I just can't clarify. What I do know is that when I'm with Ellen, I feel like I've known her for 5,764 years.

Saying Kaddish
David May

DEAD IS DEAD NOT DONE.

—GERTRUDE STEIN

Faith is the most personal (and subjective) of experiences and something I find difficult to discuss. I'm far more likely to write about my sex life than my emotional life—even when the two overlap. To write about my spiritual life is to reveal a part of me I keep far more private than I do my erotic exploits. Public displays of religiosity embarrass me. To watch two lovers kiss on the street fills me with joy; to hear someone cry out the tenets of his or her faith on the street offends, even embarrasses me.

I suspect others of my ilk share these prejudices: raised Unitarian, New England–bred. Theological discussions in our home, of which there were many, were filled with phrases like, "If there is a G-d…" We questioned dogmas, rejected absolutes, and sneered at anyone whose beliefs sprang from a fear of death. Nascent Puritans, despite being Unitarian, our parents, like most New Englanders, are suspicious of emotionalism—a prejudice we all inherited. To feel or believe something deeply is no reason to rant and rave as if one were (my parents' most contemptuous epithet) "a damn Southern Baptist!"

My relationship to G-d, then, is the most intimate one I have and not something I'm wont to discuss. Let me instead talk about *being* (though I think one is always *becoming*) a Jew, about being a part of that precious commodity we call community, and something of my spiritual life will become clear.

✡

Until my first husband, David Lourea, died, I'd been unaware the assumption among many was that I had converted for him.

"Are you still Jewish?" more than one friend has asked—even recently, almost twelve years since he had died.

At first I was startled by the question, even offended. Now I only nod, "Yes, I am."

Indeed, I think to myself, *if I hadn't been Jewish, hadn't continued to be a Jew, how would I have made it through these last ten years and not gone mad? Or even lived?*

Since I'd grown up Unitarian, becoming a Jew hadn't been quite so dramatic a step as it might have been for someone raised Catholic or Baptist. I stayed well within the realm of liberal religion, replacing the vagueness of my spiritual roots with something more defined. I grew up in a tradition that, in its avoidance of dogma, embraced questions rather than answers, an existential awareness rather than the discovery of meaning. I was, in short, raised in a faith based on doubt. Even if I was willing, perhaps even wanting, to believe in Something, I continually found myself falling short of faith with my many questions.

As a Jew I keep asking questions but now have some expectation that there might be answers. More than that, there are traditions, useful tools I can fall back on, the means to continue living when life feels (as it sometimes does) unlivable.

When David was dying he asked that I sit shiva for him, to which I readily complied, thinking I would do what he asked to honor his memory. It wasn't until he died and I was suddenly surrounded by a community set on taking care of me that I realized why he had extracted the promise from me. He knew I would need not only the comfort offered by community but looking after as well.

"But what will I do if you die?" I asked him in tears one desperate night when neither of us could sleep.

"Sit shiva, say kaddish, and look after the animals."

A sad comfort, but it worked.

The truth is, of course, death doesn't make sense. Whatever tales we tell, whatever reasons we come up with to accept our pain graciously, whatever lies we tell about G-d's will being acceptable to us: Death, so concrete and so elusive, remains absolutely meaningless. Which is, I think, why shiva and ritualized mourning are so important. For seven days the widow has the comfort of cursing G-d if she so desires, a father can blaspheme out of rage each moment he recalls the enormity of his loss. G-d, it's assumed, understands. G-d is none the worse for either our agony or our anger. And in the end, it is in G-d that we find our absolute and final comfort—our only real comfort being love.

The last time I saw a death commemorated at a Unitarian church, a candle was snuffed out to symbolize the community's loss. When David died I lit a candle that would last seven days and nights; now I prayed for the coming of G-d's dominion. I wept without shame, as I had never wept before. Had my New England ancestors seen me weep they'd have turned their heads away, embarrassed—and I would have done the same in their place.

Shiva is a luxury like nothing I had ever experienced before: the freedom to wail, to ignore people, to leave a room without excusing myself. My only obligations were to honor David's memory and eat the meals that were prepared for me. Now even eating, always a joke among Jews, became a sacred act.

One never remembers pain accurately, anymore than one remembers euphoria. The mind, clouded with the chemistry of misery or elation, has only a vague recollection of what was felt. What I remember most clearly from David's funeral, of all the images that force themselves in a jumble on my memory, is glancing down at the sleeve of my jacket and seeing it was oddly discolored in blots and patches. It took another second for me to realize it was wet with my tears. Crying being a constant for the last few days, I was oblivious to my tears, but right then I was suddenly acutely aware both them and of my pain.

Saying Kaddish

Kaddish seems an odd prayer for a funeral. There is no reference to death, no request for comfort, no refrain that tells us, this life is over; this life will go on. Instead one praises G-d, prays for the coming the messianic era, and says amen. But repeating it is comforting, especially when surrounded by community. It becomes a meditation, a time to find the spark that dares to hope despite the apparent absurdity and cruelty of death. It had been years since I'd been able to say kaddish without crying, even before David's death, the loss of so many friends impacting in so short a time on the compound fracture that was heart. Through *sloshim*, though, through those thirty days of mourning, the tears stopped coming when I prayed. A kind of peace descended, not acceptance exactly (for I am stubborn on this point and take every opportunity to bring the injustice of the early deaths of so many of my friends to G-d's attention), but a lessening of my anger and desperation. Life continues; which is why we mourn for thirty days and get on with it. When I walked the dogs though Golden Gate Park on one the last days of *sloshim,* I noticed that for the first time since David's death, they initiated play during our stroll. Mourning for them was over too. Yes, life goes on. On that, at least, G-d and I agreed.

We were called the *Davidim,* and David's death left not only the expected emptiness, that great hollow in the heart that had loved him for eight years, but with an acute sense of my new status as a single man. Not only was I alone, now I was just *David*—singular. Few things are as sad as being alone after being coupled.

David died in November, and our anniversary, having always been observed with a massive Hanukkah party, loomed before me. The first holiday season alone found me overwhelmed with a mass of invitations when I had little, if any, inclination to celebrate anything. A year later, the second holiday season found me fishing for invitations, reminding people I was still here and wanted to reunite with the world after being a recluse for the better part of a year. This reemergence led to some sad attempts at dating, dates with men who, while well-meaning, were never as smart or funny or handsome as David had been. I found myself

173

looking for excuses not to see these men again, avoided answering the phone, and felt more alone than before.

✡

"Who will take care of me?" I asked David in tears, feeling ashamed of myself for being so selfish as I saw him slipping from my life in daily decrements. "Who will look after me when I get sick?"

"I don't know," David said. "I don't know, and I worry about it all the time."

He needn't have worried. The same community that looked after me when David died looked after me through a prolonged illness that no one expected me to survive. As I was immune-compromised, my symptoms were elusive, the defining ones for what I had (what is commonly called cat scratch fever) were absent, and I lost a full a third of my body weight, having been away from work for three months and in the hospital for a full month, before a bone marrow biopsy discovered the guilty bacteria.

My community had prayed for me, I later learned. I was given *Gates of Healing* and I prayed for myself, focusing what little mental energy I had left on reading those few lines in hopes of healing. My recovery was not a miracle, not in the true sense. Rather it was a series of events, the right people saying the right thing to the right medical staff, that finally led to the bone marrow biopsy and treatment. Rather than a miracle, I call it *bashert.*

For the next few months, whenever asked how I was doing, my answer was always the same: "I didn't die!" One hears tales of gratitude from those who have escaped death, but until one has experienced it, one can never understand it, not truly. To find pleasure in every breath, to enjoy something as simple as a peanut butter and jelly sandwich, to rediscover my ability to have sex, to have regular bowel movements (for which there is *bracha*) were all joys for which I could find no words other than "*Baruch atah Adonai…*"

But I had lost so much weight I was unrecognizable, as well as incredibly weak. My beautiful *tuchas* and thick muscular legs (always points of pride) were gone. Always zaftig, I now had sunken cheeks and a waist so thin that my Levi's (worn an inch larger than my waist to accommodate the muscularity of my butt and legs and worn, sexily I thought, with no belt) slid down my hips to my scrawny thighs. I had aged years in a few months. How wonderful, though, to sit in the examining room and hear my doctor tell me: "You're job is to eat, eat, and eat!" What a joy to eat five or six meals a day and still be hungry for ice cream at bedtime. How strange to find friends forcing food on me, bringing me treats, making me meals, finding especially tasty cheeses for me (so full of fat!) to refill the hollows of my cheeks. What could I say each morning but "*Baruch atah Adonai…*"

Always vain, I found my way back to the gym to rebuild what was lost. My strength returned. My *tuchas* and legs, while never regaining the fullness of they'd once had, are no longer an embarrassment to my (considerable) vanity. My cheeks are full, and I have my tummy again. I'm back to my muscular, zaftig self, the body I was always happy to have and share with others. More important, ten years later, I'm alive.

David had hoped, perhaps even prayed, that I would be spared an early death. Fortunate beyond all right, because I was already in a research protocol at the National Institutes of Health (a program I became alerted to by a member of my *havurah*) I had access to protease inhibitors a full year before they were approved for general distribution. My ravaged immune system repaired itself. Months passed into years that no one, least of all me, thought I would ever have.

But even those grateful for their rebirth get the Empty Bed Blues. To think of how desperate I sometimes felt for want of love when I was young and still unable to understand the difference between intimacy and sex, between love and passion, between need and desire. Only when I found David and fell in love with him, did these subtleties become clear to me. Far different are the needs of an adult who knows adult pain and adult love, who understands that passion wanes and there must be something there when it fades to hold a couple together, who already understands that two people can never truly be one, just together and happy in that togetherness.

Not only is G-d great: G-d is Love.

I'd known Phil, although not well, for years before we'd started dating. Only one mutual friend thought of putting us together, an idea I resisted. It was only when I sat listening to the two of them talk one evening that I realized how appropriate a choice he might be for me. Having come close to death and no longer feeling I had the luxury of waiting for anything, I asked him point blank, "Do you want to date?"

His answer was a surprisingly shy smile before saying, "Sure."

I always had a knee-jerk reaction to gay marriage. At best it was aping heterosexist convention; at worst it was counterrevolutionary. David and I never even wore rings. Our relationship was sanctified in bed, and that was enough for us.

Phil felt differently. He felt our love was worthy of G-d's blessing and our community's support. This was hard to argue with, the points being too strong for archaic (1970s) radical thought, and I agreed to stand beneath a chuppah with him. Phil was raised Baptist but, having spent more time worshiping with our *havurah* in the past six months than he had in church in the previous five years, agreed to Jewish ritual for our wedding without missing a heartbeat.

Tears, like prayers, come at seemingly dissimilar moments. Just as I was oblivious to the extent of my tears at David's funeral, I wasn't fully aware of how much I was crying at the wedding until the rabbi handed me a tissue. Just as the funeral is a jumble of desperate images, so is the wedding a series of happy fragments. Neither event is clearly remembered. What is remembered is a happy life together with years stretching before as well as behind us. How odd now to plan for a future, to worry about retirement. How natural to wake up in the morning, and to fall asleep saying, "*Baruch atah Adonai…*"

Were I not a Jew, had I not clung to the faith that adopted me as much as I adopted it, I doubt I'd ever have understood that to experience love is to experience G-d. Thus, when a loved one dies, only G-d can comfort. To love another human being is to seek and find G-d in that person.

Kaddish or *kiddushin*, I learned, all prayers are the same.

In the Land of Anti-Semites
Simon Sheppard

I was tired of the burdens of history. I just wanted to suck some dick.

Aleppo, Syria—1989

We're on the way back to the hotel, me and my boyfriend. We've had pizza for dinner. Not the delicious Arab-flatbread-and-minced-lamb we'd grown to love, but a genuine ersatz Italian pizza. We're walking through midtown Aleppo, under the watchful eye of the omnipresent postered image of iron-fisted President Hafez al-Assad. "Look," says my boyfriend.

It's a park, a dark little park with a public restroom in the middle, its ungainly cinder-block mass glowing softly from within. A steady parade of men is strolling through the park, circling, loitering, sizing each other up, ducking inside.

"Damn!" he says. "It's a tea room. A tea room in downtown Syria!"

I've always been attracted to dark men. Blonds and redheads too, of course, but especially to Jews, to Arabs, and to their more merchandisable cousins, the Italians. I can date it back to childhood. I grew up in *goyishe*, WASPy suburbia, but just across the river Trenton, New Jersey, beckoned. Trenton, with its synagogues full of Jewish boys, its street corners brimming with Italians, its newsstand where I could sneak a look at the nudist magazines stacked semi-hidden in the back of the shop.

Further on the horizon, New York and Philly strutted their wares like cheap whores. Italian South Philly. Jewish New York. Times Square, with its full-blown dirty book stores that weren't too fussy about the age of browsers. One time a dirty old man—probably all of thirty—brushed my crotch with his knuckles while I stood drooling over an issue of *Young Demigods*. I can still feel the hot blush of shame that rose to my cheeks as I ran into the street. Even then, I knew my lusts meant trouble.

The first question on the Syrian visa application was "Religion?" It was obvious which answer *wouldn't* be welcome. Instead I wrote down bland, nondenominational "Christian," glad for once that my father had Anglicized the family name. This slight subterfuge was what enabled me and my boyfriend to travel overland from Egypt, up through Jordan and to Syria, headed eventually for the Turkish border and the heady pleasures of Istanbul. I did feel a little guilty for lying like that. Maybe part of me crossed its fingers and prayed G-d wouldn't strike me dead. But hell, I was—*am*—assimilated, nonobservant. It's been years since my last seder. Longer than that since High Holy Day services. Only Hanukkah remains, in ecumenical counterpoise to my atheistic lover's gift-laden celebration of the birth of Christ.

Which is not to say I don't self-identify as a Jew. It's not a choice, it's an orientation, right?

I've no doubt carried the image of those dark young guys from my repressed but lust-filled adolescence all the way down to the present day. For me, blue-eyed blonds carry the mark of Otherness, while dark-eyed guys with big noses are my homeboys. My boyfriend's into Jews too, but he still has his foreskin, so there's no sense in taking psychohistory too far.

I do remember this Jewish man I had a big crush on. We'll call him Mark, since that was his name. Mark let me down easy, explaining he never, ever had sex with other Jews. *Where's that at?* I thought, still horny for him. *Internalized anti-Semitism?* But you're attracted to what you're attracted to, and, as I never tire of saying, politics stop at the bedroom door. Which isn't *really* true, of course. Anyway, maybe Mark was lying to get me off his back. The Egyptians, from Cairo to Aswan and back again, mostly hadn't seemed sexy to me. Not particularly homely or anything. Just not hot.

But then we took the ferry to Aqaba. And it hit me right between the eyes, full force: *Jordanians are the sexiest men on the face of the Earth.* Yep, Jordanians, Palestinians, the guys who want to push Israel into the sea. Yep, yep, yep.

Years before our trip to the Middle East, I'd begun to feel peculiar when TV showed mug shots of "suspected Arab terrorists." Swarthy guys. Suicide bombers. Handsome guys. Mass murderers. Hot guys. The tingle I felt in my crotch was more than transgressive. It was traitorous. And yet all those guys—those dark young men with bottomless eyes and three days' growth of stubble—looked a lot like Jews. They echoed the hottest stuff about your average, stereotypical Jewish boys. Only with attitude. Attitude and plastique explosives. So familiar. So forbidden.

Once I was taking a walk with my friend Bill, who's into Semites too. We stopped into his local mom-and-pop, the sort of small, street-corner grocery that in San Francisco is often as not Arab-run. We both bought Snapples from the more-than-handsome guy behind the counter. Back on the sidewalk, Bill said, "That clerk in the store? Last time I was in there, he was reading *The Protocols of the Elders of Zion.*" The anti-Semitic classic, the book that launched a thousand pogroms.

"Really? I thought nobody read that shit anymore."

"No, seriously, he was."

"Well, he's still attractive."

Whatever my feelings about the Palestinian *intifada* (and they're complex), there's no doubt there are some Muslims out there who would as soon slit my gay Jewish throat as look at me. And damn, some of them sure are hot.

The horrors of September 11—and all that's come after—have

made things even edgier. No, not many Muslims are murderous fanatics. Only a few of them, really. But a few of them *are*. Does my dick care one way or the other? Since the fall of the Twin Towers, I've been having sex with a couple of young Middle Eastern guys, one of Iranian extraction, the other Iraqi. They're sweet, attractive kids. I like rimming them both. They get on my bed, in something like the kneel-down-toward-Mecca posture, and I stick my tongue up their asses. Simple. Though my feelings are, as I said, complex.

Jordan turned out to be a lovely place. The rose-pink ruins of Petra. Great *shwarma* for lunch. People who were genuinely friendly, so unlike the vultures on Egypt's well-worn tourist route. Beautiful men with olive skin, fine features, some with hauntingly greenish eyes. Yum.

Jordanians were doing quite well, prosperous from well-managed profiteering during the then recently concluded Iran-Iraq war. I never felt out of place there, not like I had at my *goyishe* high school, where it took me a while to realize the shouted epithet "wedge" was "Jew" spelled backward.

"I love Jordan," I said more than once to my boyfriend.

"And the *men...*" he'd reply.

There was, just once, a bit of unpleasantness. We'd gone to a police station in Amman—something about registering our tourist visas—and were sitting on a bench when three policemen dragged a prisoner into the room, threw him down a few feet from us, and kicked him and beat him with a rubber hose. It wasn't done because we were there, nor despite the fact. The cops were doing their job, same as they'd do in Brooklyn.

We got the hell out of there, quick. But even the prisoner had been sexy.

Maybe even the cops.

I never did have sex while I was in Jordan. Except with my boyfriend.

One of the good things about traveling with your boyfriend is that it takes the weight of sexual conquest off your shoulders. There's a perfect pretext, excuse, good reason not to Do It with the natives. I've never liked the prospect of being the rich (ha-ha) American tourist doing it with the poor brown-skinned (yellow-skinned, black-skinned, whatever) natives, anyway. But then, it's the same everywhere. The fleshpots of Bangkok. The backroom bars of Amsterdam. A hotel room in New Delhi. Doesn't matter where—having a partner lets you off the hook. You can look but not touch, thereby avoiding language problems, legal problems, health problems, and unwelcome, badly scrawled letters when you get back home, letters you'll feel duty-bound to answer. Male lust, which is, after all, just the life force distilled down to a few inches of dick, provides a plenty fertile ground for betrayals. Queer lust, particularly, without any issue beyond stains on the trick towel but with consequences that could be dire. The desire, the chase, the moments of sweat-soaked connection—our dicks tell us it's the way to bliss, satisfaction, glimmerings of eternity, whatever passes for heaven.

As if.

Sex, good sex, always requires a lie of some sort. Often as not, we're lying to ourselves. And as long as our own bodies remain corruptible and our own desires have the power to cause us pain, we're always sleeping with the enemy. Because we're always sleeping with ourselves.

So what's the big deal about having the hots for Hamas?

Back then, Jordan recognized part of the West Bank as a quasi-independent state, but Israel claimed it as its own. So once you crossed the Allenby Bridge, a rickety span unequal to its historic importance, you were theoretically in two countries at the same time. And therefore in no country at all. When I first saw the blue-and-white Israeli flag fluttering in the breeze, I felt an unexpected swelling of pride in my not-particularly-Zionist heart. But that didn't last. Where the Jordanians had been friendly, the Israelis easily lived up to their reputation for rudeness. Jordan had been warm and sunny. Jerusalem was cold and rainy. Yeah, some of the Israeli men were sexy. More than a few. Plenty more. But several days in Jerusalem, a side trip to Bethlehem to see where the alleged Jesus allegedly had been born, and that was enough.

We'd been treated with suspicion and contempt by the Israeli border guards when we'd crossed westward over the Jordan River. Holding American passports hadn't cut us any slack. But going back to Jordan, things were a relative breeze. I heaved a sigh of relief to be back in Amman, with its Roman amphitheater, cheap food, and stubble-cheeked hunks.

So there I was, a race traitor with a perpetual hard-on, me and my gentile boyfriend. And we were headed for Syria.

There are the Germans, of course. Most recently Rolf, a handsome, kinky German businessman who has pleasantly abusive sex with me when he blows through town every month or two. Before Rolf there was Wolf, the guy I fucked standing up in the darkroom of an Amsterdam bar. Before him, an overly sincere German hippie. And the blond boy from Bavaria who loved to be tied down and teased with a riding crop—what a charming accent *he* had. Every so often I crank up the VCR and watch him piss on himself, clothespins all over his uncut dick.

But that's different. Those boys weren't even a gleam in their papas' eyes during the…well, you know. Getting it on with a Berliner is no different from buying a VW or enjoying Wagner. More innocent, in a way. But Jordanians, Palestinians—now that's a different story.

✡

SMILE. YOU'RE IN JORDAN read the sign at the border post. Unfortunately we were headed the wrong way, into Syria. We'd already ripped the temporary Israeli visas from our passports, stuffed them in an envelope with a bunch of Israeli postcards, and mailed them home. Except for a few shekels hurriedly hidden in a crevice of my backpack, we wouldn't be carrying any evidence of our trip to the West Bank into Syria. Because, word had it, just a stray receipt from an Israeli hostel had gotten one tourist kicked out of Assad-land.

It was the most nerve-racking moment of the trip. The Israeli border guards, after all, had demanded I open my camera, ruining a roll of film. What rigors of inspection, then, would the Syrians have up their sleeves? We were escorted from the bus into the customs station, a blank little building in the middle of no-man's land. *Muslim* no-man's land.

Nothing. No search. Just a handful of Syrian soldiers, in their undershirts, sitting around on cots. Handsome soldiers. Of course. Handsome Arab soldiers with luxuriant tufts of dark hair protruding from their sweat-soaked undershirts. The stubble on their chins was better than any aphrodisiac. Dark eyebrows, dark lashes, dark, liquid eyes. I fantasized kneeling by their cots as they raised their arms so I could bury my face in their hairy pits, licking their anti-Semitic sweat. *I will gladly let them push me into the sea.*

It was one of the easiest border crossings I'd ever been through. Anywhere. A riffle of passport pages, a rubber stamp. Nobody asked that a bag be opened. Not one. For all they knew, we could have been smuggling in Uzis. Plastique. Itzhak Perlman.

Okay, so these Arab guys are my type, physically. (Or *one* of my types, since that wispy little blond Bavarian in bondage got my dick up as well.) But the question, and it's a question that may never be answered, at least not in my lifetime, is this: If peace were successfully declared, if the Arabs and Israelis found a thoroughly lasting way to live together in harmony, would it take some of the heat out of my Middle Eastern fetish?

There'd be the loss of the tang of the forbidden, a tang that, let's face it, can spice up many an otherwise dull fuck. But would I also lose something else? Self-punishment? Playing out whatever remains of deeply internalized homophobia? Internalized anti-Semitism, maybe? Or perhaps, looking on the bright side, the chance for desire to span an otherwise unbridgeable gulf? Why the fuck do I dream about having sex with men who'd hate what I am?

✡

Damascus, in those days at least, was a weird and somewhat scary place. Pictures of Hafez al-Assad hung from every street lamp, a wimpy-looking Big Brother. And maybe half the hotels proudly displayed portraits of the Ayatollah Khomeini. For the

Iranians, clearly, Syria would be a friendly, relatively temptation-free vacation spot. No bars. No pork. No open homosexuality. But not as strict as Tehran or, say, Riyadh. You might not find a copy of *The Satanic Verses* on the rack at the Damascus Airport bookstore, but a guy still could have some fun.

Oh, and one other thing: invisible women. Syria's the only Muslim country I've visited where many of the women went around in full chador, a shapeless black drape that covered them from head to toe, a gauzy black veil completing the concealment. Not a bit of flesh showed.

So there was a shortage of overt women in Damascus. One would think it would be fag heaven, then, with so few chicks visible to the naked eye. One would think I might've gotten lucky. But the mood of the people under Assad's less-than-democratic regime was, not really hostile, but *tense.* Unlike the openness of Jordan, Syrians seemed suffused with angst. And, oddly, Syrian men simply didn't have nearly as high a hunk quotient as their Jordanian brothers just to the south.

As Grandma, may G-d rest her soul, would have said, "Go figure."

✡

There's also, and let's be honest, the lure of the exotic. I'm not one to decry "political correctness." Too often, reasonable-sounding anti-PC fervor masks other, darker motives.

But guys, the days of the Raj and the White Fag's Burden are over. "Rice queen," "dinge queen"—it's not just the terms that have fallen into disrepute. The thinking behind them is frowned on as well. Why, then, does the lure of the exotic still hold sway? Face it: For many of us, difference, in this case ethnic difference, is *hot.* And if politics truly does stop at the bedroom door, then what's the fucking problem? Should any of us white guys be shtupping, or *not* shtupping, African-Americans, say, just to prove a political point? Or should we pretend we're in an ideal world where race doesn't matter, not even a teensy-tiny bit?

Oh G-d, what a tangled mess. If that black guy is an S/M bottom who wants you to play massa in an antebellum slave scene, what the hell do you do then? Play around with icky racism in a safe, consensual, maybe healing space? Or say "No, thank you" and head out the door? And then there's the thorny issue of using Nazi regalia in leathersex scenes, a kink that creates perpetual controversy among S/M aficionados. I find the SS fetish thing way beyond my limits, but I confess, when Rolf dishes out verbal abuse, I'd prefer he curse me in German. My favorite example along those lines is my good-leftist pal Max longing to play a right-wing contra in an interrogate-the-Sandinista sex scene. Perhaps history repeats itself one extra time. First as tragedy. Then as farce. And finally as porn.

✡

I'd seen drag queens in Bangkok. Boy hustlers in Costa Rica. The newspaper in Bombay carried a not-unkind article about lesbian schoolgirls. But despite a reputation for buggery, the Middle East had seemed remarkably queer-free. Until Aleppo.

When we'd checked into our hotel, the desk clerk had asked, "Are you brothers?" It's a question my boyfriend and I, similar in age and stature, get asked surprisingly often. In this case I kept matters simple. "Half brothers," I said, which accounted for our different surnames. And we got a room with one double bed. No problem. No argument.

I don't know, maybe I had been willfully blind. Maybe the desk clerk had been too. Maybe we all were part of the conspiracy of the closet. Keeping things simple. Because here we were in a park in Syria's second city, a place of souks and carpet-sellers, and the folkways of male lust were being performed—not in some off-key translation but like we'd do it back home. The pacings through the park, the looks backward, hesitations over lit cigarettes, furtive dartings into the public restroom. It could be a rest stop on the road to Sacramento. Or not. It could be Syria. Being in the Muslim Middle East sure made me feel more Jewish. Like being in Holland makes me feel short or being in India makes me feel well fed. My assimilation dropped away.

But sitting in that dimly lit park in Aleppo while my lover went into the tea room just made me feel nervous. I remembered the policemen with the rubber hose. I rehearsed what I'd say to the American consul: "He just went in to take a piss, sir." *C'mon, hurry up. Get the hell out of there.* Even so, part of me wished I could be in there as well, cruising some other guy's hard-on, some off-duty Syrian soldier's hard-on, some Muslim father of four's hard-on, some anti-Semite's hard-on, as the stench of stale urine rose to my nostrils.

✡

Being queer. Maybe that's the best analogy, the best paradigm, the best point of reference. I'm a fag, which means I desire sameness, a man, another male. But I also need difference, or else I could just spend most of my time staring into a mirror and jacking off. (And no doubt some of us gay guys do that.) So what turns me on is a person like me, but not *exactly* like me. Younger. Or chubbier. Or smoother. Or hunkier. Better hung. Or not hung as well. Without difference, there's no tension. Without tension, no lust.

And those Palestinians with flashing eyes, they're a lot like me. Semitic, in the full sense of the word. Dark. Hairy. Monotheistic. Hell, they're even cut. And yet, and yet…a gulf, wide as the distance between Arab and Jew, life and death, I and thou. Wide, yet so long as cum can rise in men's dicks and seek hot release, not unbridgeable.

You're the child of Hagar. I'm the child of Sarah. Let's fuck.

✡

It wasn't long until my boyfriend emerged from the restroom, looking a bit sheepish. I let myself breathe again. In the dim park, the cruisers continued their rites. He shrugged.

"Nothing much. Everybody seemed really shy. I stood beside a guy who was jacking off at a urinal. Not bad-looking. Pretty nice dick. He kept staring at me and licking his lips. But when I reached for him, he backed away. Boring. C'mon, let's go back to the hotel."

Seizing the Moment
Davi Cheng

I'm not a spontaneous person, nor am I the type who enjoys taking risks or seeking thrills. I follow rules diligently, and I read carefully the instructions for those home-assembled racks you buy at Home Depot. I prefer continuity and structure, and I like to know what comes next. I like to take my time and study every angle and approach before acting; even when buying a sweater, I have to think really hard just to decide between getting a medium or a large. My favorite line to Bracha, my love of twenty-five years, is "Please don't rush me."

So what happened on the morning of Valentine's Day, 2004? After work on Friday, February 13, I climbed into my car as usual, turned on the radio, and headed home looking forward to Shabbat. Traffic was especially bad because of the long weekend, with Valentine's Day on Saturday, and Presidents' Day on Monday. Stuck in bumper-to-bumper traffic, I zoned out to the NPR news playing softly in the background. Then I heard it, the announcement that the mayor of San Francisco, Gavin Newsom, was keeping city hall open through the weekend and Presidents' Day in order to beat the anticipated court injunction ending the issuing of marriage certificates to same-sex couples.

Funny how totally unrelated things can trigger memories.

When I heard the announcement, two events flashed through my mind. When I was in high school, I passed on an invitation to join the United States Youth Honor Orchestra to play music and tour Europe with the best high school musicians in the nation; and then in college, I turned down an offer to train with the United States Women's Judo team at the Olympic center in Colorado. Both times I'd been too timid to take a risk; I'd hesitated and didn't jump at the opportunities offered me. Even now, many years later, I regret the times I was too afraid to seize moment.

My heart pounded as I reached for my cell phone to call Bracha. "San Francisco's mayor is keeping city hall open this weekend to give out marriage licenses to gay couples," I blurted. "Do you want to get married on Valentine's Day?"

"Yes, let's go!" Bracha replied without missing a beat.

That was it. I'd learned from my regrets that I'd better jump at chances now and act, so that I don't live my life regretting yet another missed opportunity. Later I found out that Bracha was listening to sports news all day and hadn't even known what was going on in San Francisco until I'd phoned her.

Now, thinking back, our drive from Los Angeles to San Francisco was a bit like the story of Exodus. Just as the Israelites left Egypt hastily in the middle of the night toward freedom, Bracha and I were hurriedly packing and making hotel reservations at midnight, then getting into our car at three in the morning to make the six-hour drive. We wanted to get there before any laws could stop us, before Pharaoh hardened his heart. We too were looking forward to freedom, the freedom to marry.

Bracha and I arrived at San Francisco City Hall at ten-thirty A.M. The line of couples applying for marriage licenses was already wrapped around the large building. There were people dressed in tuxedos, gowns, and veils; couples holding flowers and vows in their hands. There were also those like us, in jeans and hiking boots, half asleep, tired and hungry. Some brought their children, some their parents. We made friends with couples in front of and behind us. Reporters and cameramen wove in and out, interviewing and taking shots. Cars driving by honked in support, and people cheered as married couples strolled by with their certificates held high in the air. A city bus passed by with a sign on its side that read: I DO, THEREFORE I AM. We cheered as confused passengers looked on. Well-wishers handed out candy and water, congratulating each couple as they walked down the line. I secretly wished there was a portable toilet somewhere. But the mood of the crowed remained jovial—we chatted, we laughed, we waited. I heard no words of complaint, no unpleasantness. As the saying goes, "Love was in the air." Hundreds of couples standing on the street, holding hands, kissing, laughing, and cheering for one another—maybe this was a brief taste of the world to come, when nothing but love abounds.

Finally, at around two P.M., we made it inside the building; a new wave of excitement engulfed us. Bracha and I were both a bit nervous—rather strange, since this wasn't the first time we had gotten married! At each stop, volunteers greeted us graciously, checked our paperwork, and congratulated us again and again as they directed us from station to station. Some of the volunteers had been married the day before and had come back to help others. The city hall chief of staff proudly stood in front of a small room and greeted each couple as we filed inside to swear in. Bracha and I took a number as they took our money, then we were sent up to a balcony under a beautiful rotunda where wedding ceremonies were taking place in multiples. It was like a marriage buffet line: Rabbi? Minister? Deputized witness? Whomever and whatever you wanted, you had your pick.

As we watched couples exchange vows and rings, then embrace and cry, Bracha and I chose not to have an elaborate ceremony because we'd already a wedding at our temple, Beth Chayim Chadashim. In fact, we'd also had a chuppah ceremony on our "chai anniversary," when we celebrated eighteen years together. When we performed our glass-breaking ritual at the end of that ceremony, eighteen friends joined us on the bimah and broke long fluourescent tubes with us. Our explanation: To us, breaking the glass symbolized breaking the "rules" and "traditions" that prohibited us from being who we are. And breaking rules and traditions is difficult to do without the support of friends, family, and community. So all of us broke the glass together.

At city hall, Bracha and I did kiss, though, when we were pronounced "spouses for life." We then were ushered back downstairs to a room where our marriage certificate was being prepared. Bracha was overjoyed as she received our California State marriage license. "This is how my parents got married," she said, smiling.

At around three-thirty P.M., arm in arm, we stepped outside the revolving doors of city hall with our certificate in hand; the crowds cheered and applauded. I'm thrilled to say I seized the moment this Valentine's Day, 2004. For what is life if you're too afraid to take the risk, especially for someone you love?

The "Jews," the "Collaborators," and the Politics of Rimming
Miodrag Kojadinović

There is a strange way in which our minds make synapses between phenomena not necessarily, or not at all, connected. Thus for me a song by Sade always evokes Seattle, Washington, even though I don't think I've heard her even once during the three days I stayed there on my only trip abroad during the self-imposed confinement in Vancouver, where I had settled in order to get a Canadian citizenship, after I had obtained a visa while working in the Canadian embassy in Belgrade during the long series of Wars for the ex-YU Succession in the early 1990s.

Seattle seemed shabby and yet strangely stately, especially after the kitschy, provincial Vancouver—I even developed a theory that since Canada had provinces, it was necessarily provincial, and that the component states made the United States stately, however narrow-minded, to the point of looking like an idiotic bully at times. Seattle was also rainy that December. It rained, and the mood on Capitol Hill to me was that easy cappuccino-bar atmosphere of Sade's "No Ordinary Love", which I'd been listening to at a friend's in a Vancouver condo, filled with balls of cat hair and overlooking the trolley buses turning south at the far end of Robson Street, just before I came…

Similarly, the gay life of Belgrade in the late 1980s remains for me forever intertwined with Jewishness. First, it was my own search for belonging, after the disappointment with what I found in various churches I tried to attend on my own at about seventeen (since my atheist father and mostly agnostic mother never gave me any religious education and the ex-Yugoslav state strongly discouraged it at school, in the army, at work etc.).

Like many gay youths, I was a lonely teenager. In our satellite town, forty minutes drive from downtown Belgrade, I withdrew from socializing with schoolmates beyond the necessary contact at school, studied languages, tried to play piano, extracted herbal oils in a homemade lab, and researched family history. That's how I dug out a Jewish ancestor, mother's grandmother's grandmother Sarah, who in order to marry a Christian converted in the mid nineteenth century and likely lived a normal life of a burgher housewife, probably fully as a Christian, to the extent that the folkloristic traditional religion of the Balkans was Christian at all.

I asked my mother who this ancestor was, but she could only vaguely remember her own great-grandmother, Sarah's daughter-in-law. I pointed to the marriage contract on responsibilities of mother's grandmother Milka and her husband toward Sarah's husband Djordje and her daughter-in-law (the one whom mother remembered, Milka's mother). Mother conceded that such contracts were untypical in a traditionalist Serbian pre-1918 society of *zadrugas* and that it was "likely" that Sarah was Jewish but added that "she could have been Armenian too."

The word in that first text read "*Jerve(i)ka*" and could indeed have equally been a misspelled "*Jevrejka*" (Jewish woman") and "*Jermenka*" (Armenian woman"), because the old-style cursive letter "j" was a variant of "i" in Serbian Cyrillic, and at the same time it was written in a manner very similar to "n": in Cyrillic it is "_", "_", "_" respectively. Well, that was enough for me—having realized that as a gay man I failed to fit in, I sought a sound enough reason to ground my "difference" in anything but gayness. Sarah had to do. Notwithstanding that the name Sarah is relatively rare in Armenian, I later found documents that indeed proved Sarah was Sephardi and her elopement had caused some uproar. But I had already made up my mind then, the summer between my freshman and sophomore years at Belgrade University.

The only remaining Belgrade synagogue was (and still is) a pre-WWII Sephardic one, as the Ashkenazi one in Zemun across the Sava (a century ago in Austria-Hungary) was sold by the city who ended up in charge of it after the Holocaust and the *aliyah* of the remaining Belgrade Jewry in 1948; eventually it was turned into a nightclub. But while remaining a static body of a building (in bad need of repair), the functioning synagogue had long overgrown the needs of its ever decreasing community. In 1980 it had difficulties gathering enough people for a *minyan,* so they never made an issue of my total lack of Jewish upbringing when I showed up one day.

Except for the beadle, there used to come just a few elderly men, a converted mother with a highly dependent son in his thirties, a middle-aged never-married woman (daughter of a second marriage of two Holocaust survivors, who became my friend and who rationalized her unsuccessful love life with the fact that she would have never been born but for the tragedy of both her parents' first families), a nephew of an Orthodox Christian priest who thought about converting, the cantor-turned-acting-rabbi (formerly a devout member of the Communist Party who suddenly rediscovered his Jewish roots in his middle age). And of course the boys…

The boys were being trained as cantors. They all had some Jewish ancestry more or less tenuous or not certain like mine, and one of the three was obviously queer. The other later married, divorced, went to Israel and became a monk with Russian Orthodox Church in Exile, and the third was officially converted in Israel and married a rich American Ashkenazi woman and took her last name…

Of course, I pretended to myself that I was looking for my "roots" in the woman whose paternal uncle was a town clerk, amateur historian, and self-taught inventor, about whose patents there is still a lawsuit going years after he died, having been hit by a car on a street crossing in Berlin.

I delved into studying Judaica with the same devotion with which I had previously read the history of Christianity and its various sects and reform movements. I started learning Hebrew at the Jewish community center, never failing to use the opportunity to flirt with cute boys who were my fellow students, as was the friend who was later to follow me to Canada, when I fled the war in ex-YU—the one of Sade's songs in Vancouver—who went on a pilgrimage to Jerusalem on the Easter week the year before and was searching for the roots of Christianity to which she returned after a brief excursion to some odd pseudo-Indian mantra-chanting cult.

There also came a seventeen-year-old boy who, even though his Hungarian grandmother used to clandestinely take him to the Roman Catholic church in the Vojvodina where he lived before his upwardly mobile (or, as I would have said in my pre-PC days, "upstart") Herzegovinan father remarried the woman powerful in the Communist hierarchy by the simple fact of being the niece of dictator Tito's wife Jovanka, had decided the grandmother was actually a Jew in disguise (!) and so therefore had also been his dead mother. He was very upset when told he would have to convert.

Eventually, inevitably, the gay cantor and I hit it off. Not only that he (as I construed it at the time) "looked Jewish," which I, with a tenuous Jewish ancestor from more than a century ago, did not—but there was another, apparently totally unrelated aspect to it: He was the son of a policeman, an epitome of the Communist regime. And because of the way my mother's family had been treated by the regime, he was the one I had to have, to take revenge on.

My great-grandmother, Sarah's granddaughter Milka, was married to a Serbian merchant and landowner Ilija, who had been a town mayor in the 1930s. During WW II, she was a potential "security risk" because of her (by then long-dead) Jewish grandmother. A more immediate, and certainly more troublesome, risk was her son, the inventor grand-uncle, who had been a salon Communist in the 1930s. So when the war started, Ilija did his best to protect the family, by paying bribes indiscriminately to the (loyal-to-the-exiled king) Chetniks, Communist partisans, the Quisling-like General Nedi's Serbian homeguard, the Germans, the Bulgarians, who—unlike in Bulgaria proper, where they sheltered the Jews—took part in the deportations of Jews in Macedonia and the parts of Serbia right at the border where they were invited by the Germans as "helpers" and whoever else showed up with guns in the middle of the night asking for food, a place to spend the night

In late 1943, after he heard through the grapevine that his "liquidation" was being prepared, and Milka's "Aryan" origins having been confirmed, he organized his own flight to England via Italy. After the Communist takeover in 1945, he was proclaimed a "traitor" and the family lost the house—which they managed to get back only years later, a few years before I was born, and only because it had been Milka's property before they married.

All this meant that I regarded the "servants of the Communist regime" as owing me something. Moreover, while street cops may have indeed been there to get after robbers (although I have my reservations about it too), the UDBA—the Yugo version of FBI, KGB, or MI5—was unabashedly evil. Not only had I repeatedly overheard in family conversations from as early as five years old, but also, on the personal side, although a couple of cruisy, sleazy public lavatories and some discreet gay contact ads in the two straight porn magazines were tolerated by the Belgrade authorities, I was made aware that the UDBA could use the old and otherwise never implemented "antibuggery law" to blackmail people any time they pleased. I was again warned about it by a gay fellow employee when I got a translator's job with the U.S. Embassy.

So N., the cantor, whose father was one of the top ten in the Belgrade "political police" hierarchy, fit my S/M urge nicely. Before him, everything I had known was to grab a thick belt, at first a brown, military-regulation one (an odd fetish for a guy who, like myself, did no military service but a two-week university students' national defense training) and hit the butt quivering before me until red stripes enveloped it and the glowing heat turned Z., my only three-year liaison, into a whimpering boy. I would then turn him around and give him my dick to suck for up to a quarter of an hour. Usually I made him jerk off all the while. As I sexually matured after the allegation that HIV and AIDS are interconnected had been made, I wouldn't dare come while another human being was touching me. To exchange body fluids was a major no-no, and at that time I still naïvely believed that life held some fun in store for me somewhere down the road. So I would build arousal by dominating Z. and then pull back to jerk off for a minute or two before I'd come.

There were moments when Z. questioned why we never switched roles, but it was always me whipping his butt or when he'd say, in that pathetic macho way of a great ladies' man that all our friends believed him to be (something I had envied since our early teens and what I was punishing him for, once I realized he craved cock and feared admitting it), that if we kept doing what we were doing, we were "gonna turn into them poofters." And, man, he did not want to be one!

I had asked him to go down on my ass several times, but he would always tantalizingly stop at my perineum, rub his youthful stubble on it, suck one of my balls into his mouth, and I'd already be pushing him away, conditioned not to come even on him, let alone in him. Well, some people naturally start with caviar and champagne; they splash excitedly as they plunge into life with insouciance that they believe to be a great style. Other, more conservative ones, are slow to dip their toes and check the water first.

By age twenty-five, I'd managed to experiment sexually with five men only and had never come while being sucked, let alone while fucking. I found it uncomfortable then, as I still often do, to penetrate a scratching orifice of a mouth—not that I'm bragging, since, although quite thick, I'm not too long. I've never even fantasized about, let alone considered, mimicking heterosexual coitus. So I guess my choices were somewhat limited, from a purely technical perspective. But as soon as my ass lips closed around N.'s lively tongue, I knew I'd found my thing. A galaxy-shattering, most magnificent sensation. A superior technique. The beautiful warmth of human touch. Even if that touch was just the tip of his tongue stretching my forever-virgin sphincter.

In the circumstances, to see and hear N. begging to eat my ass was truly a political act. It was placing the offspring of the Communists were they belonged: lower than shit, under the rectum. (Okay, I do know people get hooked on all sorts of things, and I really don't want to insult anyone—except on purpose. I'm good at reading symbols.) On the other hand, it was troubling, because we shared Jewishness, the acknowledgment of my participation in which I yearned for at the time. Moreover, his Sephardi mother and my half-Macedonian father were born in the same town in the south of Macedonia in the same year, and both had to leave it as preteen school kids, albeit for different reasons

N. was short but had good stamina. His body was frail but spoiled with his old man's belief of being above the law, his spirit was almost indomitable. He could have been a challenge in himself, were it not for his father. He learned to break gracefully and come up strong from his degradation. At rare moments he would let me see the other side of the coin—his strong guilt about his father's job—and in a most sophisticated way.

This was a watershed in my Belgrade S/M career, and by the time I met N. I had expanded the assortment of my disciplinary implements to include a black buffalo-hide belt with a huge art nouveau buckle; a patent leather one, nice-looking but not pliable enough to be really functional, matching the shoes I bought in London in my semifetish phase; a short riding crop with a pleated stem, bought at a horse equipment and tanner shop; and a rubber flogger I made by fixing stripes cut off an old Japanese briefcase to a shiny razor handle. Not too much into tits, I had some mean black plastic clothespins, just in case, but didn't invest in expensive imported tit clamps. As only the police could get handcuffs, and I couldn't talk N. into asking his father to get us a pair, I'd tie him up. Inexperienced, I'd sometimes perhaps do it too tightly, and he once complained he wasn't able to practice his harp playing for days. He loved to grovel, didn't mind bruises on his butt, and was an eager pig-boy slave. From a safe time-and-space distance, I can ascertain it was the system's attempt to buy out, before their implosion into ultranationalists in the 1990s: They were giving me one of their younglings to use as an asswipe. It was a power trip of which everything before or since is but a pale imitation.

Throughout that summer and autumn N. and I did a lot of things together, including falling madly in love with each other as in a Spanish eighteenth-century novella. Once I left him blindfolded, tied spread-eagle to a table, and went out. I returned after an hour, but he didn't know I was going to; he really freaked out that time. To run away from each other, as the relationship was getting way too heavy on both of us, I went on a trip to Copenhagen and he left for Spain ten days later. All of Europe's landmass was between us. Then two weeks later, we met at the Amsterdam Sephardi synagogue for a Rosh Hashanah service. Like two magnets, we were attracting each other across earth and air and water. Only fire had failed our test. Or, better yet, we failed its test. Passion consumed us as we consumed each other's lust.

When I came home from work one hot afternoon, I found out my apartment had been searched in my absence. Greasy fingertips were left all over the place, probably on purpose, to scare me. A Tom of Finland card sent to his parents' address from Amsterdam two months later was my small revenge. They'd probably have dragged me through the mud of their bigoted prejudice upon my return, were it not for fear that I wouldn't hesitate to describe my kick out of N.'s humiliation in spicy detail at a hearing. That winter, although somewhat apprehensive about doing it, I decided to publish, in a major Yugoslav literary journal, highly sexual poetry with references to N.'s alias. He had invented a Jewish name for himself when he joined the small congregation as an auxiliary cantor. By writing about a legally nonexistent but very factual Kalmi Koen, I was sending a message to his father: *We can stop at this, or we can fight further. You know I have this ace up my sleeve, and I can bluff if I have to; but we can stop right here. There, take your boy back*. And he took him. The system eventually bought out N.'s youthful enthusiasm, and he set for a reconciliation with his parents in return for a two-bedroom flat they got for him cheap after the civil war in ex-Yugoslavia started and organized crime openly merged with the so-called political elite.

Today, all that is bygone. There have been hundreds of other men (not thousands, of course not! What do you think I am, a slut?) on whose mouths I have sat, all the while slapping their balls lightly, pinching their tits, talking dirty. But now I am no longer political. Why should I care about what happens to the world? I've had my share, which was getting N. so early in life, and I haven't had enough of what I felt rightfully belonged to me: For instance, in Amsterdam I was deprived of a translator job because a homophobic Jordanian Palestinian, working in human resources at a U.N. agency in Holland, instead hired two Croatian women who scored lower on the Dutch language test, saying he didn't need "people who do gay studies."

So these days I travel across the world, apply for research scholarships and fellowships, rootless, disinterested, and more and more empty... The forty months of being a (for all purposes) second-class resident of Vancouver was an ultimate hell of provincialism and banality that extinguished my urge to change the world. From the days before I was scorched by the sun at the British Columbia's flag I remember a few things: Grandmother's raspberry sponge cake and healthy skepticism; dusk falling on Reguliersdwarsstraat from inside the April bar; Father's heavy smoker's cough early in the morning, the shabby hotel room in the Bay of Trieste where the bartender from Utrecht took me on a trip; Easter service at a nunnery in Eastern Serbia; how R., H., S., and I once happily laughed, high on hash, before hundreds of thousands of young, worldly people fled Belgrade for good; and, yes—of course —N.'s tongue, working enthusiastically in my chute. It sure was an act of politics. And the tyrant in me liked it, all right.

"G-d created a world full of little worlds."
—Yiddish proverb

Finding Our Place in the World

Da'at
Jay Michaelson

In the Bible, sexuality is a form of knowledge. The verb *yada*—
usually to "know"—refers to sexual relations that involve mean-
ingful intimacy. *Yada* is not anatomically different from *shachav*,
which is just fucking; the distinction is in the meaning of the act.
Growing up in the Conservative Jewish world (I've always wondered if that C really needs to be capitalized), I'd heard plenty of
explanations of this *da'at*, this "carnal knowledge," most of which
water it down to either a banal idea of romantic understanding (to
"really know" someone) or a meaningless euphemism. But *da'at* is
anything but banal.

For many years in the closet, I confused the erotic and noetic
faces of *da'at*. I sexualized my desires for intimacy, imagining the
culmination of the friendships I lacked as a teenager would be
related, in some way, to sexual consummation. It wasn't that I had
wanted to fuck my friends; it was that I wanted to know them so
well that sex wouldn't have added anything to our intimacy. I
wanted total knowledge, total closeness. There's a phrase used in
the meditation world called "naked awareness." That's what I
wanted of my friends.

Conversely, sex was, to me, primarily about self-revelation and
coming to know the other. Seeing my friends naked, in changing
rooms or camp cabins, was erotic, but erotic knowledge. Being

seen, I would think, *Now that I'm naked, he knows all about me.*
Actual, physical sex was never desired and always desired. I was so
closeted that I couldn't imagine actually touching my friends in a
sexual way, and no one initiated that contact with me. Yet I was
filled with an erotically tinged desire to have an intimate conversation, or to "hold" my friend in my arms. I would comfort them, listen to them, cradle them. I yearned for the closeness of an intimate
talk, wanted only to put my arms around a boy and tell him, it's all
right, I understand, I'm here.

Any intimacy I was able to achieve with my friends was precious—in the sense of a treasure to be hoarded. I opened up to
very few people, because I viewed "opening up" as something that
should only be done sparingly, in order for it to count. Common
friendship was cheap, but mine was dear. I was shy about my body
and shy about my heart because I felt the power of both. My adolescence was a time of great isolation precisely because of my desire
for communion.

My closest friends, if that's the right word for the acquaintances
whose company I kept, were at Jewish summer camp, with all its
typical, absurd rituals; rigorous social cliques; and intense (and
intensely repressed) homoerotic content. I probably had my first
crush on a boy at camp who's now married with two kids, back
when he was still a spindly, runty little kid who liked climbing on
the bunk rafters. I never understood these feelings as a crush—only
as a desire to get to know him better, to be friends with him, to be
the person he told his secrets. He was not the coolest kid in the
bunk, but I idolized him and pined for him. Any time I wasn't with
him, I wondered what he was doing, and assumed that where he
was—that was where fun was happening. Not only fun: reality. My
time was only well-spent when I was with him. I wanted to sit next
to him at meals, to play sports with him at free time. And I wanted
to see him naked—but only to *see* him naked, not to touch him. I
wanted the information, the knowledge, the state of direct intimacy with him that comes from knowing "everything."

Obviously, the desire to see another boy naked is homoerotic. But

I never saw it that way. I saw it as wanting to be his best friend. Best friends knew everything about each other—their likes and dislikes, their secrets, and what they looked like naked. It was as if under his shorts were the secrets that, if shared with me, meant love.

It wasn't just the one boy. There were other crushes, and sexual innuendoes at every turn. Camp was the center of my teenage emotional life, full of intensity, community, and hormones. I hated school, where I did well but had hardly any friends. At home, despite my mother's overbearing efforts to get me to socialize, I began more and more to resemble my father, who was emotionally distant and who had no friends other than those he shared with (and, I came to understand, gained through) my mother. I was a geeky kid who was too smart for my own good yet ignorant of the real knowledge I needed to get by: how to dress, act, walk, and talk. I couldn't figure it out—how I could understand Nathaniel Hawthorne but not how to get invited to parties. Summer was the only time out of the year when I felt I belonged. I knew the rules and knew other boys in a way other than from behind school desks and within the school-created boundaries of what can and cannot be expressed. At camp the barriers were lower, and fuller selves were present.

Camp was also where my first real heartbreaks were—that same boy, the same rafter-climbing, oddly shaped kid, I found out one year, had requested not to be in my bunk. He hated me that much, even though he pretended friendship. I never went back to camp after that.

In my twenties, I thought what I had lacked in my adolescence was a matter of information: There had been no one to "show me the ropes" when I was a teenager. I knew how to say the prayers in Hebrew and work the controls of the camp radio station, but no one told me what clothes, slang, or music was cool. I look at pictures of myself now and wonder how I could have been so oblivious. I wore collared shirts, tucked into my shorts, when everyone else was wearing loose T-shirts. I never knew the right thing to say but also never knew that sometimes it's best to say nothing. I was a loud, often obnoxious kid—and because, a part of me still persists in believing, I just didn't know any better. It's a miracle, I think, that I had any friends at all.

No one helped me grow up in more serious ways either. I learned wisdom from philosophy books, not older brothers. No one taught me "the facts of life" or how to masturbate or what it was like to get a blow job. Throughout my entire adolescence, I didn't know what it was like to be sexually fulfilled, and I assumed there was something wrong with my body. (I sometimes think, had the Internet been in existence during my adolescence, maybe I wouldn't have waited until my late twenties to come out.) In short, no one took me by the hand and taught me how to become a man—physically, emotionally, sexually, psychologically. My father was too awkward and distant—we never had a "man-to-man" talk in any way that allowed for real intimacy. And I didn't have an older role model or friend to convey the precious knowledge that I so desperately lacked. And all of this lack of information kept me from love, because I didn't know how to act, said stupid things, was obnoxious and easy to despise. By the time I found out all of this stuff on my own, I was too old to be a kid anymore.

In my antiquated, pre-Internet age, I pieced together how people had sex, what the terms meant, what the techniques were, from the jokes and innuendos of my peers. My lack of sexual desire made it worse—since I didn't understand gay desire, I assumed everybody had to do what I did: master a set of complicated, confused, and noninstinctual tricks in order to hook up with a girl. It was, I thought for many years, the hardest code of all to crack, and yet everybody but me had somehow had figured it out. They were just smarter, I guess. Or had been taught. It wasn't until years later that I realized they were just following their instincts, like I was when I first fucked a guy, blindly, not expecting it to work, and everything went great. *Now* I understand! No one has any knowledge—they're just following their dicks!

I felt this: If only someone had sat me down, jerked me off, explained to me how it was supposed to work, everything would have been different. I would have known how to behave, I would have been cool, I would have "gotten it," and people would have loved me.

I decided I would be this person. I would become the guide that I had lacked as a camper. Of course, I couldn't be the sexual mentor, but I could still be ninety percent of the person who I needed when I was a kid—a guide to thinking, feeling, being "cool," surviving. So, after a few years, I went back to the same summer camp, this time as a counselor and teacher.

For a while it was perfect. By helping a new generation of kids avoid the pain I had felt, I soothed the pain itself. I helped the kids who seemed like the kid I had been, and what's more, now that I knew the codes, knew the right way to win my way into the hearts of teenage boys, I was loved. Finally—because now I had the knowledge, and they wanted it—I gained the level of intimacy with some of my campers that I had never fully achieved with my friends.

This emotional fulfillment was enabled by total physical denial. I fantasized about sex, but never about sex with campers. Once in a while I'd be physically attracted to one of the older boys, but never to the ones I knew on a personal level. Though I appreciated the beauty of some of my students and campers, the beauty served only to make the nonphysical intimacy all the more delicious: such a beautiful boy is friends with *me*. To denigrate the "pure" relationship by "polluting" it with sexuality seemed a desecration, even apart from the total devastation such contact could wreak in my professional life. Sometimes the image of a camper or student would creep into my fantasies, and I would recoil, as if from the image of a parent or sibling.

Because I wanted to connect with the kids, I quickly gained a level of love and admiration from them that other counselors struggled to attain. I treated the kids as people, not as "teenagers," and it was genuine, not an act. So of course I became a beloved teacher, and attracted some followers. We created our own community at camp, a sort of miniature counterculture in the midst of Jewish suburbs-in-training. Others grew suspicious, and there were occasions on which their suspicion was actualized or verbalized. They joked that we were like a cult. But we did nothing wrong, broke no rules, crossed no boundaries. Suspect as they might, the armies of mediocre educators who wanted to treat their students only as distant and barely human objects could not find anything to pin on me.

Knowledge was always the currency of exchange. I had a certain kind of knowledge—of Jewish arcana, of the best books to read and bands to check out, of how misfits like my younger self could find their hidden communities through cultural signposts and gathering spots—and I gave that knowledge to them. They, in turn, had a level of understanding of adolescence that I never had, and they passed it back to me. I doubt they even knew how much they were giving me. Each dirty joke they would tell or moment of intimacy they would allow would be a glimpse into a secret and unknown world.

As the Greeks realized, education is an erotic communication. The relationship of teacher and student, which the Greeks sexualized and turned into the foundation for an entire culture, is one of power and transmission and submission, expression and reception. The Greek teacher sowed the seeds of knowledge in the youth just as he inseminated the youth physically. As I've said, I never consummated any physical relationship with any of my students. But as time went by, I began to see the links the Greeks had spoken of—and began to judge my actions harshly. Particularly as the age gap between myself and my students grew, I began to question my motives for wanting to remain engaged with young people—and usually, though not always, boys. Maybe this was about sex after all. I thought, *You're only doing this because you want to fuck them.* From one extreme view (it's anything but lust) I swung entirely to another one (it's just lust). I interrogated every sentence I said to every camper or student, wondering what my motives really were. *Come on,* I said to myself, *you're only trying to be so cool because you want them. All this talk of knowledge and mentorship and the life well lived is just a cover.*

For a short time my Judaism almost offered a satisfactory response. *Halacha*, as I reassured myself, focuses on deeds much more than intents. And so even if teaching was an act of sublimation, my sublimation was holy. I was a damn good teacher, and not once did I teach anything I didn't think was connected to real Torah. Even if I did possess a core of physical lust, my acts in the world were irreproachable. I was creating good, not evil.

This defense held out only so long. Eventually the psychoanalytic part of me won out over the Jewish part. I couldn't shake the doubting of my motives, no matter how many times I checked and double-checked my actions. Was I really teaching Jewish philosophy, or was I trying to impress the smart kids so they would sleep with me? And if it was the latter, was I not being utterly dishonest? And who could say I wouldn't slip up sometime in the future? What if a student tried to initiate a relationship—would I be able to resist? And how could I look parents in the eye knowing the teaching they praised came from a desire they imagined only in their worst nightmares?

So, as I finally came out—it took years—I quit. No more camp, no more school. I wasn't willing to risk that one time when my boundaries would be crossed, and I wasn't willing to live what increasingly looked like a lie. I was becoming an awful cliché: the repressed homosexual teacher, leering at his pretty boys while wooing them with words of poetry. Whitman, Heschel, Shakespeare, Solomon—what was the difference. I was whoring out the geniuses of the Jewish religious tradition to satisfy a chaste and ridiculous lust.

Coming out is itself a form of *da'at*. Other people finally can know the "real you"—I remember one time a man I met in Jerusalem's Independence Park said of his roommate, "He doesn't know anything—meaning, of course, *He doesn't know that I'm gay and I bring home tricks from the park* but saying, "He doesn't know anything." And coming out is a form of self-knowledge as well. In the case of my teaching, it showed my self-psychoanalysis and self-doubt were part of the problem. I was attracted to my male students because I created bonds of intimacy with them. Now that I can create those bonds in normal relationships, I don't depend on the ones I build with kids. And so, after a while, I went back to teaching.

I feel a lot of the time like the last queer of my generation, the last one to go through the pains of rejection and repression. Some of the kids I teach, they're gay or have gay friends, and they couldn't care less. I'm also sensitive to the fact that coming out can be a form of delusion as well as knowledge. The wounds that I was trying to heal with my students do not reduce to sexuality. They are more complex, involving loneliness, betrayal, a sense of displacement that colored my own adolescence. Just as it was a mistake to sexualize my adolescent desires for friendship, it would be a mistake to sexualize all of the healing that I searched for in my students. A successful coming-out process does not end with a blanket ascription of every pain to sexual repression. It leaves you right where everyone else is: in the middle of a thousand complicated causes and effects.

Over the course of many years, I gained the confidence to play with the erotics of knowledge in my teaching and in my personal relationships. Pretending it isn't there or pretending it's all there is—these are both wrong. The erotic component of *da'at* does not "pollute" the entire enterprise. It's there, and it's a power in which our mystical tradition immerses itself. The union of G-d and Israel through Torah. The erotic joining of the transcendent Holy One and the immanent Indwelling. The secret of the cherubs: how eros, writ large, is not a sublimation of sex but how sex is but a subset of the great desire that creates art, families, cities.

Carnal knowledge does not reduce to intellectual knowledge, and intellectual knowledge isn't sublimated sex. Both are sublimated G-d. What is the sexual act, really, but *da'at*, an act of communication, of self-expression and receptivity to the expressions of the Other? How different is sexual intimacy from the intimacy that exists between sincere and extending friends? Or the intimacy that exists between teacher and pupil?

Lischov, to fuck—this is what we are afraid of. But *da'at* can take many forms, as it is expressed in body, heart, mind, and spirit. Ultimately, *da'at* is our Awareness itself, the reflection of the great *ayin,* the primordial Emptiness That Loves. It is the root of sex and Torah and the consummation of each. And so it is impossible to expect real communication without it. We expect our teachers to be like priests, as if priests can ever exist without molestation. We suppose that we can insulate our children from all desire, and that we can teach real values without involving our whole emotional selves. Both suppositions are wrong.

Da'at is an apprehension and knowledge of that which exceeds expression, a reflection of what lies too deep even for tears. It unites the intuitive with the rational, the erotic with the intellectual, ultimately arriving at a place of simultaneous knowing and unknowing in the face of infinity. *Da'at* points toward, gestures toward, what is beyond boundary.

The moment of revelation: taking off the shirt, the socks, the underwear. Our clothes are masks we wear to reveal and to conceal, but our bodies are ourselves as we did not choose them. I have no interest in the embodied masks of Chelsea gym boys. The imperfect, not-up-to-ideal Jewish body, in its delicate, pre-Zionist shape; pale and skinny, as if fragile, utterly without pretension in presentation—I want the honesty of it. I want to see each potential flaw, delight in every hidden vein, sinew, and bone. When the naked body is revealed, we stand two men "face-to-face," as the Zohar and the Ari describe the highest, most concealed form of Divine union, and as Buber and Rosenzweig and Levinas would later employ as their metaphor for the most complete form of knowledge. When we look into the face of the Other, we see that which is not ourselves in a way that nothing else in the world can ever be. We see the New.

In the openness of learning we are entered by Newness and expanded into It. Our mouths stand slightly agape, as if ready to lick the words of the text, dribbled with honey by our teachers.

Is this lovemaking? Sometimes we act as though all that is important must be concealed. Our genitals are called "privates" and hidden

211

away. Although our bodies seem designed to call attention to our sexuality, most of our clothing acts like it isn't there—even, as in the case of men's pants, crushing a man into the shape of a Ken doll. And what else is "private"? Our intimate thoughts on any subject. Our relationship or lack of one with G-d. Our family histories. Anything that might be an answer to "a personal question." That which is concealed, our "privates," is that which informs. And secret knowledge can only be known experientially. Is the feeling of "nakedness" that I perceive in writing this essay merely a projection of a wish, a fanciful metonym for anatomy?

No: Full knowledge, full truth, naked *da'at* radiant and carnal, lies in the brain and the body and the spirit and the heart, and beyond all of them. The pathology of language is pornographic, replacing the knowledge that can only be known beyond it. While in the closet, I collected three degrees, wrote four full-length books, tried three or four different careers, and spent a decade thinking my way through everything and everyone that has occupied my attention. Now I am tired of substitute information. I want to know a knowledge that unites the knower and the known: the love of G-d and men, the primordial Torah that existed before words were ever written.

Good Luck in the Real World
Shifra Teitelbaum

"*Good luck in the real world with a name like Shifra Teitelbaum.*"
This wish came from a classmate at Yeshiva of Flatbush High School in Brooklyn, when he learned I was transferring to public school. I recognize the humor, the disbelief, even the fear and envy he must have felt, as I was about to cross the line and move outside of our bubble into that thing known as the "real world."

Six years later, across the continent, I began the process of coming out as a lesbian. My sheltered Jewish childhood was so far from my new lesbian life in Los Angeles, yet many of the lessons I learned in my early Jewish community helped shape my views about life in the real world, and the kind of lesbian I wanted to be in it.

I was born and raised in Boro Park, Brooklyn. When I lived there in the 1960s and '70s, it was an insulated Chassidic Jewish neighborhood, and it remains that way to this day. Jewish friends from other parts of New York, the "real world," often gawked when they first visited me at home. It does not look like New York, or America, as most of us know it.

What can I tell you about Boro Park that will explain? That will help give you the mental picture you need? First let me tell you that Jewishness was the air we breathed and water we drank. It was overt and explicit, yet the subtleties were not taught, were not named, they were inhaled. I don't remember learning I was Jewish, I always was. Everyone I knew was Jewish, except the woman who cleaned our house twice a month, and Jewish was unquestionably normal. I learned to sing the alef-bet song at the same time I learned my ABC's. Most lessons were not imparted in specific moments, or with direct instruction; they were absorbed through my pores, and were part of every breath I took.

Storefront signs were as frequently in Yiddish as in English. It was impossible to buy anything treif in the neighborhood, even at the local Waldbaum's supermarket. I suppose you could have bought kosher meat and kosher cheese and mixed them on a sandwich for spite...

In a setting with that kind of uniformity, the subtleties of different practices become chasmic: Who doesn't take their dishes to the mikveh before they use them? Who lets their kids carry stuff for them on Shabbas? Which kids don't get in trouble for using a car as base when playing tag on Shabbas, and who isn't allowed to touch a car on Shabbas? These and other nuances were deeply significant here; there was an unspoken hierarchy of Good Jews, and these subtle differences in practice were what made up your ranking. Needless to say, the more observant, the higher on the scale, the more honored your standing in the community, and, of course, the closer to G-d. My family never ranked very high, but we tried to be inconspicuous about it.

Religious norms seemed to me to be maintained by an invisible Committee, commonly referred to as "They." What will They think? Who will They tell? They never meted out direct punishment that I was aware of, but the overall fear of Them, and of Them spreading the word of one's violations among the community, loomed large and kept people in line, or at least hiding their violations.

Most men wore Chassidic clothes—black pants, white shirts, long black overjackets, *payes* (sidelocks), and *streimels* (round fur hats) all year round. Rarely did you see a woman in pants, not to mention anything less modest. I learned to recognize a *shaytel* (woman's wig) from a mile away, even if it was a really "good" *shaytel* made from real hair. From a child's perspective, I was swimming in a sea of men in black; it was often hard to distinguish one fish from another, or to see these men as anything less (or more) than one large organism, functioning effortlessly, with many eyes, arms and legs carrying out its wishes.

I lived with my family, directly across the street from the Rebbe—the religious and communal leader of the Boro Park Chassidim—and the boys' Yeshiva. My home was front-row orchestra seats to all the action in the neighborhood—prime real estate, in other words. People regularly offered to buy our house, for astronomical sums, to be this close to the action.

There were interesting ramifications that came with living in this esteemed location. My street was closed to traffic every Shabbas and Jewish holiday. It wasn't clear that this was actually legal, but They (these members of the Committee were affiliated with the Rebbe and the Yeshiva) managed to secure a wooden police horse, and used it to block the street whenever they wanted to prevent disruption by strange cars, who shouldn't have been driving on Shabbas in this neighborhood anyway.

Everything is closed in Boro Park on Saturdays and Jewish holidays, even holidays the average American Jew has never heard of—like Shmini Atzeret (the eighth day of the eight days of Sukkot). Of course, December 25 is the most ordinary of days in Boro Park—all stores are open, and everyone goes about their usual business, as if "Silent Night" only meant there was a power outage…

My family, living within this ultra-Orthodox world, was best defined as Guilty Conservative. This was a sort of theology, never explicitly articulated, that suggested Orthodox Jews were right about Judaism and we as Conservative Jews were too lazy or too busy to go to the trouble of that level of practice. We lived a hybrid existence in Boro Park; we clearly did not dress or look like the Chassidim, but we went to great lengths to *pass* in regard to our more overt violations.

My father is a Jewish scholar but a true atheist. He seemed clear that observance was a waste of time, but was he was fearful of upsetting his mother, who lived downstairs from us. His way of coping was to keep our level of Jewish observance in the closet. My mother felt more guilt about our lack of observance. I think she believed she would have been more observant had she married a different man. We were out to her parents, who lived three blocks away, as Conservative Jews. They knew we didn't lead the kind of observant lives they had hoped for us, and it was a source of conflict between them, but they never knew the extent of it, and my mother had no intention of spelling it out. (As an aside, none of my grandparents would eat at my home; although the details were unspoken, it was clear that our *kashrut* did not meet their standards.)

In this context, my parents' great concern was to prevent neighbors from telling my grandparents that we had been spotted in violation of one or another Jewish law. In an effort to avoid conflict and exposure, we parked our car on the edge of the neighborhood on Shabbas and holidays. So we strolled through the neighborhood nonchalantly, secretly on our way to the car. Once we got there, we were home free, able to run errands, go shopping, whatever we pleased outside the neighborhood, as long as we left our purchases in the car until after Shabbas and were not actually spotted in the car by any neighborhood Jews on Shabbas. On dangerous occasions, we ducked and covered, slinking down in our seats so that the Shabbas walkers couldn't actually see us. I am sure people suspected us, but as long as we weren't caught in the act, didn't leave any fingerprints, we could not be found guilty.

Our Conservative Jewish affiliation included sending me and my younger brother to a Conservative Jewish Day School located in a neighboring community. I learned to read and write Hebrew alongside English, in addition to studying Torah, holidays, and Jewish and Israeli history. My education, although more liberal than my neighborhood, provided me with the knowledge and context to understand the practices and beliefs of my people, and the ability to read the Yiddish or Hebrew signs. I enjoyed school; my education helped provide fluency in the ways of Boro Park. I had little to compare it with, knew nothing other than that which was totally Jewish.

It didn't take long for me to realize, though, that Judaism expressed itself in different ways outside of Boro Park. Apparently, many of my classmates who did not live in Boro Park were not under the spell of the Committee. Some even did things as flagrant as trick-or-treating for Halloween—an unthinkable heathen crime in Boro Park. I was mortified and yet slightly envious, especially of all the chocolate.

It was safe to be Jewish in Boro Park, safe and completely normal. And yet my family's more liberal relationship to Judaism and Jewish practice meant we were marginal in our own way in that community. It meant we were openly, proudly Jewish, yet *passing* as more observant than we were. It meant we felt protected by the community, but I also felt suffocated in such a small world, with no anonymity and such rigid and confining norms.

A friend of mine, growing up in a real diaspora town in Southern California, was asked by her fifth-grade teacher to tell the class why the Jews crucified Christ. When I was a child, I remember watching a public television show about art that frequently referenced Jesus. When I asked who he was, my mom responded, "He was just a guy; you don't have to worry about him." The amazing thing about that response is that it worked. I was not faced with Jesus or Christianity as a child, so I didn't have to "worry" about him.

In this world, Shifra Teitelbaum was a long name for a little girl to learn to spell but not a particularly strange one. And from this world, I decided, at fifteen, that I wanted to go forth and broaden my horizons, and explore the greater world of the non-Jews of Brooklyn, by attending public school, after finally persuading my parents it would be safe.

I didn't begin to really analyze or criticize my environment, or all its givens, until my teen years. It started small; I began to wonder what other people, non-Jews, were like. I wanted access to primary sources, to see if everything we had been told was true, and what it felt like from/on the outside. These questions led me to push my parents to send me to public high school. They both worked in public high schools, and their experience made them reluctant to let me go. They feared for my physical safety, they believed public school was academically inferior, and they feared assimilation and intermarriage. Ultimately, a new public high school opened that was praised by enough of my father's colleagues, so with my persistence, they ultimately relented.

✡

What began as a real-world adventure in public school, continued with a move across the country, and soon after, my coming-out as a lesbian. In relative terms, coming out was rather painless for me. I suppose the transition from Boro Park to America made any other changes understated.

Growing up in Boro Park, although surreal and suffocating at times, taught me many lessons that I took with me to the real world of public high school and beyond. There's an old joke that says that between any two Jews, you'll get three opinions. Well, in many ways, growing up in Boro Park offered me three conflicting lessons for every experience. These contradictions can be confusing for others, but I learned to navigate them with the air I breathe. It's only when I try to dissect them, to explain them to people who haven't lived it, that I see how many layers and contradictions exist in the fabric of my upbringing. Complexities and confusion about pride and passing, about community and conformity, and about integrity and integrating were all part of the obstacle course I learned to maneuver.

It's hard to translate the most fundamental of ways we see and learn about the world as children, the things we absorb that don't involve specific language or explicit learning, that aren't transmitted precisely. Yet I am a reflective adult, and I live far from that world now, so to connect with others (and most have not had this experience), I strive to comprehend and then explain, so I can build bridges and be understood.

Four enduring lessons have traveled with me from my days in Boro Park to lesbian adulthood in California.

I give no thought to being a visible Jew. I cannot consider hiding it, or even being self-conscious about it. I take it for granted, like I do my gender, my self. When I voice an opinion, when I spell my name, when I take time off from work for Jewish holidays, I give no thought to how I will be perceived as a Jew, to the possible threats, judgments, or rejection, to the cost of being a visible Jew in a Christian society that doesn't particularly embrace difference. I no longer live in an insulated Jewish world. There may be costs, but I cannot choose differently; I don't even notice myself choosing.

When I was a new lesbian, at twenty-one, I liked the feeling of pride and normalcy that Boro Park had taught me as a Jew; I wanted to be that kind of lesbian. I didn't like the passing and deference to Orthodoxy that I had learned, and I wasn't willing to be a closeted or apologetic lesbian.

The way I am Jewish set the standard, reminded me that there should be nothing to be ashamed of as a lesbian, that being and feeling normal is internally defined, not contingent on acceptance from others. It taught me to assume that if I am comfortable with myself and who I am, others will have to be too. I practiced coming out nonchalantly to people at first (scripted spontaneity is amusing), but it was a goal I believed I could ultimately achieve, and I did. I also realized that as I came out nonchalantly (or pretending to be), others would respond nonchalantly (or do their best to seem that way).

Community creates the fertile ground from which identity sprouts. Community shelters me and nurtures me. Community helped teach me who I am and continues to help me create the kind of world in which I want to live. As a visible Jew and an out lesbian, I feel safer because I have community, draw like-minded people to me, feel power in numbers. When we are hiding, we are isolated, and we are weaker, vulnerable, and more afraid.

A community of peers has a normalizing effect—it takes that item off the agenda, so we can proceed with the business of living. As a Jew among other Jews, we can disagree on everything (which we often do) and we do this knowing we are not being judged for being Jewish but simply for our outrageous opinions. In a community of lesbians, I can argue about LGBT politics, criticize lesbian and gay community leaders, and explore heterosexism or internalized homophobia without worrying about perpetuating stereotypes or wondering how this is being filtered through heterosexual people's perceptions. Sure, I have these same conversations in mixed company, but in these cases I am sensitive to my role as an educator and an interpreter of experiences of Jewish or queer culture and community.

My communities also help me understand the wider world. They help me figure out what is bias and what is cluelessness, and identify strategies for taking care of myself.

On the other hand, community can feel smothering to me at times and make me feel invisible. In Boro Park I was neither a member of the community (Chassidic or observant), nor an outsider. I walked among them as something of a go-between, an interloper. I had entry, I knew the language, the customs, but my entry was limited since I was not a member. I had a similar status as a girl in a traditional Jewish community. As a prewoman, I could enter the places where men worshiped, even sit beside them, yet not as a participant, and my access would soon expire.

In community, people tend to want to see you as just like them, not just like "me." I sometimes feel like the parts of me that don't fit aren't invited, or aren't seen, and that any one community can't contain all of me.

I lived in the margins in Boro Park and have grown attached to margins. For me, the margins give me the best of both worlds—one foot in, a great view of the community landscape, easy access to escape. I can get the nourishment I need, and get out for fresh air whenever I have had too much.

If community is the incubator, growth means branching out. The Jewish community and a lesbian community are not the limits of my social world. They are the anchors, and these have enabled me to move outside of the familiar, to feel open and curious about other people, to feel comfortable talking about who I am, and confident we all bring valuable things to the exchange.

What I have learned about myself, and my identity within community, is strengthened and clarified as I take it on the road, testing it on my own, without members of my communities beside me. Who I am as a lesbian and a Jew is planted firmly inside me. It's nice to have people in my communities reflect that back to me at times, but it is also exciting to change the picture in the mirror, to see other faces and hear other stories that are new, anchored in completely different perspectives and experiences and that teach me about the wider world.

The lessons of Boro Park have stayed with me in the twenty-two years since I have left, and have shaped my view of myself and the world. Ironically, Boro Park has prepared me, in ways I or my parents could never have anticipated, for life in the real world, especially with a name like Shifra Teitelbaum.

Hasidism and Drag Queens
(Or, Memoirs of a Contrary Son)
Bruce Shenitz

Sometimes I feel Hasidim are following me. Not me in particular, but secular, relatively assimilated Jews as a group. Whenever I hear the sinuous rise of a recorded clarinet on the street, I immediately look around for a "Mitzvah Tank," an RV fitted out as a mobile enforcement unit for religious Jews who come to Midtown streets to herd their assimilated brethren back to the fold. They are not interested in conversion, only in outreach, so they must first establish who's Jewish and who's not. They use a simple, direct method: They ask. Presumably, they do some sort of racial/religious profiling, and only pose the question to the more likely candidates.

I never understood how they could always find me. I certainly "look" Jewish, but I also look like a lot of people in New York: dark hair, a nose that proclaims my family arrived sometime after the Mayflower—a sort of all-purpose ethnic. I've been asked for directions by natives in Trieste and Stockholm, so I suppose I look vaguely European—whatever that means.

One time, I was crossing Sixth Avenue heading toward Macy's, lost in thought. A young boy in a yarmulke and *payes* shot through the crowd, homing toward me like a heat-seeking missile.

"Are you Jewish?" he asked, in what sounded like a hopeful tone of voice. Knowing a simple "yes" would lead to an invitation to go into the tank to say a prayer or perform a holiday ritual, like the blessing over the *etrog* and *lulav* (the citron and palm frond that mark the fall festival Sukkot), I never knew how to the answer the question. These are the responses I've rehearsed but never used:

Yes, but not in a way you'd approve of.
Yes, but my boyfriend isn't.
No. (This last one would end the whole transaction quickly, but short of a life-threatening situation, I can't imagine using it.)

✡

"Are you Jewish?"
When I was in a Conservative synagogue youth group in the years between the Six-Day and Yom Kippur Wars, the big question was "Are we Jewish Americans or American Jews?" In a way, that question posed a more direct challenge: if a day arrived when loyalties came into conflict, which side would we be on?

As I shift between "I" and "we," I'm reminded of the Passover story of the four sons. Each son symbolizes a response to Judaism, ranging from the observant to the apostate; the "contrary" son asks "What does this seder mean to *you*?" and consciously excludes himself from the Jewish community by using the word "you." The haggadah never suggests that the contrary son may, on the other hand, contain the seeds of his own survival: After all, as the Russian writer Ilya Ehrenburg famously said, he'd remain a Jew so long as there was a single anti-Semite in the world. Not a terribly positive basis for forming a cultural identity, but one that still carries some weight in a world where Jews are still sometimes viewed as an alien—if infinitesimal—presence.

While most American Jews under age forty have probably experienced little if any anti-Semitism, that level of comfort is a source of concern to many rabbis and religious leaders. It is, they say, both the cause and effect of the high rate of intermarriage among American Jews. One of the rabbis who led the synagogue where I was bar mitzvahed used to talk about "rubbing-shoulders Judaism," a condition he described as endemic to New York. He meant that one "feels" Jewish simply by being around Jews, without having to attend synagogue, keep kosher or observe the Sabbath. (Nonpracticing Jews in Israel might be considered an extreme example of this phenomenon, but they are usually granted some latitude by virtue of living there.) The symptoms of this condition include the substitution of a religious fetishization of, say, lox or pastrami, to the detriment of, more traditional rituals.

If I have to plead guilty to being an adherent of this unorthodox sect, I'm also one of those people who sometimes devotes the same vigor to seeking out Jewish communities when I travel abroad that I have often spent avoiding them when I'm at home. But I suppose this is yet another facet of being a "contrary son."

When I was in Budapest in 1988 to write about dissidents during what turned out to be the waning days of Communism, I also visited some of the state-recognized Jewish community institutions. My Jewish translator's daughter, who was substituting for her ailing mother that day, offered to introduce me to some of her friends, mostly in their twenties and thirties, who were trying to develop some form of Jewish communal life outside of the state-sanctioned structures. "Please don't tell my mother about this," she said as we walked from a streetcar stop to a friend's apartment one evening. We were going to a Jewish social gathering and Mom wasn't supposed to know? I was intrigued already.

The apartment reminded me of a prewar upper west side residence: heavy, dark drapes, comfortably worn overstuffed armchairs and sofas. The people also looked like Jews who had surrounded me growing up in New York. The sat in small groups around the living room, playing Monopoly (with a Hungarian board), talking, or reading. One of these "unofficial salons" had been raided by the police not long before, and though Hungary had loosened up about as much as they ever would before 1989, people were still cautious about having a foreign visitor.

I've always been attracted to the notion of people stepping outside the norms of their surroundings: abolitionists in the antebellum South, German resisters to Hitler, a middle-aged married female psychologist who proclaimed in the mid 1950s that gay people were psychologically normal. I've written about all of these subjects over the years, a contrary son in search of like-minded company.

✡

"Is he Jewish?"

When I was growing up, my parents and grandparents often asked this question about friends or acquaintances. If we happened to be out in public, at a restaurant, for example, the word "Jewish" was usually silently mouthed or spoken in a whisper. The same precaution was used if we were talking in the kitchen, which was located near our apartment's hallway and in hearing range of the neighbors. In recent years, the question *"Is he gay?"* has been added to the repertoire of questions my parents ask me about new friends of mine they hear about or meet. I make fun of this voice-lowering habit and scorn the fears that lie behind it, but I too have been known to do the same thing when I'm about to speak the same words. (Not long ago, a friend gleefully pounced on me as I lowered my voice to whisper the word "lesbian"—while we were sitting in the gay synagogue. You can't invent irony like that.)

✡

I returned to Hungary in December 1990, shortly after the fall of Communism, and again found myself searching for Jews. My translator, the one with the mildly subversive daughter, had told me there would be a public Chanukah party at the Rabbinical Seminary in Budapest. I found the address without too much trouble, but from my previous visit I remembered that the seminary occupied a couple of the upper floors in an old apartment building. I was wandering in the hallway when I saw an elderly woman who looked approachable. Knowing that relatively few older Hungarians spoke English, I asked "*Beszel nemetul?*" ("Do you speak German?"), which about exhausted my knowledge of Hungarian. "*Ja, ich spreche Deutsch*" she smiled. Before I was ready to ask if she knew where the seminary was, I hesitated for a moment. I had to remind myself that whatever residual anti-Semitism there might be in Hungary, I didn't have much to fear from a small, slightly stooped woman with gray hair. She smiled, and told me she was heading for the Chanukah party as well, and took me in hand.

As I stood in the room listening to the singing and watching the celebration, I saw a youngish man whom I recognized as one of the rabbinical students I'd interviewed on my earlier visit. When I introduced myself, he immediately remembered me, and ran to his dorm room to show me he still had my business card, now dusty and worn. I remember his telling me his grandfather had gone from Poland to Budapest around the turn of the century, around the same time my maternal grandfather was journeying from Poland to New York—a tragic decision, like Anne Frank's family's move from Frankfurt to Amsterdam to escape the Nazis in the late 1930s. Of course, these observations are astute only with hindsight, and moving to Budapest was probably reasonable at the time, and clearly a step up from life in Poland. I wondered about the life I might have led—or not been permitted to lead—if my grandparents had made that trip instead of the one across the Atlantic.

✡

One time a friend was driving past the endless stretch of cemeteries in Queens, and without thinking said, "*Everyone's* grandparents live there," and then burst out laughing when he realized what he'd said. Continuing the thought, he added, "I can just see it: They all gather at night to drink tea and discuss the grandchildren." I'd like to think they have other things to occupy them during eternity than *kvelling* (or for that matter, *kvetching*) over their descendants. It has occasionally occurred to me that if they could see what happened in the next generations it might amaze and astound them more than frighten them.

When I was a grad student in Northern California, I dated a third generation Japanese-American. We talked about our families occasionally, and I realized one day that at roughly the same time my grandparents set off from Poland and Russia, his were leaving Japan. Both our families, as if exhausted from their wrenching uprootings, stopped on the coast where they landed in the United States and apparently vowed never to move again. When I continued the journey by heading west, where James and I met, we each brought our grandparents' voyages to a destination they'd never imagined. In a way, it's a classic American story, though we never contributed to the genetic melting pot of the next generation.

✡

"Are you Jewish?"

I used to promise myself that the next time I faced the question from a Lubavitch Hasid on the street, I would respond with a speech about the oppression of women and gay people under Hasidism, the narrowness of their point of view, their intolerance for Jews who had chosen a different balance of the ancient and modern worlds.

I've never given that speech, though I have made it to friends who already agree with me, and declaimed it to my more religious brother, who doesn't. Why haven't I ever had this imaginary conversation with my Hasidic counterpart? Was it a fear of self-exposure or of self-revelation? One of my college friends may have figured out the answer more accurately than he realized. Years ago, I made fun of the stereotypically uptight and reserved ways of WASP families, including his. "There's no one nearly as uptight as third-generation assimilated Jews," he chided me, and I conceded he had a point. Call it the anxiety of ancestry.

Philip Roth described the phenomenon in his short story "Eli, the Fanatic," in which a Jewish lawyer is sent by his suburban neighbors to persuade the Orthodox head of a yeshiva to be less conspicuous. By the end of the story, the lawyer has donated his most expensive suit to one of the Hasidim and begun to wear the long black coat and hat of his counterpart.

We who can pass as non-Jews until we choose to say otherwise may sometimes suspect the Hasidim we pass on the street are the "real" Jews among us. But because they make visible what can generally remain undetected by the *goyim¸* they arouse anxiety and fear.

Years ago my father asked me whether it didn't bother me to see drag queens in public, especially at gay pride marches, because "they ruin things for the rest of you." The scorn he expected I would feel would be based on what I call a move-the-velvet-rope theory of social change: I won't challenge the general idea of selectively admitting only certain people to the club du jour, I'll simply lobby the management to move the rope enough to get me admitted—and promise not to worry about anyone else who is still being excluded.

I explained to my father, with the slightly patronizing patience that only an adult child can bring to a discussion, that the drag queens were in the front lines at the Stonewall riots and that I wanted to see a world made safe for every kind of difference. My own behavior often falls short of the professed ideal; when I interviewed some transgendered people for an article I was writing a few years ago, I wasn't as comfortable with the subject as my personal politics told me I should be.

I've always done well with speeches that charge straight past my own discomfort and ambivalence. When I "pass," whether as non-Jewish or straight, I either laugh at my triumph as an invisible spy who has successfully penetrated enemy lines or become enraged that no one has bothered even to take note of my carefully concealed otherness.

✡

"They're Jewish!"

I live in a New York apartment building where about half the apartments on my floor have a *mezuzah*. I have one too, though I'm not observant. One of my friends, who was working at the time in Germany, a fact that made her acutely aware of her own nonpracticing Jewish identity, looked at my hallway with wonder. "Welcome to the land of many *mezuzahs*," she said. It seemed to make her nostalgic for a Jewish past that was even more tenuous than my own.

✡

"Are you Jewish?" a young Hasid asked, as I strolled past the Mitzvah Tank parked near Lincoln Center a couple of years ago. Something has shifted, and occasionally, I don't walk through the crowd hoping to avoid recognition. These chance meetings now feel like a game, as if I'm saying "Come, find me." Perhaps it has something to do with taking a Yiddish class a few years ago—my small attempt to reconnect nonreligiously with my past. I imagine trying out my meager knowledge of the language with one of these young men, then realize I don't know what it is we could talk about together.

I smiled and refused the menorah and candles he was handing out. "*Chag sameach,*" I said. "Happy holiday. I'm going home to light candles." I'm not one of the wayward you tend to, I might have added. "*Chag sameach,*" he smiled back. "So you already have a menorah?" I nodded and continued home, and wondered if he envied or despised what he imagined my life to be—or whether he gave it any thought.

The Idea of Home
Sara Marcus

1.

"I have a thing for Jews," Diana confessed to me over dinner on our three-month anniversary.

"I guess," she added cautiously, "you might call it a fetish."

"A Jew fetish?" I stared at her. She was pale and blond, a product of the Catholic school system of Orange County, California. Should I be offended? Was she exoticizing my people? What was there in Ashkenazi culture to exoticize, anyway? All the culture I'd grown up with seemed white and dull to me, consisting mainly of bland, beige-to-tan foods: cheese blintzes, bagels, noodle kugel, lumpy challah loaves purchased already sliced from the Giant bakery counter.

True, I had recently started learning about other ways to be Jewish. Barely a year earlier, my best friend at college, a grandson of Communist Party members, had played me a Klezmatics CD that included the lyric "We're all gay, like David and Jonathan," and given me a crash course in radical Jewish history. In my Hebrew school lessons about the Triangle Shirtwaist fire, no one had ever told me this workplace tragedy had inspired radical Jewish girls to get fired up and fight for a union, bellowing strident chants in Yiddish and English. I had no idea New York City had traditionally been home to a rich community of Jewish anarchists, communists, and socialists, all speaking the same language my grandmother had sung to me in lullabies.

Why hadn't anyone taught me this history when I was growing up? These stories could have counteracted all the conclusions I'd reached about Judaism by looking around my hometown and my parents' temple: Jews were materialistic, status-obsessed, and apolitical; Jews were worried only about the well-being of other Jews; Jews were so preoccupied with continuity and childbearing that queers like me had no place in the family or communal structures. I had grown up alienated and lonely, a radical queer out of place in a conformist suburb, and Judaism had seemed like part of the problem. I was still trying to figure out where I might feel at home and where being Jewish could fit in.

Diana nurtured her own private image of Jewish identity. "Jews are some of the only white people in this country who still have a culture," she said. "I know so many activists in New York who use that cultural identity as a rallying point for some fantastic organizing. And Jewish lesbians are all smart and obsessed with books; and they're tall and swarthy and nearsighted, which is my physical ideal." She trailed off, her gaze growing misty.

Diana had picked me up at the gay pride celebration in D.C. the summer after my first year of college. I was collecting petition signatures for the union where I was an intern; she'd strolled up to me and started arguing with me about the petition. "So what if you win this law requiring public hearings?" she said. "Will anybody actually come? Do you have that organizing in place already?"

I was immediately smitten by this fast-talking girl with the word LOGIC tattooed in block letters across her biceps. Within a week we were sleeping together in her crumbling apartment in Northeast, where she was spearheading a rent strike. Because she was two years older than me and several affairs wiser, Diana considered herself my first real lesbian and took her job seriously. She took me to New York for my first Dyke March, my first New York pride parade. In the big parade, we marched with the anarchists she used to live with in a squat on the lower east side. We swaggered downtown in our torn cutoffs and punk band T-shirts, yelling Diana's favorite chant:

Pussy, pussy, we love to eat 'em
No government can ever give you freedom

At the end of the summer, Diana moved back to New York and I returned to school in Connecticut. Every other weekend that fall, I stuffed my course books into my backpack and rode the Metro-North to spend the weekend in Diana's six-by-eight room over a hair salon in Park Slope. We would read in bed all day, then go out to buy dinner ingredients at the food co-op as the sun was setting. She told me Marxist theory didn't hold water; that I was really an anarcho-syndicalist and just didn't know it yet. She told me we were perfect for each other. She told me she'd convert to Judaism when we got married.

She had all the qualities I'd ever wanted in a girlfriend, but for some reason I couldn't fall in love with her, so we fought bitterly and broke up messily and didn't talk for almost a year after that. Then it was Yom Kippur again, and I realized Diana was the only person I hadn't made up with.

"You're just calling me because it's Yom Kippur, aren't you?" she said as soon as she heard my voice. I couldn't tell if she was angry or just messing with me.

I tried to explain I viewed the day as a useful milestone, a reminder for me to set things straight with people I'd been meaning to be in touch with.

"I don't mind," Diana said more gently. "I understand why you called, because I went to Rosh Hashanah services with my girlfriend last week. In fact, I've sort of been waiting for your call. So let's talk."

2.

East Tennessee in March was refreshingly balmy. The Smoky Mountains, rising above the four-lane highway, gave the landscape a sense of motion I hadn't expected to find in the South.

To be honest, I wasn't sure what I had expected to find when I went to Unicoi County to meet May's family. We'd been dating for just under a year. I tried hard to be polite, respectable, helpful. I had many factors in my favor: I had a real job; I did all the dinner dishes without being asked; and I wasn't the first of May's girlfriends to meet the family. The first such meeting, famously, included May's father waving a shotgun in the air.

I was also alien to them: a college-educated Northerner, with the rapid speech patterns to prove it. And then there was the Jew thing.

"Well, I've never met a Jewish person before," May's mother, Ida, said with easy grace and curiosity. "We don't have too many of them down here. So I hope you don't mind me asking you, Sara," she turned to me, laying down her fork, "what's the Jewish religion like?"

I looked at Ida and pictured the small brick Freewill Baptist church where May had gone to youth group, where her mother got saved in revivals summer after summer. Where should I start?

"Judaism is much less based on faith and belief than the Baptist Church is," I began seriously. "The measure of whether a person is a good Jew doesn't have much to do with faith or other internal things. It's more about following certain codes of action. I guess Judaism is mainly about ordering time in a certain way, and creating community with other people who order their time the same way."

Ida wrinkled her brow. I tried to simplify. "I mean, I think it's more about what you do than what you believe."

May jumped in to rescue me. "Mom," she said, "Jews don't believe Jesus was the son of G-d."

Right. I knew I was forgetting something.

3.

It's summer 2002. My first-ever Jewish girlfriend has just broken up with me and traveled to the West Bank to protect the Ramallah hospital from army raids. May is in Tennessee introducing her new girlfriend to her mother. But Diana is with me for New York City pride this year, exactly six years since the last time either of us marched in a pride parade—unless you count the year Diana and her affinity group chained themselves across the parade route to block Mayor Giuliani from marching.

Diana's most recent girlfriend moved back to Israel and marched last week with Black Laundry, a queer Israeli anti-occupation group, in Jerusalem's first-ever gay pride march. Today the New York Black Laundry contingent is marching in solidarity. There are thirty of us, mostly Jewish. I march between Jacob, a queer rabbinical student, and Hannah, whom I met at shul last summer. Hannah and I have been in an anti-racism study group together all year. Her sign says FREE LOVE/FREE PALESTINE. Mine says ARIEL SHARON = DANGEROUS TOP. We chant:

Bulldykes, not missile strikes
End the occupation

Hannah thinks we should chant:

Talmud, mishnah, and kaballah...
IDF out of Ramallah

but Diana vetoes this one. "How many people hearing us will know IDF means Israeli Defense Forces?" she argues. "We have to keep our message clear and obvious."

In front of the Stonewall Inn, the march stops while we wait for a red light to change at Seventh Avenue. Spectators are lined up six deep on the sidewalk, laughing and giving me the thumbs-up when they see my sign. Somewhere ahead of us a sound truck is playing dance music, so Hannah, Jacob, and I circle up, arms on each other's shoulders, to do an anti-occupation Jewish folk dance on Christopher Street. But which dance? Hannah crosses her feet awkwardly, attempting a hora. Someone else joins and dances us into the middle of the circle. *Mayim mayim mayim mayim.* Clap! *Hey, mayim bisason.* Jacob prances around with his right arm bent back over his right shoulder. "Come on, you guys!" he shouts, humming an old melody and clapping—two right, one left—until the rest of us catch on.

The Idea of Home

I know the melody Jacob is singing. It goes, *Tovu, tovu ohaleinu:* How good our tents are. These times are dangerous ones, and the tents we build for ourselves often seem scant protection. The lines between acceptable and unacceptable ideas are drawn ever more sharply throughout America, and many Jewish communities seem so narrow that people feel in danger of being shut out. If I went back today to the temple of my youth, if I walked into that space with my short hair and my boy's clothes, my criticisms of Israeli policy and my vocal dismay at American Jewry's shift toward the right, I would be less welcome than ever. My mother has told only three people at temple that I'm queer; she's afraid how anyone else might react.

Meanwhile, synagogues are being firebombed in France; Jewish teenagers are bulldozing Palestinian homes in East Jerusalem; Israeli families are terrified of suicide bombers in Haifa; a Jewish American is doing human rights work in the West Bank as Jews send his family death threats in Brooklyn. We suffer from the violence that others inflict upon us, and we are diminished by the violence we inflict on others.

How good our tents are. I spent years searching for lovers and communities that would help me make sense to myself, that would finally make feel at home. Now I live in the radical Jewish homeland of New York City, where I celebrate holidays and life-cycle events with a raucous, magnificent, left-wing, mostly queer Jewish community. Sounds like a happy ending—but it's not really an ending at all. Home isn't something we stumble into ready-made, like a snail finding a new shell and sliding in. It's an ongoing process of wishing, a regimen of hard labor. People are such hodgepodges of identities and passions that the mythical perfect fit is probably impossible. But the idea of home continues to exist—in partial, hungry form—as the work we do to give life to our relationships, our communities, and the marvelously rowdy cacophony of our irreducible selves.

A Jew in the South
Rob Rosen

My family moved to Hilton Head when I turned fifteen, just in time for me to start high school. We drove from my childhood home in New Jersey to our new home in South Carolina, eight hundred miles into the unknown. Driving down the coast with your parents is no fun when you're a teenager. Though I'm pretty sure it wouldn't be fun at any age. Having a Jewish mother in close proximity for more than several hours at a time can truly break your spirit. Every sudden stop resulted in a quick jab at the breaks followed by her arm slamming into my chest to prevent my head from crashing through a windshield, or so she assured me. Though I was sure she got a certain thrill out of beating me, however inadvertently. There were also the ten hours of incessant Neil Diamond and Barbra Streisand tapes. Corporal punishment for a growing boy. It was no wonder my Irish Catholic stepfather drove his car up separately.

The industrial North slowly gave way to smaller and smaller sleepy Southern towns until, after what seemed like an eternity, we arrived. Stepping into the searing heat was the first clue that my life would be considerably different. The surrounding wet marshlands, the white egrets flying overhead, the proximity to the ocean at all times, and the lack of skyscrapers, or any tall buildings for that matter, ended what little hope I had left that I'd retain a semblance of my old life. I was in the South now. But what exactly did that mean?

A Jew in the South

Hilton Head is an island off the coast of South Carolina. It's the second largest island on the East Coast, the largest being Manhattan. But that's where the similarities end. There are no large suburbs on Hilton Head, only gated communities known as plantations. Another sign that something wasn't quite right. I imagined cotton fields and log cabins in our backyard. I hummed a little of "Swing low, sweet chariot" as we pulled up to our new home. I had already noticed, along the way there, that there were no downtown shopping malls, no downtown period, actually. No city parks, no city streets, no city sidewalks, no city. And, what I was soon to discover, no Jews. This was back in the early 1980s, mind you. I'm sure there are some there now. But not back then. None that I knew of, anyway.

The scary thing is when it dawned on me that I was now a stranger in a strange land. My parents moved to Hilton Head to get away from the hustle and bustle of the big city. The lure of warm ocean breezes and a complete lack of traffic enticed them down there, with me in tow. And they eagerly started a new life with a new business: a bakery and juice shop. Guess who they hired to work behind the counter that first summer? Yep, me. My first job. And it was during that first week I knew I was in trouble. A good half dozen people walked into the bakery that week and floored me with an unexpected question as they pointed to the bakery case and the sign sitting on top of it.

"What's a bagel?" they asked.

What's a bagel? They were kidding, right? Everyone knew what a bagel was. I'd been eating them my whole life. Passed innumerable bakeries in New York and New Jersey that sold them. Had seen countless Lender's bagel commercials on television. How could this be? The answer is: no Jews, no bagels. It was as simple as that.

Though I still wasn't sure. I mean, I had an inkling. And to be certain, no one coming into the bakery that summer looked anything like me. Gone were the Semitic features I had grown accustom to in my youth. No dark-skinned, large-nosed, wavy-haired people with New York accents anywhere. They were replaced by

237

fair-skinned, largely blond, and overly Southern strangers, all with a propensity to say ma'am and sir with every sentence and always with a conspicuous drawl. They were polite, but noticeably stand-offish. Not at all like the exuberant, emotive adults I had grown up around, most of whom had been Jewish.

And still I hoped I was wrong. Maybe the Jewish kids went off to summer camp, like I had done in my youth. But nothing I had seen so far led me to believe there were Poconos-style Jewish retreats near-by. It wasn't until I started high school that my hunch proved correct.

My parents, in their infinite wisdom, decided to send me to private school, something they never let me forget. The public school system in South Carolina was and still is among the worst in the country. That was the threat they'd hang over my head when I was bad, to send me off to public school. Like it was prison or something. As a result, I was now to be in a very homogenized setting. Public school might have offered me a worse education, but at least there would be other minorities there. Other people I could associate with. A mix.

My school went from kindergarten to twelfth grade, and there were perhaps only about three hundred students in total, twenty-eight of whom were in my freshman class. All were white and rich, and not a Jew in the bunch. There were no steins, bergs or gardens anywhere on the roster. And not one other minority. It was like a big bowl of mayonnaise. And it was quite obvious from the get-go that I was a novelty item. A Jew in a land of Baptists. A land that was to be my own private desert to wander around in for the next four years.

Though quite honestly, I never really experienced any preju-dices as a result of my uniqueness. Perhaps it even made me instantly acceptable. Or perhaps it was just my stereotypical out-going, Northern personality. In any case, I was accepted. Still, I always felt outside the norm. There were always little reminders that I was a Jew among non-Jews.

In school, when anyone had a question about Jews or Judaism, I was always deferred to. I was the instant expert. But I'm a Reform Jew, which meant that I had a limited knowledge base to work with. Like most of my childhood friends, I went to Hebrew school to get bar mitzvahed, but once that was over I rarely stepped foot back in my temple, save for the High Holy Days and the occasional Purim festival. And it was hard to explain that not all Jews are alike; that we have different backgrounds and levels of religiousness. This always made me feel guilty, like I was letting my team down. It didn't help that I went to a Baptist church most Sundays so I could spend the day with my friends. I wanted to be a proud Jew, a member in good standing in my tribe, but it was nearly impossible considering my circumstances. There was no temple, no rabbi, no Jewish friends or adults to fraternize with. There was just my mom and me. And what fifteen-year-old likes to pal around with his mom?

Then there was the time that the headmaster of my school, who started each school day off with a prayer, asked if I wanted to say something from the Old Testament one day a week. I knew he was being kind, but I emphatically said no thanks. I certainly didn't want to call attention to my differences, especially over a loudspeaker. But again, I felt guilty. At the time, I didn't know guilt is just a part of being Jewish. A big part, actually. My mother passed that trait along to me, as did her mother before her. But at the time, I thought I was being a coward, afraid to face my religion.

One of my best friends even had a sign over her television that asked, WOULD JESUS WATCH THIS? Yes, my friends' parents were that Baptist. I even had a few friends who warned me that I shouldn't tell their parents that I was Jewish. They would not be as accepting. So I never did. Why rock the boat? I went along with the crowd, like most teenagers are apt to do. Though I certainly never would have denied my heritage. I was just lucky that, back then, few Southerners knew a Jewish last name when they heard it. And most people attributed my outgoing and exaggerated mannerisms with being a Northerner, not a Jew. So again, I fit in, but I never really felt like one of them.

And life went on. Freshman year rolled into sophomore year and so on, and then my other unique quality started rising to the surface. Oh, I certainly knew I was gay; that I had always been gay, since the first fleeting homosexual fantasies ran through my brain. But it was hard enough to be the only Jew. What would it mean to be the only Jew who was also gay? For a fact, my Southern Baptist friends would have had a harder time accepting my gayness more than my Jewishness. And being in such a small school meant I couldn't come out to one or two friends without the entire student body finding out. So I accepted that I was gay, within my own head and heart, but I never filled anyone else in.

I never went on a date, never kissed a girl, never experienced what my friends were experiencing. I didn't have the money they had, or at least that their parents had, so I worked after school and on weekends and every summer. No time for dating. It was a strange blessing. But it stunted me sexually. I never learned how to flirt, to kiss, to date, to have sex. I learned how to make money and be responsible. My Jewish forefathers would have been proud.

So when it was time to go to college, I was thrilled to leave my small-town surroundings and head for the big city. I decided on Emory University in Atlanta. My mother was happy because I'd still be close by. I was happy because Atlanta was a real city. Like the New York I remembered as a child. But I didn't know what Emory was known for, besides its close association with Coca-Cola. I found out immediately, once I arrived.

Emory, apparently, is called the Brandeis of the South. A place where Jews could get an excellent education, but not be forced to reside in the chilly environs of the north. Not Ivy League, but not a state school either. And Emory didn't just have a strong Jewish presence—it was *awash* in Jews. When I enrolled, the freshman class was nearly sixty percent Jewish. I was in shock. Culture shock. Now I was facing a new problem, the reverse of the one I'd experienced four years earlier. I had forgotten how to interact with my own kind. How to be a Jew among Jews. I hadn't been friends with another Jew for so long and, frankly, I wasn't sure I wanted to be.

I had nothing in common with them now, save for a smattering of Jewish genes and a long forgotten ancestry. I had no experience with Hillel or Hadassah, with Shabbat dinners or Yom Kippur fasts. I passed, outwardly, as one of them, but inside I again felt like the outsider. Their Northern accents were jarring, their lack of manners disconcerting, their unfamiliar jargon off-putting. I had, unbeknownst to me, become a Southerner. A gay, Jewish Southerner. My unique attributes were blending, but still I was an outcast.

And as much as I hid my Jewishness in high school, I hid my gayness even more in college. I joined a fraternity, immersed myself in my studies, and filled my remaining free time with extracurricular activities. Again, as in high school, I didn't date, only kissed women when drunk and in the fraternity house, and tried my best to hide my homosexuality like I had hid my Judaism for four years. If I did go on dates, it was with Jewish girls who I knew didn't want to have sex with me. If one wanted to go further than I was willing to go, I'd feign inebriation.

And I was a success. Not having to hide my religious affiliation allowed me to better cover my gay tracks. Besides, living in a fraternity house meant no chance of having gay sex or for even the possibility of a boyfriend. But this wasn't as bleak as it sounds. Having no experience whatsoever with dating or with anything even remotely sexual, I was ill-prepared for these things that seemed so far out of my reach. I neither wanted sex with men nor knew how to find it. And the thought of finding it and then not knowing what to do with it scared the hell out of me. So I abstained—from Judaism, which I no longer knew anything about, and from being gay, which I didn't know anything about to begin with.

It was strange being both gay and Jewish, but not really being either one. Are you Jewish if you don't practice Judaism? Are you gay if you don't make it with someone of your own sex? I certainly didn't think so. And again, life rolled along. Freshman year became sophomore year and so on, and I was too busy to notice that I had no social life, either religiously or sexually. But then, as it's natural to do, my hormones finally caught up with me.

My senior year meant that my life slowed down. I had taken easier classes in my second semester, dropped most of the clubs I belonged to and was getting too old to party like I had the three years prior. I was nearly twenty-one years old and still a virgin. Though that never really bothered me. I wasn't ready to have sex with men, either physically or emotionally, until then and I knew it. No, what bothered me was that I was about to go into the real world and I hadn't learned anything about how to interact with other people on a sexual level. Something had to give and I knew I was running out of time.

Looking back on it, I believe gaydar—the ability gay people have to spot other gay people—is innate. No one had ever come up to me while in college and flat-out said they were gay, but I had a feeling that more than a few of my friends and fraternity brothers were. The bells and whistles definitely went off when I was around them. What's funny is that I think there's a Jewdar as well. Granted, it's easier to spot a Jew because of the physical characteristics, but even without that, I almost always know when someone is Jewish.

Still, it was a scarier thing to rely on my gaydar more than my Jewdar. But I had to do something. I couldn't imagine graduating without having at least one man-on-man sexual encounter. And so, during Christmas break of my senior year, my needs outweighed my fears and I made my move. There were only a few brothers staying in the house over break. Most people went home for the holidays, but I had a job in Atlanta and stayed there rather than venturing back to Hilton Head. One of the other brothers that remained always set my gaydar off, so he was the one I decided to take a chance with. Besides, I told myself, we were pretty good friends and I doubted he'd make too big a deal of it if I was wrong and he was actually straight.

Of course, he wasn't straight. He was shocked that I made a move, but not upset. And after a few brief, awkward moments, Mother Nature took control and I was on autopilot. You don't need lessons to do those things; you just need imagination. And I was fine. *Free*, actually, is a better word for it. For the first time in my life, I was free to be who I really was. Gay. And it felt amazing. Between the sex and being gay at last, my mind was racing. I had finally kissed a man, had sex with a man, embraced a man. Thank G-d all before I turned twenty-one.

I had sex with two other guys before I graduated. One was another fraternity brother. The other was another guy that lived in a fraternity house nearby. It was nerve-racking having sex in my fraternity house, but it was better than the alterative: no sex at all. And so, I graduated with at least a modicum of experience and was ready for the real world.

But the real world turned out to be Atlanta. I stayed at Emory for eight more years as a clinical biochemist in the pediatric department. But, it turns out, the Jews I went to school with all went back up North once they graduated, back to where their families and better paying jobs were. And once again, I was a Jew among non-Jews. Atlanta is indeed a city, but it's a Southern city. And Jews were few and far between. Certainly there were temples and Jewish organizations, but these were populated mostly with adults much older than me. Besides, I had never practiced my religion in college and wasn't prepared to start after I graduated.

So again I went back to being a novelty. I had one or two Jewish friends, but, for the most part, I was the only Jew at parties, at the bars, and in most social settings. This, as it turned out, was not necessarily a bad thing. Lots of men found it intriguing, even titillating, to have sex with me simply because I was Jewish. And I was the first and only Jew most of my partners had sex with. Naturally, it wasn't surprising that I worked the Jewish angle once I found it to be a sexual advantage, but I always felt like it was a hollow victory shortly after these men left my bed and my life.

And again, life continued on. My twenties passed by and I never dated one single Jewish guy. Never even had sex with one. But it wasn't something that I really noticed. If you're born deaf, hearing isn't something you necessarily miss, having never have had it. That was the same way with me and Jewish guys. I never had them to begin with, so I didn't miss having guys in my life. But something was missing. Atlanta was beautiful, but it wasn't me. It wasn't fast and vibrant and rich in textures, like I imagined a big city to be. These are the things I discovered in San Francisco.

After eleven vacations in the City by the Bay, I decided to make a life altering decision and I broke my lease, sold my car, quit the only job I'd ever had. and moved to the land of my people, San Francisco—my people being gay people—but as it turned out, it was also a land full of minorities of every race, nationality, and religion, especially Jews. For the first time in my life, since I was a child anyway, I had several close Jewish friends. And then, finally, I had a Jewish boyfriend.

That really brought me full circle. It was wonderfully comforting to date someone with the same background as me, someone with a similar childhood, family stories, and religious memories. Someone who knew the same Yiddish words as I did, understood what it was like to have a Jewish mother, knew what it was like to have Jewish guilt. Even our personalities were similar. Through him, I saw glimpses of myself. I was able to see what other people saw in me as well. It was incredibly eye-opening. And for the first time since I came out, it was also freeing. I was about to have my second coming out, this time as a Jewish gay man.

It was that first Jewish boyfriend who reintroduced me to the joys of temple, of communing spiritually with people of my own kind. Living in San Francisco afforded me the opportunity of finding not only a synagogue but a gay one at that. These were people truly like myself: gay and Jewish. It was an unbelievable experience to sing the songs I sang as a child. To speak Hebrew again for the first time in seventeen years. And to be holding the hand of another man as I did this. I finally found my home, and for the first time in my life, I belonged.

Aggrieved
Jill Dolan

Our genetic imprint defines my family by a narrow pool of sanctioned traits. Our DNA codes us with an unshakeable desire for things to stay the same, in the same place, for people to remain the same, in the same place. In a battle between nature and nurture that I've commanded nearly from birth, I somehow corrupted one of those genes, and placed myself in an ambivalent relationship to family dynamics and imperatives that others took up without question. For my family, every absence or death, every change or loss, prompted a profound trauma so painful they could only cover it with layers of denial. Laughter substituted for pain; frequent and fervent togetherness kept at bay the demons of solitude and singularity. Probably because of my own resistance to their insistent denial, I measure my life by loss. I'm regretful about things I didn't say or didn't do; I yearn to make right relationships with people who've died or otherwise vanished from my life into some obscure future whose location is impossible to map, let alone visit to ameliorate mistakes, to assuage pain and guilt.

I watched the family practice its response to loss at funerals, where I learned they suffered absences and deaths and their own regrets only with louder, more insistent demonstrations of the tribe's impervious solidity. My first lesson came when I was twelve, before the arbitrary induction to womanhood that my bat mitzvah

heralded the following year. We'd been at the synagogue for Rosh
Hashanah. We left B'nai Israel's main sanctuary after the long service and poured with the crowds onto the street like school children
released for recess. Outside, someone told my father that his mother,
my Bubbie Rosie, who'd been living in a rehabilitation center after she
had a stroke, had just "passed away." I was already disoriented, standing in sun that seemed too warm for September, too glaring after
the dim stained-glass light of the shul. The news seemed too sad,
right after the happy freedom of the High Holiday service's end,
and too private, on a street full of traffic ignorant of the holiness
of the day and now, its sudden coloration with loss. I watched as
my father's face crumpled and closed, as the pain seemed to collapse him. Soon, his posture was shaded by something that looked
like rueful relief, as well as sorrow.

After his initial unguarded response, my father resigned himself
to the tasks and the details of death, helped by my mother's parents, who lent their house on Shady Avenue for the shiva. I was old
enough to be ushered into the house of mourning, if not quite old
enough to understand the particulars. When I ran up the cement
front steps to Nana and Zedie Dave's house and opened the screen
door to their living room, I found a long box covered with sheets
under their mantel, already burdened by heavy Jewish women crying. The mirrors too were covered. I had no real attachment to my
own image, but I found it unnerving to stand in a room without
reflections. I felt unmoored, as though the house itself and the
family with it were in an unrecognizable state of transition, something that looked like moving out but turned out to be moving on.

Zedie Dave took me aside, which in that small house meant that
he cornered me under the thermostat in the proscenium arch of
his tiny dining room, crowded me up against their china cabinet,
with the playing card holding its glass door closed. He told me that
Bubbie Rosie had died and we were mourning for her now. I
remained concerned that those women—relatives I avoided,
because I never knew their names—were sitting on my grandmother's coffin, that the long sheet-draped box contained her.

Throughout the shiva, I avoided the living room and tried to reassure myself that if Bubbie Rosie's dead body were stored in this little house, she'd by now have started to smell.

Men in dark coats with scraggly gray hair came for the minyan, wrapping themselves in prayer shawls as big as bath sheets and tying on their leather tefillin, swaying and mumbling around the dining room table. I knew these strangers were praying, but I wasn't sure what any of it had to do with Bubbie Rosie. She was a quiet, resolutely inconspicuous woman who would have been appalled by all this high drama on her account. Here were these religious men, making noises out of the sides of their mouths, rocking back and forth, and holding books they didn't consult, to make prayers in her honor. I was sure everyone who came for the shiva was communing with ghosts—mumbling to them, singing to them, sitting on them, consuming food meant to respect them, food that, to me, seemed to *be* the flesh of the dead. I had no where to go to make sure that life outside this little house, with its mysteriously self-contained system, was still normal.

My family could hardly be called wandering Jews. Once my Nana and my six great-aunts and great-uncles immigrated to Pennsylvania from the Saskatchewan prairie, where their parents had immigrated from around Kiev, Pittsburgh became a home base so insistent and imperative that the two great aunts who chose Chicago instead were always branded with a not-so-subtle outsiderness. Their choices bore certain emotional costs. When the whole tribe gathered, the great-aunts from Chicago protected themselves from an insidious snubbing by assuming a critical position, as outsiders who could see the unwavering borders of the Pittsburgh family as exclusive, narrow, parochial. The great-aunts' critique shielded them from what they knew they missed, living a thousand miles away: instant community, continual if quotidian support, and a ready-made place to call home. Their righteous outsiderness was always tinged with loss.

I grew up inside the Pittsburgh tribe but adopted the outsiders' critique early on, for reasons that puberty exposed, when my sudden, horribly strong desires strayed to women. Earlier, I began to push myself to the edges of the inside when I read Nancy Drew mysteries and anything else I could find that described a world larger than my own, one where secrets were unraveled and revealed instead of being held in tacit agreement, silently. In fiction, people talked to me, described the workings of the world in a way my family never found necessary. Family insiders presumed knowledge; no initiation rites taught the codes for how to use such privileged citizenship. Insiders assumed that genetics would work their trick and each newly formed family subject would accept the encoded family rituals and ideologies, naturally evolving to go to college (preferably nearby), marry Jewish, raise children, and assume their own place as middle-class homeowners in the predominantly Jewish neighborhood of Squirrel Hill, extending the family's real estate holdings and adding to the clamor of the clan. Straying from this presumption, whether prodded by new knowledge or new desires, spelled only loss.

I grew up in the late '50s and early '60s as part of this hearty Jewish clan. My family shielded me with people, always in groups, of four or ten or fifty. Filling up the space between us, my family warded off the vulnerability that shadowed the rest of Jewish life. None of us stood alone; we rarely even stood in pairs. More than one person always surrounded me, making noise, making plans, making food, driving cars, making trips, saying hello, and taking the most regretful, unimaginably painful goodbyes. Leaving meant betrayal. I learned very young that safety meant remaining within the family's outlines, at whatever cost. My aunt and her husband once left for a mandatory two-year stint with the Army in Germany. Everyone in the family went to the airport to see them off. The tense and horrible spectacle as they walked out to climb the stairs to the jet persuaded me that this airplane ride would surely be another form of death, that the long, sheet-covered box would soon be out and the house on Shady Avenue would again adopt the strange postures of mourning. But eventually they did return and took up their lives among the family with great relief.

Aggrieved

My family taught me being Jewish means remaining in one place, means pressing individual relatives into a singular tribe, and means an impenetrable sense of "we-ness" that's used as a source of pride and as a club of exclusion. Because I couldn't keep my turbulent emotions still, and because I soon grew tall enough to see past the tribal forest to other trees, I learned to be both inside and outside at once. My latent queerness gave me second sight, critical distance, and a canny ability to see through surfaces, which left me only frustrated, because I couldn't yet interpret the signs of my own or others' discontent. The synagogue, where I enrolled in Hebrew school lessons and Sunday school classes, was poised to teach me to think of myself as part of the family of the Jewish race, but I continued to feel inside and outside the presumption of cultural and spiritual similarity. Barely competent teachers told me what it meant to be a Jew; the topic wasn't discussed, it was announced, prescribed. I found myself dubious, resisting a commonality I had yet to feel.

I was vaguely frightened about the Holocaust. The story never quite cohered for me, but it represented how being different could be lethal, which both intrigued and terrified me. The assistant cantor, who led our youth services in the small chapel below the opulent main sanctuary at B'nai Israel, had survived the camps. Occasionally he or someone else referred to his status as someone who'd "lived." My childhood was full of cautionary tales like this that never started at the beginning. This man had survived something unspeakable, too horrible to fully explain. People referred to his past in hushed tones. He earned respect not necessarily through who he was but through what he'd suffered, with its irrevocable reminder penned in blue numbers on his arm. I was appalled when other students disrespected him, when they squirmed in the hard wooden pews and talked and laughed through the services he tried to lead. I too found the liturgy deadening, but to act out in the face of the history he represented seemed an affront to human suffering. The origin of his pain attracted and bemused me—pain was something tangible, something I could examine and measure myself by. The mysteries of death and its rituals still eluded me, but pain was already shaping my emotional life, speaking softly without words, a personal liturgy I thought was original and singular.

The synagogue wasn't where I learned what it meant to be a Jew. I learned from non-Jews, who overwrote my presumptive people with coarse cultural stereotypes. I learned since my last name is Dolan, people assumed I wasn't Jewish. In the acting classes I began taking in eighth grade, I learned to tone down my gestures and inflections, to erase my Yiddishisms of hand and voice, and to quiet the shorthand expressions and the too-appropriate exclamations that sometimes only Jewishness can provide. People outside the family and the neighborhood somehow couldn't read my Eastern European features as Jewish and had no way to know that when my father's Poland-born father registered to fight in WWI as an American citizen, they shortened his name from Dolinsky to Dolan.

At the Pittsburgh Playhouse, where I took my acting classes, or during my summer at the Pennsylvania Governor's School for the Arts, or at Papa Joe's, the hamburger shop near the university where I was a waitress and short-order cook throughout my teens, I understood my cultural identity wasn't necessarily something to boast about. Because they thought I was Irish, people mistook me for Christian and told me anti-Semitic jokes. These were often people I liked, people I'd become intimate with, in my casual, superficial way. They revealed their racism blithely, expecting me to laugh, to confirm their suspicions, to share their sarcastic antipathy and their blatant disgust. I never corrected or chided them. I never told them the truth. I collaborated with their prejudice. I stood frozen and bruised by my new knowledge of people's hatred. I was ashamed and slightly afraid, and I learned how to be cautious and guarded so that this secret (on top of my other secret) would remain so. I hid all the facets of my neophyte identity, terrified they would show only their flaws and perversions under public (or family) scrutiny.

I left when I was eighteen. Once gone, I knew I could never

come back to stay. I had to leave because I was queer and because, despite the perils I knew it might hold, I wanted a bigger world than the one that suited the family. By the time I was a teenager, my yearnings extended into places my relatives couldn't imagine, places I couldn't describe, so alien were they to everything intended for my future. When my parents drove me from Pittsburgh to Boston for my first semester at college, I stumbled out of their car filled with desperate ambivalence: relief that I was on my own; sadness because I knew I wouldn't be back; guilt because they were enabling my escape and didn't know it yet.

At Boston University, I learned that both of my foundational identities—the lesbian and the Jew—required announcement, needed performance to be seen. I knew how to perform Jewish when it seemed safe and appropriate, to resurrect the Yiddishisms of gesture and say, "Oy vey!" and roll my eyes with resigned and amazed understanding. I had to learn how to perform my sexuality, which took a year of quiet observation and unspoken initiation at the BU Women's Center. Performing lesbian, I accrued even greater cultural risks. But in downtown Boston dyke bars, on the empty streets after businessmen finished their work hours, my body learned how to signal its desires, how to speak in signs the marks of its difference. I became adept at performing Jewish and lesbian subcultural codes for initiates to read; I sent them quick bursts of light that signaled what circumstance too often required stay dark.

I returned to the family, often for the shivas, to see if I could recognize myself in a place where people presumed to know me without my lesbian subcultural accessories and without my heightened performance of Jewishness. I returned to play my older role as the good student, the good girl, the first child of the good Jewish family's newest generation. The small house on Shady Avenue was like a haunted stage; with each shiva, the set design and the props remained the same. Only the person playing Death changed. But over the years, my relationship to the family's pact to deny their losses grew tenuous and taut.

Both my grandfathers died on the same day, fourteen years after we buried Bubbie Rosie. Nana buried Zedie Dave—my mother's deeply religious, garrulous father, who worked tirelessly for a small Orthodox congregation called Share Torah—in another synagogue's cemetery, in a plot Nana had reserved beside her own, surrounded by her family. Standing among the well-groomed graves, we paid visits to the already dead and tried to avoid, without speaking, the grassy spaces left open under joint headstones that would eventually be filled. We buried Zedie Jake—my father's father, who after WWI had performed briefly with a vaudeville circuit, then spent the rest of his life driving for Yellow Cab—in a forsaken place with no caretaker. We stood in the rain by the cracked asphalt road while the non-Jewish gravediggers pulled from the ground the leg that had been amputated earlier because of his high blood sugar and, following the rules of Orthodoxy, placed it in the casket with the rest of Zedie Jake's body. Bubbie Rosie now had company, although I thought the two of them would be lonely here, separated from my mother's larger clan.

After two different trips to these two different burials, I walked up the now broken stairs to Nana's house choking on cemetery dirt, my eyes tearing with images of shovels lifting clotted mounds onto pine caskets. At twenty-six I was an avowed lesbian, in graduate school in New York City. My outsider's critique of the family had hardened into its own shield, one that protected me as I moved through a new queer world without the security of family support, wondering where I would find my next home and if it might be congenial. But at my grandfathers' shiva, I suffered the ambivalence of being a mourner with her own perspective on this unspeakable grief, one that left me alone in the family crowd. The ritual eating and laughter and crush of live bodies and loud talking about everything but our loss struck me then as mysterious and as foreign as the men chanting kaddish in the dining room had been when Bubbie Rosie died. Both of my parents had lost their fathers at once. But I was supposed to know how to set the grief aside. When I collapsed in Nana's kitchen after the funerals, sobbing and

lost, my great-uncle Mike took my arm and whispered, "Pull yourself together." He broke the seal on Nana and Zedie's liquor cabinet, and poured me a glass of my grandfather's still-full bottle of
cheap whiskey. I learned that in this family, if you had emotions, it
was better to torch them with liquor, so that they smoldered, but
didn't flame.

The family contract decreed that we'd move on, that our band-
ing together as closely as possible physically would substitute for the
hugeness of the loss we felt emotionally, would suture the enormous
gaping hole that these two deaths blew into our lives. The contract
demanded that we fill the empty space as soon as we returned from
the burials, by forcing our shoulders together and presenting an
impermeable front. When I was twelve, I worried about the ghosts I
thought haunted the house; now, I wanted to conjure them against
this apparent speed of forgetting. As an outsider still (always) presumed to be inside, I trembled from the friction of what I felt and
what I was supposed to do chafing against my soul.

All our family deaths occur in the fall, around the High
Holidays. September and October are anxious months. The year
Zedie Dave and Zedie Jake died, the weather was warm enough to
sit on the cement front porch of the house on Shady Avenue without a jacket. The September sun let me park myself outside there
all day and not feel suffocated by the people packed into the house,
which seemed even smaller, now that I'd moved away. The porch
retained its allure for me; everything in the family began and
ended here. Each cement crack was written over with a memory of
one of those comings and goings. The small porch with its green
canvas awnings is where the new babies were brought, where relatives arrived from out of town, where the family left for their trips,
where eight-millimeter cameras caught them jerking through silly
gestures, waving goodbye in blurry blue light, waves that said, Here
I am, here we are, still here, always here, nothing more. Their gestures implied, This is where we live, this is where time freezes us.
We don't leave here. You must always come here and see us waving,
entering and exiting this house.

The films are silent, but I can almost hear the cacophony, the people from inside yelling to people out on the porch and back, the telephone ringing, the screen door slamming, the porch glider squeaking, a house full of activity that never stopped, not even for death. The house of mourning rocked with vitality, with the warmth of people crowding together with nowhere to sit, fighting their way into the dining room or the even smaller kitchen, out to the misshapen backyard and around the rocky driveway to the front porch, where they could repeat the journey again, shouting and joking and jockeying for position. My family panicked facing death, and tried to outrun it with slapstick shtick. They grieved with laughter. I sat on the porch glider at the shiva, observing myself decide how I could perform my own pain in the midst of their lively comedy.

When Nana died, twelve years later again, we mourned at my parents' house. Nana had moved from the house on Shady Avenue; she gave up the family stronghold to everyone's sentimental regret, a harbinger of the unsettledness that came with her death. This time, at thirty-eight, I knew the family's gaiety in the face of grief was performed to keep the semblance of tribal invulnerability intact. We'd lost our matriarch and our shoulders couldn't press close enough together to hide her gaping absence. The scenery of family mourning fell, its always-flimsy flats toppling to reveal the hardworking stage machinery of denying grief. I watched from outside in, seeing as though the eight millimeter films had been freeze-framed to show the yearning space around each person, even in the middle of the always present crowd. Finally, I began to see myself in them and knew that each of them, in their own way, struggled with the rules of denial. I felt weighed down by the sleeves of my family's coat of armor. But as much as I tried to shake it off, I knew my own responses were just a different part of the protective costume.

We didn't talk about Nana and how much she meant to us, each of us, differently. We just talked. The more voices raised, the less possible to hear grief and loss resonating in your head, the more possible to drown out the echoes of the voice that used to be loudest, in song, in joy, in praise. Hers was the voice that heard, that responded, that saw through sharp eyes the outline of each individual against the family crowd. Nana knew me; she was the only person in the family who objected to my silence, who wanted to hear more from me, more of me, who told me being a lesbian was no reason not to share my life with her. She offered to see me in my own milieu, to look at me through the performances of adult identity I suspended when I was with the family. She reveled in the tribe but saw its constraints, even when she so proudly assumed its leadership. Nana, more like her Chicago sisters than I'd imagined, was always a bit outside, always the Jewish Canuck, who inserted "O Canada" into each family songfest. Once her voice was gone, we all had to talk at once, so that no one could hear its quieting.

At Nana's shiva, the wall of sound for sound's sake made me reel. I now saw myself as inevitably part of this loud, unwieldy clan, but I remained silent, individual, and alone, frozen in the family film's frame. Voices talking over each other sucked up my space, didn't leave me room to learn my own grief, to find its shape and extent, its depth and colors. I boxed it up and choked it down. I set grief aside until I could take it out privately and figure out what I'd lost. When I returned to New York after the shiva, I carried my grief around like a battery leaking acid. I didn't know how visceral grief can be, how long its shelf-life is extended when you let it live deep in your system, when it travels your capillaries and clogs your arteries, when it constricts your vessels and your heart pumps in spite of it, with blood rusted by its bitterness. I thought I understood my pain, that I'd sat it out at the shivas, that I'd placed it in some emotional storehouse I'd draw from when I seduced lovers, or found a rare contemplative moment on a west side pier in Manhattan, looking across the Hudson toward those I'd left behind in Pittsburgh. I didn't know that grief is so active, that it rides with you, that it shifts and turns and reshapes itself into something else, attaching itself like filings over a magnet, reappearing like a picture on an Etch-a-Sketch. I didn't understand the importance of mourning, didn't know the rules, because the ones I was taught instructed me to move on, to bury the dead and return to my life, not to bring anything along but what can be captured on old silent movies.

But now I grieve. I grieve that I can't be of them, in the same way I was when I starred in those family movies as the first and favored granddaughter, before my dawning knowledge of myself began to shade my face and move me away from the center of the small, clicking frames. I grieve that it takes straddling muddy graves on slightly chilled, brilliant fall days to let us show emotion that the family turns too quickly from sorrow to forced laughter. I grieve the comfort I could give when those tears fall, if only I'd learned how to respond to the grief of others and learned how to simply express my own. I grieve that in my family, being a lesbian with an outsider's critique marks my difference, and being a Jew isn't enough to make me the same. Outside the family, propelled in circles by my ambivalence, I dance uneasily along the edges of queer and Jewish worlds.

Nana and Zedie Dave visited my dreams, shortly after they died, in images of sudden, golden vitality, each alone in vague situations of movement or travel. Asleep, I felt the air cold, brisk, even business-like, as death proceeded through its itinerary. But those last singular passport photos of Nana and Zedie Dave were captured in bright, warm light, and my grandparents were vital and joyous as they told me goodbye without speaking. Those dreams were benedictions. Moving into an in-between space where, despite my agnostic atheism, I believe that their spirits still return to watch me, to watch us, sometimes, Nana and Zedie Dave told me it was all right to dance between two worlds. The family would always keep me inside, even when my own life failed to resemble its insistent ritualized presumptions, born of their own historical terror and their own fear of losing the strength of their numbers, of their own difference from the world.

My aunt tells stories about visiting Nana and Zedie Dave's graves, placing stones on their markers, updating them on family events. When she visited before her daughter's wedding, she asked them for a sign, so she could be comforted, knowing they too would still be present in the family that would gather to celebrate. As she walked back to the car, a buck slowly came out of the trees around the cemetery. Soon a doe followed him out to the edges of the lawn. The deer watched as my aunt got in her car and drove back to downtown Pittsburgh. When I visit the cemetery, I swear I'll never be buried there, preferring to think of my ashes flung out over the wind, dissolving on a wave. But like the deer, I'll always be there, on the edges, watching, with joy and trepidation, ambivalence and fear, love and pride.

Identity Crisis:
Tales of a Wandering Jew
Steven Cooper

I'm a Jew trapped in a *goyishe* body.

What else explains the blondish hair? The bluish eyes? My average penis? What, I ask?

Then there's the name.

Jews and gentiles alike have taken me to task on my surname. No, it doesn't sound Jewish. No, it wasn't shortened from Cooperman. Or Cooperstein. And no, once and for all, I haven't had a nose job.

Look at my profile, for chrissake!

(You see, I'm even invoking the name of the world's most famous Jew in defense of my Jewishness...talk about a cross to bear!)

I grew up in an Irish Catholic town and had Irish Catholic friends who accused me of impersonating a Jew so I could get into show business.

"But I don't want to be in show business," I begged. "I want to be a psychiatrist!"

"That's a Jewish job too," they'd insist, dismissing me with pity. "Your parents just want you to get a good job and make a lot of money."

Don't be mistaken. My friends were not anti-Semitic. In fact, many of them admired the accomplishments of famous Jews. They simply refused to accept me as a Chosen One.

"Why the hell would they choose you?" I remember Margaret O'Callahan asking. "You're always the last one picked when choosing sides in gym."

"Ha! I told you! That's me. Jews are terrible at sports!"

Even the teachers didn't believe me.

"Raise your hand if you will be staying home for Rosh Hashanah…" they'd say.

Nervously, I'd raise my hand.

"That's not funny, Steven," they'd warn me. "We don't make fun of anyone's religion here."

"But I won't be in school tomorrow. I have to go to temple."

"Bring a note from your parents," they'd say. "And get it signed by the rabbi."

I'd show them. I'd show them all. I was nearing thirteen and soon, I prayed, I would have pubic hair, and a bigger penis. My voice would crack and get deeper, and in that deeper voice, the voice of a young man, I would stand on the bimah at Temple Israel and chant the *haftorah*.

And so I studied devoutly. I learned to sing on key. In Hebrew, no less. Such *naches* I would bring my family!

My parents fitted me for my first three-piece suit and decided on a Pierre Cardin because nothing was too good for their little *boychik*. Well, almost nothing. Thinking it more elegant and posh and ultimately more fabulous, I did want an evening soiree at splashy hotel (this should have been the first hint that their little *boychik* would grow up to covet other *boychiks*), but instead I got a luncheon at the country club. It was *almost* fabulous (open bar, a nice piece of chicken, and the Herbie Weinbaum Orchestra)—but not *absolutely* fabulous. And sadly it did nothing to prove my Jewish identity.

Hundreds came. I had insisted on cordially inviting dozens of my Irish Catholic friends if for no other reason than to put an end, once and for all, to the prevailing opinion that I was one of them. But it turns out the only reason most of them came was to see if I could pull it off.

"It doesn't mean you're Jewish just because you can talk in tongues," one of them told me. "My mother says they do that at the black churches all the time."

"That was Hebrew," I insisted.

"How much did your parents have to pay the rabbi guy to let you hold up that big-ass Bible?"

"That was the Torah," I explained.

It wasn't until my junior year in high school that I finally got the recognition I was looking for. I went to a party. The underage gentiles were playing that age-old game of Quarters, drinking beer when required. There were many, many teenagers, a virtual cluster-fuck of acne and heavy petting, and the crowd broke off into several, smaller games of Quarters. Trouble was, we were short on change.

Kevin Malley had a solution. "Turn that homo Cooper upside down. He's a Jew. All sorts of change will fall out!"

I'm thinking that was an insult, and I suppose I should have been offended.

But I felt vindicated.

Finally, in the eyes of the drunken gentile, I was a Jew!

But was I a homo?

The thought hadn't seriously occurred to me. One identity crisis at a time was about all my tender psyche could handle. And when you consider that my childhood crushes ran the range of Julie Andrews, Dolly Parton, and my buxom seventh-grade math teacher whose mini-skirts were up to her *pupik,* well, you can see where I may have been confused, but not necessarily queer. While the other homos coming of age were pining for Barbra, Liza, and Ms. Ross, I chose the oddest collage of women, not divas, to occupy my fantasies. Women. Not men.

Go figure.

Later, in my barely post-pubescent years, the object of my affection was the Tic-Tac lady. She had lovely skin, I thought. That was a long time ago, so I assume she's living in a nursing home these days. With minty, wonderful breath, mind you, but in a home nonetheless.

And then, of course, came Stevie Nicks.

What could explain my crush on the fairy-goddess high priestess of rock and roll?

The crush struck me late in high school, the first time I heard her dreamy, throaty voice that admittedly still haunts me today. I'd marry her tonight.

What the hell is that?

Little did I know, however, that when I graduated from high school I would also graduate from heterosexuality. And what a commencement it was.

His name was Eric.

He was dark-haired and dark-eyed, and he wore a sexy shadow of a beard way before it was fashionable. Eric traveled in my sister's social circle, which meant he was four years older than me—which felt sexy and dangerous unto itself. He wore his shirts unbuttoned just low enough to reveal a fine meadow of black hair across his chest. I remember wanting to dive right into his manliness, and the eagerness in my eyes must have been obvious whenever he was around because my sister called me on it.

"You like Eric, don't you?" she asked.

"What do you mean?"

"I mean you *like* him, like him."

"Yeah, right."

"It's okay if you do. He thinks you're really cute."

I nearly wet my pants. He thought I was cute? *He* thought *I* was cute? Could this mean he would soon be lying naked on top of me?

It could and it did.

Essentially, my sister arranged the whole thing. Not really a *yenta* in the purest sense of the word, or a matchmaker in the spirit of *Fiddler on the Roof,* my sister did have a knack for getting people together to fuck. It happened one night during those first promising weeks of summer when anything seems possible and considering my parents were abroad at the time, anything probably was. Nancy and her boyfriend Nick showed up at the house with food, wine, and Eric.

I don't remember what we ate, but I do remember what happened next. Nancy and Nick retired to the upstairs, presumably in carnal pursuit, leaving me in the family room with Eric and a flavorful, aromatic French merlot. There I was with a man I desired and an unopened bottle of wine. What would you expect me to do?

What, I ask?

Eric smiled. I smiled. I laughed nervously as the wine melted inside me. I don't know which got me higher: my first sexual encounter with a man or the flavorful, aromatic merlot. I believe it was the sex, the pure burst of discovery, the unrolling of my secret desires, a tidal wave of truth—intoxicating in itself. I slept well that night with the knowledge that I had found myself not only in the arms of Eric but that I had, indeed, found myself. It was truly a *mitzvah*. The merging of my two identities, intertwined like the restless bodies of new lovers. After all, could it be any sweeter that my first sexual encounter with a man should be with Eric Levinson, a nice, nice Jewish boy?

What should have ended right there in the softness of fond memory-making came to a jarring and abrupt halt the following morning when my sister bolted into my room, woke me up, and pushed Eric aside. "Get up, you two…someone's coming in the back door!"

"Huh?" I asked from my daze of splendor.

"The back door," she repeated. "Someone's coming in."

It was not my parents. Thank you, G-d (there were not enough Yom Kippurs on the planet to atone for this, I knew).

We heard almost instantly the clank of dishes. It was Fiona, the housekeeper, doing the dishes we had left precoitus in the sink. Lovely, demure, grandmotherly Fiona. How the woman would have swooned into cardiac arrest had she discovered the sin abounding throughout the house. We pushed Eric and Nick out the front door, ducking them out of sight, ushering them into a curbside automobile before lovely Fiona sensed even a sliver of suspicion.

If she did suspect, lovely Fiona never said a word. She kept to her chores, like any Monday morning, stopping for tea at half past ten, never raising an eyebrow or, when she came across the open jar of Vaseline, bristling at the notion of misdeed.

The encounters with Eric continued. He was sublimely kosher (not in the dairy-versus-meat tradition, just simply delicious and clean and most certainly rabbi-approved). But he was not college-educated, which, for a Jew in those days, was a *shanda*. I would have a hard enough time telling my parents I was gay; dating a man without an education was unthinkable. And yet there I was, off in the fall for a higher education of my own.

I realized I had made the best choice for college. I would attend a university where two birds would be killed with one delicious stone, where that merging of identities would have the perfect home. I would enter Brandeis University—where Judaism was practically a prerequisite, a circumcision presumed—and hopefully sleep with many nice Jewish boys and, for the first time in my life, not be mistaken for a *goy*.

Once at Brandeis I settled in among the Rothsteins, the Goldbergs, the Rabinowitzes. And the African-Americans.

If you were not Jewish at Brandeis, you were black.

How, then, did I land behind yet another veil of suspicion?

"You're *Jewish*?" Rhonda Klineberg cried.

"Do I look black?"

Still the grilling continued.

"You're *Jewish*?" Andy Leibowitz asked. "What kind of Jewish name is Cooper?"

Oy, I was back in third grade.

I had assumed that, as a Jew in the Promised Land of Brandeis University, I would fit right in like a gentile at, say, Sears.

But the skeptics with their dubious stares persisted.

"*Jewish?* You're not *Jewish*."

"Must I show you my circumcision?" I begged.

"Yes, you must."

Frankly, I didn't mind. The request came from Josh Manheim, whom I wanted to fuck.

Even then, even after the fuck, even after I had *davened* my way through midterms and finals, even after I had forsaken bacon just for the hell of it, I still had the reputation for being a *goy* on an athletic scholarship.

"You've got to be kidding me. I can't play sports," I desperately explained.

Still the reputation stayed with me.

I hung out briefly with the *goyim* on campus, white-like-me gentiles who admittedly ran faster, jumped higher, threw farther than the average Jew. I figured, fine, I'll be a *goy*. If that's my destiny, I'll embrace it.

I'll eat ham and cheese.

Buy in bulk.

Use Ivory soap and feel guilty about sex.

Guilty about sex? Wait…isn't that a Jewish thing?

"No," Donna Finnegan told me after I had spent the night with a black man named Rex. "Catholics feel guilty about sex. Jews feel guilty about feeling guilty about sex. Jews are the true neurotics."

And didn't that describe me? Didn't I sweat neurosis from every pore?

Donna Finnegan spoke the truth. In fact, guilt about guilt ruled my brief relationship with a woman (we'll call her Madame Ovary) in my sophomore year at college. Though we never indulged ourselves in talk of future implications, for me, almost every orgasm was predicated by a terrifying image of Madame Ovary and me facing each other on the bimah of no return, exchanging vows, smashing the glass, and committing to a life of falsehoods. I felt guilty about the guilt that followed our sex. While Madame Ovary basked in the afterglow (I'm giving myself the benefit of the doubt here) of our coitus, as she crawled innocently into the arms of dreamy expectations and innocent assumptions and into the clasp of a sacred trust, I was dodging bullets of regret. How insulted she would be. How hurt she would be. How unfair of me. Bad, bad gay Jew, I scolded myself.

My friends thought I had lost my mind.

Her friends called me a closet heterosexual.

Everyone called me a *goy*.

Oy vey, I'm gay! I cried.

Let's face it: I needed help.

I sought professional counseling from a Jewish psychotherapist forty miles from campus.

"What brings you here?" Dr. Birnbaum asked.

"I'm having an identity crisis."

"Crisis? That's a strong word," she said.

After a few sessions she zeroed in on my sexuality. "What does it *feel* like to be gay?"

I so badly wanted to say: It depends on the lube; sometimes it hurts.

But I didn't.

This was costing seventy-five bucks a pop.

I told her it *felt fine* being gay. She checked my "psychological pulse" for internalized homophobia. She didn't find any.

Then she asked about my family. "Your identity is *so* tied into your family of origin," she chanted, not unlike a transcendental guru perched high upon a misty mountaintop.

"My family of origin is slightly insane," I told her. "But I'm not making this forty-mile shlep every week to talk about my family. That's not the antidote to my crisis, Dr. Birnbaum. That's just more oil in the fire…"

"Did you say 'shlep'?"

"I did."

"You're Jewish," she said. It was a statement, not a question.

I decided to answer anyway. "I am."

She looked at me with conspicuous revelation in her eyes. "Now, *that's* why you're in therapy."

Yes, I conceded silently. That's why I was in therapy. Jews have two choices: You see a shrink or you become a shrink. It's a toss-up.

A few thousand dollars later I graduated from therapy, and tens of thousands of dollars later I graduated from college.

Such a *mitzvah* it was, I tell you.

Finally, my family came to campus, blended in swimmingly with all the New York families—they were just as loud and as hard to please—and finally, by observing the insanity of my *mishpuchah*, my fellow graduates could see, that yes, indeed, my roots came from fertile Jewish soil. I was a Jew. *L'chayim, mazel tov,* and all that.

✡

So as a Jew, a *born-again* Jew, I marched forth into the world.

I moved from Boston to New York, the domestic equivalent of *aliyah.* I learned how to talk fast, walk even faster, and whine very slowly. There were Jews galore. Even though Brandeis University should have opened the door to a world of Jewry, it wasn't until I immigrated to Manhattan that I could truly stake my claim. No one dared challenge my religious roots.

Well, to be more truthful, no one cared.

How's that for irony?

Huh?

I'm finally standing there on the brink of independence, like Moshe Dayan or Golda Meir surveying the Promised Land half a century before me…and nobody gives a shit.

Fine, then. I'll get a job. I'll forsake the Promised Borough of Manhattan and move on.

And so I left with my fate in one hand, my faith in the other, and in my back pocket a very good recipe for *kreplach* from Mrs. Ruth Winkler, the old lady who lived below me on East 20th.

✡

Much to the chagrin of my family I landed in journalism, a career that would zig-zag me across the country not unlike the wandering Jews of biblical times. "Am I not honoring one of our richest traditions?" I begged my family as I packed my bags for the fourth or fifth time.

"You are not," they told me.

Identity Crisis

I had broken both the 11th and 12th Commandments:

11. Thou shalt go to medical school.
12. Thou shalt at the very least go to law school.

I visited and considered many places in my self-imposed diaspora.

Back to Boston: Nice for the Jews.

Chicago: Quite Good for the Jews. But Cold for The Jews.

Washington, D.C.: Not Bad for The Jews. Fairly Transient, So Not Enough Time to Find the Jews.

Not knowing it was Mormon country, I landed in Arizona. Not knowing the man who ran my company was a Mormon, I took a job there. I soon learned Mormons aren't so fond of people who aren't Mormons. But I also learned they pray in a temple, so I figured that's one thing we had in common, so maybe it wouldn't be so bad after all.

It was bad after all.

Jewish: strike one.

Gay: strike two.

Openly Jewish and openly gay: Well, does the word *pogrom* mean anything to you?

I adore the desert. Physically it is such an open place, its wide burnt valleys cradled by huge, red mountains. So open, there has to be room there for more than one faith. And there is a spiritual vibe that says yes, there's room, plenty of room, let your faith resonate and echo in the canyons.

But there are also people, and among them dwell stupid, provincial, never-saw-a-Jew people. And I would find these denizens of the desert messengers of things to come. So many Americans, so much ignorance.

Wal-Mart: Tempe, Arizona.

I stood in the checkout line with all my bargains. Just some innocuous, inconspicuous *tchotchkes* for my new home that no one would ever suspect or assume came from Wal-Mart, the national retailer of all things *goyishe*.

"That'll be one hundred eleven dollars and sixty two cents," the pasty-faced cashier told me. ("You live in the desert! Get some sun already!")

I smiled and said, "Wow, one hundred eleven dollars, that's a bargain for all this crap...er, stuff."

"Not really," she told me. Then, leaning forward surreptitiously, she whispered in my ear, "You can get a better deal at the swap meet."

I crinkled my forehead. I had never heard of a swap meet. Was it a desert thing? A Mormon thing? Did they swap wives?

"Uh, okay," I said. "Can you tell me where this swap meet is?"

"Mesa. On the weekends. Way out there, off of Higley. You can really Jew 'em down."

"Excuse me?"

"I said you can really Jew 'em down. Don't ever pay full price."

"No kidding?"

"No kidding. Have a nice day."

I complained to the manager, who offered a dispassionate apology. "Would you like help out to the parking lot with your bags?" she asked.

"No need," I told her. "My people carried their own things when they fled centuries of oppressors. I can do the same."

Okay, I didn't actually say that. I wish I had, but nothing came to me in those moments of disbelief. In the middle of Americana, I stood insulted, offended, heartbroken.

I did enjoy the melodrama of my own misery because there are some Jewish traits that are more than skin deep, but I have not been back to a Wal-Mart since.

I told all my Phoenix friends, gentiles and Jews alike, about my Wal-Mart experience. They have boycotted the dump too. Incidentally, my Phoenix friends never doubted my Judaism. Apparently, when you tell someone from Arizona that you come from the Northeast, they assume you must be Jewish or Italian or a Kennedy. However, those same friends had a problem with my sexuality. It wasn't a homophobia kind of problem; it was a credibility problem.

"No self-respecting gay man has a refrigerator this empty," Allysa told the others who had gathered at my backyard pool.

"You live like a single straight guy," Linda groaned. "And not a very good one."

They chastised me for not having, among other things, an ice bucket, and—Lord have mercy—tongs.

"Nothing worse than a gay impostor," someone said. "A gay opportunist, someone in it for the notoriety."

"The notoriety?" I begged.

"The whole exotic thing, the trendiness, the trappings…"

"Sorry," I informed them all, "there is nothing exotic about waiting for a lover to douche his bum."

"And you don't even have gay lighting," Allysa retorted. "Jesus!"

Well, a homosexual can take only so much scrutiny, and a Jew can only take so much of the desert. And so, three years later I wandered out of the desert and landed not in Eretz Yisrael, but Florida. Close enough, you think?

No, not *that* Florida.

Not the early-bird special, Mr. and Mrs. Seinfeld, such a nice day, who-ordered-this-weather Florida.

Not Boca.

Or Delray.

Not Fort Lauderdale or Miami.

Not even the Jewish enclaves of the West Coast.

Let's talk Central Florida. Let me sum it up for you:

It's Jesus meets NASCAR.

It's the Southern Baptist Convention (wives will be subservient to husbands, Jews will be converted, and gays will burn in hell). It's Holy Land—a theme park (theme park!) dedicated to the New Testament and, again, to the conversion of Jews. It's Jesus, Jesus, Jesus, twenty-four hours a day.

On bumper stickers: REAL MEN LOVE JESUS. I wanted to put on a bumper sticker of my own: REAL JEWISH MEN DON'T LOVE JESUS BECAUSE IT WOULD KILL THEIR MOTHER.

On road signs: JESUS IS LORD OVER CENTRAL FLORIDA. Except

over the Jews, I tell you. He skips over the Jews just like that angel does at Passover .

On the wall of a car dealership: wwjd? What Would Jesus Do? He wouldn't pay sticker price. He'd bargain like a Jew, what do you think?

Oy gevalt.

Get me some lox.

Welcome to the best-kept secret notch in the Bible Belt.

Here, the question is not whether I look Jewish or have a Jewish-sounding name.

There are no questions.

No, there is a big (or should I say "supersize"?) assumption instead.

People assume everyone is Christian.

This is what I have learned about America.

There is no separation of church and state; this is a Christian nation, not because it is but because people assume it is and no one tells them otherwise. I face Israel every day and ask for strength. I send her some of my own. My soul makes *aliyah* about twice a week. And yet I feel this is where I must stay. I must stay here until my identity resonates with America, until my Jewish homosexual self is as much a part of the landscape as Chevrolet and the McChicken sandwich.

I must stay here until the assumptions cease and desist.

I must stay here until someone can come up with an explanation of how the charming little organization that saves men and women from homosexuality through Jesus got to be named Exodus. Use your own testament, for G-d's sake.

I must stay here until people stop making anti-Semitic remarks in the general course of conversation.

It happened last night.

Pierre, my righteous gentile lover, had a visitor. A coworker with a shaved scalp. Despite our heartfelt desire to give everyone the benefit of the doubt, shaved scalps make Jews nervous. If only for a second. And truly it only took a second for me to feel comfortable and engaged with this man, knowing he had shaved his head for no other reason than because it's so damn hot in Florida.

We talked politics mostly, derided the Bush family,

Pierre cooked dinner. I stayed with the visitor. He had a wonderful, brilliant smile.

I mentioned *naches*. Soon Pierre emerged from the kitchen with a plate of tortilla chips and salsa under a bed of melted cheese food. "Did someone say nachos?" he asked.

I laughed out loud. The humor eluded the visitor who had clearly not understood, as well, what I had meant by *naches*. In fact, he dug into the nachos and made a comment about Pierre being such a good wife. "Ask and ye shall receive," he barbed, scooping a chip from the mound in front of him.

We talked politics again. And corporate greed, corporate corruption. I told him to read Michael Moore. Good vibe.

Then he stood up to leave. Said he couldn't stay for dinner. But he would love to cook for us some day. He learned from his grandfather, he said. Not only a master chef, but a wonderful man as well, a former politician, actually, who was honest and caring, a "real exception," he said proudly. "But just like a Jew! My G-d, he could be stingy like a little Jew. I mean a real honest-to-G-d Jew!"

I looked at Pierre. Pierre looked at me. How had this happened? A seemingly kindred spirit, a politically savvy articulate young fellow whom I might have even nominated for Mentsh of the Month had pushed me back into the Jewish Closet?

I came right out and told him.

Suffice it to say he left our home red-faced—red-scalped, in fact. He apologized profusely, but it was hard to make out his words, what with both feet jammed in his mouth.

Out came the same old, same old: "I didn't mean it personally. I didn't mean to offend. Really, no offense."

He left. Once again I faced Jerusalem and asked for strength. She came through unconditionally. But I didn't have to make *aliyah* to be the out-of-the-closet-Jew I wanted to be.

"You don't have to do *anything* to be the Jew you want to be," Pierre said as we feasted on dinner. We sat there at the table contemplating a home invaded by the cancer of ignorance. Malignant or benign? It was hard to tell. We put it under the microscope and examined. Would it spread? Was there a cure? Did I need to warn others?

His loving eyes comforted me, guided me through the microscope and back. Patiently. "Thank you," I told him.

"You know," Pierre said to me, "it's not important what other people think of you."

I knew that.

"And it doesn't even matter if it does in fact matter to other people," he added.

I don't think I knew that.

I had to repeat the thought to myself. I had to consider it like one might that first sip of merlot.

"I suppose you're right" was my verdict.

"Be the best Jew you can be," he said. "And be the best homosexual you can be too."

"Where were you thirty years ago?"

"In my own identity crisis…a biracial French kid landing in America without a stitch of English."

"That must have sucked."

"Paris to Omaha? Half-black, half-white? Oh, yes, it sucked indeed."

Before we turned in for the night I felt it only fair to share with him the true meaning of *naches*. "It's something wonderful you can bring your family," I said. "The purest joy, the purest pride."

"Gay pride and *naches,* two different things, right?"

"Not necessarily," I replied. "But neither should be served with Velveeta."

The Whole Jewish Thing
Bonnie J. Morris

THIS HAS BEEN THE CENTURY OF STRANGERS, BROWN, YELLOW, AND WHITE. THIS HAS BEEN THE CENTURY OF THE GREAT IMMIGRANT EXPERIMENT...BUT IT MAKES AN IMMIGRANT LAUGH TO HEAR THE FEARS OF THE NATIONALIST, SCARED OF INFECTION, PENETRATION, MISCEGENATION, WHEN THIS IS SMALL FRY, PEANUTS, COMPARED TO WHAT THE IMMIGRANT FEARS—DISSOLUTION, DISAPPEARANCE.
—ZADIE SMITH, *WHITE TEETH*

To be a Jew and a lesbian, to live openly and comfortably as both—healthy, successful, published—is a fist in Hitler's face. I learned to think this way in college, when I was coming out as both Jewish and woman-loving, devouring the history of Judaism and the history of lesbians simultaneously, at age eighteen, nineteen. I won the top awards in my Jewish history major at American University and was one of the first two students to graduate with the women's studies minor. But devouring books is one thing; internalizing the moral lessons of the Holocaust and homophobia is another. How often I would have died, been burned, been judged unfit to live, in other periods of world history. How terrifying to understand this, as a teenage bookworm. Were there still folk who wanted me—us—dead? I quickly discovered there was plenty of homophobia in Judaism, plenty of anti-Semites in the larger gay community. I was nonetheless alive and free, in my generation. But I was not procreating, not multiplying into a hopefully even more enlightened time. I chose not to have children. There's a jaunty gay T-shirt that says the family tree stops here, and that's a sober thought for childless gay and lesbian Jews. Is that a "posthumous victory for Hitler," to use philosopher Emil Fackenheim's phrase? Or is my thriving membership in *two* of Hitler's scorned tribes the last word in revenge?

During the High Holidays this year, I had a long talk on the phone with my mother, and heard myself say, "I chose to perpetuate the culture, not the family tree."

My Washington, D.C., is, was, and forever shall be shaped by the contributions of proud, out Jewish dykes. This is where Judy Dlugacz conceived the idea for Olivia Records (the women's music soundtrack of my coming-out years). This is where Evelyn Torton Beck teaches—she who compiled and edited the groundbreaking 1982 book *Nice Jewish Girls: A Lesbian Anthology*. This is the home of Joan Biren (JEB), whose photographs (and, later, videos) of lesbian images created the visuals reflecting our real lives. This is where Amy Horowitz and Roadwork began producing Sisterfire, the D.C. women's music festival. These women—not too much older than myself—were distant role models, awe-inspiring "elders," whose lives eventually crossed with mine: *Blessed are the role models.*

I would not have believed it, though, as a raw gay teenager in 1980, if some fortune-teller had shown me the crystal ball and said: You will teach a guest class for Evi, you will work on one of Judy's Olivia cruises, you will appear in one of JEB's videos, you will network with Amy for your own book on festival culture. Probably the butchest thing I ever did was to hail a cab for Jewish dyke entertainer Maxine Feldman, also a friend now, when she came to D.C. for the recent photography exhibit honoring JEB's career.

The daughter of an intermarriage, I grew up thinking both Jewish culture and non-Jews' respect for Jews' contributions to society were *normal*, since I worshiped my parents, whose lives and endless love affair embodied these concepts. When we moved to the D.C. area, we understood that the Beltway basically connected Jewish Montgomery County with Jewish Baltimore. My brother and I attended an affluent suburban high school top-heavy with Jews; in Montgomery County it was normal to have the Jewish holidays off. I went to a very Jewish college in D.C., the American University, taking my junior year abroad to study Judaism in Israel; I earned my Ph.D. at a very Jewish "public Ivy" in upstate New York, Binghamton University, where I wrote my dissertation on feminist approaches to the study of Hasidic women. After leaving grad school I founded the Jewish women's program at the Michigan Womyn's Music Festival, did a one-woman play about being the daughter of intermarriage, taught the first-ever graduate seminar on Hasidic women at Harvard, then returned to D.C. to teach at the other very Jewish school, George Washington University. The first and only guy I ever slept with was the Jewish son of a Holocaust survivor; the first girl I made love with was a nice Jewish girl from Baltimore, also the child of an intermarriage; she became a second daughter to my mom. My students and my friends include huge numbers of Jewish feminist/lesbian activists.

Yet, for all this—for all my life, my mind, body, family history, love life, books, and dreams—we are a tiny minority. Less than one—that is, less than one percent of the American population. Un-Christian, hated, feared

If I came of age in suburban Jewish subculture, then studied in urban but Jewish institutions, moving to D.C. as an older gay grown-up and living across the street from the Christian Coalition's hotel convention reminded me: *less than one.*

Remember that much of D.C. is a black Christian church town, bristling, voting rights, in the shadow of a paternalistic white Christian government, with white congressmen heading home at day's end to even more Christian Virginia, just across the Potomac. There is black-Jewish conflict and gay-Christian conflict, resentment of Montgomery County's better schools, Nation of Islam rants against Jews on D.C.'s primarily black campuses (Howard, UDC), and a gay synagogue, Beth Mishpachah, that has to meet in a church for

High Holiday services (with crucifixes hanging over the Torah and shofar). What I eat and how I talk and where I fit into the nation's capital is built on a lifetime of assuming Jewish reality; but on my block in the hippest part of town I've seen angry guys waving signs saying abortion and AIDS are both plots against black babies, led by Jewish doctors. At the Capitol South Metro stop, newsstands sell *The American Spectator,* with its anti-Semitic rants. Or consider the following chunks of dailiness:

Visitor's logbook, the Holocaust Museum: The first entry I turn to reads, "What a sad legacy. It's proof that we will only be united when Our Savior the Lord Jesus Christ returns."

Woman sitting in my apartment lobby, to her friend, as I pass by: "This was a Christian country until the devil took hold."

Cashier at the Safeway on 17th Street, the gayest block in town: "What *is* this? Matzy-ball soup? *Can we have a price check on matzy-ball soup?* I never heard of such a thing. Who eats this?"

The Promise Keepers come to D.C. for a giant convention on the Mall. I have to take Metro that day and end up crammed into a subway car where I'm the only person not going downtown to the prayer rally. I'm also the only woman in the car. I'm also the only Jew. I'm also the only homosexual. Sweat breaks out under my arms. These are nice guys, but they're here to take back the male-dominant role in the traditional family in the name of Christ. Me? *I live here.* And I'm also a nice guy.

Kensington, Maryland, a wealthy D.C. suburb, is in an uproar during Christmas season 2001—some Jewish families have objected to the township's plans for an elaborate Christmas-Santa display. Santas pour into Kensington from across the country as an angry, incredulous media picks up the story, and soon scary people show up with handmade signs: CAN'T WE BAN THE JEWS?

When I go to the D.C. Jewish Community Center to hear a panel of lesbian rabbis speak, I'm asked for identification and have to sign in with security. The event, the JCC, all of us—targets.

Standing in line at Starbucks, Dupont Circle, the heart of gay D.C., I overhear two men behind me discuss the plight of Bosnian and Albanian refugees: "Have we really done *one thing* to reach out to those people?" the first man demands, in anguished tones. His companion then gives a learned explanation of the difficulties in refugee work: "Well, but there are the Serbian Orthodox, the Bosnian Muslims, the Croatian Catholics, the Albanian communists, the Gypsy/Roman clans," he sighs. I'm poised to join this sophisticated dialogue when, suddenly, the two men relax into big, conspiratorial smiles and conclude: "Of course, it doesn't really matter. In the long run, we'll bring 'em all to Jesus."

There's no question that the "millennium" (2,000-plus years since the birth of Jesus, and even my diploma in Jewish studies is stamped Anno Domini) has been rough for progressive Jews in D.C. A new U.S. president set the inaugural mood with state-sponsored benedictions in the name of Christ, then appointed an attorney general infamous for his evangelical beliefs. Born-again lobbyists and pundits ranging from David Duke to Pat Buchanan to Paul Weyrich freely declare America to be a Christian nation and lick their chops in anticipation of government funding for "faith-based" social programs. For most of my Jewish feminist cohorts, relocating to Israel is not a solution we'd choose or recommend, and we watch in helpless frustration as a different sort of religious government, obsessed with turf and population numbers, wages war on Palestinian autonomy. At various peace demonstrations in D.C., liberal activists are eager to confront and condemn American Jews, whom they see as monolithically complicit with genocide for avowing Israel's existence. But these same folks don't always want to hear how panicky the powerful Christian lobby makes Jews feel.

Though my Washington is a city packed with educated talking heads, I rarely hear anyone use airtime to confront the new Christian supremacy. Every denomination competes daily for my soul. Walking to my job as a professor at George Washington University, I'm handed conversion literature by Mormons, "ex-gay" ministries, Jews for Jesus, and Scientologists.

Of course, I also teach at (Jesuit) Georgetown University, an institution doing a good bit of soul-searching of its own

(Hanukkah menorahs smashed two years in a row) on whether to follow the new Vatican directive that most hired faculty should be practicing Catholics. Assigned to serve bacon during Georgetown's faculty-student "midnight breakfast" last December, a culinary irony I appreciated, I reeled as a student cramming for next day's theology final raced up to ask, "You're all Christians, right?" And without consulting me, my colleagues told him, "Yes, we all are."

During the six years I've lived on Connecticut Avenue, Jewish food began to vanish from the neighborhood. Sutton Place Gourmet, where I once bought my challah, turned into a Xando coffeehouse. The bagel place next to the Janus movie theater became a Comfort Zone shoe store. Market Day, where I bought measured ounces of smoked whitefish to eat on the train to New York when I commuted to a Jewish girlfriend on Long Island, is now an Italian deli. Safeway still sells Shabbos candles off a shelf in the back, but sometimes I jump in the car and head out to the Giant grocery of my Bethesda adolescence: an entire Passover section, endless challah, endless Jewish women like my mom, a store where everybody knew my mother's name and the fruit grocer once called out to her with love and affection, "Myra, we got some of your 'hometown' oranges today," meaning, Jaffa oranges. From Israel.

My pal Noa and I sit together at an open-mike poetry slam, trade sexual Jewish puns, call ourselves Burning Bush and Chanukah Bush. She's just returned from a ski trip in Austria and scribbles in my journal, "I had a lovely time skiing in Osterreich—defying the obvious, stark lack of Judaica in the area." Noa and I are separated by seventeen years, almost a generation, but we share the Jewish lesbian instinct for assessing situations and writing ourselves into them as though we have a right to shape hegemony. She tells me, "At dinner one night I didn't realize my chai was hanging out of my shirt...got some stares. How can you tell the difference between stares and a dead look in the eye?"

What we share—what everyone in my extended Jewish dyke posse understands—is that odd experience of being *really attracted* to a non-Jewish woman who at some point in the relationship (courtship, dating, drunken one-night stand) says something so *stupid* about Jews and Jewish culture that it ruins everything. Just completely wilts your hard-on. (What's the lesbian-feminist parallel to losing one's erection? It's such a vivid analogy that I can't resist.) I who go merrily back and forth between Jewish and non-Jewish lovers, as befits my odd heritage as daughter of a Jewish mother and gentile dad, can make my own list of deflating moments:

- Girlfriend lights cigar off my Shabbos candle.
- Girlfriend says "Do you think there's a *reason* the Jews are so unpopular?"
- Girlfriend calls another woman's clothes/hair/makeup "JAPPY."
- Girlfriend calls me a "princess" (and she doesn't mean like Princess Di).
- Girlfriend says, "I'm so sick of hearing about the Holocaust."
- (Black) girlfriend tells me, "Jews are oppressors."

In contrast, when a Jewish woman speaks Yiddish to me in bed, I come instantly. If a dyke has a nice long stereotypical Jewish nose, I'm ready to get married. While I'm prudent about disclosing my personal love life in front of my classes, I'm hugely aware of being a Jewish *feminist* in front of my classes. My GWU students are, disproportionately, young Jewish women finding their way in D.C.— as I was. As I did. Far from their own Jewish mothers, they aspire to government internships where they may end up serving senators totally immune to Yiddish humor. They quickly learn to act "professional" (i.e., gentile). Anorexia and bulimia are now epidemic amongst my Jewish students; how did these sweet young women lose that link to fat-based dairy delicacies, come to see sour cream, cream cheese, blintzes, latkes, macaroons, kugel, as bad things, a heritage to *purge*? For one thing, Calista Flockhart, Gwyneth Paltrow, and Britney Spears aren't Jews. Hollywood still serves up Jewish women as overly busty clowns—Roseanne, Bette Midler in the old days, Fran Drescher. The best-known nice Jewish girl to fulfill her ambitions as a political intern was Monica Lewinsky: both stylish *and* clown *and* warning bell: Oy, don't shame the tribe! And so, fearful of failing, of taking up space, my students starve themselves.

The point is, if you're young and gay, you always have other role models, as I found in D.C. in those otherwise difficult Reagan years. Gay role models—until Ellen DeGeneres—never looked or acted "Hollywood." Barney Frank, Capitol Hill's best known and most effective out gay Jew, is no pretty boy—he's only a godsend to progressives. Moses allegedly had a lisp too: "I am slow of speech."

The Jewish obligation of *tikkun olam,* repairing the world, has inspired many Jews to be leaders in social activism, in huge proportion to their numbers in the U.S. population. Look at second-wave feminism: Who was testifying on Capitol Hill? Betty Friedan, Gloria Steinem, Bella Abzug, Elizabeth Holtzman. Who taught my undergraduate feminist studies classes at American U? Roberta Rubinstein, Muriel Cantor, Myra Sadker, Pam Nadell, Rabbi Mindy Portnoy. Who were we reading? Dorothy Dinnerstein, Ellen Levine, Shulamith Firestone, Cynthia Ozick, Grace Paley, Rosabeth Moss Kantor, Vivian Gornick, Barbara Bergmann (who lived around the corner from my parents), Roslyn Rosenberg, Emma Goldman, Naomi Weisstein, and, eventually, Alice Kessler-Harris, who became my teacher.

In my college years there was no *debate* over the role of smart Jewish feminists in shaping history. There was a role model for everyone. The question was how many honors to pursue, which graduate program to apply for. Except that in all my studies, from undergraduate through grad school, no one ever introduced the history and contributions of *lesbians,* Jewish or otherwise.

That education, that cultural literacy, I had to pursue on my own, off campus and in libraries, in women's bookstores, at women's music festivals, in the truly "separate spheres" of D.C. and beyond. I found—surprise!—that the lesbian cultural movement and its scholarship had also been led by Jews: Karla Jay, Joan Nestle and Deb Edel (who founded the Lesbian Herstory Archives), Lillian Faderman, Alix Dobkin, Robin Tyler, and Maxine Feldman. Much later, the emerging transgender movement was likewise sparked by feisty Jew Leslie Feinberg and hir groundbreaking novel *Stone Butch Blues*.

Yet these role models were not presented to me as such in the classroom, even all the way through a very good Ph.D. program. So now I teach *my* classes wearing a Jewish star with a black triangle overlaid on silver—the symbol for lesbians who were sent to Hitler's death camps. My students know me—all of me—in what role modeling I present. This has been no problem even at Georgetown (where the women's studies department is chaired by loud and proud Jewish dyke Suzanna Walters). But working in academic D.C., as a writer surrounded by politicians and movers and shakers in positions of real power, I keep my eye on the Christian right—wondering, wondering if one percent will be enough to stem their tide. Fact is, no amount of education about centuries of church-based anti-Semitism and state pogroms seem to curb evangelicals' creed that it is loving kindness to convert Jews. Such conversion would supposedly grant us everlasting life, though diminishing yet further the population of living Jews. Jews don't seek to convert gentiles, so there are all kinds of imbalances right off the bat when we all sit down at faith-based roundtables for idealistic, ecumenical chitchat. Unless you accept Jesus as your personal savior, you'll never be a moral equal in a fundamentalist's eyes, whether you're an unbaptized Nobel Prize winner, a rabbi, or a Native American tribal chieftain. You can forget about pluralism and diversity if the Christian right takes power, because most of us won't measure up to their biblical standards. Though often leery of "one-world government," occasionally insistent that Zionist bankers control global destiny, fundamentalists seek to make the entire world one flavor of *their* theology and practice. (This is also becoming tragically apparent in Islamic fundamentalism, which of course offers its own hatred of Jews and homosexuals.)

How am I entitled to issue this warning, that the Christian right is bent on nothing less than an American theocracy? Because I've infiltrated some of their conventions.

Living in D.C., we all bitch and moan about the federal government, with our multivarious complaints: laws that are sexist, racist, and homophobic. But how to complain about the creeping author-ization of the larger percentage's Lord without seeming ungra-cious? Whatever credibility I have as a concerned Jew is compro-mised by my identity as an out lesbian, at least as some would see it—including many Jews. What can I do? Am I doing enough? "If I am not for myself, who will be for me?" cried Hillel.

In her great stand-up show, "In the Beginning," Ellen DeGeneres parodies the media frenzy that accompanied her coming-out and talks honestly about overcoming her need for approval. "It's an addic-tion. I'm on the patch now," she jokes, but the gay audience gets it. Noble activists we may be, with a legacy of role models we each dis-covered and claimed in our own secret self-educations, but no mat-ter how many awards, good jobs, cute kids, university appointments, science grants we pile up, we read in the paper *every day* that our kind is loathed, that this state or that just voted to ban gay marriage or gay adoption. The Catholic Church and the Mormon Church have invested the most money in defeating gay rights initiatives, making gay oppression both state and Christian business. The lack of "approval" is writ large in our lost custody, our unrecognized civil unions. And so much of this flows from Washington.

I love it here. And I am loved. The whole Jewish thing, the les-bian quest for tolerance, the energy of Jewish dykes who built a world I walk in, here and now—I live within this beautiful tension, this friction from all sides. My students pay big tuition bucks for a good political education here, inside the Beltway.

And I make sure they get it: the honors and ironies I had to hunt for: that "America the Beautiful" was written by a lesbian, that GWU itself hosted the first Jewish lesbian comedy night in D.C., 1982, the year my students were born.

"I did not die, but lived long enough for other stories to fill up my days and nights. It's terrible how much has been forgotten, which is why, I suppose, remembering seems a holy thing."

—Anita Diamant, *The Red Tent*

Stories From Our Lives

She Koogled Me?
Tania Katan

It started with a lump. It always starts with a lump. No, actually it started with a girlfriend who found the lump. Wait. It started before the lump, before the idea of having girlfriends even entered my mind; it started five years earlier when I was sixteen years old. See, my oncologist told me that by the time you find cancer it's been growing for at least five years.

The Breast Clinic. A clinical setting or…a lesbian mixer? As a lesbian and optimist, I choose the latter. I'm here to get a little lump checked out. I'm a bit nervous. I didn't anticipate being nervous—it's not my first trip to the Breast Clinic—and when I'm nervous I tend to pretend I'm somebody else, somebody less nervous than me, like a politician, or a therapist or a…rock star. Today I'm a rock star. I sign in while verbally asserting my presence, "What up? I'm Tania Katan." It's working. I feel infinitely more calm. Maria, the hot young receptionist, looks at me like she wants to hump me, or she has something stuck in her throat. According to the pastel yellow sticky note with my name on it next to her computer, I'm a VIP at the Breast Clinic. My breast cancer survivor status has kicked me up to platinum level. Maria, my groupie, hands me a clipboard's worth of paper and instructs me to "Fill out all the forms and then I'll take you back…stage, Miss Katan."

She blushes and turns away.

Name: Tania Katan
Age: 30
Date of Birth: 9/28/71
(Other info, such as address and phone numbers have been omitted due to the high volume of groupies trying to get a piece of me.)
Sexually active: extremely
Form of birth control: lesbian sex
Have you ever had a mammogram? yes
Have you ever had an ultrasound? yes
Have you ever had breast cancer? yes
If "yes," at what age? 21
Did you have surgery? Yes, a modified radical mastectomy. Buh-bye, right booby. Hello, six months of chemotherapy.
If "yes," did you have reconstructive surgery? No, I opted for tattoo surgery performed by Stag, the Venice Beach artist who dons a pop-top tattoo on top of his bald head. Blue Shield didn't cover that.
List any prior surgeries (and at what age): Removal of a nine-centimeter fibroid tumor attached to my uterus. Age: 23
Why are you here today? I found a lump in my remaining breast.

Maria leads me to my dressing room. The walls are a mosaic of mirrors stained with red wine and cocaine. She licks her glossy pink lips and asks me to take off everything from the waist up. She tosses me a flimsy, obviously Mizrahi vest to put on. Wait, this whole rock star thing isn't working. I'm not a rock star. Even in tight leather pants and a chunky silver chain, I'm still a nerdy Jewish lesbian with one breast, you know? And right now, as I'm surrounded by the smell of disinfected medical equipment, the reason I'm here feels very real. I wrap the paper vest around my cold and anxious upper body. I pull back the curtain. There is no audience waiting for me.

The first event in the Early Detection Decathlon is the Mammogram. The nurse conducting the mammogram seems sweet, sort of nondescript, like someone else's mom, not ugly or unattractive but definitely not someone you'd think about having sex with unless you were on a reality show or forced to wait a long time in a doctor's office. Nurse Someone's Mom asks me to disrobe.

"Great tattoo. Keith Haring, right?" she says in response to the tiny colorful dancing men in place of my right breast. She read my chart. You can always tell when they know your history because they compliment you. A lot.

"Great glasses! Where did you get them? Look at your earrings! Do you have anything else pierced? You're just...fun!"

I'm positioned in front of the sci-fi machine as Nurse Someone's Mom pulls on my A-size booby. Like someone who works with taffy, she stretches and folds until it lies just right on the cool flat surface. She runs behind the curtain and gently yells, "Hold it...hold it," as she flips a switch that activates the Booby-Smusher-Downer, which in turn sends a signal to the Intense Atomic Ray, which then radiates through my booby. We are successful. We have imaging. It's time for the next event at the Early Detection Decathlon: the Ultrasound.

I lie on the table that's barely large enough to accommodate one of my butt cheeks, let alone two. I love Ben & Jerry's. Dr. Comack comes in; he's very kind, kind of young, and maybe queer, like Richard Chamberlain in *The Thorn Birds*.

Nurse Someone's Mom quickly places a round rubber disc on the Ultrasound Wand. She's rolling it down when I realize what IT is—a condom! Where am I? And when Nurse Someone's Mom squeezes a mountain of lube on the condom-clad wand, I know where I am: on the set of this hot new lesbo porno, *The Magic Wand*. I'm the star awaiting my first scene. The nurse is, in fact, the fluff girl and the doctor is the lascivious director. The nurse is just about to show me a "magic trick," when the slap of the cold, slimy wand, winding around my breast snaps me back to the Breast Clinic. The three of us stare at the screen like it's Must-See TV.

"Okay, see that? It appears to be..." Dr. Chamberlain leans into the screen. "A junky cyst."

A what? "What's a junky cyst?"

"A benign cyst that's filled with fluid. Nothing to worry about."

A junky cyst, huh? I kinda like the sound of that, like my cyst wears a beret, smokes colorful European cigarettes, and shoots up heroin for fun. My junky cyst is intriguing, cunning, and usually running from the law. We're looking for chicks, for kicks, for our next fix, me and my junky cyst.

The Early Detection Decathlon has become a Titty Triathlon, and the final event of today's games is the Core Biopsy. Dr. Chamberlain explains this procedure to me.

"I will start the procedure by injecting your breast with one of the 'Caines': Nova, Lyda…Michael." He smirks and continues. "You're going to hear a loud noise, something akin to a gun being fired, as I shoot this tremendously large, hollowed-out, steel cylinder, which we will refer to as a *needle,* through your breast. I will shoot your breast three times." He pantomimes shooting a gun with a lot of kickback. "A nice cross section of your mass, which means chunks of bloody and fibrous tissue, will be gathered. You won't feel a thing, assuming we gave you enough anesthetic." He laughs. "You may experience some discomfort, light bleeding, intense fever, excessive bleeding, light bruising, horrible bruising, for a day or two or six. Don't shower for two days. This will take about five seconds. Ready?"

"When will I know the results?"

"We'll give you a call either Thursday or Friday. Okay, are you ready?"

In all honesty, I'm not ready, but what other options do I have?

"Yeah, I'm ready."

✡

It's two A.M. and I'm lying next to the lump that found my lump, Sharon, aware this will be the last time we sleep together. In the morning, I will break up with Sharon. The reason I'm breaking up with her is simple: Sharon is toxic. Am I thinking too loudly? How many times have I been thinking loudly in someone else's bed? I can't sleep. Why am I even here? These sheets are so stiff. Low thread count. That should have been the first Red Flag. Never date a girl with less than 300 threads. Tania, please, try to sleep. I can't sleep. Okay, just try not to think. Why did I leave San Francisco? Why am I in Long Beach, California? Why am I working at a crappy job? What if my lump is…something? How does one know when they've reached rock bottom? How long is Long Beach?

Long Beach, or Idaho by the Sea, is a mishmash of newlywed, nearly dead, quirky queens and outdated dykes, all set to the backdrop of stucco strip malls and the *Queen Mary*. I moved here from San Francisco six months ago to transition out of being a poor but produced playwright into a salaried and successful sitcom writer. I set up temporary residence at my father's more-than-humble Long Beach apartment. My writing partner, Daniele Nathanson, and I would meet twice a week trying to write the definitive *Will & Grace* spec script. We were determined to find an agent, land a job, and become amazingly wealthy before our respective cushions ran out. My cushion consisted of $4,000. My monthly bills consisted of $2,000. Although I was never good at math, I knew I had about three months to "make it." Two months into our Southern California tour, our cushions, our steam, and our connections all ran out. I took to watching television, a form of research, if you will. I mean, the last time I really watched TV was when Gilda Radner was on *Saturday Night Live,* and if I was going to write for TV, I needed to fully understand TV. Who knew TV was chock-full of crap? Why didn't anyone tell me this? I would have reconsidered the whole writing-for-TV thing. The only two channels with any artistic merit, and an obvious connection to one another, were the Food Network and the Spice Channel. For months I flipped back and forth between *Hot off the Grill* and *Hot on the Girl*. After several failed attempts at writing a *Will & Grace* spec script, in which Will fell in love with a chef and Grace fell in love with a porn star, I decided it was time to go to therapy or start dating. The latter was cheaper…initially.

✡

She's snoring. In the five months we've been together, I don't think I've ever heard Sharon snore. That pinched, tense look she usually carries between her eyes and on the sides of her nose seems to be smoothed out. She looks sweet right now. They always do that, you know, look sweet before you break up with them. Wow, I just realized this is the first time I've ever felt completely comfortable around Sharon. Two-thirty A.M. epiphany: When the only time you truly feel comfortable around your lover is when she's asleep, it's time to break up, right?

✡

Six months ago I was living in San Francisco. My five-year relationship, with a woman eleven years older than me, had ended and I was ready to start anew. San Francisco seemed like the right place for a single, twenty-seven-year-old lesbian who had always felt out of place in Arizona. All the kids from high school who had ever been ridiculed for being ugly, silly, witty, nerdy, or edgy colonized San Francisco. Wearing glasses, supporting the arts, and being disheveled was hot. I had finally found my peeps. The most important thing I found in San Francisco, however, was that attractive women found me attractive. Everywhere I went there seemed to be a cute queer girl who wanted to meet me: at a coffeehouse, in a grocery store, on the street, near a boat, next to a goat. I was in the lesbian version of a Dr. Seuss book: *One Girl, Two Girl, Three Girl, New Girl!* In San Francisco my status shifted from nerdy to sexy. I loved San Francisco.

Long Beach was a different creature, a South-Going Zax, if you will. After being a single babe in S.F. for the past three years, I was ready to scope out the Long Beach scene. I arrived in Long Beach to find that all of the cute lesbians were clearly on vacation, leaving their older, Trans Am–driving, cigarette-smoking, Alcoholics Anonymous–attending, stereotypical counterparts to hold their places at the neighborhood bar named, quite cleverly, after the street it was on, Broadway. I would not be going to Broadway unless it was to see Patti LuPone in a show. Just driving by Broadway brought back images from the Bar Scene in Arizona, complete with characters like Michelle, the faux Euro babe with the homemade accent and raspberry red lipstick who used her sex appeal to seduce naïve girls—me—dump them, seduce them again, dump them, seduce them one more time for good measure, then dump them for good. The Bar Scene also brought me random make-out sessions with stalkers, psychos, and sycophants. The Bar Scene was the dysfunctional undertow that crept below the cocktail-stained carpet, constantly trying to pull me back into its clutches. I would not be seduced by Broadway's promises of two-for-one's.

✡

Ow! Lester just bit me. I know *hate* is a strong word, and G-d will probably punish me in some theatrical way for saying this, but here it goes: I hate cats. I wish I could sleep. I wish I didn't have a lump. I wish I didn't have to break up with Sharon. I wish she had asked me some questions, or even one question. It was the questions that started it. Two months into our five-month relationship, when I emerged from the blissed-out-sex phase of our connection, I realized Sharon never asked me questions, ever. She never asked about my childhood, my goals, my bout with cancer—nothing. When someone doesn't ask you questions it can only mean one thing: They don't want to know you. Eventually I confronted Sharon about it. She told me she didn't ask questions because her parents taught her asking questions was rude and intrusive. As I'm a Jew, we had a problem.

✡

A friend of mine suggests an alternative to the Bar Scene, to take a trip to a planet far, far away: PlanetOut: a place where lesbians of all shapes and sizes can love each other in two dimensions. The love of my life was just a "Click here" away. A pop-up message informs me to "Sign up now in order to receive great personal services for as low as $9.95 a month." It seems a small price to pay for love, but I'm a broke writer in search of a day job. Can a Jew "Jew" someone down? I'm not sure that's kosher. I grab my only remaining credit card—the rest are thriving in the '90s—and optimistically enter the numbers. My entrance into the lesbian dating world is…accepted.

Snapshots of my future girlfriend appear with catchy headlines like, "Looking for HOT Bisexual PUSSY?" and "Snuggle up with this fifty-something recovering crack addict" and "I've suffered a great deal of emotional trauma, but now I'm ready for fun!" I click "next" so fast and furiously that I almost bypass the butch girl with the spiky hair and cool glasses whose headline reads, "Semantics"—right now I think "Semantics" is a succinct way of saying, "I'm smart," but later I'll learn it was a Red Flag waving: "You can expect a life time of arguments and clarification if you pick PlanetOut girl #55."

She's a lesbian into Middle Eastern food and foreign films who lives within a ten-mile radius. Perfect. I shoot off an extremely clever e-mail—I'm certain—and wait for her response. After 2.5 days of checking my email every 8.5 minutes to no avail, I hear the mellifluous cries of the Bar Scene Siren beckoning me to, "Come back to earth, Tania. You can't meet a girl in cyberspace. Come to Broadway. One-dollar well drinks and all the cute girls in Long Beach will be here. Come, come, come, come, milady. Sugar pie honey. I'll make your knees weak... You make me go crazy."

✡

Broadway. The cocktails are priced according to size, and for one dollar I get a Dixie Cup cosmopolitan. It is a tasty hors d'oeuvre before the main course of three Dixie Cup cosmopolitans, and by that time I'm too drunk to realize I paid four dollars for one regular-size drink, so I have another and head over to the pool table.

You become an instant superstar when you're running it, you lean on it when you're drunk, and you hide underneath it when your ex enters the bar. The pool table. Stability in an unstable environment. My father taught me how to play pool the summer I came out to him; I was nineteen years old and he lived next to a gay bar. At the Crowbar, with sailors and naval officers as onlookers, my dad showed me how to chalk, break, stroke, masse, and jump my way into coming out on top. As we would leave the Crowbar victorious, my father's hand around my shoulder, the older guys would give my dad a sort of thumbs-up nod.

"What's that about?" my dad would ask.

"They think I'm your boy, Daddy. You're like the king of NAMBLA around here. I'm hot property."

Once at the pool table, barely able to stand, I chalk my cue, shake my opponent's hand, and proceed to kick her astonished ass. My daddy taught me well. Six opponents down, eight cosmopolitans down—which is really like two regular-size drinks—I wind down and watch as the two cutest girls in all of Long Beach walk into the bar and sit near me: Carrie and Sharon. Carrie is a girly-girl: lipstick, midriff, and seductive smirk. Sharon is barely a girl: retro boy's glasses, faded Hot Wheels T-shirt, and a hyphen for a mouth. I approach them with all the confidence of a fraternity guy at a high school party.

"Hi, how are you girls doing?" I slide into their booth, because if I don't sit down I might fall over. Carrie, my aesthetic ideal, is the first to respond.

"Great, now that you're here."

I let out an audible gulp.

The other girl, Sharon, seems a bit tentative. "Fine," she says.

I'm immediately attracted to Carrie, whose honey-brown hair seems to oscillate whenever she looks at me.

"You girls look too cool to be from Long Beach. Where are you from?" I ask.

"San Francisco." Carrie says. I am in love with Carrie.

"Me too! What part?"

"Noe Valley."

"I love Noe Valley!" We have so much in common already.

"I'm from Long Beach." Sharon says with an impish grin.

"I know you live in Long Beach, but you weren't born and raised here? I mean, no one's really from Long Beach, right?"

"Yeah, actually I am," she says, again sporting a sneaky smile.

I'm not sure if Sharon has a nervous facial tic or if she's a touch "special." For the next twenty minutes Carrie and I play out a scene from a lesbian romance movie: We discuss early childhood trauma in slow motion, we laugh spontaneously while feigning falling off of our chairs, we talk about past lovers and all of *their* issues; we are falling in love.

Sharon finally says something. "You know, you responded to my personal ad on PlanetOut."

What? This was the butch girl into foreign films and hummus?

"How come you didn't mention that when I first sat down?"

"Sorry. I thought it was kind of fun that I knew and you didn't." Sharon smiles, finally coming to life. I'm feeling a little exposed, but she intrigues me. Here's a girl who appears to be completely removed from the conversation, when in fact she's hyperaware, totally engaged, a bit sneaky, but definitely present. I like that. There's something to this Sharon, some substance. My focus shifts from Carrie and our easy banter to Sharon and her intrinsic mystery.

✡

Sharon is still snoring, Lester is still biting, and I'm still unable to sleep. Doomed to repeat the story of how I got here over and over in my head until the alarm goes off in about three hours, and I'll turn to her and say, "Good morning. I'm breaking up with you. Do you want some coffee?" Why does hindsight always beat foresight to the punch? If you listen, people will tell you exactly who they are and how they'll handle situations within the first few hours of meeting them. The difficulty comes when we don't listen, when we see a Red Flag waving and choose to view it as a decorative banner rather than a giant foreboding gesture. Red Flag #1— was waved during month one of our five-month relationship, in the form of an e-mail.

She Koogled Me?

E-mail to: Sharon
Subject: Hey, Super Cutie!
Sharon—can't wait to have coffee with you Saturday. Do you mind if my friend Julia comes? I'd like for you guys to meet, since I adore both of you. Hope you're having an amazing day!
xo,
Tania

E-mail to: Tania
Subject: I'm going to count to ten…
I thought just YOU and I were going to have coffee. What's up with inviting Julia? I'm going to count to ten, 'cuz I'm really pissed. Call me.
Sharon

I took note of the Red Flag, but I also knew I was ready to be in a relationship—and there's nothing more powerful than being ready.

Sharon e-mailed me the minute she got home from the bar:

Email to: Tania
Subject: I wouldn't give Carrie your e-mail address…
because I wanted it all for myself! Sorry I didn't return your PlanetOut message sooner…didn't realize you were so cute in real life. Can I take you out to dinner sometime?
Cheers,
Sharon

I e-mailed her back the next day:

Email To: Sharon
Subject: I'm a cheap date sexually…
but when it comes to a culinary encounter, I can be very expensive! Dinner sounds great. How about Saturday? Let me know.
Take care,
Tania

✡

Saturday night arrives, and Sharon shows up at my door carrying flowers. *She* brought *me* flowers. As a rather androgynous woman who has historically been attracted to girly-girls, I have fallen into the role of the Boy (different from the Boy of my pool-playing days with Daddy at the Crowbar. Being gay is complicated), which means paying for things, making reservations, and buying flowers. It takes a lot of energy to be the Boy. I don't know how real boys do it. Sharon's chivalry is not lost on me. I love it. Not since Dawn have I encountered a butch girl who wanted to help with dating duties. Sharon leads me to her car, and when I ask her where she wants to go for dinner, she confidently responds, "I've already taken care of it."

✡

I've given up on the idea of sleeping altogether. I'm obsessed with the Red Flags that make up the fabric of our relationship, like Red Flag #2: Sharon conceals information. Red Flag #3: She prefers *not* talking to talking. Red Flag #4: Sharon's intimacy policy: Don't let anyone in, because when they leave, which they *always* do, you won't get hurt. Red Flag #5: Her father is insane. Red Flag #6: She believes Armageddon is coming in 2005, so she's a bit tentative about making long-term plans. Red Flag #7: I'm the first Jewish person she has ever met. Red Flag #8: She's a devout Catholic. Red Flag #9: She calls herself a drummer but never actually drums. Red Flag #10: the gifts.

✡

Sharon is a focused driver—so focused, in fact, that when I casually ask her the usual getting-to-know-you questions—Do you have siblings? Any dietary restrictions? Have you been to therapy?—she answers in a quick, stiff manner, "Two, no, and definitely not." At least we won't get into a car accident.

The restaurant is an homage to the '80s set directly on the beach. Nagel prints displaying girls with names like Rio and Hungry adorn the walls in this odd '80s Disneyland. When a gay guy in a Hawaiian shirt seats us, I'm not sure why Sharon brought me here. Didn't I mention that I'm an expensive culinary date? I look down at the menu to find the most incongruous cuisine: filet mignon and potatoes au gratin—twenty-three dollars; chicken stuffed with spinach and cheese—eighteen dollars. It goes on. That's why gay restaurants never seem to make it; they can't get the camp-to-cuisine ratio figured out. I easily decide on the lamb (sorry, vegetarian sisters), while Sharon selects the chicken. We settle into our spaces, but Sharon still isn't engaging in conversation.

"So how do you know about this restaurant?" I try to spark something.

"I've been here before."

"Oh, is this where you bring all of your dates?" I'm joking, of course.

"No." Sharon is not joking.

"Sorry, I didn't mean to…"

"I'm sorry. I'm just a little nervous."

We drink. Drinking is a good first-date activity. Sharon begins to loosen up as a result of too much alcohol and first-date adrenaline. Her pale Irish face becomes flush as she allows herself to talk. I mean, really talk. I can't get her to shut up. Don't get me wrong, I love it. It's actually in this moment, of Sharon's effortless verbal eruption, that I decide it would be all right for us to kiss at the end of the date, and if she's so inclined to feel me up, that would be all right too, but that means…the Speech. Which one should I use tonight? How about the organic one? *Sharon, if you try to touch my breasts, which I strongly encourage, you will find that I do not, in fact, have a right breast. The one on the left, however, is in great repair and really loves being touched!* Then I segue into the after-school-special version of *Why Tania Doesn't Have a Booby.* Or I could go with the surprised speech. *WHAT? No breast? Are you sure? Shit! I've got to go.* There's always the McDonald's explanation. *Yeah, see, I ordered a cup of coffee at McDonald's, and you know how hot their coffee is..well, it spilled and…it burned right off!* I wait for Sharon to provide me with the perfect segue.

"And I said, 'I'm sorry, but I can't, sir.' And the guy says…"

Thank you, Sharon. "Cancer? Did you say cancer?" I ask.

"Oh, no, I said, 'can't, sir.' "

"Sorry, it sounded like cancer, which reminds me of a story that goes a little something like this: When I was twenty-one years old, I…"

Sharon interrupts me.

"Look, Tania, I have to confess something…I Googled you."

"You Googled me?" Google? Oh my G-d, she's trying to relate to me in Jewish terms! That's so sweet! "Oh, Sharon, it's koogle. You made me a koogle? With raisins?"

"No, Google, it's a search engine. When you told me you were a playwright I decided to look you up online, to Google you. I know all about the breast cancer and your plays and—"

"Why would you do that? Why wouldn't you just ask me about my playwriting? I would have told you."

Sharon clams up. She reaches into the pocket of her jacket to retrieve something. "I have a gift for you." The gift is a stick in the spoke of our conversation. An overt redirection. She hands me the tiny box. If it's a ring I will scream, then laugh, then run out of the restaurant as fast as I can.

"Thanks." I rip it open. "Wow, it's a…well, it's pink, but what is it exactly?"

"It's an angel. As a devout Catholic, I believe angels have healing powers. I don't mean to sound too out-there, but I just came back from this retreat, and when I read about you and your plays, I thought, well…everyone can use an angel. I hope I didn't offend you—I know you're Jewish. I just care about you."

I'm not offended, maybe a little freaked out. I mean, first of all you Googled me, which is duplicitous and icky, and second, how can you be a devout Catholic and a homosexual at the same time? But on the other hand, I am ready for a relationship, and how exciting to have someone take the initiative to find out about me, albeit indirectly, but still. And the gift. What a thoughtful gesture. Sure, it's an angel—I would have preferred a gift certificate to Starbucks—but you took the time to give me something that had meaning to you, and if your religion allows you the space to be open and thoughtful, then an angel is okay by me!

"Thank you for the angel, Sharon."

✡

How come I never noticed that her copy of the Dalai Lama's *A Simple Path* is covered in dust and cat scratches? At four A.M. one notices many things, like the pile of gifts she has given me in place of language and conversations that needed to occur. It started with the angel, to avoid the *Sharon, I want you to know I had breast cancer* talk; then the bottle of champagne, to eschew the *Sharon, why do you hate my loving family?* discussion; then the fancy steel commuter mug, to dodge the *Sharon, why is it that you only open up after a couple of cocktails?* remark; and finally the plastic dreidel filled with chocolate coins, to avert the *Sharon, why aren't you supportive of my writing?* declaration. As the pile has grown, I have become less interested in presents and more interested in talking, in sharing, in something that is not gift-wrapped.

✡

Sharon have been together four months and seven days, but it feels longer, and not in a good way. Today is my cousin's wedding, and Sharon is coming with me. It's her first Jewish wedding—hell, it's the bride's first Jewish wedding. My cousin is the only Jew in the equation and he's not the most religious guy, but they agreed to be married by a rabbi. When I come to pick Sharon up at the designated time, she isn't ready. Not only is she not ready, but she seems angry, and she's wearing a dress. Now, let's stop right here. Sharon might have been born a woman, but that's merely a formality. Her usual style is akin to that of an adolescent boy: grubby sneakers, baggy jeans, and oxford collars sticking out of V-neck Gap sweaters. It's most often the case that people mistake Sharon for a boy rather than a man. A dress? I address the issue with sensitivity.

"Wow. I've never seen you wear a dress before. Are you going to wear that to the wedding?" The vague anger I felt from her before feels directed now, more specifically at me.

"Why? Doesn't it look good? I like wearing dresses. I used to wear dresses all the time. Do you have a fucking problem with it, Tania?"

"No. I want you to feel comfortable. If wearing that makes you feel comfortable, then wear it. It looks great." It's hard to muster sincerity when your girlfriend looks like Arnold Schwarzenegger in a dress. She then proceeds to apply makeup. I pray quietly to G-d that she will look more like one of the boys from 'N Sync than a drag queen. She simply looks weird.

"Let's fucking go already," she says, so defiantly that her lipstick almost smears.

As soon as the rabbi announces, "You may kiss the bride," Sharon turns to me and snarls, "Can we fucking go?"

Huh? We drove fifty-five minutes to get here, we've been here only twenty-five minutes, and you want to leave already?!

"No, I'm sorry, but this is my family and I'd like to hang out with them. Is everything all right, Sharon?" Sincerely, I don't know what's going on with her.

"Jews. Everyone here is a Jew. I don't fit in. I want to fucking go." That's when I feel toxicity emanate from her body. In a few seconds I can actually see the poison oozing out from the pores on her face. The lipstick and eye shadow she took so much time to apply are being forced down her face by sweat and anger. Streaks of mascara and lipstick stream their way down to her chin and drip off like she's a human candle. I want to tell her that makeup doesn't suit her; instead I say, "We're going to stay until we're both ready to leave. I'm going to say hello to my aunts and uncles. You're welcome to join me." She sulks until I decide to leave. On the drive home I turn on NPR as loud as I can. I want to hear about conflicts that don't involve Sharon or me.

✡

Sharon has invited me over because she wants to talk about something. I'm happy to let her talk. I hope she wants to break up with me.

"What's going on?" I cut to the chase.

"Umm...I have to tell you something, but why don't you open this gift first."

"I don't want the gift—I want to know what's going on."

"Okay, open the gift, then I promise I'll tell you."

"Tell me first and then I'll open the gift."

"Well...I was thinking about the wedding last night and...the reason why I acted the way I did was...well, it's because I'm scared."

"Scared of hanging out with Jews?"

"Will you please open the gift? It will help explain."

I tear open the package to reveal...

"*Not Just One in Eight*?" This is a book that contains stories of how breast cancer survivors and their families have coped with illness. My story, as told from the twenty-five-year-old Tania Katan perspective, is in this book.

"How did you know about this book?"

"Google."

"Did Google tell you it would be more cost-effective to ask Tania Katan about the Tania Katan story?"

"Tania...I'm not sure how to say this."

"Try words."

"I'm scared you're going to get cancer again."

"Huh?"

"I'm scared you're going to get cancer again and then...and then...die. It's my biggest fear."

Whoa! Why don't you get your own fears? Why don't you give

reality-based fears a try, like dogs, heights, or guns? Why don't you read *Codependent No More*? Sharon has never asked me about my one-night stand with cancer, and whenever I bring up the subject, she disengages.

"Thank you for your concern, Sharon. I've been cancer-free for almost ten years now. I'm happy, healthy, and not about to drop dead anytime soon, so don't cancel any dinner reservations."

"I'm just concerned."

"I'm concerned too."

The Letter...and the Word
Hinde Ena Burstin

Author's Note: "The Letter...and the Word" was written in 1996, in response to a coy invitation from Generation Journal of Australian Jewish Life and Thought. *It is believed to be the first time that a Jewish journal in Melbourne, Australia, had solicited and published lesbian content, and many were surprised I chose not to hide behind the "complete anonymity" that the editor offered. "The Letter...and the Word" now reads as a herstorical piece, offering insight into how much change we have brought about in a short time.*

The letter's in the mail. It didn't arrive at my work today, although I ran to the letterbox to check five times. I guess it will arrive on Monday, which means I may not be the first one to open it. I hope I won't get into trouble.

I know the letter is coming because she rang for my address. I've never met her, though the name is familiar. She told me she was sending an invitation to write something for her journal. I asked her what about. She said it was for an issue on man/woman. I wondered whether she thought I could write on men.

Then she added, "Maybe your partner could write something too." My partner publishes on acetylcholinesterase. Chuckling, I wondered if that was what she wanted. I wasn't even sure if she knew who my partner was. So I asked, "Who recommended me?" Her reply told me she knew.

Euphemism. It was all left so unsaid. She did not name me over the phone. I wonder whether she will. I spent the day checking the letterbox, because I wanted to see how she'd worded her letter. Had she said the word? Or had she just alluded to it?

Did she expect me to just allude to it, to dance around the flame but never touch it? Allusion—it's such an illusion. Will it shatter?

Does it matter? I'm wondering already what I should write.

Should I describe how it feels to be always alluding, never saying, never spelling it out, always wondering who knows, who's wondering, and what will happen if it is all out in the open? If I tell her, "Imagine having to drop the word 'Jew' from your vocabulary, to describe it but never say it," will she understand?

Or should I talk of Jewish pride, of being raised never to be ashamed of who I am, never to allow injustices to be rained upon me because of being a Jew. Will she understand if I say that is rooted deep inside me, so that I will not allow another to make me ashamed of anything that I am.

Oh, she said it was about relationships. So should I tell her that no matter how many men I tried, they didn't cut it with me? Should I tell her that the first time I explored a woman's body, I finally understood what aliyah meant? I felt like I was coming home to the Promised Land. And it was flowing with milk and honey.

Should I mention, in passing, that there's no law of return that shuts me out of my promised land? And no part occupied without consent?

Perhaps I should talk about love, how it feels to catch those dark Jewish eyes smiling at me, to watch those soft Jewish lips shaping lush Yiddish words. About how sweet it is to share my life with a Jewish woman, this Jewish woman.

Perhaps she wants to know how I got here. Maybe I should describe the feeling, like trying to unstick bubble gum, of trying to break free. Should I depict the aching loneliness when I was the only one I knew? Should I tell of the strength, the courage, the sheer guts it took to be what I had not been taught to be. What I had been taught not to be.

Maybe I should mention the things people say. Like the time recently when someone said, "I'm very private. The thing about coming out is that people know what you do in bed." I wondered why she thought she knew what I did in bed, when she hadn't been there. And did she worry that people knew what she'd done when she was pregnant? And did she know it wasn't just about beds? After all, is she a Jew just in shul?

Perhaps I should write about another time recently, when a man said "Jewess. The word makes you think of men raping and pillaging." I was confused. "Jewess" rolls off my tongue deliciously. When I think of Jewess, I think of beautiful women, round like eggplants, succulent, bold, with a bit of a bite. I laughed, "No, it doesn't make me think of that at all. But then, we move in different worlds."

Maybe I should tell her about *tsouris*. Like two balabostes in the kitchen, each swearing her latke recipe is the greatest. Or premenstrual tension twice a month. Or being expected to live as if we are straight without any straight privileges. Should I tell of the fear of losing my work, my home, my safety because of who I am? Will she understand if I tell her of being hated, called unnatural, silenced?

Would she feel for me, if I told of the heartache of not having the words to name myself to my Booba, in her language, my language? The frustration of discovering the dictionary had not translated me. Should I try to describe how it felt to have had to travel a day and a night by plane just to find someone who dared to name me, in my mother tongue and out loud? Could I capture how it feels now be able to hear myself named that way in my home and in the world outside my door?

I don't know what to write for her. I don't know yet what she expects. I only know she has asked me to write for an issue on woman/man. Whoops, man/woman.

I gather she doesn't want me to write about man. I wouldn't know what to write on that topic. I do know I don't hate men the way that women who have to live with them do. But what else could I say?

So, I guess she'll want me to write about woman. And about woman, I could tell her a story or two. But I'm not sure what she wants to hear. I won't know until the letter gets here.

So I guess I'll spend the weekend wondering, did she skirt around the edges, did she phrase things oh-so delicately?

Or did she dare to say the word…"lesbian."

The Chutzpah
Faith Soloway

Though I'm Jewish, I'm not what you would call a "practicing Jew." And while I've been in a committed lesbian relationship for eleven years—complete with toddler and mortgage—I'm not what you would call a practicing lesbian. I guess that's why I have an artistic life—so I can ditch my nonconfrontational stance for my raunchy stage personality and jump up and down manically on stage yelling "Look at me look at me! I'm a Jewish lesbian!."

Okay, so I don't literally do that, but I'm somewhat known in Boston as the lil Jewish lesbo who could do that. I write, direct, and star in my version of rock operas—"schlock operas," I call them. I'm a real pioneer all right, a real button-pusher too. Yup, that's me—keep 'em laughing and squirming at the same time. Put a real message in there, somewhere under all the bawdy musical stuff so they have something that sticks in their craw a little. Thanks to my latest show, *Jesus Has Two Mommies,* I have a fairly large Christian group sticking in my craw. They're not laughing or digging my message either. My guess is they don't appreciate the title of the show. Yes, the American Society for the Defense of Tradition, Family, and Property (uh, I don't get the property part) is planning a protest the likes of which hasn't been seen since *The Last Temptation of Christ* (At least that's what they're promising on their Web site.) Oy. Now I'm forced to reconcile my off- and onstage personae by defending my Jewish lesbian position to the Boston press. I didn't know I had one. Maybe I can whip up some sort of saucy sound bite: "Think of it as a Nativity scene done up in flannel and Birkenstocks." Any angry Christians laughing yet?

I can be cavalier on the outside, but on the inside I'm trembling. This is the first time I've been called to task about my material. I feel so utterly underprepared to defend myself or my religion. I don't even know my own people's story very well—where do I get off retelling the greatest gentile story ever told? The chutzpah. When I started writing this show I called on my Christian friends, some actual divinity school graduates, to set me straight on all things Christian. Though I was aiming to take a few liberties, I still needed to get the basic Nativity idea down. Now I even know my apostles from my saints. Wait, aren't they the same thing?

It's not like I should be surprised that certain people are upset with the title of the show. If I were to be one hundred percent honest, I'd say I asked for this. It's also not the first time I've had a controversial show title. Try inviting your relatives to *The Miss Vagina Pageant* and you'll have some idea of what kind of life I've cut out for myself. And if I were to be one hundred percent honest, it's not the controversy that's keeping me up at night, nor is it the thought that there could be hundreds of angry Catholics protesting. I'm not even sweating the thought of my grassroots gay-friendly audience getting all backlash sassy and spraying right back into the throngs of Christ defenders. That's the fun stuff, really. It brings out the camera crews and sells tickets. What keeps me up at night is this call to all Christians to come and "protest the defiling of the Virgin Mary." Surely someone might consider it their personal call to fuck with my show. What keeps me up at night is the thought of that one person who comes all the way from Scranton, Pennsylvania, buys a ticket (prays first), and then quietly waits for an opportune moment to stand up and shout something that will leave me, at my most vulnerable: speechless.

I'm trying in vain to predict when this indignant wail of protest will happen. Will it be when Mary first meets the soft butch Jo, a tool belt–wearing carpenter at the Desert Depot? Will it be when they share their first kiss at the Burning Bush, the local Nazareth lesbian watering hole? Or will it be when G-d (a sexy, tall, Pam Grier '70s G-d) seduces the horny couple into having a hot, tantric three-way love dance at the Burning Bush? I know it's outrageously scandalous. I mean, Mary is only fourteen and she's in a bar! And what will my mystery protester say? Will it be a gashry of outrage fueled by the seven-hour drive to see just what this lesbian Jesus show is all about? Or even worse, will it be a calm but clear prayer complete with rosary beads, and all the more intimidating because it will be in Latin?

As I continue through the Rolodex of awkward possibilities, I get a phone call from Fox News. This is the right-wingy cable station that hosts shows like *The O'Reilly Factor, Geraldo Rivera,* and *Hannity & Colmes.* The *Hannity & Colmes* producer calls me to ask if I would like to appear on the show and have a "discussion" with Bill Donohue of the Catholic League. Now I'm making the national television airwaves with my show? The debater in me is very freaked out, but the producer in me is very Jewish. I accept the offer thinking that if anything, it could help promote the show as well as prepare me for the loose-cannon protester of my nightmares. All of the sudden I feel stronger in my resolve to defend my Jewish lesbian take on all things Christian and holy.

The next night when I arrive at the studio where I'm scheduled to go live via satellite to television sets in living rooms across the nation, I see it's a big setup. While I sit in a small windowless room in Boston facing a camera, my opponent Bill gets to be cozy and elbow to elbow with the show's hosts back in New York. My confidence peels a bit. I'm given earplugs in which I'll receive the live audio feed, but I won't be able to see who I'm talking to. A technician tells me to look into a camera lens. My heart is thumping as I hear the New York producer tell me through my earplugs, "Hey, Faith, just be prepared—Bill is a real piece of work." They've obviously had him on the show before and they know what he's capable of. He's had actual television experience baiting and attacking unassuming freethinkers like myself who have no idea what they're getting into. I'm sure he did a Google search with the title "Jesus" to see what popped up. I popped up and bit like the sucker he knew I was. I start wishing I could have thought of a more innocent show title like *My Lil Lesbian Jewish Christmas Story.*"

"Okay, Faith," the smooth, tiny voice in my ear says, "we're in the break now and going live in thirty seconds. Are you ready?"

"As ready as I'll ever be," I respond. How cliché and real at the same time.

We're ten seconds into the show when Bill proves to be the stereotypical fanatical right-wing raving lunatic I was warned he'd be. He keeps referring to some quote I made in *The Advocate* two years ago that had to do with my middle finger.

"How dare you stick your middle finger up to the Virgin Mary!" he seethes.

"I'm not doing that!" I limply retort.

Though I can't see him, I swear he's foaming at the mouth. He keeps repeating there's no way he would ever see my show.

"So, Bill, if you will never see my show, then you'll never know it's about love and acceptance and Jesus is at the center of it. And yes, I'm Jewish and a lesbian and in crisis because even though my partner and I have a child, I worry all the time because in this world there's not a lot of acceptance for our new family. See, Bill, G-d comes to me and tells me this alternative story in order to nurture and bless our decision. This is a version of the story that G-d knows I will listen to. It's quite a warm and fuzzy spiritually life-affirming show after all."

Bill isn't feeling me. He sticks to his attack-dog position, and in some very safe way, I'm really glad he—and hopefully others like him—will never ever ever ever see my show. Ever.

I come home that night feeling pretty defeated. I'm bruised from the pelting of Bill's well-rehearsed religious rhetoric and feeling like I never should have done *Hannity & Colmes*, never ever ever ever ever should have come up with a show title that included both the name "Jesus" and the phrase "two mommies." But at the same time I'm angry. Why can't I even fictionally suggest that Jesus might have been parented by two women? Why is that offensive and degrading? Now I'm feeling like both my lifestyle and my religion are being attacked. Even though my show has a loving theme at the core, Bill will never know that, nor will the people who are protesting. I start rethinking my grand-scheme agenda and wonder if I'm preaching my schlock operas to the converted.

My partner taped the show for me. I look like a Jew caught in headlights. I have to turn it off. My anger gives way to my fear. My Fox experience only worsens my anxiety about the show. If I'm unprepared for Bill, a known and planned-for quantity, how can I manage the unpredictable dreaded showstoppers? I become obsessed with thoughts of pulled fire alarms and bomb threats to the theater. I immediately want to cancel the show. My partner and I have a ten-month-old girl whose safety we need to consider, and now random people can look me up and hunt me down if they want to. I imagine an angry mob of people surrounding our house yelling, "Jesus has one mommy and so should your daughter!"

I go online to compose an e-mail to my production partner explaining why we should cancel the show and find I have sixty-five new messages. This confirms it. I'm getting hate mail now. I have the justification I need to cancel the show. I open up the first e-mail with a fearful eye.

It's not the response I'd expecteed. Neither are the others.

"I just wanted to tell you that even though I'm not gay or Jewish, I really appreciated where you were coming from," reads the first one.

Huh? He's from Tennessee! I open up another.

"I have to say I've never been so embarrassed to be a Catholic as I was when I saw your debate with Bill Donohue. He doesn't speak for me or any other Christians I know. You handled yourself with such grace and dignity. I would say you are more of a Christian than Bill could ever be."

What? Me? A Christian? Okay, if you say so Helen from New Londonderry, Connecticut. I open the others and am welcomed by more and more supportive letters from non-Jewish, non-lesbian types from all over the country. I do get a small percentage of angry responses more along the line of Bill's ranting nasty-speak, but for the most part, people are—dare I say—proud of me.

As the countdown to opening night progresses, I start to feel ready. Ready for anything. Ready for the protests, the press, and even the random unpredictable live and crazy person. I have on a life vest that I didn't have before. I'm buoyed up by faceless Christians—Laura from St. Louis, Matt from Albany—who, despite their devotion to Jesus, support me and my right to explore my personal story. I start to think that for every one protester out there, there are ten supporters. I'm kept afloat by the divine thought that Jesus just might dig where this Jewish lesbian is coming from. And if someone does buy a ticket just to mess with my show, he or she might just be the key that winds up my back.

My Rabbis and Myself
Arthur G. Marx

I grew up in a Reform temple in Pennsylvania. My parents, skeptical liberals, carpooled us kids to Sunday school. We found our way to Wednesday afternoon Hebrew school ourselves. The family attended High Holiday services—Mother's hat was the central event of the season—and the rare other occasion for an outstanding speaker or musical program. Dad made a habit of taking his sunglasses along should sleep prevail.

I went as far as bar mitzvah in my formal Jewish education. But I continued to feel inspired by our rabbi, Richard Roth, who spoke more of Selma, Alabama, and the antics of the House Committee on Un-American Activities than of godliness and holiness. He often suffered the slings of outraged board members for inviting Martin Luther King Jr. or César Chávez to address our Friday night audience—in the '50s and '60s, when they were dangerous! Not like now, their memories sanctified by our achingly PC leaders. The week after he earned tenure, as if to force his commitment to controversy down the congregation's collective throat, Rabbi Roth gave a sermon on the local Jewish Federation and the parochialism (you should forgive the expression) that kept it disengaged from the roiling social movements of the times.

Though I had stopped going to temple, for a time in my college years I entertained the thought of applying to rabbinical school. Like

Rabbi Roth, I wanted to lead my flock on social issues—more than lead them to G-d, in whom I didn't trust. But in the end, I felt too sharply the contradiction between unbelief and communal leadership, and abandoned my rabbinical fantasy. What remained was a certain sexual attraction toward men of the cloth, an excitement at the naughtiness of it. A few years ago, cleaning out my childhood bedroom in anticipation of my parents' move to a retirement community, I finally discarded the twenty-year-old course catalog from Hebrew Union College I had sent away for.

Rumors circulated about Rabbi Roth, who had never married. Whenever he came to our home for dinner, two or three times a year, he'd announce to my younger sister—this began when she was about five—that when she grew up he was going to marry her. She would scream in a confusion of hilarity and terror, in part inspired by his shocking tangle of thick white hair that we called, evoking the fashion of the day, his "Hebro."

Angrily I deflected the unsubstantiated rumors before friends and relations, like a true lawyer's son. "Where's your evidence?" I demanded. How easily now I see my instinctive protectiveness of him as my own defense, though I had neither the vocabulary nor the self-knowledge then to recognize myself as a fellow lover of men.

Had I been older, I would have heard in Rabbi Roth's sermons the coded references that inescapably mark us, above all his exegeses on popular Broadway shows, Bernstein, Sondheim—with whom rumor further had it he was personally acquainted. He certainly made no secret of his periodic theatre trips to New York and of the pied-à-terre he kept there. Once or twice a congregant spotted him in an orchestra seat, next to a much younger, not very Jewish-looking bodybuilder. My imagination then did not extend so far as to speculate what he might do après-show in the Big City.

My brother Bern, older by six years, sees Rabbi Roth a little differently. What filtered down to *me* was rumor. But Bern says it wasn't just rumor: Although not made public, Rabbi Roth's homosexuality was quite well known. And Bern feels that our congregation, even in those times, chose to overlook it in exchange for his outspoken moral leadership on other fronts. Which confirms a thesis I've had for years: that alongside the horrific patterns of ignorance, hate, exclusion, and the rest, another story of benign tolerance and understanding awaits, largely untold.

As a pregay and inevitably troubled youth in those before-Stonewall years, I was given to morose silences that, as I reflect on them now, signified a kind of aphonia. Not a true inability to speak, but a willful retreat into self when what I needed to express—my feeling for other boys and men—remained unspeakable, even to myself.

My dutifully sympathetic parents asked me if I wanted to talk with Rabbi Roth. I replied with a sullen "Okay," but the rabbi preferred not to take me on for counseling. Did he intuit my problem and choose not to chance self-revelation? Would he have wanted to suggest—or even appear to—a solution of graceful acceptance? Indeed, what counsel might he have given in the 1950s? *Wait, Arthur, you're still growing. If you turn out to be homosexual, well, it's not the end of the world. Homosexuals may never be happy, but they manage to function.*

Instead, the good rabbi recommended a well-regarded psychiatrist associated with a university medical school and a member of the congregation. After a few sessions, I was advised to enter psychoanalysis with Dr. Sachs. "It's not for everyone, but for you it would be helpful." Later I learned, from other memoirs of psychoanalysis, that this line was a popular come-on for this profoundly self-absorptive process. I felt helplessly swept along by the course of these successive referrals. Sick people need treatment.

Psychoanalysis for a teenager? It sounds so disproportionate, so misguided now, when almost no one indulges in it. For several years I stretched out on the couch four and five mornings a week, tripping around the subject of homosexuality. It arose from time to time when I "acted out," but never emerged, as it should have, as the core issue of my thwarted personality. Again, it's a question of the lack of vocabulary. True, there existed in the world a handful of untraditional psychiatrists who prescribed acceptance of homosexuality as a normal state of being. But Dr. Sachs was not one of them. Some years later, after I had come out, my mother sent me his obituary. He had died in a "hiking accident," but people who knew him widely assumed suicide.

Fast-forward ten years or so. Between finishing my graduate school coursework and taking my doctoral exams, I spent several months studying at home. One night I dropped into the local gay bar, finding a most attractive young man to chat up. Jeff's ebony hair lay stylishly long, '70s-style, against his neck. His eyes laughed. His hands brushed softly, suggestively, against mine. He called himself a social worker, but my passion for detail soon uncovered the fact that he now served as assistant rabbi at my old temple. Not something he would have breezily dropped on any trick.

For the rest of my stay in town Jeff and I carried on a scalding romance, both of us titillated by our temple connection. He looked up my bar mitzvah records, even found a copy of my speech. A few weeks after we met, he gave me his hilarious impression of my mother, who had attended a Sisterhood canasta party. It had all the frisson of a forbidden, back-street affair. He gave me a ring of sardonyx—talk about gemstones reflecting character—that still draws comment when I wear it. I tried to ignore Al, the guy in New York he went in to see every other weekend—and with whom, so far as I know, Jeff lives now. I doubt Al ever knew about me.

Aside from Jeff's own liberal views, which the senior rabbi wished to promote in the Reform rabbinate, Rabbi Roth was clearly physically attracted to him as well. Jeff was stunningly good-looking, smart, well-read, well-theatered. Rabbi Roth might well have pictured Jeff coming to the temple as, in effect, his partner and *rebbetzin*. Among our secret sharings of the heart were the episodes Jeff told me of Rabbi Roth constantly trying to put the make on him. Jeff felt confounded with emotions—flattered, but mostly harassed and angry. After the minimum apprenticeship, Jeff moved on to head another, smaller congregation somewhere. I heard that after a while he came out loud and proud as a gay rabbi in the Reform movement. I occasionally see his name on a liberal masthead or petition.

Years passed. Rabbi Roth retired to New York City. One summer day, with my lover Michael, I ran into him on Third Avenue. He was sitting outside a coffee shop and, not in any hurry, we joined him for half an hour. The subject of homosexuality did not need to be mentioned. All was understood. Not long after his seventieth birthday he had a sudden heart attack and died in the lobby of an off-Broadway theater.

I often think the progressive sympathies of my two rabbis stood in for a wider tolerance. All through the 1940s and '50s, and into the '70s and beyond, gay people supported every other human right in the world but our own, to live freely, to love freely. Did they imagine eventually our turn would come? Was it our way of creating for ourselves a tolerant community to fall back upon for support? Was that community—alongside the world of theater—a place to cruise?

I owe the biggest part of my social consciousness to Rabbi Roth. (I also credit Rabbi Jeff with showing me a thing or two, but not so much in the social consciousness department.) I continue to marvel at the way Rabbi Roth used his pulpit so courageously in the spirit of the prophets, while so personally vulnerable to disclosure and scandal. When gay liberation came, I joined marches and protests, found out there were millions like me. I never needed another psychiatrist.

Three years ago I buried my partner Michael in an Orthodox Jewish cemetery. He died of AIDS at age thirty-six, an ironic double chai. Though not very observant, his family had belonged to this modern Orthodox shul in New England for three generations. By Jewish law, as Michael's unrecognized lover, I wasn't considered an official mourner. Rabbi Swerdlick therefore permitted me to serve as a pallbearer, walking Michael's casket to the grave, pausing seven times, in that short march from hearse to that awful earthen hole, so it shouldn't appear we were too gladly rushing his spirit away.

The night before the burial, the rabbi spoke with me privately about my nine-year relationship with Michael so he could prepare the eulogy. We talked far longer than he needed to. He took well to me, this divorced father of two teenagers, and asked me to contact him again whenever I wanted to. He made it clear that he meant for more than continued spiritual counseling. The next day, at the funeral parlor, the rabbi gave his eulogy. I would understate it if I said I was feelingly mentioned. In fact, he extended his remarks as far as he could toward acknowledging the love and care I gave Michael, especially in his last year of life.

Nu? Yes, Orthodox Rabbi Swerdlick, with the neat, trimmed beard and the knitted *kippah,* is gay too. I was probably the only one out of one hundred fifty people in the room who knew it.

A year later, it was time to put up Michael's stone. The gravestone designer submitted the Jewish calendar dates and the standard Hebrew formula "beloved son and brother" to Rabbi Swerdlick for approval. After consulting me, he added *v'khaver*— "and friend."

So rests in eternity my beloved friend Michael, with everlasting rabbinic blessing.

Mouna in Flight
Sue Katz

Although she was well-treated in the Catholic orphanage, Mouna ran away when she was eighteen years old. This was not a simple matter. The Swiss orphanage in the West Bank is about twenty kilometers from Jerusalem, and Mouna, sheltered for so many years in this religious institution, had little experience of flight.

Because there was no public transportation, she had to spend some of her miniscule savings to take a group taxi to the city. Using powers of persuasion she did not know she possessed, she convinced the driver to let her sit in the front, next to him, and by wrapping her headscarf around her and remaining rigidly forward in her seat, she managed to avoid the kind of questioning the other passengers, all male, would generally feel justified in mounting. Her greatest luck was that an important local football game was being broadcast on the radio and the men found that even more compelling than a woman traveling alone.

The smallest coincidence had changed her whole life. While escorting one of the elderly nuns to the medical clinic, Mouna had happened upon a leaflet advertising a rape crisis service for Arab women operating out of the predominantly Jewish women's center in Jerusalem. She was not a rape victim, but she had heard about feminists. People often referred to them disparagingly as lesbians and man-haters.

Mouna had come to understand and accept her own romantic desire for women. Her long, sustaining relationship with one of the other girls in the orphanage was annihilated when Nabilla, against her will, had been married off several months before to her distant cousin. This left Mouna mourning, alone with her secret. She realized it was just a matter of time before her brothers forced a similar fate on her.

The director of the orphanage, Mrs. Roshardt, was a strict Catholic, and although she was like a mother to Mouna, the girl knew Mrs. Roshardt would consider Mouna's feelings for women sinful. Her extended family was no source of comfort for, of all things, Mouna most feared the plans her brothers and cousins might be making for her. She knew they would condemn her involvement with women as a smear on the family name and honor. After so many years living in the orphanage, she had no close allies in the family who might protect her. Her father, like so many Palestinian men, was in jail, and her mother, Sister Mary often told her, was with G-d. She hoped at the women's center to find a way to escape, to live her own life.

I just happened to be at the Jerusalem center the day Mouna arrived. Ruthie, a member of the center collective and an old friend of mine, had invited me to come from Tel Aviv to talk about teaching a self-defense class in their center.

Mouna, her long brown hair moist with perspiration, arrived in the middle of our conversation. She knew no Hebrew, but her English was pretty good. She didn't say anything about being a lesbian. Her main concern was finding employment and a roof, and she wanted to know the legal implications of her living in West Jerusalem, the Israeli half of the city. As a daughter of the West Bank, she was very clear that she could never settle alone,in East Jerusalem or anywhere in the occupied territories. Who would rent a room to a single woman? Who would hire a young girl on her own? They would want to know the name of her village and they would immediately contact the men of her Hamula, her clan. She would be returned to the orphanage, at best, or to the hands of her brothers. Even this one day on the road, alone, put her at great risk of punishment.

Ruthie and I were pessimistic about finding her a room to rent. We invited her to join us at a nearby café, as it was lunchtime. After breaking bread with this determined girl, we were profoundly moved by her situation. She was not, in fact, the first young woman who had turned to us for help in avoiding an unwanted arranged marriage. The Bedouin girl from north of Beersheva who had been murdered last year by her uncles had been our most glaring failure. On her father's orders, they had snatched her off the streets of Jerusalem, where we had placed her with a sympathetic family, and dragged her back to her village to be wed against her will. On the night of her wedding, she stabbed her groom when he tried to take her by force. Ironically enough, her father attempted to protect her, but her uncles insisted on extracting a price for family honor.

Ruthie offered to let Mouna stay at her own home until she could get set up, and the girl trembled with gratitude and relief. When we returned to the office, Ruthie phoned a friend who ran a mixed Palestinian-Jewish child-care center, to see if Mouna could work there. They did not need any more care workers, but the woman agreed to take Mouna on as a cleaner with the chance, later, to apply for any openings. The pay was very low, but the opportunity was huge. Mouna, with her tiny carrying case, entered our lives.

We drove Mouna to Ruthie's house and watched her closely while we explained that Ruthie lived with her lover, Dalia, and Dalia's two sons. As Mouna's smile took over her face, Ruthie and I exchanged the happy looks of friends confirming their suspicions. Within a week, Mouna had quietly confided in Ruthie.

Their house was the social nexus for a whole community of lesbians. Mouna drank in feminism with great gulps and fit into Ruthie and Dalia's scene with the ease of a foot into an olive-oiled sandal. Mouna used her talent for sketching caricatures of people to keep us all entertained with doodles of ourselves. She flattered me with a portrait of a woman with massive fists. We all giggled at the family portrait she did in which the two boys, lovely spoiled children whose demands dominated the house, were about twice as big as Ruthie and Dalia. Despite her lack of Hebrew and without any experience of the feminist subculture, she soon became everyone's little sister.

The first apartment she rented was in the Katamonim, a big government-subsidized housing slum. She sublet the place from a friend of someone in the center's collective, thus avoiding any face-to-face contact with the landlord. However, a neighbor, a Jewish Iraqi immigrant, became suspicious when he realized she didn't understand Hebrew. He addressed her in Arabic. Her mistake was to answer him. The neighbor called to complain to the landlord, who arrived within the hour to throw her out.

Ruthie found her the next apartment and, to be safe, signed the lease in her own name. Mouna was able to stay there safely for a couple of months, but then some of her relatives from the village managed to locate her through the postmark on a letter she sent to Mrs. Roshardt to reassure her that she was doing well.

"It was terrifying," she told Ruthie later. "Four of them turned up and banged on my door. I didn't open it so they stood outside screaming in Arabic, 'You whore! You're ruining the family's good name. Get back to the orphanage. How will we ever find you a husband?'"

"What did you do?" Ruthie asked, holding the girl's hand.

"I climbed out the bathroom window and escaped through the yard. They're probably still there trying to break down the door."

Mouna stayed home to baby-sit while Ruthie and Dalia went to the apartment to collect Mouna's things. They found the landlord and the upstairs neighbor waiting inside the apartment.

"What the hell is going on?" he demanded. "My tenants call me to say they are under attack by terrorists living in my apartment." He was sweating with fury. "I thought you were living here."

"And so I was," Ruthie answered. "But if you intend to break into my apartment all the time, I'll just take my stuff and get out."

Mouna stayed in touch with Mrs. Roshardt but wouldn't go into the territories to see her, afraid to be trapped either by her cousins or the Israeli border police. Like so many people from the territories, she didn't have any papers allowing her to stay overnight in Israel. If she got stopped by the police, even once, we feared she would be jailed.

Ruthie and Dalia asked me up to Jerusalem to help Mouna plan a future that would prevent her from becoming a prisoner of someone's kitchen or of someone's jail. Dalia felt strongly that the only solution was to get Mouna out of the country. Ruthie and I came to agree, since we couldn't come up with many ideas of how to move things forward here. Mouna was reluctant, though, knowing that such a move would be permanent. Despite all the difficulties and threats, for the first time in her life she had found friends sympathetic to her deepest feelings. We convinced Mouna that if she went to London, she would find much bigger lesbian communities, including other Arab women. Ruthie had friends in London and she promised to arrange a meeting for Mouna with them.

Eventually Mouna too faced the facts and accepted Dalia's idea. We drew Mrs. Roshardt into the planning. Not only was she ready to help because of real fondness for Mouna, she was also feeling guilty about having put Mouna in danger by showing her brothers the postcard. She contacted a colleague of hers in London to request a letter of sponsorship. We were trying to get Mouna enrolled in a London school for kindergarten teachers, but because Mouna was officially stateless and did not have a passport, arranging travel papers was an ongoing headache that was stretching out the process.

One summer weekend Ruthie and Dalia organized a group trip to the Sea of Galilee in honor of three London friends who were visiting. Using her church connections, Mouna succeeded in getting us rooms at a monastery on the edge of the sea. Two cars from Jerusalem met up with our carload of women from Tel Aviv. In total we were thirteen women, quite a party.

We had exclusive use of one entire dormitory. It was divided into twenty cells, each furnished with a set of bunk beds and a storage box. Once we unloaded the cars and changed into our bathing suits, we ran down the path to the stony beach. For our visitors, it was their first time at the Sea of Galilee, and they were amazed to see that it was, in fact, just a lake. Ruthie made the introductions all around and I cannot deny that I experienced an instant attraction to Courtney, a muscular carpenter from London. Despite her peculiar hairdo, a windswept blond mass that appeared to have been generated by curlers, I felt a strong message of desire in her glance.

We quickly found some time alone, swimming out from the beach and floating as we talked, and by the time we returned to the crowd on the shore, she had agreed to share my cell with me. Since my old friend Yaffa was already in my room, it might have been awkward. Yaffa, however, just laughed and wished me luck as she gathered up her stuff to move down the hall.

Later I realized that while I had been swimming with Courtney, Mouna was getting along exceedingly well with Gail, a good friend of Courtney's. Since Mouna was in charge of cell assignments, she simply put Gail in a cell by herself. This prevented Mouna from having to suggest moving to her roommate Leila, her dear straight friend from the orphanage. It also ensured that she and Gail could have some privacy if things went that way.

I got more than the vacation romance I was anticipating. Courtney was a complex woman in trouble, and she was hoping I would serve as a life raft.

"You're the first other woman I've slept with in the eight years that I've been with June," she told me. "It's not that we're really a couple—I mean, there's even a bloke in her life right now. He's actually been around for more than a year. But she's got a bit of a problem with my seeing someone else."

"What kind of problem can she have," I asked naïvely, "if she herself is messing around?"

"Well, the last time I was attracted to someone—not that I acted on it or anything—June broke my nose."

"Broke your nose? And you're still with her?"

"I told you, she's got this problem."

Later that night, when I mentioned the conversation to Ruthie, she nodded sadly. "Wait till you see her naked. You'll find more chapters to that depressing tale."

She was referring, it turned out, to the jagged scar that ran along the inside of Courtney's left breast.

"It was my birthday," she told me, "and June and I were supposed to go out to dinner at an expensive restaurant. She turned up a couple of hours late—but only to pick up a leather jacket she had lent me. When she saw the disappointment on my face she mentioned—as an aside—that she couldn't go out with me because she had made a date with that guy. I started crying, and she got furious that I was attempting to delay her. She grabbed a kitchen knife and stabbed me. Of course, I knew how much she hates it when someone tries to guilt-trip her."

"So what happened?" I asked.

"Well, she left."

"She left you stabbed and bleeding?"

"Not really. Actually she called Gail and told her to come over to take me to the hospital. They removed about half my left lung, because it had collapsed altogether." The entire recitation had been done in such a disinterested voice that it was hard to make sense of it.

I spent so much energy trying to figure Courtney out that I hardly noticed the intensity of the intimacy developing between Gail and Mouna. By the end of the weekend, in classic lesbian form, they were in love and making plans to live together in London. We all quietly agreed that it was a timely and convenient affair.

By the time the London contingent returned to England, I was relieved to say goodbye to Courtney. Both in and out of bed, she carried an air of surrender that, for me, quickly lost its appeal. I was looking for a peer not a servant. But Gail provided Mouna with a massive motivation, and she entered into her travel plans with a vengeance. She wrote letters, made appeals, got a lawyer to help her establish stateless travel papers, and set up contacts with the English church folks. She moved around a good deal, eluding her brothers and cousins.

My job was to check into British immigration regulations. At one point I sat down with Mouna to go over the possibilities.

"You'll only get a six-month tourist visa when you enter," I explained, "because you haven't been officially accepted into kindergarten-teacher school yet. It you get accepted and the church people pay your fees, then you can change to a student visa. But if nothing else works out, the local lesbians will try to fix you up with a marriage of convenience."

"I'm going to England to be with Gail, not to marry some damn man!" Mouna was adamant. "When I left the orphanage, I took an oath never to marry a man."

"But this isn't really a marriage. It's just so you can stay there and be safe and be with Gail. Otherwise you'll have to come back after half a year. And imagine what your family will do after you've been abroad unchaperoned."

"I have my principles," she said quietly. "I'm not marrying any man."

Ruthie had taken on the job of raising funds for Mouna's ticket and her early days in London. Mouna had won so much affection from the community that all the small donations added up. But we had a nervous sense that time was running out. Finally her papers came through, and the next day a travel agent friend of mine managed to get her onto a flight. Seven of us accompanied her to the airport, to give her a massive farewell and to make sure her departure went smoothly. We weren't only worried about the treatment she would get from the Israeli security people, we were also scared that Mouna's family might turn up to restrain her. But it all went smoothly.

Mouna wasn't much of a writer, but Ruthie was in touch with Gail regularly. She and Mouna only lasted a couple of months together. Mouna had some trouble adjusting. She had a fiery personality and wanted to be utterly independent. It was hard for her to reconcile her own self-image with her new circumstances. She was alone in a foreign land. She was in need of help. The last we heard was that after staying unhappily at Gail's for a couple of months, the church placed her in a boardinghouse for single women, where she hated being bound by their rules and restrictions.

Meanwhile, Ruthie and Dalia were having horrifying trouble with Dalia's not-yet-ex-husband. He was threatening to take the kids away from her, an easy enough task for a Jewish man appealing to the rabbinical judges. He was ready to expose her as a lesbian in order to win exclusive custody, if she didn't give him the apartment, the car, and all their savings. Because only the rabbis can grant divorce, the lawyers told her she didn't have much choice. Ruthie, Dalia, and the boys were suddenly poor and homeless.

In the middle of that crisis, Courtney called. She had just been released, she told me, from the hospital. She offered to break totally with her violent girlfriend if we could be together. I replied that I didn't feel suited to the role of the knight on the white horse.

That winter I went to London for a two-week visit at Gail's invitation.

"You'll never guess what," she told me when she picked me up from Kings Cross Station. "Mouna is living with this gay guy she married."

"Great. That's what we wanted her to do."

"Wait a minute. That's just the beginning. Apparently she's pregnant!"

"Now, there's a set of principles if ever I've seen one," I laughed.

"It's actually quite sweet. Her husband is this dear little thing who's terrified of AIDS. Neither of them feels like they've gone straight or anything. They feel the timing is good and they both want to raise a child. They say they're in love."

"How do you feel about it?" I asked her.

"What can I tell you? They've asked me to be the godmother. I wish them luck."

"And what's with Courtney? Last I heard, her girlfriend had put her in the hospital again."

"I don't see Courtney much. June bought a dog and

Courtney spends her life taking care of it. She walks it twice a day, feeds it twice a day, grooms it twice a day—she's a busy little canine tender."

"So why doesn't the woman take care of her own dog?"

"Courtney says that she's allergic."

"What made June get a dog, then?"

"She thought it would be a nice joint project for her and Courtney, especially while Courtney is recovering."

Exile
Aaron Hamburger

In 1994 I moved to Prague to escape the capitalist grind of San
Francisco and the swallowing up of all the creativity and intelli-
gence in the world. A month later, my mother came to visit me.

We did the obligatory walking tour of the Jewish Quarter. I was
the only one with green hair. Our guide, "Zara," was as tall as a man
and wore a suede hunting jacket.

"Do you know of a nice shul for him to go to services?" my
mother asked with a disapproving glance at me.

"I attend a small alternative community with the name of Bejt
Ahava," Zara said, rolling her r's. "You should check it out."

"You have a beautiful accent," my mother said. "Where are you
from?"

Zara seemed startled by the question. "New York City," she
replied.

My mother and I stopped for lunch at a pizza place called KGB
that offered Lenin and Stalin "plates." Lenin was green pepper, and
Stalin anchovies.

"Those huge eyes, and that accent," my mother *kvelled*. "I
think she's striking." She picked at a glass bowl of Bulgarian salad
I'd recommended: shredded cabbage and feta soaked in oil.

"Yeah, like an Amazon," I said, wielding an imaginary club in
the air. "Wham!"

Her fork froze. "Remember how serious you were as a child? On Halloween you used to dress up as your favorite rabbi, whatever his name was."

"I don't remember anymore."

His name was Johanan Ben Zakkai. He'd escaped from Jerusalem in a coffin.

"Why don't you try that synagogue some Friday night?"

"To meet a nice Jewish girl from Eastern Europe?"

"Well, if you're interested. I think it'd be a waste if you didn't reproduce."

"Heartwarming." I flashed a monkey grin with all my teeth, even the gums.

"Ha, ha." She pushed away her bowl. "Too much oil. This is not a salad."

✡

I felt lonely when my mother left, her suitcase loaded with marionettes and T-shirts printed with I SAW THE GOLEM! She'd been the most company I'd had in a while.

One Friday night I thought, what the hell, and took a taxi to Bejt Ahava. I didn't care for the green in my hair anymore, so I bleached it.

Bejt Ahava was on a gloomy block named after Uruguay, in a gray cement building with bars over the windows. The synagogue was in the basement with two street level windows painted with menorahs and smiling faces. All the lights were off.

I rang the bell, and after a few minutes I heard a dog barking. The door opened and a woman with a strong nose and two angry black holes for eyes glared from the dark vestibule. She pulled up a barking chocolate lab, which was missing a patch of hair on its back. The lab bared its teeth at me.

Another woman was hiding in the shadows. She was young and pretty, with black hair brushed smooth and a tight button of a mouth painted strawberry red.

Exile

The woman with angry eyes looked me up and down. "Come in, come in," she said in a tired voice, as if I were imposing.

Our breath turned to mist in the dimly lit hall, which stank of cabbage. The plaster walls had been stained a color between olive and aqua not found in nature and otherwise only in Eastern Europe. Straddling the yapping brown lab, the woman unlocked an iron gate. We walked down a steep flight of stairs to a cramped, freezing basement room where a dozen folding chairs sat in a sloppy circle. A plastic lemon hung over the door.

The woman tossed her keys on a brown upright piano wedged in the corner. Letters of the Hebrew alphabet, chopped crudely out of construction paper, were Scotch-taped above a silver velveteen Torah cover that sagged on the far wall.

"No Torah," she said. "But a Torah cover, which is very important."

The young woman ran upstairs with the dog.

"Sit comfortably," commanded the angry woman, leaning against the piano as she gnawed on a hangnail. "You're new," she said, as if "new" were an adjective of contempt. "I'm Sylvie Wittmanova. And what brings you to Prague?"

"I'm not a tourist," I said, to clarify things. "I live here. I'm an artist."

"Another of these young men fucking teenage girls like Henry Miller in Paris." Just then a bell rang, like at the end of a boxing match, and she ran upstairs to get the door.

I was checking out their library, a low shelf crammed with paperbacks in English like *Golda's Story* and *Portnoy's Complaint,* when a tall man in a pea coat entered alone. He had a high, sloping brow and wide-curled hair that he kept twisting between his fingers.

"Hey, dude. Are you American?" I asked.

The guy let go of the curl he'd been teasing. "Er, no," he said as if startled.

"So then, let me take a wild guess…you're Czech?"

"Er, yes." He took out a notebook and pen and began taking notes.

Several congregants then entered at once, led by a boy with a delicate doll-like face, frighteningly deep blue eyes, and blond fore-locks. He wore a long dark coat and a fur-trimmed black top hat like a Hasid.

Sylvie and her young friend with the button-mouth returned. But no dog.

A few more foreigners filed in: two doubtful-looking couples from Indianapolis—"Is this the right place?" "Sit, sit," Sylvie replied—and a rabbinical student with a British accent—"Didn't you get my letter?" "I don't know from any letters. Go sit."

Sylvie stared at us, then mumbled in Czech. "Start, start," she said in English. "Why look at me? It's your service. Sing something. Lenka, give them what to read."

The young woman with the bright red mouth handed out sta-pled prayer booklets with goldenrod covers. My cover had a big X in black marker. A quote on the first page read: "The boulder that the builders neglected became the cornerstone."

"They don't even have real books," marveled one of the ladies from Indianapolis as we sang "*Ma Tovu*," printed in Hebrew, English, Czech, and Czech transliteration.

"It's a miracle they have anything at all," said her friend.

We'd used pamphlets like these at Hebrew Day School, where from the ages of five to thirteen I attended morning services in the dusty gym. I carefully mouthed each syllable of the prayers because our rabbi explained it was a sin to mangle a word or miss one. The other boys stared wistfully at the basketball nets. I watched them out of the corner of my eye, certain that if they'd caught me admir-ing their hair or the curves of their necks, they'd have punched me to death.

When I graduated from day school, I worshiped G-d at B'nei Tzedek Synagogue, the largest shul in Northern California. The soaring wedge-shaped tabernacle was as enormous as a battleship. From our padded seats in the audience, we'd have needed binocu-lars to make out the face of our rabbi, enthroned in front of a mar-ble ark.

Sylvie interrupted my daydreaming. "I'm bored. Why don't we skip to the kiddush?" Stopping without finishing had never occurred to me even as an option. And yet here she and her pretty friend were already blithely passing around plastic cups of wine with and wisps of *vanocka,* or "Christmas bread," as the Czechs called challah. As I turned in my booklet, I felt exhilarated, like I'd gotten away with something.

The young Hasid in the fur-trimmed top hat continued to pray silently. Meanwhile, the British rabbinical student told Sylvie, "I've heard so much about you."

"What did you hear and who from?" she shot back.

"Everyone. They say the work you're doing over here is amazing."

"Well, here I am." She stuck her thumbs in her ears and wagged her fingers. "We are quite small. Maybe twenty, not counting the Americans—they're impossible to keep track of. And Maria. She's Catholic—I think she goes to church too on Sundays. Still, she always comes. I don't give blood tests at the door like our Rabbi Kahn at the official Altneu Synagogue who asks for official paperien—*Achtung!*—to prove you are one hundred percent Jew."

"Then what do you think makes a Jew?" asked the student, and I inched forward in my chair because I was curious to hear the answer myself.

Sylvie settled in a chair and put her feet up on the piano keys. "You know how I knew I was a Jew? One day I came home from school with a report saying I am a Zionist. I thought, okay, you want me to be a Jew? Why not."

The young man with the notebook was putting on his coat. I followed him, so we'd happen to leave at the same time. He wasn't bad-looking.

"I like her," I said, holding the door as we went outside. "What is she anyway, some kind of rabbi?"

"Not rabbi. She began Reform seminary in London, but they expunged her for subverting statements. She disapproves of Chief Rabbi of Prague Kahn, because he says only Orthodox Jews are legal Jews. However, he himself was not real Jew because his mother was not Jewish, only father, so he converted in absolute Orthodox way."

His name was Lubos, and he shook my hand with moist fingers. He studied theology at Charles University and had been visiting Sylvie for a few weeks.

"Rabbi Kahn says rumors that Sylvie raises money for drugs or her group engages in illicit liveliness. But you see it is not so. You witnessed poor Daniel, this growth-deficient youngster next to piano who looks as Hasidic boy? He attempted to attend official services, but Rabbi Kahn expunged him in belief he is trying to mock them."

"So was anyone in that room actually Jewish?" I asked above the roar of the train.

"Sylvie, yes. And Daniel thinks he is Jew. He owns video of *Fiddler on Roof.*"

"But you don't convert to Judaism because you like *Fiddler on the Roof.*"

"Perhaps." Lubos shrugged. "Actually, I am now very intimate with foolish Daniel, who has few friends his age. He asks me often to visit Budapest with him to meet Jewish girls. Germans did not arrive there until 1944 so there still exists sizable Jewish community. But it is foolish idea when we do not speak Hungarian."

I asked if he'd be at Sylvie's next week.

"Yes, I will be there," he said with a tight, mysterious smile that looked like gas.

✡

Friday evening, I rang the doorbell on Uruguay Street fifteen minutes late. Zara the Amazon answered with a glazed look in her matte grey eyes.

"Don't you remember me?" I asked. "From the tour last week?"

"Oh, yes," she said slowly, as if she'd forgotten the words in English. "You are late. I hope you will find some free chair."

I wasn't worried, but the room turned out to be almost full. Daniel the Hasid, in the same fur hat and black coat, prayed to himself behind the piano. I waved to Lubos.

"*Sh'ma Yisrael!*" Daniel cried out and pulled his hat brim over his eyes.

"Jesus, he scares me," I whispered as I sat down next to Lubos. "That kid is going to end up a juvie delinquent."

"No, no. Daniel is very serious. I admire him. He almost eloped to England for conversion in Reform way, but parents uncovered his plans and stopped him in anger."

There were no *yarmulkes* because Sylvie had left them on her tour bus to Terezin, and it felt strange to pray with nothing on my head. Sylvie had also forgotten the wine for kiddush so we used Becherovka, a Czech liqueur that tasted like pumpkin.

"And I told that bastard Kahn, the Reform is the most religious branch of Judaism we have," said Sylvie, a bit tipsy on Becherovka. "When a Reform decides to put on a *yarmulke* or to fast on Yom Kippur, each act is a conscious decision. To me, this is much better than your super-Orthodox *yeshiva bochers* who run around in black and argue if it's permissible to drink a glass of milk five hours after eating a steak instead of six."

I fantasized about Sylvie hauling our morose rabbi down from the stage at B'nei Tzedek, dragging him through the congregation by the hem of his black robe.

Lubos whispered to me, "May we go? There seems small possibility of cake."

I took him to Meduza, a parlor of plush red chairs lit by candles dripping over empty wine bottles. Our waitress was a tall willowy woman with spiked hair. A Jewish star on a silver chain glittered below her gaunt white neck.

"All things Jewish are fashionable now in Prague," Lubos explained. "May I ask, what is the nature of your religious belief?"

"Art is my religion," I told him. "I've never been a big fan of Judaism. It excludes certain groups, like women." I paused. "And gays."

Lubos thought a minute. "I think if some gay wants to attend service, he is able."

"Not openly."

I thought he'd be shocked or embarrassed, but instead he went on with our argument. "Why is it important openly? One does not discuss sexual life in synagogue."

Suddenly I was the one who felt embarrassed. "It's not just your sexual life. It's who you sit with in synagogue. Lots of things." But I was skirting dangerously close to sounding like I gave a fuck, so I changed the subject.

✡

The crowd at Sylvie's the next week was the largest yet. The Torah cover was tacked up properly to the wall, and the faded Hebrew letters had been replaced with crisp new ones. Sylvie assigned us seats.

The service proceeded properly from start to finish. Sylvie sat quietly in her chair, and when she stood for the kaddish, she clutched Lenka's elbow and read piously from the prayer booklet they were sharing.

After a rousing "*Adon Olam,*" Sylvie announced: "Today we are honored by the presence of a special guest, Rabbi Samuel Adler of the Beth Israel Reconstructionist Synagogue in Washington, D.C., a key supporter of our work here. Welcome."

As Sylvie translated her introduction into Czech, I realized the reason for this dog and pony show was money. Of course. Whenever something doesn't make sense, the answer's always money.

Rabbi Adler leapt to his feet as his plump wife beamed at his elbow. His hair was lush and dark like a carpet, and his cheeks gleamed as if he'd scrubbed them with Brillo.

"My friends, after two visits, I feel at home," he said. "Sylvie, would you...?"

"Yes, yes," she said, and translated his message like a dutiful servant.

Rabbi Adler announced he would deal with a difficult subject: the Holocaust. He got along fine until he tried to explain about how the Germans hated the Jews.

"Rabbi, I must interrupt," Sylvie called out.

Finally! Prepare to be demolished, I thought, wanting to laugh out loud.

"Your information is incorrect. The Germans did not hate the Jews. 'Hatred' is the wrong word. To the Germans, the Jews were a sickness, a thing, like a diseased tooth. You don't hate a thing. You simply extract it, and into the garbage. That the Germans hated Jews, it's a big propaganda to raise money for Israel."

As Sylvie repeated herself in Czech, Rabbi Adler grinned and leaned over to assure his indignant wife, "It's all part of the act." I guess the guy enjoyed being made a fool of.

During kiddush, which was served in antique shot glasses with gold trim, Sylvie punched my arm. "You're becoming a regular," she said and smiled. "You with your friend."

I blushed.

I was still thinking about what Sylvie had said about Lubos and me while we were waiting at the corner for the traffic to clear. That must have been why I blurted out, "So I was thinking instead of coffee we could grab drinks at this gay bar I know. It's not far."

Lubos jerked his head back. "Er, no. I am not homosexual."

"I was kidding," I said quickly. "Or actually, I was hoping. For myself."

He asked me how to recognize if someone was a homosexual. "I did not recognize you as a gay," he said. "Of course, immediately I knew you look Jewish."

I blushed again. "I never tried to hide that I was gay. It just didn't come up."

"Surely," he said. " Of course, Sylvie and her girlfriend, they are homosexuals."

"Sylvie's a lesbian?" I couldn't have been more surprised if he'd said she was American. Sylvie? She was almost a rabbi. How could she be a lesbian? Who's her girlfriend? Then I remembered Sylvie clutching the arm of Lenka, her "assistant," during kaddish.

"Everyone knows," he said. "But she never talks about it openly."

So even the fearless Sylvie had her limits. This supposed maverick, so eager to spring to the defense of Reform Jews and Nazis, refused to crusade for the gay Jews too, even though she was one of them, she and her Lenka.

She was a hypocrite, a faker like all the rest of them, like that Nazi Rabbi Kahn.

✡

I stopped going to Sylvie's. One night I met Lubos at Meduza after services to help him translate a Jewish book written in English. He needed it for his thesis.

"Has she asked about me?" I said.

"Sylvie would not ask about an American," he explained.

A few weeks before Christmas, I decided to leave Prague. My plane ticket home was open-ended, but what about the rest of my life?

On my last day in town, I met Lubos in Old Town Square and together we visited my favorite cathedrals. I hardly saw him anymore. He was always in the library or synagogue.

"So now what?" I asked as we watch the sun sink behind the clock tower.

He seemed embarrassed. "Er, tonight is Friday. Many synagogues are not far…"

I cut him off. "I'll go with you to Sylvie's."

"Really?" Lubos clapped his hands.

Lenka let us in this time. She'd just returned from England and her face glowed like she was pregnant.

When we entered the basement, I heard, "You are returned from the dead," and turned to face Sylvie. She was shorter than I'd remembered.

"I've been out of town," I said, not afraid to meet her eyes for once.

She rolled her eyes. "Enough excuses. Find a chair."

I made a point of being friendly to everyone except Sylvie. I shook hands with newcomers and Zara the Amazon, who told me she'd gotten a grant. "Oh, *good*," I said with special emphasis. I sat next to an old man from New York with a Brooklyn accent who'd moved back here to die after a fifty-year exile. "I speak Czech like an American now and I didn't even know it. They all try to cheat me, in all the stores."

I felt sorry for him. "Why do you stay when they don't want you?"

"I have no choice," he said with a weak smile. "I feel it in my skin."

I watched Sylvie and her girlfriend closely, but I didn't see any signs of endearments until Sylvie chose Lenka to slice the challah.

At the end of kiddush, I tried to bid Sylvie a casual goodbye, but she pinched my arm and said, "Will we see you next week?" I didn't answer quickly enough and she added, "Why do I bother? You Americans are all gypsies."

"I want to ask you something," I said. "Isn't it true that if you follow the Torah strictly, you're supposed to reject gays? You're supposed to stone them."

"I'm glad you asked this question," Evzha said and repeated my challenge aloud in Czech so everyone could hear. "Let me tell you a story about Hillel and Shammai."

Here we go, I thought. Hillel and Shammai, the famous Jewish good cop–bad cop routine.

"Shammai believed you should obey all rules of Torah strictly, to the letter. But Hillel said, 'G-d gave us the Torah as his gift. He wants us to obey the rules in the way that will make our lives better.' Today, we study the words of both men, but Hillel's words are now the law."

"You still didn't answer my question," I said after she translated her sermon.

"Didn't I?"

"I mean, you didn't come out and say if you believed in excluding gays."

"Didn't I?" she repeated with a wink and folded up a chair.

On our way to the metro, Lubos said, "I would like to go to America, to go to a land where it is not strange to be Jewish."

"You're more Jewish than they are. More than I am. You chose it."

"There is no choice," he said. "In Holocaust, you would have died, not me."

When we said goodbye outside my apartment, he handed me a folded slip of brown paper. Inside were several bills, one, five, ten, twenty, and fifty marks. Terezin marks, play money for a concentration camp. "I collect them," he said shyly.

I handled the weirdly beautiful money by the corners. Each bill featured an oval portrait of Moses with the Ten Commandments. Each denomination had a different color, pale green, pink, and blue.

"Lubos, you can't give me this," I said, feeling dizzy. "It's too precious."

"I can find more. I know a special source," he said. "You keep it."

I was going to argue, but I looked at him and choked up. I didn't know if he was Jewish, but he was strange and so was I and he was my friend. "Thank you," I said.

✡

I live in New York now, and I attend services at a gay synagogue that meets in a church.

Lubos still writes me letters. Once he sent me an article about Sylvie that made no mention of her lesbianism. In the photo, Sylvie didn't smile, just looked up eerily from the shadows like a prophet. There was an account of a former fiancé from twenty years ago, a Mongolian dissident who'd agreed to convert to Judaism so they could get married. Before that could happen, the government expelled him from Czechoslovakia.

Today he lives in Mongolia and is married with a family.

The Great J. (Jewish) Gatsby
David Rosen

Uncle Art was the unacknowledged patriarch of my family, a former professional minor-league baseball star, and, possibly, Buffalo, New York's number-one most eligible Jewish bachelor (if anyone compiled those sorts of lists back then—say in the 1930s, '40s, '50s, and '60s).

In the F. Scott Fitzgerald version of my childhood, I'm Nick Carraway and Uncle Art is the Jewish Jay Gatsby of our clan, an enigmatic über–role model of colossal—and problematic—proportions.

He was a pillar of the Buffalo community, universally respected for being a businessman with a lot of heart. However, once you got to know him well (not unlike everyone else in my family, or everyone else in the world, come to think of it), you learned this loca superstar Jewish mover-and-shaker *macher* was actually kinda loco, kooky, weird—nothing less than a tangle of public and private eccentricity.

He was born (around 1900 or so) one Aaron Arthur Fisher. No one I know ever called him Aaron. He sometimes went by A. Arthur. His business was called Art Fisher Tire Co. (It was located down on Main Street, right near this great doughnut bakery, and not as far downtown as the famous Anchor Bar (of Buffalo chicken wings fame).

To all of Art's legions of intensely devoted and loyal employees of one sort or another (clerks, maids, cooks, mechanics, gardeners, Chinese delivery boys, salesmen, and so forth), to whom he referred in conversation as "the help" or "my boys" or "my men" or, as appropriate for the gender and the times, "my girls," he was always "Mr. Fisher."

He was lanky—or at least to me he seemed lanky, for a post-middle-aged Jewish businessman, that is—and handsome in that dome-headed captain-of-industry way. One of those polished bald men who, ever insinuating their way into any number of upper-crust social settings, always manage to turn others' heads.

I never saw Uncle Art wait in line for anything. He could cut a swath through a crowd like the razor-edged prow of a sailing vessel. If he couldn't manage it himself, he'd hire someone to wait or shlep something heavy or park his car for him. "Where's our man?" I remember him asking quite often, when we were shopping or at dinner or in a parking lot. Sometimes it was my brothers or my sister or me he'd hire—to work in his office, to rake leaves, cut lawns, paint his cottage, or the like. The pay was ridiculously generous: twenty-dollar bills, savings bonds, snow tires, cars…

That this impressive yacht of a successful Jewish man was also often at the epicenter of my family's most perfect storms of dysfunctional dramas, few of his business associates (and all his friends, who of course had some sort of business connection to him) ever suspected.

I myself was no stranger to stirring up my own heavy-weather hurricane of growing-up dramas. In 1963, when I wasn't yet four years old, I was forever sitting three inches away from our family's black-and-white RCA television, and so it was soon discovered that I was intensely nearsighted (like -20, if you understand the opthal-lingo). And so I was forced to wear mega-Coke-bottle-bottom glasses. Even at this young age, I picked up real quickly that being so oddly, so majorly, so freakishly bespectacled, I resembled those kids they'd always show on TV as "retarded" or "awkward" or "bookishly awkward and retarded." I was so often called Hey Four Eyes, Hey Retard,

Hey Sissy, Hey Homo, and worse, that by age six I was of course withdrawn. I must have outwardly exhibited a rather shell-shocked, hyper-self-conscious kind of social disdain. When I could muster something to say in public, my voice was squeaky-high. I often played the clown, just to spin hordes of unwanted attention into more jovial sorts of attention I controlled. Hmm…gay Jews: born to entertain?

I often retreated to the bathrooms in any houses of relatives or friends we visited, as a respite from scrutiny or the usual social demands—like playing any sort of game with others. "I bet you love to read books!" the kinder folks would say to me at first meeting. Every kid I met and most adults were transfixed at the sophisticated optics involved in what enabled me to (minimally) see—the hundreds of concentric circles that were contained in my glasses' lenses. People openly gawked. Small children and dogs couldn't look away to save their lives.

As I grew up, I was always trying way too hard—unsuccessfully, I'm now quite certain—not to look or act like a retard or sissy or genius—for that matter, to not act like anything, really.

To me, Uncle Art was the walking definition of what I could never, ever be: a potent male archetype, one I was equally drawn to and deeply disturbed by. How could I ever grow up to be that? So confident, so in control, so suave, so…manly? He was self-assured, cologne-scented sexy, successful. To my megamyopic eyes (and mindset), he presented to the world what it was to be a man a cut above—eagle-like, important.

It didn't hurt my inchoate (and, of course, illusory) idol-worship of Uncle Art that he was (and this part is true), as we Buffalonians would say, "fucking filthy rich," a self-made rags-to-riches millionaire.

But that's making it sound all so neat and tidy. Nothing in my family, in any family, is altogether ship shape, now is it? Uncle Art's place in my little nearsighted familial world was particularly puzzling, hard for me to square away, as much as I bowed and scraped (everyone did) at his beneficent altar. For starters, he was my *great-* uncle. Not my father's brother but my father's *mother's* brother—one of those just-complex-enough relational and relativistic relative ideas your mother has to explain hundreds of times to you when you're a kid until it vaguely sinks in. Looking back now, it seems so funny how, in feeble attempts (often transparent) to save some measure of little-kid face, I recall after each helpful retelling of who this man was to me, I'd still feel compelled to whine "I know, I know, Mom. You told me already."

Uncle Art belonged to a hotsy-totsy private city (not country) "club," the Montifiore. People "dressed" for dinner there, for drinks there, for being there. So each year like clockwork, he'd take my brother Rick (three years older) and me to Buffalo's bastion of gentlemanly fashion, Kleinhan's Men's store, to buy us sport coats and shoes and raincoats and such so we'd be suitably tony and presentable at Mother's Day and Passover meals at "the club." For a few years in my teens, we went almost every Sunday—all dressed up, us Rosen and Fisher Family Royals.

I, for one, loved going to the club exactly because we got to dress up. The prospect of which, I—unlike every single other young boy in Buffalo—absolutely adored. I have always loved clothes. Men's clothes, ties, suits, tuxes, and such. I loved the Montifiore Club's oversize chandeliers and floral arrangements; the tables bedecked with stacks of gold-edged china, the multiple weighty-in-the-hand flatware settings; the way everyone (family, servants, strangers too) all looked in the crystalline glow-the sheer shimmering, expensive showiness of the place. My idea of boyhood bliss!

This was a club that had separate "lounges" for men and women. (Only the men's had access to a bar, which was called "The Library.") Women could be accompanied by men there, but this was often subject of drunken jokes. All the waitstaff and other "help" were either over seventy years old, or Asian and eighteen, or black. We Fisher and Rosen men were addressed as "Sir," and I'm almost certain gold-edged place cards graced the table, mine always reading "Master David."

To be fair, this was surely no Brideshead upbringing, but we pretended to be classy as all get-out. I can't help confess that I loved being someone on the outside looking in, an invited guest to the ball. I knew we weren't rich, but we could pull it off when it counted.

I really didn't know how to act like a boy. "David, what do you want to be when you grow up?" everyone forever asked me. "A doctor? lawyer? How about a fireman or astronaut?"

"A girl," I'd answer.

And everyone would think I was a little budding comedian. A mini-Jackie Mason. Couldn't anyone tell I was really a little budding *faygeleh*?

By the time I was six, I'd run through the house, with a towel trailing off my head like long flowing pretend girl's-hair, shouting "I wanna be a girl" so all the world could hear. "A girl, a girl!" Why?

Well, I really didn't want to be a girl. I just didn't want to be a boy either.

I hated any sport that required anything to be done with a ball. If pressed for the reason why I'd pick being a girl over a boy (which rarely happened), I had it all figured out. Because girls got to wear all the pretty clothes; girls could have long beautiful bouncy straight hair, like Cher and that Prell model (and my sister, who bought a really happening wig called a "fall" when she went to college); and girls didn't get drafted and get themselves maimed and killed in Vietnam. (My father and my brother Bruce were always talking about "the war" and my mother would always say we'd all move to Canada should her son ever get picked.)

For the longest time it seemed more than logical, actually rather essential, that you would be able to choose which gender you would grow up to be. And from my perspective, I was absolutely certain girls had the better end of the deal. In the early 1960s no one was forcing them to play baseball and football and such. And girls just had better hair.

You see, this hair-obsession thing, for me, and truth be told, for my entire family, was as constant as western New York State's lack of sun, the Friday night Sabbath, and the five months' worth of snow beneath our feet. Hair mattered, big-time.

My father (not as master-of-the-universe successful as Uncle Art, but no poor schlub in the business arena, himself) was tall and waspy-handsome for a Jewish guy. But like Uncle Art (and certain American eagles) he was also bald.

Unlike Uncle Art, my dad in later life (after fifty) became vain and adventurous enough purchase a toupee from some Hair Club for Men in Toronto and so donned a not entirely unconvincing and rather flattering hairpiece.

All throughout my childhood, teens, and early twenties, my father forever sung praises to my utterly unruly, wavy, bird's nest hair (onto which I forever applied liberal amounts of water and Vitalis and Breck hair spray to smooth it down like the Monkees' hair—and every other cool guy of the moment's). My dad would take one look at his greasy-kid-stuff-lathered kid, yell "stop plastering your hair down," and finger-brush my poor attempt at ultracool bangs off my forehead. He'd scold, "If only I had wavy hair like yours! Like a matinee idol!" I didn't know what a matinee idol was, but I knew Jews weren't supposed to worship idols. And if they had out-of-style wavy hair, I didn't want to look like one. "It looks messy all wavy," I'd retort. "I like it smooth." A follically challenged control-freak-in-training?

One of Dad's favorite proud-papa stories: When I was a baby and he wheeled me around in the stroller, all the passersby oohed and aahed how gorgeous the curly locks of this adorable baby *girl* were. The story goes that they got tired of correcting folks on the gender-confusion thing. "How could you blame us?" he'd ask by way of a feeble attempt of a defense. "For the longest time, your mother and I couldn't force ourselves to cut your beautiful curly blond hair! Such pretty hair on a boy!" my Dad would recount with glee.

I wonder if this is a Jewish thing: hair envy spread rampant through several generations. Uncle Art (permanently *un*-toupeed) was also fixated on hair—color, texture, and length. (In the 1960s and '70s, it felt to me that everyone was always and only talking about either hair or the war. The musical *Hair* must have just nailed the cultural flash point that converged the two in everyone's imagination. To this day, when I hear the word "Vietnam," I see a bone-skinny man with a beard and long hair. Christ and Vietnam are permanently fused in my mind's eye.)

But my family (around the dinner table, in bathrooms, in the car, on the porch or on the beach, in parks, watching TV) mostly just talked about hair. All hair all the time. My mother was always "doing" her hair, applying acrid-smelly chemicals in plastic squirter bottles, and then sitting under the cone of a hair dryer. My sister Scotch-taped her hair into place each night, which I'd listen to while falling asleep. It was a comforting sound, a repeated screech and snap. Screech and snap.

Sitting under the beneficent half-cocoon of my mother's hair dryer, with its gentle shower-cap halo of toasty air, its block-out-the-rest-of-the-world hum, was also unbelievably comforting—which my brother and I were allowed to do after baths and showers "so we wouldn't get a chill." Only when I was about thirteen or fourteen did I realize how wussy this must have looked to my poor WWII-veteran dad, and so I therefore stopped.

Most folks my age measure the big events of their growing up with vivid memories of stuff like the Kennedy and Martin Luther King Jr. assassinations, the Neil Armstrong walk on the moon, or even the day their family got their first color TV. I too recall, vividly, with great rushes of emotion, these earth-shaking events—where I was and what I was doing when each occurred. But right up there in my private pantheon of "Days the World Changed" is that blessed Saturday afternoon in the winter of 1974 or '75 when my father carted home a hand-held hair-drying device—designed for men. The planet shifted on its axis.

The glossy box of this "electric hair-styling nrush," as it was called, boasted a handsome guy with a Farrah Fawcett–like layered mane, a mustache, and a beard. Maybe a little Robert Redford-ish in honey-blond color and texture. Inside was this fabulous, tool-like, tortoise-shell gadget (that oddly matched the color of my eyeglass frames), which had more attachments than our Hoover. I spent much of my high school years (when I wasn't shoveling snow or watching *Bowling for Dollars* on my mini TV) performing an endless ritual of wetting and rewetting, spraying and gooping, and drying and redrying my disturbingly unmanageable, wavy hair. All in efforts to make it fall into place like that guy on the box, or like everyone on TV. Often, my hair would get so static-filled and bone-chilling dry, the only thing that would make it settle down was to put on a ski cap. This I often resorted to even in the heat of summer, before particularly significant "appearances," like walking downstairs to breakfast, or running the garbage out to the cans we kept back by the garage.

How Hair Care 101 is tied to Uncle Art: Uncle Art's preferred form of interaction with my brother Rick and me for at least an entire decade revolved around hair. Often he'd answer our "Hi, Uncle Art" greetings by grabbing the hair that trailed just over our collars (as was the fashion for mildly faux-rebellious but essentially wimpy parent-pleasing young men like us to wear during those polyester pre–disco party years). He'd yank on our mini-manes until it hurt, say "What's all this?" and then proceed to slip us ten or twenty bucks (which felt like a fortune back then, and probably was).

"Now you boys can afford to get a haircut."

We never, not even once, used Uncle Art's faintly tire-smelling money to get a haircut. My brother Rick spent his windfalls on his hobby of collecting Spiderman and Green Hornet comic books; I myself, set upon the self-appointed task of amassing a full-spectrum collection of Flair fine-point felt-tipped colored pens, which I'd purchase one by one from the Leader Drug store across the street from the comic book store at the end of our block. The Flairs were pressed into service when we traced covers of the comics and filled them in, paint-by-number style. Soon, by age seven or eight, I moved on to tracing boxes and circles from my sister's geometry text, when superhero art started to lose its allure. My figurative phase gave way to abstraction, akin to most twentieth-century doodlers, artistes, and their appreciators.

Uncle Art, come to think of it, was like our own private Jewish superhero. You've got trouble? Mister moneybags to the rescue. He was generous, to be sure, a veritable font of bills and coins, unsolicited Polonious-tedious advice, and, oh yeah, how can I ever forget about…the fruit.

Here's the set-up: Every Friday night my family staged an "Ozzie and Harriet" adaptation of the ritual Shabbos (now irritatingly referred to by most Jews as Shabbat) candle-lighting scene in *Fiddler on the Roof*. My mom and dad and their brood of four gathered round the dinner table in suitable, upstanding Reform Jewish family fashion. We'd divide up the prayers like parts in a play: Mom would bless the candles, Dad the bread, and either Bruce or Rick wine, and I would get to say the Shema. Mom really loved this time of blessing (we never said grace on other nights, but on Fridays the dining-room TV, usually chattering away, was silenced), and she would try to keep this time, well, *sacred* is the right word. But more times than not, our tiny hallowed slice of spiritual sanctuary, our own private, quiet, eternal kiddush-cup moment, was unceremoniously shattered by the honk of Uncle Art's horn.

The hulking luxury car du jour (endlessly changing from a Mercury to Lincoln or, in later years, a Caddie) would swing into the drive. He'd honk again.

"Boys, Uncle Art is here!" my dad would announce. "Don't make him wait." My mother would begin her Shabbos-interruptus sulk, corralling the platters and bowls of food back into the kitchen to keep them warm.

"Boys," my father would repeat. This was our cue. My brother Rick (light-years wiser than I in his skills of shirking chores such as this) would often stop at the bathroom en route to doing anything he didn't want to do. Darn nervous stomach!

What we were supposed to do on cue: The dutiful pair of bright-eyed young Jewish boys race with joy out to their great-uncle's fancy car to help him lug huge boxes of near-rotting fruit from his trunk.

"Do you have a job yet?" Uncle Art would bark. I remember this question being posed week after week, year in, year out, when I was five (and six and seven…and seventeen).

"I'm only five (or six or seven or seventeen)," I'd say.

"You're never to young to learn the value of work. Boys have to learn responsibility. You boys have it so soft. Come down to the store and I'll find work for you to do. At the very least you two should have a paper route. Jesus Christ, you boys are spoiled."

Now, I ask you, why did all my Jewish relatives (and most Jews I grew up with) say "Jesus Christ" all the time? Curious, isn't it? Were they too thinking of the fabulous long hair?

So Rick and I (or more often than not, just I) would cart the moldy-bottomed boxes of apples, oranges, and my favorite, sour pink grapefruit—whoopee!—into the kitchen. *Please don't let me drop the box,* I'd pray. *Please don't let the bottom fall out, like it did once—fruit rolling down the driveway into the street, all of us shouting and being shouted at, scrambling like fools for all the neighbors to see.*

But most of the time, the Delivery of the Fruit was accomplished sans disaster, and my brother and I (especially if an attendant "Get a haircut" speech was in the offing) made out like bandits. Uncle Art would then continue on his mission of delivering fruit to his major "accounts."

Another weird fact of Uncle Art life: This sixty-something ladies' man—who owned a cottage across the Peace Bridge in Canada that boasted a garage plastered with 1950s *Playboy* "nudie" pinup shots of women—this most eligible bachelor lived with my grandmother. It was unclear who took care of whom. We called her Nanna (to distinguish her from my mother's mother, whom we called Nanny). Nanny looked like a grandmother should—gray hair, sweet, bubbly, always taking pies out of the oven, and wearing an apron she'd made herself. My father's mother, Nanna, on the other hand, Uncle Art's dear sister, was the spitting image—with her diaphanous scarf-y outfits and teased-frizzed red-blond hair and blue eye shadow and fake long lashes—of Endora from *Bewitched.*

So Uncle Art lived with Endora in this huge rambling ranch house just outside Buffalo's northeastern limits. Uncle Art's room was vast. His bathroom smelled like Millionaire aftershave (remember the huge pyramid-shaped bottle?). My father, my brother, and I would go there to do boy things, like polish our shoes on Uncle Art's electric shoe shiner. This was long before the Sharper Image marketed these handy gentlemanly items to the general public, but sometimes you'd find them in men's rooms at hotels, or at the Montifiore Club men's coat room.

One night I will never forget: Uncle Art asked us to accompany him into his huge walk-in closet. He called it a "wardrobe." A silk bathrobe in dry-cleaning see-through plastic was hanging on the door. Suits were arranged in impeccable order like they displayed them at Kleinhan's. Dress shirts in boxes marked as such—also fresh from the dry cleaner's—were stacked next to a collection of hats. The closet smelled like a dry cleaner's. "Look, boys. Want to see my beautiful shirts?" We looked, and oohed and aahed.

And piled atop a dresser-like built-in storage chest, in a fanlike arrangement worthy of Busby Berkeley, were some twenty or more packages of dress shirts, still in their original plastic wrappers. Mostly white and light blue, with maybe an ecru or yellow here and there for accent.

"And boys," Uncle Art began, and the three of us edged closer to share in the secret of his holiest of holy, inner sanctum. "See these. The finest money can buy."

"But you haven't even opened them yet," my father observed. "You have more shirts than you can ever wear!"

"No. I'll get to them... Maybe," he defended. "Here, you're missing the point. Just knowing I have them, that I could open up a new shirt whenever I want, to wear...whenever—just knowing I can buy the finest shirts they make, that's what it's all about."

"Huh?" we all gasped in shared confusion, disbelief.

"What what's all about?" Dad queried.

"Having all these expensive shirts is what. They remind me every day that I've made it. That I'm a real *mentsh*. That I have to be that good to deserve them. That's what."

About the Mentshen

HARLYN AIZLEY is the author of *Buying Dad: One Woman's Search for the Perfect Sperm Donor* (Alyson Books). Her writings have appeared in magazines and anthologies, including the *Berkeley Fiction Review, Boston Magazine, The South Carolina Review, Best Lesbian Love Stories 2004, Look Shook My Heart,* and *Scream When You Burn.* Despite having graduated from Brandeis University, Harlyn still has no idea what *Shimini Atseret* is.

JEFFREY BERNHARDT is a Jewish educator, licensed clinical social worker, Jewish communal professional, and freelance writer in Los Angeles. He is the author of *Day's End,* staged in Los Angeles in May 2000, and is the author of *Who Shall Live…?* which has been staged at synagogues and Jewish settings throughout the country. While he grew up in a mainstream Jewish synagogue in a small New Jersey suburb, he now belongs to the world's oldest GLBT synagogue.

WARREN J. BLUMENFELD is the editor of *Homophobia: How We All Pay the Price;* former editor of the *International Journal of Sexuality and Gender Studies;* coauthor of *Looking at Gay and Lesbian Life,* author of *AIDS and Your Religious Community;* coeditor of *Readings for Diversity and Social Justice: An Anthology on Racism, Antisemitism, Sexism, Heterosexism, Ableism, and Classism;* coeditor of *Butler Matters: Judith Butler's Impact on Feminist and Queer Studies;* and coproducer of the documentary *Pink Triangles.* He is a visiting assistant professor in the Department of Educational Studies at Colgate University.

HINDE ENA BURSTIN is a secular *dykele* who spends lots of time down under. She is a founding member of Jewish Lesbian Group of Victoria (Australia), and a feminist, anti-racism, disability action, and peace activist. She teaches "Yidish far Lezbiankes" and other courses. More than fifty of her poems, short stories, and feature articles have been published in Australia, the U.S., Canada. and Israel. She is currently compiling and translating a commissioned collection of Yiddish children's poetry.

DAVI CHENG serves as president of Beth Chayim Chadashim, the world's first gay and lesbian synagogue, founded in Los Angeles in 1972. Davi cofounded the synagogue's klezmer band, Gay Gezunt, and plays the trumpet and French horn. She also designed the stained-glass windows at BCC. In addition to her interests in art and music, Davi holds a second-degree black belt in Judo. Born in Hong Kong, she immigrated to the U.S. with her family in 1971, at age fourteen. She holds a B.A. degree in biological science from the University of California, Berkeley, where she met her life partner (twenty-five years and counting!), Bracha Yael. Davi is currently the in-house graphic designer at a medical research laboratory in Southern California.

EDWARD M. COHEN's novel *$250,000* was published by Putnam; his nonfiction books by Prentice-Hall, Prima, SUNY Press, and Limelight Editions. He has just completed a new novel, *Golden Boys and Girls*. He has published more than thirty stories in quarterlies and won honorable mention in the Lorian Hemingway Story Contest, Arch & Bruce Brown Short Fiction Contest, and Evergreen Chronicles Novella Contest.

STEVEN COOPER is an Emmy award–winning television news anchor and reporter. Born and raised in Massachusetts, he also calls Orlando and Phoenix home. He is the author of the novels *With You In Spirit* and *Saving Valencia* and is currently working on the movie musical *Pomp & Circumcision*, based on his college years, to be directed by Mel Gibson (not).

About the Mentshen

JILL DOLAN is the author of *The Feminist Spectator as Critic; Presence and Desire: Essays on Gender, Sexuality, Performance;* and *Geographies of Learning: Theory and Practice, Activism, and Performance.* Her story, "Exorcism," appears in *Best Lesbian Love Stories 2003.* She teaches at the University of Texas at Austin.

RABBI LISA A. EDWARDS, PH.D., has spent the last decade as rabbi of Beth Chayim Chadashim ("House of New Life") in Los Angeles. Founded in 1972 as the world's first synagogue for gay and lesbian Jews, BCC continues to be a community for queer and progressive Jews, allies, and friends. She lives with her partner of eighteen years, Tracy Moore, oral herstorian and editor of *Lesbiot: Israeli Lesbians Talk about Sexuality, Feminism, Judaism and Their Lives* (Cassell Press, 1995). Rabbi Edwards has published essays in a variety of Jewish books and journals, including *Lesbian Rabbis: The First Generation* (Rutgers, 2001). An interview with her appears in *Outspoken: Role Models from the Lesbian and Gay Community,* a book for adolescents and teenagers (Beech Tree, 1998). Rabbi Edwards holds a Ph.D. in English from the University of Iowa and received ordination from Hebrew Union College-Jewish Institute of Religion in 1994.

DAN FISHBACK is a performance artist and songwriter living in New York City. In 2003, his band Cheese on Bread released its first album, *Maybe Maybe Maybe Baby.* In February 2004 he premiered his first one-man show, *Assholes Speak Louder Than Words.* Dan is part of New York's anti-folk community and performs solo acoustic material regularly at the Sidewalk Café. It's been two years since he wrote his story for *Mentsh,* and he's no longer feeling so melodramatic.

INA TURPEN FRIED is a writer and journalist in San Francisco, where she lives with her partner, A.J., and her mischievous cats, Chuppah and Kiva. A few words that often describe Ina are: sporty, sarcastic, transgender, busy, culinary, softball-obsessed, queer, and married. She's thankful to her family and to the pioneers of the women's movement, the civil rights movement, and the gay, lesbian, bisexual, transgender, and intersex liberation movements for making the world a safer place for all of us.

CAROL FRISCHMAN is a daughter, sister, friend, student, teacher, coach, lesbian, feminist, vegetarian, Jew, and jock. She embraces these labels fully and wholeheartedly.

AARON HAMBURGER is the author of *The View from Stalin's Head* (Random House, 2004), a story collection about Prague. His first novel, set in Jerusalem, will be published in 2005. His writing has appeared in *Poets & Writers, Out, The Village Voice, Time Out*, and *Nerve*.

SIOBHÁN HOUSTON is a writer, mother, priestess, and doctoral candidate in Western esoteric history and spirituality at the University of Wales, Lampeter. A graduate of Harvard Divinity School, she has had her work published appeared in numerous journals of spirituality and religion as well as in *Weird Sisters, We' Moon 2004*, and *Best Lesbian Love Stories 2003* (Alyson Books). She lives with her spouse, Rae Miller, near Boulder, Colorado.

DANIEL M. JAFFE's gay-Jewish-themed novel *The Limits of Pleasure* was a finalist for a *ForeWord Magazine*'s Book of the Year Award and was excerpted in *Best Gay Erotica 2003*. He is the editor of *With Signs and Wonders: An International Anthology of Jewish Fabulist Fiction* and translator of Dina Rubina's Russian-Israeli novel *Here Comes the Messiah!* Visit his Web site at www.danieljaffe.tripod.com.

BONNIE KAPLAN lives and works in the San Fernando Valley. She holds an MFA in film/video/performance art from the California College of Arts and Crafts. Interpersonal comedy is at the core of much of her creative work in live performance, video art, and public-access television.

About the Mentshen

TANIA KATAN is an accomplished playwright, professional lesbian, and a soon-to-be memoirist. In 2003 she was an artist-in-residence at the Creative Center in New York. In addition, she has appeared half-clad in both *The Advocate* and *Girlfriends* magazine. Her memoir *My One-Night Stand With Cancer* is forthcoming from Alyson Books.

SUE KATZ has published journalism and fiction on the three continents where she has lived. Full-time writing is her third career, after having been a martial arts master for twenty years and then an executive in the nonprofit world. She has just completed a novel that takes place in Israel during the 1982 invasion of Lebanon and is looking for an agent. For fun, Katz is a Latin American dancer and rebellious activist.

After completing two master's degrees and a few research scholarship residencies, MIODRAG KOJADINOVIĆ feels he may eventually have to finish his dissertation. In the meantime, he writes poetry, nostalgia, erotica, travelogues, reviews, and academic papers; he also translates works of gay authors from seven languages into Serbian and English, coordinates and coteaches queer studies, does astrology charts, S/M escorting, some media work, and more. Make him an offer at Concomitantly@yahoo.com.

After a successful career in Hollywood as a producer and talent executive, BEVERLY KOPF was hired by Barbara Walters to create the voice of a new show, *The View.* Beverly went on to win a GLAAD Media Award and an Emmy award for her work as writer for *The View.* In 2000, Beverly and her life partner, Bobbie, joined forces to create their own television production company, TVgals. Beverly has also written her first screenplay, *Unleashed!!* about coming out in Hollywood, and is at work on her first play. She mourns the loss of her mother, who died in January 2004.

ROY LIEBMAN is a (mostly) retired university librarian (California Institute of Technology and California State University, Los Angeles).

About the Mentshen

His decade-long interest in silent and early sound film history has led to the publication of four books, including his latest, *Vitaphone Films* (McFarland, 2003), as well as numerous articles, reference book entries, and countless book reviews. He also wrote a produced script for a television documentary. Roy currently works part-time for the Los Angeles Public Library.

SARA MARCUS is a freelance writer living in Brooklyn. She is also the politics editor at *Heeb,* a magazine of progressive Jewish culture and politics. Her work has appeared in *The Advocate, Time Out New York,* the *Philadelphia Inquirer, Venus,* and *A Girl's Guide to Taking Over the World.*

DAVID MAY was a nice boy from a good family who fell in with the wrong crowd. He first made his mark writing for *Drummer* and other gay skin magazines in the 1980s and is the author of *Madrugada: A Cycle of Erotic Fictions.* His work, both fiction and nonfiction, has appeared in numerous magazines and journals as well as in more than a dozen anthologies, including *Best Gay Erotica 2003, Afterwords, Kosher Meat,* and *Flesh and the Word 3.* He lives in Seattle with his husband and cat.

JAY MICHAELSON is the director of Nehirim: A Spiritual Initiative for GLBT Jews (www.nehirim.org), and the chief editor of *Zeek: A Jewish Journal of Thought and Culture* (www.zeek.net). A teacher of kabbalah, spirituality, and embodied Judaism, he was a finalist for the 2003 Koret Young Writer on Jewish Themes Award. Jay's recent work includes *The Inflected Letters: Stories of Faith and Desire* and *The Gate of Sadness: Enlightenment and the Broken Heart* (forth-coming). He lives in Brooklyn.

BONNIE J. MORRIS lives and writes in Washington, D.C., and is the author of five books, including *Eden Built By Eves* and *Girl Reel.* When not teaching women's history (at George Washington University, Georgetown, and most recently on a ship going around the world for the Semester at Sea program), Dr. Bon works at women's music festivals and Rollerblades past embassies in her extremely hip neighborhood.

Liz Morrison is a San Diego–based freelance writer. Her articles have appeared in several local and national publications. Her short stories have been published in *Sinister Wisdom, From These Walls, Storied Crossings,* and *Testimonies.*

Lesléa Newman has written many books that explore the dual identities of being a lesbian and being a Jew, including the novel *In Every Laugh a Tear,* which details the relationship between a nice Jewish dyke and her 99-year-old bubbe. Her other work includes the short story collections *A Letter to Harvey Milk; She Loves Me, She Loves Me Not; Girls Will be Girls;* and *The Best Short Stories of Lesléa Newman* as well as the children's books *Heather Has Two Mommies, Felicia's Favorite Story, Runaway Dreidel!* and *Matzo Ball Moon.* Visit lesleanewman.com to learn more about her work.

Eric Pliner lives in Brooklyn, New York, and works in education. He thought about going to rabbinical school but changed his mind. Instead he writes plays, stories, and e-mail (epliner@earthlink.net). Eric enjoys chopped liver but hates gefilte fish.

Adam Seth Rosen is a twenty-five-year-old composer, performer, and writer in St. Louis, Missouri. In June 2002 he made his professional debut as a composer with an original theatrical score for the St. Louis premiere of Moisés Kaufman's *The Laramie Project.* Adam is currently music director for Ed Reggi's Paper SLIP Theater, an improv comedy troupe. Last year he played keyboard for (Mostly) Harmless Theatre's premiere of a new rock musical, *Jouet.* Adam's *bashert* can reach him at tequilamock@hotmail.com.

David Rosen is the editor in chief of InsightOutBooks, which he cofounded in 2000. He has been active in LGBT publishing and bookselling for twenty years. He has been an editor at the Quality Paperback Book Club (QPB) since 1989 and is currently QPB editor at large. Before that, he was assistant editor at *The Advocate* in the 1980s. In 1994, David's work making gay and lesbian books available through book clubs won him a GLAAD Media Award. In 2001, his work at InsightOut and the Triangle Classics Library that he edits were honored with the Lambda Literary Foundation Pioneer Award. He lives in New York City.

ROB ROSEN lives, loves, and works in San Francisco. His first novel, *Sparkle: The Queerest Book You'll Ever Love,* was published in 2001 to critical acclaim. His short stories have appeared on such literary sites as SoMa Literary Review, Unlikely Stories, Ten Thousand Monkeys, Thunder Sandwich, Willow Lake Press, Muse Apprentice Guild, Defenestration, Zygote in My Coffee, DriftersOasis, and Acid Logic. Visit him at www.therobrosen.com or e-mail him at robrosen@therobrosen.com.

RONNI L. SANLO is the director of the UCLA Lesbian Gay Bisexual Transgender Center. Dr. Sanlo earned a bachelor's degree from the University of Florida, and a master's and doctorate in education from the University of North Florida in Jacksonville. Her research area is sexual/gender identity in higher education, and she has written numerous books and articles on these subjects. She's a proud mother and grandmother, the daughter of outrageous PFLAG parents, and she's single!

BRUCE SHENITZ is executive editor of *Out* magazine and editor of the Lambda Literary Award–winning anthology *The Man I Might Become: Gay Men Write About Their Fathers* (Marlowe & Co., 2002). His writing has appeared in *The New York Times,* the *Los Angeles Times Magazine, Newsweek,* and other national publications. He lives in New York City with his partner, Stan.

About the Mentshen

SIMON SHEPPARD is the author of *Kinkorama: Dispatches From the Front Lines of Perversion* and the short-story collections *In Deep* and *Hotter Than Hell,* all from Alyson Books. His work appears in more than 100 anthologies, including many editions of *The Best American Erotica* and *Best Gay Erotica,* and his Sex Talk column is widely syndicated. He lives in San Francisco with his charming *shaygets* of a boyfriend and can be found at www.simonsheppard.com.

Hollywood native RAPHAEL SIMON writes chiefly for film and television but is also a closet prose writer. His essays and articles have appeared in the *Los Angeles Times Magazine, Premiere,* and *L.A. Weekly,* among other publications. A graduate of Yale and of the University of California, Irvine, Raphael has also taught courses in writing and critical theory, most recently at California Institute of the Arts.

FAITH SOLOWAY has been hailed by critics and audiences as one of the best and brightest of the Boston area's singer-songwriters. Whether singing with her animated, energetic band, The Faith Soloway Crisis, or creating and performing in one of her many comedic "schlock operas"—which include *Jesus Has Two Mommies, Miss Folk America,* and *The Lezboat*—Faith has built a large and devoted following throughout Boston and beyond. She is also the creator of the nationwide stage show *The Real Live Brady Bunch,* which she directed with her sister, Jill. Faith lives with her partner, writer HarlynAizley, and their daughter Betsy.

SHIFRA TEITELBAUM has been an educator for more than twenty years. She is the director of youTHink, a program that serves public schools in California, engaging students in contemporary social issues and community involvement through art. Shifra lives and makes trouble in Los Angeles with her partner, Melissa.

CHANA WILSON is a psychotherapist and writer who lives in the San Francisco Bay Area. She is published in the anthology *The Next*

Step: Out From Under, and the forthcoming anthology of lesbian love stories *I'm Home: What It Is Like to Love a Woman*. She is currently at work on a book-length memoir about her relationship with her lesbian mother.

Hebrew and Yiddish Glossary

Hebrew words are designated with (H). Yiddish and Hebrew spellings are not "official," as the only correct way to spell Yiddish and Hebrew words is with Hebrew letters. Instead, the words are transliterated. Likewise, the usage of Yiddish words may vary according to where one is from. Lastly, many Yiddish words have adopted English suffixes (i.e., *shmoozing*), as Jews who came to America learned to speak English and sprinkled this new foreign language with words from the *mama-loshen* (mother tongue), which really do lose something in the translation. (**Editor's note:** I've added a few Yiddish words here that do not appear anywhere else in this book, merely because I love them so much. Maybe I'm a little *farblondzhet*?)

Adon Olam: literally, "Master of the World." A very old poem recited at the beginning of morning prayers.
Aleinu (H): literally, "It is our duty." Prayer recited near the conclusion of the Shabbat service.
aliyah (H): to go up, to become a citizen of Israel
alter kocher: an old Jewish man
Amidah (H): silent prayer recited during a prayer service
Ashkenazic: of Eastern European Jewish descent
bar mitzvah (H): a formal ceremony to commemorate a thirteen-year-old boy's entry into manhood
Baruch atah Adonai (H): "Blessed are You, Eternal our G-d."
bashert (H): destiny or, commonly, one's soul mate

bat mitzvah (H): a formal ceremony to commemorate a twelve-year-old girl's entry into womanhood

bimah (H): a pulpit, stage, or raised platform in a synagogue

boychik: a Jewish boy

bracha (H): a blessing

bris milah (H): Literally, bris means "convenant" and "milah" means cutting. Ritual circumcision performed on male Jewish infants on the eighth day after birth. Often shortened to "bris."

bubbe: grandmother

bubele: darling or sweetheart

bubkes: nothing, but less than nothing if possible. "They had *bubkes* in the Passover aisle!"

Chag sameach (H): literally, "joyous festival." An appropriate greeting for just about any holiday but especially appropriate for Sukkot, Shavu'ot, and Pesach (Passover), which are technically the only festivals (the other holidays are holidays, not festivals).

chai (H): two Hebrew letters representing "life"

challah (H): beautiful braided bread eaten on Shabbos and holidays

Chanukah (H): festival of lights lasting eight days and commemorating the Maccabees' victory over the Syrians and the rededication of the Temple at Jerusalem

chavurah (H): literally, "friends." A group of people, generally within a synagogue, who learn, celebrate, and socialize together.

chuppah: a marriage canopy

chutzpah: nerve

daven: to recite Jewish prayers

dayenu (H): "It would have been enough for us."

fachadick: extremely confused

fahklumpt: another word for confused

famisched: confused, mixed up

farblondzhet: lost, bewildered, confused. Yet another in the group of mixed-up words. By the way, not an easy word to rhyme with.

faygeleh: a gay man. Often used disparagingly.

feh: interjection used to indicate disapproval or displeasure, as in, "*Feh*, don't touch that pork chop!"

Gottenyu: oh, my G-d

goy: a non-Jew (pl., goyim; adj., goyishe)

haftorah (H): one of the biblical selections from the Books of the Prophets read after the Torah portion in a synagogue service

haggadah (H): the prayer book used during the seder ritual

hamish (H): warm, welcoming

Hashem (H): literally, "the name." A term used to describe G-d.

kaddish (H): mourner's prayer

kedushah (H): holiness

ketubah (H): a Jewish marriage contract

khaver: a friend

kibbutz: a communal farm or settlement in Israel

kibbutznik: someone who lives on a kibbutz

kiddush (H): a ceremonial blessing pronounced over wine or bread in a synagogue or Jewish home

kiddushin (P): Jewish marriage

kippah (H): a skull cap

kosher (H): fit to eat according to Jewish dietary law

kreplach: square or triangular dumplings filled with ground meat or cheese, boiled or fried, and usually served in soup

kugel: a baked pudding (as of potatoes or noodles) usually served as a side dish. Can be sweet or savory.

kvell: to swell with pride

kvetch: to complain

latke: a potato pancake (traditionally eaten on Chanukah)

L'chayim (H): "To life!" Toast offered before drinking wine or any other alcoholic beverage.

Ma Tovu (H): a collection of verses (from Numbers 24:5 and Psalms) said upon entering the synagogue in the morning.

mameleh: literally, "little mother." An endearing term for one's mother or daughter or granddaughter (based on the assumption that all women will eventually become mothers one day—oy vey).

matzo: unleavened bread

matzo ball: a dumpling made of matzo meal, eggs, oil, and salt, usually served in chicken soup

matzo brie: a fried dish consisting of eggs and matzo served with jam, honey, sugar, or syrup

Mazel tov (H): "Good luck!"

mentsh: a person of character, someone you can count on, someone who struggles to do the right thing

meshugeh: crazy

mezuzah (H): a small oblong container holding parchment with biblical passages, affixed to the doorframe of many Jewish homes

mikveh (H): Jewish ritual bath

minyan (H): a quorum for public prayer consisting of ten Jews

mishpacha (H): family

mitzvah (H): a good deed, blessing, commandment

momzer: a bastard

naches: the purest joy, the purest pride

nosh: a snack

nu: an all-purpose word that doesn't really mean anything, like "well," "so," or "hmm?"

oy: an expression of surprise, fear, sorrow, pain, excitement, etc.

oy gevalt: oy, oy, oy

oy vey: oy and then some

oy vey iz mir: woe is me

Passover/Pesach: the eight-day holiday commemorating the Exodus of the Israelites from Egypt

payes: sidelocks worn by Orthodox men and boys

plotz: Literally, to burst, as in, "I just about plotzed when I found out Jeffrey was a faygeleh."

pogrom: any systematic massacre of a group of people. Often refers to Tsarist destruction of Jews in nineteenth-century Russia.

pupik: bellybutton

Purim (H): Feast of Lots, or feast of Esther, taking place on the fourteenth day of Adar.

rebbetzin: a rabbi's wife

Rosh Hashanah (H): the Jewish New Year

rugelach: literally, "little horns." Delicious crescent cookies filled with poppy seeds, jams, nuts, chocolate, or fruit.

sabra (H): a native Israeli

schlock, schlocky: junk, junky, something that is cheaply made, or corny, as in "He's got a schlocky sense of humor."

seder (H): the traditional meal eaten the first two nights of Passover (literally, "order")

Sephardic: a Jew of Spanish or Portuguese Jewish origin or ancestry.

Shabbat (H): the Sabbath

Shabbos (Y): the Sabbath

shah: hush

shanda: a shame

shayna: beautiful

shayna maidel: a beautiful girl

shiksa: a non-Jewish woman. Often used disparagingly.

shiva (H): seven-day period of mourning following the death of a close family member

shlep: to drag, carry, or haul

The Sh'ma (H): a specific Jewish prayer (see below)

Sh'ma Yisrael, Adonai Eloheinu Adonai Echad (H): the most common Jewish prayer. Many Jews try to die with this prayer on their lips. (Literal translation: "Hear O Israel, the Lord our G-d, the Lord is one.")

shmaltz: excessive sentimentality (literally, "rendered chicken fat")

shmendrick: a jerk, but so much more.

shmuck: a jerk (literally, "penis")

shtetl: a small Jewish town or village formerly found in Eastern Europe, usually plagued with crowded, impoverished conditions

shtup: to have sex with, as in, "Harriet is shtupping Leah."

shul: a synagogue, but literally "school"

siddur (H): Jewish prayer book

simcha (H): joy, a joyous event

sloshim (H): thirty-day period following the death of a close family member

tallis (H): a prayer shawl

Talmud (H): the authoritative body of Jewish tradition comprising the Mishnah and Gemara (which itself comprises rabbinical commentary)

tashlich (H): ritual that takes place on the first day of Rosh Hashanah in which Jews gather to recite prayers and symbolically cast away their sins by throwing bread crumbs into a body of water such as the ocean or a lake.

tchotchke: a knickknack

tikkun olam (H): the transformation, healing, and repairing of the world so that it becomes a more just, peaceful, nurturing, and perfect place

Tish B'av (H): a day of mourning to commemorate the many tragedies that have befallen the Jewish people, many of which coincidentally have occurred on the ninth of Av

Torah: the first five books of the Hebrew Bible

tsouris: troubles, problems

tuchus: buttocks

tzadik (H): a righteous person (in Yiddish, "lamed vovnik"). There is a teaching in the Talmud that says that in every generation there are thirty-six true tzadikim, and the very existence in the world depends on these hidden, humble, righteous people.

yarmulke: skull cap

yarzheit: the annual Hebrew date on which the death of a loved one is commemorated

Yasher koach (H): literally, "straight strength." A way of congratulating someone for performing a mitzvah or other good deed, most commonly used in synagogue to congratulate someone after he or she has participated in some aspect of the service.

yenta: a female blabbermouth or one who meddles. Also: a matchmaker.

Yeshiva: Torah academy

Yidden: Jews

Yiddishkeit: literally, "Jewishness." Suggests perhaps more an emotional attachment, and a feeling of identification with the Jewish people, than full commitment to a lifestyle based on observance of biblical commandments (mitzvot).

Yom Kippur: (H) Jewish day of atonement

yontiff: holiday

Western Wall: the holiest shrine of the Jewish world. The Western Wall (also referred to by some as the Wailing Wall) is part of the retaining wall supporting the temple mount built by Herod in 20 B.C.E. Today it is a site where Jews from around the world gather, pray, and insert written prayers into the cracks between the wall's stones.

zaftig: plump

Resources

Organizations

The Agudah: The National Association of GLBT in Israel
10 Nahalat Binyamin St.
P.O. Box 29523
Tel Aviv 61290
972 (0)3-5167234
E-mail:sppr@012net.il
Web site: www.aguda-ta.org.il

Ahava Collective
c/o Hillel
1429 Hill St.
Ann Arbor, MI 48104

AVIV of Arizona
P. O. Box 7313
Phoenix, AZ 85011-7313
(602) 952-1612
E-mail: avivsocialaz@yahoo.com

Gay/Lesbian Concerns Committee—L'Cha Dodi
5801 West 115th St., Ste. 203
Overland Park, KS 66211-1824
(913) 327-8100
E-mail: jcrbajc@jewishkcorg
Web site: www.jewishkc.org/agencies/jcrb.htm

Resources

Greater New York Council of Gay and Lesbian Jewish Organizations
c/o JCC on the Upper West Side
15 W. 65th St., Floor 8
New York, NY 10023

HaAsiron HaAcher: The Other 10%
The Gay and Lesbian Student Union of the Hebrew University
c/o Daniel Hoffman
P.O. Box 24156
Mount Scopus
Jerusalem 91240
972 (0)2-581 8414
E-mail: asiron_jer@walla.co.il
Web site: www.gay.org.il/asiron/

Haverim
913 Allendale Road
Mechanicsburg, PA 17055
(717) 764-4407

International Association of Lesbian & Gay Children of
Holocaust Survivors
c/o Congregation Beth Simchat Torah
57 Bethune St.
New York, NY 10014
(212) 929-9498
info@infotrue.com

Israel AIDS Task Force
P. O. Box 4071
Tel-Aviv 61040
Israel
972 (0)3-5100520
E-mail: iatfec-s@internet-zahav.net
Web site: www.aidsisrael.org.il/hebrew

Resources

Jerusalem Open House: LGBT Community Center, Advancing the
Cause of Social Tolerance
P. O. Box 33107
Jerusalem 91330
Israel
972-2-6253191
joh@gay.org.il
Web site: www.gay.org.il/joh (Hebrew)
www.gay.org.il/joh/eng/home_eng.htm (English)
(American Friends of Jerusalem Open House: P.O. Box 1851,
New York, NY 10185-1851)

Jewish Lesbian Daughters of Holocaust Survivors
P.O. Box 75
Hadley, MA 01035
(888) 340-1122

Keshet
58 Glen Rd. #3
Jamaica Plain, MA 02130
Phone: (617) 524-9227
E-mail: keshetboston@yahoocom
Web site: www.boston-keshet.org

Keshet Ga'avah
3500 Holmes Ave.
Minneapolis, MN 55408
(612) 824-4226
E-mail: keshetgaavah@mac.com

Kolot: The Center for Jewish Women's and Gender Studies
1299 Church Rd.
Wyncote, PA 19095
(215) 576-0800 ext. 149
www.kolot.org

Resources

The Leo Baeck Education Center Foundation
250 West 57th St., Ste. 730
New York, NY 10107
(718) 796-1879
gsilver@attglobal.net

Long Beach Jewish Community Center Lesbian and Gay Havurah
3801 E. Willow St.
Long Beach, CA 90815
(562) 426-7601
E-mail: havurah@compupix.com

Mishpachat Alizim
P. O. Box 980136
Houston, TX 77098-0136
(866) 841-9139 ext. 1834
mishpachat@onebox.com

New Jersey Lesbian & Gay Havurah
P.O. Box 2576
Edison, NJ 08818-2576
(732) 650-1010
E-mail: info@njhav.org
Web site: www.njhav.org

NUJLS: National Union of Jewish LGBT Students
31 Gardner St. #12
Allston, MA 02134
(617) 254-8590
E-mail: info@nujls.org

The Political Council for Gay Rights in Israel
P. O. Box 11999
Tel Aviv 61116
972(0)54-878117

Resources

E-mail: PCGRI1@icqmail.com
Web site: www.geocities.com/pcgri2/index.html

Shalom Chavurah
c/o Kleinerman
1617 Chevy Chase Dr.
Brea, CA 92621
(714) 529-4201
E-mail: margyk@earthlinknet

Spinoza (LGBT study and social group)
P.O. Box 6112
Bloomington, IN 47407
(812) 331-1973
E-mail: spinoza@indiana.edu

Valley Beth Shalom Response
15739 Ventura Blvd.
Encino, CA 91436
(818) 788-6000
Web site: www.vbs.org/response/

World Congress of Gay, Lesbian, Bisexual, and Transgender Jews:
Keshet Ga'avah
8 Letitia St.
Philadelphia, PA 19106-3050
(202) 452-7424
Web site: www.glbtjews.org

LGBT and LGBT-Friendly Synagogues

Am Tikva
P.O. Box 1268
Brookline, MA 02446-0010
(617) 883-0893

E-mail: info@amtikvaorg
Web site: www.amtikva.org

Bet Mishpachah
P. O. Box 1410
Washington, DC 20013
Phone: (202) 833-1638
E-mail: office@betmishpachah.org
Web site: www.betmishpachah.org

Bet Tikvah
P. O. Box 10140
Pittsburgh, PA 15232
(412) 362-7025
E-mail: info@bettikvah.org
Web site: www.bettikvah.org

Beth Chayim Chadashim
6000 West Pico Blvd.
Los Angeles, CA 90035
(323) 931-7023
E-mail: bcc@bcc-la.org
Web site: www.bcc-la.org

Beth Rachamim Synagogue
719 Arlington Ave.
St. Petersburg, FL 33701
(813) 839-4911
E-mail: tpanolgy@tampabayrrcom
Web site: www.bethrachamim.org

Chevrei Tikva
P. O. Box 18120
Cleveland Heights, OH 44118
Phone: (216) 932-5551

Resources

Congregation Ahavat Shalom
P. O. Box 14392
San Francisco, CA 94114-0392

Congregation Bet Haverim
P. O. Box 309
Decatur, GA 30031-0309
(404) 607-0054
E-mail: cbh@mindspring.com

Congregation Beth El Binah
P. O. Box 191188
Dallas, TX 75219
(214) 521-5342 ext. 1784
E-mail: dptaffet@aol.com
Web site: www.bethelbinah.org/

Congregation Beth Simchat Torah
57 Bethune St.
New York, NY 10014
(212) 929-9498
E-mail: office@cbst.org
Web site: www.cbst.org

Congregation Beth Torah
6100 W. 127th St
Overland Park, KS 66209-3683
(913) 498-2212

Congregation B'nai Jeshurun
100A W. 89 St.
New York, NY 10024
(212) 787-7600 ext. 325
Web site: www.bj.org

Congregation Etz Chaim
2455 E. Sunrise Blvd., 10th floor
Fort Lauderdale, FL 33304
(954) 714-9232
(954) 714-2650
E-mail: congregation@etz-chaim.com

Congregation Kol Ami
1200 N. La Brea Ave.
West Hollywood, CA 90038
(323) 606-0996
E-mail: staff@kol-ami.org
Web site: www.kol-ami.org

Congregation Kol Simcha
P. O. Box 17871
Irvine, CA 92623-7871
(949) 551-2072
E-mail: kolsimcha@earthlinknet
Web site: www.home.earthlink.net/~kolsimcha

Congregation Or Chadash
c/o Second Unitarian Church
656 W. Barry Ave.
Chicago, IL 60657
(773) 248-9456
E-mail: mlw507@aol.com

Congregation Sha'ar Zahav
290 Dolores St.
San Francisco, CA 94103
(415) 861-6932
E-mail: shaarzahav@igcapc.org
Web site: www.shaarzahav.org

Resources

Congregation Tikvah Chadashah
1122 E. Pike #734
Seattle, WA 98122
Phone: (206) 329-2590
E-mail: tikvahchadashah@yahoo.com
Web site:
www.geocities.com/tikvahchadashah/GLBT_Jews_Seattle.html

Web Sites

CLAF-Israel's Lesbian Feminist Organization:
   www.aquanet.co.il/vip/klaf/
Do-It-Yourself Rainbow Kippah!:
   www.usc.edu/isd/archives/oneigla/tb/TheRainbowKippot/index.html
Frum Gay Jews: www.orthogays.com
Gay Guide to Eilat: www.gaynation.org/eilat/
Gay/Lesbian Jewish Ring: www.eskimo.com/~rmisaac/gayjews.html
Haifa Gay Community Home Page:
   www.geocities.com/WestHollywood/5574/
Jewish Feminist Resources: www.jew-feminist-resources.com/
Jewish Gay Men: www.clubs.yahoo.com/clubs/jewishgaymen
   (an online meeting place for Jewish gay men)
Jewish Women's Archive: www.jwa.org/index.html
Like an Orange on a Seder Plate: A Lesbian Haggadah:
   www.ruthsimkin.ca/
Nice Jewish Girls: www.geocities.com/WestHollywood/3222/
   (e-mail discussion list for Jewish lesbian and bisexual women)
OrthoDykes: www.orthodykes.org (Web site for Orthodox Jewish
   lesbians)
Pink Triangle Pages: www.pink-triangle.org (the history of the
   gay male and lesbian experience during World War II)
Social Action.com: www.socialaction.com (online Jewish magazine
   dedicated to pursuing justice, building community, and repairing
   the world)

Resources

Twice Bliced: www.usc.edu/isd/archives/oneigla/tb/ (the Jewish LGBT archives online)

Books

Aimee and Jaguar: A Love Story, Berlin 1943, Erica Fischer (Alyson Books, 1998).

The Best Short Stories of Lesléa Newman (Alyson Books, 2003).

Beyond Flesh: Queer Masculinities and Nationalism in Israeli Cinema, Raz Yosef (Rutgers University Press, 2004).

Confessions of a Jewish Wagnerite: Being Gay and Jewish in America, Lawrence D. Mass (Cassell Academic, 1999).

Dancing on Tisha B'av, Lev Raphael (St. Martin's Press, 1991).

The Devil and Daniel Silverman, Theodore Roszak (Leapfrog Press, 2002).

Engendering Judaism: An Inclusive Theology and Ethics, Rachel Adler (Beacon Press, 1999).

The Escape Artist: A Novel, Judith Katz (Firebrand Books, 1997)

Found Tribe: Jewish Coming Out Stories, edited by Lawrence Schimel (Sherman Asher Pub, 2002).

Friday the Rabbi Wore Lace: Jewish Lesbian Erotica, edited by Karen X. Tulchinsky (Cleis Press, 1998).

A Gay Synagogue in New York, Moshe Shokeid (Columbia University Press, 1995).

Half the Kingdom: Seven Jewish Feminists, edited by Francine Zuckerman (Vehicule Press, 1998).

Girls Will Be Girls: A Novella and Short Stories, Lesléa Newman (Alyson Books, 1999).

Hidden Holocaust? Gay and Lesbian Persecution in Germany 1933-45, Gunter Grau (Cassell, 1995).

Hot Chicken Wings, Jyl Lynn Feldman (Aunt Lute Books, 1995).

I, Pierre Seel, Deported Homosexual: A Memoir of Nazi Terror, Pierre Seel (Basic Books, 1995).

Independence Park: The Lives of Gay Men in Israel, edited by Amir Sumaka'i Fink and Jacob Press (Stanford University Press, 1999).

Resources

Journeys & Arrivals: On Being Gay and Jewish, Lev Raphael
(Faber and Faber, 2000).

Kosher Meat, edited by Lawrence Schimel (Sherman Asher Pub, 2000).

Lesbian Rabbis: The First Generation, Rebecca Alpert et al
(Rutgers University Press, 2001).

*Lesbiot: Israeli Lesbians Talk About Sexuality, Feminism, Judaism,
and Their Lives,* edited by Tracy Moore (Cassell Academic, 1999).

A Letter to Harvey Milk: Short Stories, Lesléa Newman (Firebrand
Books, 1988).

Like Bread on the Seder Plate, Rebecca Alpert (Columbia University
Press, 1997).

The Men With the Pink Triangle, Heinz Heger, (Alyson Books, 1980).

Miriam's Well: Rituals for Jewish Women Around the Year, Penina
V. Adelman (Biblio Press, 1996).

The Nazi Extermination of Homosexuals, Frank Rector (Stein and
Day, 1981).

The Pink Triangle: The Nazi War Against Homosexuals, Richard Plant.
(Henry Holt and Company, 1986).

Nice Jewish Girls: A Lesbian Anthology, edited by Evelyn Torton Beck
(Beacon Press, 1982).

Out of Our Kitchen Closets: San Francisco Gay Jewish Cooking
(Congregation Sha'Ar Zahav, 1987).

Queer Jews, edited by David Schneer and Caryn Aviv (Routledge, 2002).

Queer Theory and the Jewish Question, edited by Daniel Boyarin et al
(Columbia University Press, 2003).

Running Fiercely Toward a High, Thin Sound: A Novel, Judith Katz
(Firebrand Books, 1992).

The Same Embrace: A Novel, Michael Lowenthal (Penguin USA, 1998).

She Loves Me, She Loves Me Not: Romantic Fiction by Lesléa Newman
(Alyson Books, 2002).

Standing Again at Sinai: Judaism From a Feminist Perspective,
Judith Plaskow (Harper San Francisco, 1991).

Stone Butch Blues: A Novel, Leslie Feinberg (Alyson Books, 2003,
reissue edition).

Resources

Twice Blessed: On Being Lesbian, Gay, and Jewish, edited by
   Christie Balka and Andy Rose (Beacon Press, 1989).
An Underground Life: Memoirs of a Gay Jew in Nazi Berlin, by
   Gad Beck, et al (University of Wisconsin Press, 1999).
*Women and Jewish Law: The Essential Texts, Their History, and
   Their Revelance for Today,* Rachel Biale (Schocken Books, 1995)
*Wrestling With G-d and Men: Homosexuality in the Jewish
Tradition,* Rabbi Steven Greenberg (University of Wisconsin
   Press, 2004).
Yentl's Revenge: The Next Wave of Jewish Feminism, edited by
   Danya Ruttenberg (Seal Press, 2001).